KENT HISTORY PROJECT

7

GOVERNMENT AND POLITICS IN KENT, 1640–1914

KENT HISTORY PROJECT

ISSN 1352–805X

Already published

Traffic and Politics: The Construction and Management of Rochester Bridge, AD 43–1993, ed. Nigel Yates and James M. Gibson

Religion and Society in Kent, 1640–1914, Nigel Yates, Robert Hume and Paul Hastings

The Economy of Kent, 1640–1914, ed. Alan Armstrong

Faith and Fabric: A History of Rochester Cathedral, 604–1994, ed. Nigel Yates with the assistance of Paul A. Welsby

Early Modern Kent, 1540–1660, ed. Michael Zell

Kent in the Twentieth Century, ed. Nigel Yates with the assistance of Alan Armstrong, Ian Coulson and Alison Cresswell

Volumes in progress

Kent to AD 800, ed. John Williams

Early Medieval Kent, 800–1220, ed. Richard Eales

Later Medieval Kent, 1220–1540, ed. Nigel Ramsay

GOVERNMENT AND POLITICS IN KENT, 1640–1914

EDITED BY

FREDERICK LANSBERRY

THE BOYDELL PRESS

KENT COUNTY COUNCIL

First published 2001
The Boydell Press, Woodbridge, and
Kent County Council

ISBN 0 85115 586 3

The Boydell Press is an imprint of Boydell & Brewer Ltd
PO Box 9, Woodbridge, Suffolk IP12 3DF, UK
and of Boydell & Brewer Inc.
PO Box 41026, Rochester, NY 14604–4126, USA
website: http://www.boydell.co.uk

A catalogue record for this book is available
from the British Library

Library of Congress Cataloging-in-Publication Data
Government and politics in Kent, 1640–1914 / edited by Frederick Lansberry
p. cm. – (Kent history project, ISSN 1352–805X ; 7)
Includes bibliographical references and index.
ISBN 0–85115–586–3 (acid-free paper)
1. Kent (England) – Politics and government.   I. Lansbury, H. C. F.
II. Kent (England). County Council.   III. Series.
DA670.K3 G68 2002
942.2'3 – dc21   2001035616

This publication is printed on acid-free paper

Printed in Great Britain by
St Edmundsbury Press Ltd, Bury St Edmunds, Suffolk

Contents

Illustrations

Maps

Tables

Notes on Contributors

Brian Atkinson   took both his first degree in history and his doctorate at Oxford, joining the University of Kent in 1966. He has published work on Bristol but regards his main achievements at Kent as teaching history to generations of undergraduates and playing a prominent role in launching part-time evening courses such as the Diploma in Local History and the BA in English and History. Now retired, he still teaches on part-time courses such as the Diploma in Kentish History and the Certificate in Modern History whilst also seeking to initiate the Japanese students of Chaucer College, Canterbury, into the mysteries of Modern European History. He has also contributed the chapter on Politics to *Kent in the Twentieth Century*.

Bruce Aubry   was born at Oakland, California, into an immigrant French Canadian family. He spent five years at the University of California, Berkeley, and Ruskin College, Oxford, studying politics, economics and history. After his degree and diploma he came to live in England where he taught in secondary schools and technical colleges, including nearly twenty years at Mid-Kent College of Higher and Further Education. During a three-year break from teaching, he was the key worker in a SSRC-sponsored project at the University of Bristol's Department of Politics, during which he listed the papers of Keir Hardie, Bruce Glasier, and the Independent Labour Party. He published 'Socialdemokratiet og kristendommen. Stauning og Keir Hardie 1913' in *Arbog for Arbejderbevaegelsens Historie 4*, Copenhagen, Denmark, 1974, and 'Een zomer van agitatiede Antwerpse dokken in het teken van de internationale solidaritiet: juni-september 1896' in *AMSAB Tijdingen*, Gent, Belgium, 1983, in collaboration with Michel Vermote. The first volume of his history of the Medway labour movement, *Red flows the Medway*, was published in 1999.

Jacqueline Eales   is Reader in History at Canterbury Christ Church University College. She is the author of *Puritans and Roundheads: The Harleys of Brampton Bryan and the Outbreak of the English Civil War*, Cambridge 1990, and *Women in Early Modern England, 1500–1700*, London 1998, and editor, with Christopher Durston, of *The Culture of English Puritanism, 1560–1700*, London 1996. She has also contributed a chapter on the rise of ideological politics to *Early Modern Kent, 1540–1640*.

Paul Hastings   read history at the University of Birmingham where he also secured his master's degree. A specialist in English social history, he has lived and worked in Warwickshire, Herefordshire, North Yorkshire, Cleveland, Durham and Kent. He was awarded his doctorate by the University of York for research into 'Poverty and the Treatment of Poverty in the North Riding of York-shire c.1780–1847'. He has been sometime schoolmaster, head teacher and Principal Lecturer in History at a college of education. From 1980 to 1993 he was inspector for history for Kent Local Education Authority. He combined this post with that of Senior Inspector (Secondary Education) 1983–8. He has written some forty books and articles and three programmes for BBC television. Since 1960 he has also worked at intervals as a part-time lecturer in history for the extra-mural departments of the universities of Birmingham, Durham, Leeds and Kent and taught undergraduate history part-time for the Open University and the Humanities Faculty of the University of Kent. He left Kent County Council in 1993 to become an independent educational consultant but was forced to retire by serious illness in 1995. He has also contributed to two other volumes in the Kent History Project, *Religion and Society in Kent, 1640–1914* and *Kent in the Twentieth Century*.

Bryan Keith-Lucas,   who died in 1996, was a leading authority on the history of local government. After a period as an assistant solicitor to the corporations of Kensington and Nottingham, he was elected to a fellowship of Nuffield College, Oxford, during which time he was also Senior University Lecturer in Local Government and an elected member of Oxford City Council. In 1964 he was appointed the first Professor of Politics at the University of Kent and was, from 1970 to 1974, Master of Darwin College. He served on several commissions relating to local government in the United Kingdom, Fiji, Mauritius and Sierra Leone, and was for six years Chairman of the National Association of Parish Councils. His publications included *English Local Government in the Nineteenth and Twentieth Centuries* (1977), *The Unreformed Local Government System* (1980) and *Parish Affairs: The Government of Kent under George III* (1986).

Frederick Lansberry   was employed by Oxford University Delegacy for Extra-mural Studies to teach Kentish history to adult students in Kent. In 1975 this responsibility was undertaken by the newly created School of Continuing Education of the University of Kent at Canterbury for whom he has taught sessional and residential classes in Kent history and associated subjects. *Sevenoaks Wills and Inventories in the Reign of Charles II*, published by the Records Committee of the Kent Archaeological Society, was the product of one such class. He is at present working on a diary and account book of Sir Edward Dering, 2nd Bt.

Elizabeth Melling   read history at Durham University and holds a Diploma in Archive Administration from Liverpool University. She worked as an archivist in the Kent Archives Office (later the Centre for Kentish Studies) in Maidstone from 1950 to 1981. While at the KAO she was responsible for a number of the office's publications, particularly the *Kentish Sources* series, vols I to VI (1959–69), and also wrote *History of the Kent County Council, 1889–1974*

(1975). After taking early retirement she wrote for the Cobtree Trustees *Sir Garrard Tyrwhitt-Drake and the Cobtree Estate, Maidstone* (1988). The history of local administration has long been one of her particular interests. She has had close links with the Kent Archaeological Society over many years, becoming a member in 1953; she has been on the Society's council since 1975 and a vice-president since 1984. A member of the Society's publications committee, she has recently become its secretary.

General Editor's Note

The Publication of *Government and Politics in Kent, 1640–1914* marks the completion of those volumes in the Kent History Project covering the period from 1540 to the present day. The three remaining volumes, scheduled to appear in 2002–3, will cover the history of the county from earliest times to 1540. The editorial board wishes to thank all those who have edited or contributed to the volumes published to date and also those two bodies that have provided the funding for the project as a whole, Kent County Council and the Rochester Bridge Trust.

Abbreviations

AA	*Ashford and Alfred News*
BL	British Library
BPP	*British Parliamentary Papers, Dublin reprint*
CCA	Canterbury Cathedral Archives
CJ	*Journals of the House of Commons*
CKS	Centre for Kentish Studies, Maidstone
CN	*Chatham News*
CO	*Chatham Observer*
CSPD	*Calendar of State Papers Domestic*
DNB	*Dictionary of National Biography*
KE	*Kentish Express*
KG	*Kentish Gazette*
KH	*Kent Herald*
KM	*Kent Messenger*
LJ	*Journals of the House of Lords*
MG	*Maidstone Gazette*
MJ	*Maidstone Journal*
NS	*Northern Star*
PP	*Parliamentary Papers*
PRO	Public Record Office
SEG	*South East Gazette*
SS	*Southern Star*
VCH	*Victoria County History of Kent*

Introduction

FREDERICK LANSBERRY

Government is about power and politics is about how that power is grasped. President Jack Kennedy said the first question to be asked about government is 'Who's in charge?' This volume attempts to answer that simple question in relation to Kent. The answer, even for a single county, is complex and comes in the form of chapters which are arranged largely chronologically and are descriptive of administrative and legal institutions and of political movements and ideas, but is in no sense a linear political history.

Our study begins on the eve of the most radical and potentially revolutionary time in English history. On 30 January 1649 Charles I stepped through the window of Inigo Jones' classically inspired Banqueting House on to the scaffold in Whitehall, having passed under Rubens' paintings of the apotheosis of his father, James I. Could a greater irony have been stage managed than that a monarch who, through the masques of Inigo Jones, had been encouraged to regard himself as apart from and floating above the mundane, should step upon a stage of black crepe to face reality and the keen edge of his subjects' rejection?

Although regicide and usurpation were common enough practices in medieval England and the divinity that hedges about a king would have been viewed as ludicrous, not to say blasphemous in pre-Shakespearean days, the debate about the nature and limits of ultimate power was propounded by two Kentish idealogues, Sir Robert Filmer and Colonel Algernon Sidney. Filmer was a member of the ubiquitous Kent gentry; Sidney was a scion of the comparitively rare Kentish aristocracy. Filmer's *Patriarcha* extolled hierarchical family values, and as his title implies, the precedence and rule of the male as the head of the household and the subservience of the female and children.[1] An impeccable descent from Adam and Eve to Charles I was constructed. Obedience to a divine and hereditary order of things was implicit and wayward subjects were to be treated as wayward children. It has been argued that hereditary principles and Divine Right formed an essential prop in the political theories of both Whigs and Tories until well into the eighteenth century, and that Sidney's theory of a

---

[1] Modified in practice in his own family, see M.J.M. Ezell, *The Patriarch's Wife*, Chapel Hill 1987.

natural order of government was every whit as divinely ordained as that of Filmer's.[2] Be that as it may, Sidney's *Discources concerning Government*, which like Filmer's *Patriarcha* was not published in the author's lifetime, was produced in manuscript at Sidney's trial. In it Sidney set out the case for republicanism in a form which was even more extreme than William Penn had envisaged for his constitution for Pennsylvania and altogether too much for Charles II. Sidney was executed on a charge of treason which was based largely upon his writings rather than his actions.[3]

Between these two extremes lay the bulk of Kentish political opinion, an opinion which was most readily recorded and broadcast by the gentry of Kent. But the gentry were by no means the only institution or social grouping which held views about how the county and, less immediately, how the country should be governed. However, the gentry, particularly in the half century following the restoration of Charles II in 1660, were for a variety of reasons, the medium through which government was transferred from London to the provinces, and their domination of the House of Commons gave this narrow social élite an unprecedented role in government.[4] The growth of a powerful resident gentry between 1560 and 1660 and the concurrent expansion in the functions of the justice of the peace has been termed the greatest revolution in social control ever to have occurred in rural England.[5] Seated in Quarter Sessions the gentry, with a few beneficed clergymen, formed the most august and powerful judicial and administrative body in the county. Seated upon their estates, the gentry represented a hierarchy and a pecking order within society, recognised by their own kind, if not by the population as a whole.

Urban centres, such as Maidstone and the Medway towns, fostered dissent and radicalism. At first focussing its refusal to conform to the Church of England, established to unify Christian worship, dissent acquired a political agenda. The radical pulpit was supplemented by a radical press as a means of spreading political awareness. The patrician and patriarchal concepts of the gentry were challenged by the concepts of co-operation – the earliest examples were in Kent – and later by workers' organisations and trade unionism. Led by their more educated members, combinations of artisans formed corresponding societies and, until they were suppressed, contemplated real alternatives to government policies. For a short time the red flag floated over the Medway and the Thames estuaries. But until parliamentary representation was widened, riot not rebellion was the usual response to want and oppression. The Swing riots, the most successful workers' protest movement of the nineteenth century which began in Kent, destroyed property but not life. However, when a Messianic leader did appear to lead the agricultural paupers, a ferocious battle occurred,

2   J.C.D. Clark, *English Society 1688–1832*, Cambridge 1985, pp. 121–41.
3   A report of the trial, allegedly Sidney's own, is printed in *Cobbett's Complete Collection of State Trials*, vol. ix, London 1811, pp. 118–205.
4   F. Heal and C. Holmes, *The Gentry of England and Wales 1500–1700*, London 1994, p. 241.
5   L. Stone and J.C. Fawtier Stone, *An Open Elite? England 1540–1880*, Oxford 1986, p. 202.

more sanguine than Peterloo, more memorable in peasant consciousness than Waterloo.

Parliamentary reform, when it did come in 1832, extended the franchise to some but disenfranchised others. The redistribution of the 140 seats taken from the smaller boroughs nation-wide was perhaps more significant. Not only was the proprietory reign of the Derings over New Romney ended, but the government's loss of seats like Queenborough meant that party became more important than patronage, and party became clearly divided into Liberals and Conservatives.

More radical than parliamentary reform was the Municipal Corporations Amendment Act of 1835. Under the guise of abolishing 'old Corruption', private property rights were confiscated and their financial proceeds devoted to public use. New councils were created to become 'useful and financially responsible instruments of local government'. Instead of the rights of property, lauded by Locke, and applied to the advantage of property owners for a century and a half after the Restoration, *pro bono publico* became the shibboleth of reformers and centralisers alike. Furthermore, the attack upon the established church by the repeal of the Test Act, Catholic Emancipation and the Tithe Redemption Act made a dent, but only a dent, in England's *ancien regime* of monarchy, aristocracy and established church, which had survived the Napoleonic wars more or less intact.

Gradually, during the nineteenth century the great changes evolved which shaped the county's administration into forms which we may still recognise today. Public boards replaced privately sponsored statutory authorities; ratepayers replaced bondholders as the financiers of highway and sanitation boards and of a county police force. County Hall, literally backed by a county gaol, had become more important than the country seat and the squire's parlour as a concept and locus of local government.

1

Kent and the English Civil Wars, 1640–1660

JACQUELINE EALES

(1) Introduction

During the English Civil Wars and Interregnum the proximity of Kent to Parliament's power base in London meant that the political and military control of the county, with its supplies of food and timber, strategic coastal defences and routes to the continent, was of vital importance. Parliament therefore took early and decisive action to subdue royalist opposition within the county's borders even before Charles I declared war on 22 August 1642 at Nottingham. Earlier that month, parliamentarian troops led by Captain Edwin Sandys had seized arms from leading royalist and catholic families in Kent, intimidated the cathedral clergy at Rochester and Canterbury, and prevented the execution of the royalist military commission of array. Parliamentarian forces also made their presence felt at Chatham, Maidstone and Dover, and made a number of arrests.[1] Some Kent royalists had already joined Charles I, but those who remained in the county were largely overawed and a parliamentarian administration was set up consisting of a number of committees, which formed the basis of local administration in the county during the 1640s and 1650s.

Despite the early successes of the parliamentarian authorities in the county Kent has been regarded as an area where the majority of the inhabitants were anti-Parliament and Alan Everitt has argued that this was in part the response of a tight-knit community, which resented the interference of outsiders.[2] One of the principal aims of this chapter will be, therefore, to redress this impression by investigating evidence of support for Parliament in the county. The active participation of the inhabitants of Kent in the varied disputes of the civil war at both local and national levels will also be stressed. Most of the published histories of Kent during the civil war period have concentrated on the experiences of the

---

[1] *Journals of the House of Lords*, London 1846, V, 284, hereafter *LJ*; *Calendar of State Papers Domestic, 1641–1643*, London 1887, pp. 374–5, hereafter *CSPD*; *LJ*, V, 289, 313, 314, 318; *Journals of the House of Commons*, London 1803, II, 731, hereafter *CJ*; see also footnote 53, below. For a list of the 75 commissioners of array see Northamptonshire Record Office, Finch-Hatton MSS 133, unfoliated. I would like to thank Richard Cust for this last reference.

[2] A. Everitt, *The Community of Kent and the Great Rebellion, 1640–60*, Leicester 1966, p. 94; M. Stoyle, *Loyalty and Locality: Popular Allegiance in Devon During the English Civil War*, Exeter 1994, p. 252.

gentry, but the active engagement of other social groups, particularly the clergy, in the ideological disputes of the 1640s and 1650s will also be an important theme here.[3] Before going on to consider the various patterns of allegiance in Kent, a brief account of the impact of the civil war on the county will help to explain the context in which such political choices were made.

Throughout much of the 1640s the most influential political figure in Kent was Sir Anthony Weldon, who headed the central parliamentarian county committee until his death in late 1648. Weldon had strong personal reasons for hostility to the Stuart regime since he had been expelled from court office in 1617, but his discontent was also expressed in more general terms in his book *The Court and Character of James I*, an attack on the corruption of the early Stuart court published posthumously in 1650.[4] In 1642 Parliament tried to ensure that other key administrative officials in Kent, including the lord lieutenant and the lord warden of the Cinque Ports, were also men with parliamentarian sympathies. It was not just the maintenance of a military presence in the county, but also the control of these posts, which helped to sustain parliamentarian dominance there during the 1640s. Although Robert Sidney, Earl of Leicester, had been nominated as lord lieutenant by Parliament in March 1642, his reluctance to issue commissions to his deputies resulted in his resignation and replacement in early August 1642 by Philip Herbert, Earl of Pembroke. Leicester's sons, Philip and Algernon, did accept military commissions from Parliament in the 1640s and 1650s, but the Sidney family withdrew briefly from the political scene at the execution of the King in January 1649, when the Earl recorded that he and his sons were at Penshurst with the young Sir Henry Vane of Fairlawn, who 'had long absented and retyred himself by scruple of conscience'. Vane and the two Sidney brothers soon resumed their seats in the newly purged Rump of the Long Parliament and Algernon's republican sympathies eventually led to his execution for treason in 1683.[5]

At the start of the Civil War Parliament also agitated for the replacement of the King's cousin James Stuart, Earl of Richmond and Lennox, as lord warden of the Cinque Ports. This was strongly resisted by Charles I as the warden was one of the most influential patrons in the region and it was not until November 1643 that the parliamentarian Earl of Warwick was appointed instead. With the passage of the self-denying ordinance, the wardenship was placed in the hands of a parliamentarian commission in April 1645 and later transferred to the

---

3   The history of Kent during the years 1640–60 has been dealt with at greatest length by H.F. Abell, *Kent and the Great Civil War*, Ashford 1901, Everitt, *The Community of Kent*, and T.P.S. Woods, *Prelude to Civil War, 1642: Mr Justice Malet and the Kentish Petitions*, Salisbury 1980. See also M.V. Jones, 'The Political History of the Parliamentary Boroughs of Kent, 1642–1662', London Ph.D. 1967.

4   For Weldon see *Dictionary of National Biography*, hereafter *DNB*, which states that a second edition of his book appeared in 1651 with the addition of *The Court of King Charles*.

5   *CJ*, II, 713; *LJ*, V, 701–2; J. Scott, *Algernon Sidney and the English Republic, 1623–1677*, Cambridge 1988, pp. 92–3.

council of state in February 1649.[6] By this time the traditional independence of the ports of Sandwich, Dover, Hythe and New Romney in matters of taxation, provision of military force and parliamentary elections had been vigorously challenged by Parliament and by the county committee in the course of the war effort against the King.[7] The argument for the independence of the Cinque Ports had been based on the costs to the inhabitants of their defensive role against foreign invasion, but such special pleading was no match for the demands of civil war. The instability of the wardenship in this period also meant that its in-fluence was largely wielded by the warden's deputy, the lieutenant of Dover castle. This post was filled first by Sir Edward Boys of Nonington, MP for Dover in the Long Parliament, until his death in 1646 and then by his son Sir John, who was replaced by Captain Algernon Sidney at the height of the Second Civil War in 1648. The lieutenancy went in 1651 to Thomas Kelsey, a Londoner and army commander, who used it as a power base to establish himself as the most influential figure in Kent for much of the 1650s. Kelsey was a staunch supporter of Oliver Cromwell and under the Protectorate he was appointed major-general for the counties of Kent and Surrey in 1655.[8]

During the First Civil War of 1642–1646 the main field armies did not enter Kent, but the county was highly destabilised both by active royalism and by anti-parliamentarian sentiment aimed against the powers of the county commit-tees, the high levels of parliamentary taxation and Parliament's reforms of the Church. As a result localised insurrections took place in 1643 and 1645, and in 1648 Kent was one of the main centres of resistance to Parliament in the Second Civil War. All of these risings were firmly put down by parliamentarian troops, although after the execution of Charles I Kent continued to be regarded as an arena of potential royalist conspiracy. Security in the county, particularly during the first naval war against the Dutch in 1652–54, and the observation of the movements of known royalists there such as the Earl of Richmond and Lennox, Sir Thomas Peyton of Knowlton, Richard Thornhill of Olantigh and Sir John Boys of Bonnington, became key policies of the successive republican and Cromwellian regimes from the death of the King until the Restoration of Charles II in 1660.[9] The spread of extreme religious radicalism in the county was also perceived as a threat to central governments especially after the missions into Kent in 1655 by the Quakers Ambrose Rigge, Thomas Robertson, William Caton and John Stubbs, who claimed to have made many converts despite meeting with persecution for their egalitarian beliefs. There is also evidence that

---

[6] M.V. Jones, 'Political History of the Parliamentary Boroughs of Kent', p. 322; *Acts and Ordinances of the Interregnum, 1642–1660*, ed. C.H. Firth and R.S. Rait, London 1911, vol. 1, p. 669, II, p. 13.

[7] Everitt, *Community of Kent*, pp. 135–7; M.V. Jones, 'Political History of the Parliamentary Boroughs of Kent', pp. 351–418.

[8] M.V. Jones, *ibid.*, pp. 323–4; Scott, *Algernon Sidney and the English Republic, 1623–1677*, pp. 90, 97–8; *CSPD, 1656–7*, p. 88; for Kelsey see also *DNB*.

[9] P.G. Rogers, *The Dutch in the Medway*, Oxford 1970; D. Underdown, *Royalist Conspiracy in England, 1649–1660*, New Haven 1960, pp. 23–4, 109–10, 266–8; A. Rhodes, 'Suspected Persons in Kent', *Archaeologia Cantiana*, xxiii (1898), pp. 68–77.

a few of the more extreme Fifth Monarchists, who believed in violent opposition to civil government in order to achieve godly rule, were also active in Kent in the 1650s.[10]

The years from 1640 to 1660 have been seen not only as a period of political revolution but also of social revolution since the exclusion of royalist gentry from local office meant that men of lower standing were increasingly called upon to administer the county. One of the complaints of the Kent rebels in 1648 was aimed at 'these deputed governors for the Parliament. Their weak fortunes, weaker wits and yet less merit to such a high calling of public rule. Their obscure parentage and education.'[11] Certainly there was a significant power shift in county government, but it took place, as Alan Everitt has pointed out, within the landed classes as members of the minor gentry took over positions previously held by major gentry families. Although this did not constitute a fullscale social revolution, it was nevertheless an important departure from tradition and the use of new men was particularly marked after the crisis of the Second Civil War of 1648 and the regicide in January 1649, when there was a political purge of both county and town governors. The newcomers were, however, regarded by central government largely as administrators and not as old-style gentry power-brokers. A similar process has been observed by Madeline Jones in the four parliamentary boroughs of Kent and the four Cinque Ports where, despite the influx of new men, the majority of office holders were still drawn from 'the ranks of the minor gentry, the professional and the upper trading classes'. After the death of Oliver Cromwell in September 1658 central government became increasingly unstable and there was a conservative reaction in these towns where governors were once again chosen from the old ruling families.[12]

The enforced sale of land owned by prominent royalists, the Church and the Crown in the 1640s and 1650s certainly helped some individuals to gain wealth, but it did not mark the establishment of a new class. The sequestration of royalists' land commenced in 1643, but in Kent no more than fourteen small estates were sold outright. The properties of the Church and of the Crown were on sale from 1647 and 1650 respectively and went mainly to men who already had enough money to speculate. Although tenants were given a first option to buy Church lands, only the wealthiest did so, such as Sir John Roberts of Canterbury, who bought marsh and woodland in the manor of Chislet, and Sir Robert Honeywood, who bought St Gregory's priory and the manor of Lecton where he

---

10 G.F. Nuttall, 'Dissenting Churches in Kent before 1700', *Journal of Ecclesiastical History*, xiv (1963), pp. 175–89; M.V. Jones, 'Political History of the Parliamentary Boroughs of Kent', pp. 472–8; R. Acheson, 'The Development of Religious Separatism in the Diocese of Canterbury, 1590–1660', Kent Ph.D. 1983, pp. 228–71, 329–38.

11 A.B. *A Letter from a Gentleman in Kent Giving Satisfaction to a Friend in London*, London 1648, p. 1.

12 Everitt, *Community of Kent*, pp. 143–4; M.V. Jones, 'Political History of the Parliamentary Boroughs of Kent', pp. 251, 254. The parliamentary boroughs were Canterbury, Dover, Hythe, Maidstone, New Romney, Queeenborough, Rochester and Sandwich.

was the chief tenant. John Blackwell was a typical London speculator, who bought the manor of Reculver and half of the archbishop's palace at Canterbury amongst other properties. The transfer of these lands was seen as a hindrance to the Restoration of the monarchy in 1660, but most ecclesiastical and crown lands were recovered peacefully and the deprived owners received some compensation.[13] In Kent the Restoration marked a return to the pre-war status quo in terms of wealth and political power but, as this chapter will argue, it also left a powerful legacy of religious and political dissent amongst the wider population.

(2) Ideology and Allegiance

Any consideration of the events of the English Civil Wars and their aftermath in Kent must take account of Alan Everitt's pioneering work, *The Community of Kent and the Great Rebellion, 1640–1660* published in 1966, whilst also observing how civil war scholarship has developed in the intervening years. Everitt saw the activities of committed royalists and parliamentarians in the county as atypical, the work of newcomers and outsiders. He described the natural leaders of county society as a group of between twenty and thirty closely related gentry families, most of whom had been settled in Kent since Tudor times or earlier, including the Boyses, Derings, Diggeses, Finches, Haleses, Honeywoods, Knatchbulls, Oxindens of Deane, Scotts and Twysdens. Their reaction to the crisis was essentially conservative and politically insular, and they increasingly withdrew from public life in this period. They wanted to preserve the legitimate powers of the monarchy and the tolerant traditions of the established Church, and they resented any outside interference in local affairs. Their patriarchal influence over their tenants, neighbours and the parish clergy served to create widespread support for this moderate stance. Everitt's interpretation has had a considerable influence over subsequent work on civil war Kent, as well as on other counties, such as Cheshire and Sussex, yet it is open to a number of criticisms. Indeed, Peter Laslett had earlier described Kent gentry society as altogether more cosmopolitan, with intellectual links both to the continent and to a national political culture centred on London and the universities. Similarly, Peter Clark's study of pre-civil war Kent, which was published in 1977, drew attention to the contribution made by the county to some of the central religious, political and social developments that took place in England between the Reformation and the Civil War.[14]

---

13 G.B. Tatham, 'The Sale of Episcopal Lands during the Civil Wars and Commonwealth', *English Historical Review*, xxiii (1908), pp. 91–108; I. Gentles, 'The Sales of Bishops' Lands in the English Revolution, 1646–1660', *English Historical Review*, xcv (1980), pp. 573–96; I. Gentles, 'The Sales of Crown Lands during the English Revolution', *Economic History Review*, xxvi (1973), pp. 614–35.

14 For Everitt's influence see for example J. Morrill, *Cheshire, 1630–1666: County Government and Society during the English Revolution*, Oxford 1974, and A.J. Fletcher, *A County Community in Peace and War: Sussex, 1600–1660*, London 1975. For interpretations of Kent that are different from

Everitt not only seriously underestimated the strength and nature of ideological commitment amongst the major gentry of Kent, but he also made a misleading distinction between individuals with national concerns and those who were more interested in local issues. For example, his assessment of Sir Thomas Peyton as a 'firm opponent of Charles I', who had been driven to support the King 'principally by the violence and injustice' of Weldon and the county committee takes no account of Peyton's clearly expressed earlier support for ship money and the royal prerogative in the wake of the dissolution of the Short Parliament. In May 1640 Peyton had confided to Henry Oxinden of Barham that 'since wee will nott give, the king must take . . . I thinke the king may use the goods of his subjects *nolentibus volentibus* . . . for the conservation of the more universall and generall good'.[15] Similarly, Everitt depicted Weldon's parliamentarianism as the vengeance of a disappointed courtier, yet it should not be overlooked that Weldon's books attacking James I and Charles I fit into a general pattern of legitimate political criticism of the early Stuart court which, as Linda Peck has shown, centred on the issue of corruption.[16]

Charting the patterns of religious and political allegiances during the civil war period is a notoriously difficult task for the historian, since political and military events developed at such speed that party groupings were intrinsically unstable. Even Members of Parliament are not always easy to label, although two of the Kent representatives to the Long Parliament, Sir John Culpeper and Sir Thomas Peyton, clearly absented themselves from the House of Commons because of their royalist sympathies and were subsequently disabled from sitting in the House. Another three, Sir Michael Livesey, Augustine Garland and John Dixwell were regicides, who signed the death warrant of the King. Livesey was also a parliamentarian regimental commander and some men can be identified as committed supporters of one side or the other because they were enthusiastic military leaders.[17] Sir John Mayney of Linton has been described as the 'most eminent' of Kent's 22 royalist colonels who served during the First Civil War, a group which included Sir John Boys of Bonnington, Sir Anthony St Leger of Ulcombe and Richard Thornhill of Olantigh.[18] A number of gentlemen with Kent connections also died whilst campaigning, including Edwin Sandys, Mark

Everitt's see P. Laslett, 'The Gentry of Kent in 1640', *Cambridge Historical Journal*, ix (1948), pp. 148–64; P. Clark, *English Provincial Society from the Reformation to the Revolution: Religion, Politics and Society in Kent, 1500–1640*, Hassocks 1977, and D. Hirst, 'The Defection of Sir Edward Dering, 1640–1641', *Historical Journal*, xv (1972), pp. 193–208.

15 Everitt, *County Community*, p. 279; *The Oxinden Letters, 1607–1642*, ed. D. Gardiner, London 1933, p. 173.

16 Everitt, *County Community*, p. 134; L. Levy Peck, *Court Patronage and Corruption in Early Stuart England*, London 1990.

17 M.F. Keeler, *The Long Parliament, 1640–1641: A Biographical Study of its Members*, Philadelphia 1954; D. Brunton and D.H. Pennington, *Members of the Long Parliament*, Cambridge (Mass.) 1954; D. Underdown, *Pride's Purge: Politics in the Puritan Revolution*, Oxford 1971. I am grateful to Dr Stephen Roberts at the History of Parliament Trust for supplying me with a list of all Kent MPs for 1640–60.

18 P.R. Newman, *The Old Service: Royalist Regimental Colonels and the Civil War, 1642–46*, Manchester 1993, pp. 282–5.

Dixwell and Sir William Springate for Parliament and Sir William Clerke, Sir William Butler and Sir Thomas Bosville for the King.[19] Yet those who chose not to fight, or otherwise confront the soldiery or adminstrators, in these uncertain conditions cannot automatically be assumed, as Everitt claimed, to have been moderates.

The reaction of Henry Oxinden of Deane to the demands of King and Parliament has been widely quoted as exemplifying the quandary of the moderate majority not just in Kent, but in the country as a whole.[20] In July 1642 Oxinden described his condition 'beetwixt the commission of Aray and ordinance of Parl[iament]' as being like 'his that is between Silla and Carybdis, and nothing butt Omnipotentcie can bring mee clearely and reputably off'. In the same letter, however, he also declared in a much less frequently quoted passage – 'I will much rather quitte my place then obey, or serve under any commission without co[n]sent of, much lesse against the Parl[iament] ittselfe and our owne lawes and liberties.' In fact Oxinden and his father, Sir James, served as active parliamentarian administrators in the county until the outbreak of the Second Civil War in 1648. Henry Oxinden was returned as MP for Winchelsea in 1645, but could not be persuaded to sit in the House after the King's execution. He later represented Kent in the Protectorate Parliaments of 1654 and 1656.[21]

Genuine neutrals, those who refused to support either side, were rare and in Kent they suffered for refusing to endorse Parliament. Sir Roger Twysden, for example, maintained a consistently neutral stance by rejecting the more extreme claims to power of both King and Parliament. After he had encouraged subscription to the Kent petition of March 1642, Twysden was regarded by Parliament as a royalist and his estates were sequestrated in May 1643.[22] Neutrality could also take the more common form of trying to obey both sides in the conflict, but in the light of Parliament's hegemony in Kent this form of insurance policy was not as frequently practised as it was in counties whose control was more directly under dispute.

Recent research on the Civil Wars has also suggested that it is important to

---

19 Sandys died of wounds sustained at Worcester in September 1642, see *DNB*; Dixwell died at the siege of Arundel in December 1643, see *The Oxinden Letters, 1642–1670*, ed. D. Gardiner, London 1937, pp. 39, 43; Springett died after an illness at the garrison of Arundel, see H. Dixon, 'Original Account of the Springett Family', *Gentleman's Magazine*, October 1851, pp. 369–71; Clerk and Butler died at Cropredy Bridge in 1644, see M. Toynbee and P. Young, *Cropredy Bridge, 1644: The Campaign and the Battle*, Warwick 1970, pp. 98–9; Bosville died at the Oxford garrison in May 1643, see Newman, *The Old Service*, p. 284.

20 See for example, J. Morrill, *The Revolt of the Provinces: Conservatives and Radicals in the English Civil War, 1630–1650*, London 1976, p. 40. Patrick Collinson is right to describe Oxinden as a 'strong parliamentarian': P. Collinson, 'The Protestant Cathedral, 1541–1660', *A History of Canterbury Cathedral*, ed. P. Collinson, N. Ramsay and M. Sparks, Oxford 1995, p. 195 n. 8.

21 *The Oxinden Letters, 1607–1642*, ed. D. Gardiner, p. 312; Underdown, *Pride's Purge*, p. 197; see also *ibid.*, p. 382 where Professor Underdown mistakenly claims that Oxinden was secluded.

22 *Certaine Considerations upon the Government of England by Sir Roger Twysden, Kt and Bart.*, ed. J.M. Kemble, Camden Society 45, London 1849, pp. v–lxxxv; P. Bloomfield, 'The Cromwellian Commission in Kent, 1655–57', in *Studies in Modern Kentish History*, ed. A. Detsicas and N. Yates, Kent Archaeological Society, Maidstone 1983, p. 18.

consider the role that was played by groups other than the gentry in helping to shape the conflict at local level.[23] In particular, it will be argued here that the lead of the clergy was highly important since, as members of a national institution, they were likely to see religious reforms, at least, in terms of national policies.[24] Kent was unique in being the only English county to have two diocesan centres, Canterbury and Rochester, within its borders, and the clergy in the diocese of Canterbury were also directly exposed to the ecclesiastical changes, which were introduced after the election of William Laud as Archbishop in 1633. The importance of the clergy is reflected in the very high level of clerical ejections in Kent, which ran above the national average. Everitt calculated that 233 Kent benefices and canonries are known to have been sequestrated or forcibly vacated between 1642 and 1660 from a total of 450.[25] Ministers were ejected for a variety of reasons including negligence, for High Church or Arminian doctrines and practices, for royalism and for not using the *Directory for Public Worship* endorsed by Parliament in 1645 to replace the *Book of Common Prayer*.[26] The high level of clerical ejections in Kent in the years from 1643 to 1662 testifies to the importance which successive central governments placed on securing the support of preachers in their quest for a political settlement. For this reason lay preachers, who had not been formally ordained and who were difficult to control, were regarded with particular hostility by the civil powers, especially if they were women. The ferment of the Civil War did give some women the opportunities to involve themselves in these debates and in 1641 the preaching of Joan Banford of Faversham and Susan May of Ashford was decried in an anonymous pamphlet. In 1646 Thomas Edwards complained of 'a preaching woman, an Anabaptist, who . . . doth meet other women' at Brasted and at Westerham.[27]

The history of the Civil Wars in Kent, in fact, reveals a considerable amount of political and religious commitment amongst the gentry, the clergy, urban groups and the wider population of freeholders and peasants. Opposition to the Crown was strongly linked to religious dissent and was at its strongest in the urban centres of Kent particularly Canterbury, Cranbrook, Dover, Maidstone and Sandwich as well as in the parishes of the Weald and in the east of the county. These were areas which had traditions of religious nonconformity reaching back to the reign of Elizabeth I or earlier, but the inhabitants of these

[23] Hirst, *op. cit.*; D. Underdown, 'The Problem of Popular Allegiance in the English Civil War', *Transactions of the Royal Historical Society*, 5th ser. xxxi (1981) pp. 69–94; C. Holmes, 'The County Community in Stuart Historiography', *Journal of British Studies*, xix (1986), pp. 54–73.

[24] J. Eales, *Puritans and Roundheads: The Harleys of Brampton Bryan and the Outbreak of the English Civil War*, Cambridge 1990, pp. 106–7, 128–9.

[25] I. Green, 'The Persecution of "Scandalous" and "Malignant" Parish Clergy During the English Civil War', *English Historical Review*, xciv (1979), pp. 522–3; Everitt, *The Community of Kent*, p. 299.

[26] *Walker Revised*, ed. A.G. Matthews, Oxford 1988, pp. 209–28; for ejections in the diocese of Canterbury see G.L. Ignjatijevic, 'The Parish Clergy in the Diocese of Canterbury and Archdeaconry of Bedford in the Reign of Charles I and under the Commonwealth', Sheffield Ph.D. 1986.

[27] Cited in Acheson, 'The Development of Religious Separatism in the Diocese of Canterbury, 1590–1660', p. 289.

areas were not united in their opinions. In the rural parish of Minster-in-Thanet in East Kent Richard Culmer, the presbyterian cleric, believed that his puritan and pro-parliamentarian ministry was opposed in the late 1640s and early 1650s by a combination of royalists, religious sectaries and Levellers. In 1655 Luke Howard, the Dover Quaker, recorded the opinions at an inn there of 'Baptists, Independents, Brownists and Episcopals', who 'all agreed in one voice, that they [the Quakers] were deceivers, and so cryed them down'.[28] Some historians have suggested that the spread of radical religious ideas followed a common social, economic and geographical pattern in the early modern period. Towns were clearly centres of social mobility and provided a focus for the exchange of news and innovative beliefs, while large parishes with scattered habitations in woodland or pasture areas, such as those of the Weald, offered refuge from the authorities for those with unorthodox ideas.[29] The development of religious radicalism also relied, however, on a number of other factors including lay patronage and family traditions, which also need to be taken into account.[30]

Lower down the social scale men from Kent fought on both sides and at least three Kent towns, Ashford, Canterbury and Cranbrook, enthusiastically raised volunteer forces for Parliament before the formal declaration of war by the King in August 1642. Enlisting may have been an attractive prospect for some of the men affected by the localised depression in the cloth industry, but it cannot be assumed that they were all solely motivated by economic concerns. According to his wife's later memoirs, Sir William Springate raised eight hundred volunteers for Parliament in the autumn of 1642, most of whom like Springate himself were puritans – 'professors and professors sons', as she termed them.[31] Religion has been seen as one of the crucial determinants in civil war allegiance since the role of the Church in buttressing the Crown meant that any criticism of the ecclesiastical hierarchy or the established liturgy could be interpreted as an attack on the monarchy. Thus in 1642 when two weavers, a yeoman and a husbandman were indicted at the assizes for their presence at a conventicle, attended by 100 people and held on the border of the Weald in the parish of Ulcombe, they were accused of 'denigrating and opposing the King's authority in ecclesiastical causes'.[32] In particular the issue of reform of the episcopate was central in raising support for Parliament from both moderate anglicans, who wanted the powers of bishops curtailed, and puritans who divided into presbyterian and independent camps, but by and large were initially united in their desire

---

28 R. Culmer (the younger), *A Parish Looking-Glasse for Persecutors of Ministers*, London 1657; cited in M.V. Jones, 'The Political History of the Parliamentary Boroughs of Kent', p. 485.

29 D. Underdown, *Revel, Riot and Rebellion: Popular Politics and Culture in England, 1603–1660*, Oxford 1985; Stoyle, *op. cit.*

30 See for example Eales, *Puritans and Roundheads, passim.*

31 C. Russell, *The Causes of the English Civil War*, Oxford 1990, p. 226; the Kent towns form a high proportion of the 22 communities identified here by Russell; Dixon, 'Original Account of the Springett Family', *Gentleman's Magazine*, October 1851, p. 367; *CJ*, II, 714.

32 *Calendar of Assize Records, Kent Indictments, Charles I, 1625–1649*, ed. J.S. Cockburn, London 1995, p. 439.

to abolish episcopacy. The rejection of a national Church organisation by many of the independent congregations also went hand in hand with a refusal to accept the intervention of civil goverment in religious affairs and by the mid-1640s the relationship between the presbyterians and the independents was to become increasingly acrimonious and polarised.

(3) The Opening of the Long Parliament, 1640–42

Religion was not, of course, the sole issue at stake between the two sides and the 1640 elections to the Short and the Long Parliaments brought considerable numbers of grievances about Charles I's rule to the fore in Kent and other counties, including the imposition of ship money and the absence of Parliaments in England in the 1630s. Moreover, Kent traditionally shouldered heavy responsibilities in guarding its coastline and the approaches to London, thus the additional demands of impressment and taxation for the military campaigns against the rebellious Scots in 1639 and 1640 had caused particular disquiet in the county.[33] The High Church, or Arminian, policies of King Charles and the Archbishop of Canterbury, William Laud, also raised considerable fears of a rapprochement with the Roman Catholic Church, particularly amongst the puritan critics of the Crown.[34] These fears were reinforced at parish level in Kent by Laud's contentious attempt in the 1630s to suppress the independent congregations of the stranger communities, the French and Dutch Protestants, in Canterbury, Maidstone, and Sandwich in order to bring them into conformity with the practices of the English Church.[35] At Laud's trial for treason, which led to his execution in 1645, he was accused of suppressing these congregations in order to create discord between the English Church and the continental reformed Churches to give 'Papists' the advantage in the 'overthrow, and extirpation of both'. The cases of a number of ministers, who had been punished in the 1630s for not reading the *Book of Sports*, were also cited at the trial. The *Book* endorsed physical recreations on Sunday afternoons and was abhorred by observers of the sabbath. In Kent five puritan ministers, Richard Culmer then curate at Goodnestone, Thomas Hieron of Hernhill, John Player of Kennington, Lawrence Snelling of St Paul's Cray, and Thomas Wilson of Otham, had opposed these directives by refusing to read the *Book* to their parishioners. They

---

[33] K. Fincham, 'The Judges' Decision on Ship Money in February 1637: the Reaction of Kent', *Bulletin of the Institute of Historical Research*, lvii (1984), pp. 230–7; M.V. Jones, 'Election Issues and the Borough Electorates in mid-Seventeenth Century Kent', *Archaeologia Cantiana*, lxxxv (1970), pp. 19–27; F. Jessup, 'The Kentish Election of March 1640', *Archaeologia Cantiana*, lxxxvi (1971), pp. 1–10.

[34] P. Lake, 'Anti-Popery: The Structure of a Prejudice', in *Conflict in Early Stuart England: Studies in Religion and Politics, 1603–1642*, ed. R. Cust and A. Hughes, London 1989, pp. 72–106.

[35] J. Bulteel, *A Relation of the Troubles of the Three Forraign Churches in Kent*, London 1645; see also A. Oakley, 'Archbishop Laud and the Walloons in Canterbury', *Crown and Mitre: Religion and Society in Northern Europe since the Reformation*, ed. W.M. Jacob and N. Yates, Woodbridge 1993, pp. 33–43.

were suspended from their ministry, which caused considerable local concern amongst their supporters, and their evidence against Laud was eagerly heard at his trial.[36]

When the Long Parliament assembled in November 1640 the King faced a united opposition led by men with considerable sympathy for the Scottish rebels and determined to curb his power. One of the first acts of the Parliament was to draw articles of impeachment against the Lord Keeper, John, Baron Finch of Fordwich, who had upheld the King's right to levy ship money in John Hampden's case of 1637. Finch wisely fled to the Netherlands at the end of 1640 and became the first Kent exile of the civil war. The execution of Charles I's minister, the Earl of Strafford, in May 1641 exemplified the punishment feared by Finch; it also caused the first major split in the parliamentarian ranks. As the demands of Charles' opponents became increasingly more radical, they alienated a substantial number of their colleagues, who began to form a coherent royalist party. As we have seen, one of the key issues which divided the two parties was the support of the parliamentarian leadership for the abolition of episcopacy, which was a matter of principle, but was also vital to retain the goodwill of their Scottish presbyterian allies. Another important sticking point was the militia, the only permanent military force in the English shires, which Parliament attempted to control in 1642 through the mechanism of the militia ordinance (the legality of which was severely criticised by royalists) while the King utilised commissions of array to the same purpose. A third area of conflict concerned the power to choose the members of the privy council, which Charles refused to relinquish.[37]

In response to these political developments at Westminster, Kent became the scene of a series of popular petitioning campaigns from late 1640 until the outbreak of war. The petitioners were almost exclusively men, many of whom probably already exercised a measure of political authority through their ability to vote in parliamentary elections or as members of parish vestries. Sir Edward Dering estimated that 10,000 freeholders assembled to vote in the county election for the earlier Short Parliament of 1640 and such men expected their representatives to voice their concerns in Parliament.[38] In the opening months of the Long Parliament Sir John Culpeper and Sir Edward Dering, as the two knights of the shire, were the most active of the Kent MPs in presenting grievances from the county to the Commons. In doing so both men displayed a clear awareness of the relationship between national and local politics. In the first week of the Long Parliament Culpeper delivered a speech to the Commons in which he set out the complaints of the inhabitants of Kent against Charles I's government. His speech, which was subsequently printed, was anti-catholic and anti-absolutist in tone and showed a firm grasp of how local issues were part of the wider political

---

[36] W. Prynne, *Canterburies Doome*, London 1646, pp. 27, 33, 388–409, 539–43, 504–6.
[37] For an account of the early stage of the Long Parliament see C. Russell, *The Fall of the British Monarchies, 1637–1642*, Oxford 1991; for Finch see *DNB*.
[38] Jessup, *op. cit.*, p. 4.

debate. After complaining about the military levies on the county for the campaigns against the Scots, he turned to ship money and, in words that could have been framed in direct answer to the judgement of Sir John Finch and his fellow judges in Hampden's case, argued that if the law gave the King the power to raise emergency taxation, then '[all] that we have is left to the goodness of the King not to the law'.[39] In January 1641 when Dering presented a petition to the House from 2,500 inhabitants of the Weald against episcopacy, he drew attention to the relationship between this petition and its model, the Root and Branch petition of December 1640 from the City of London, with the words 'the same grievances which the City groans under are provincial unto us and I much fear they are national among us all'.[40]

In early 1641 Culpeper and Dering continued in broad agreement with the attempts of the parliamentarian leadership to restrict royal power, but by November both men opposed the Grand Remonstrance, which set out the failings of Charles I's rule under 204 separate headings. Culpeper was appointed as chancellor of the exchequer in January 1642 by the King and he subsequently attacked the measures designed to give Parliament control over the county militias. He joined the King at York in May and later accompanied the young Prince of Wales into exile. Culpeper played a leading role amongst the King's moderate advisors, who have been described as constitutional royalists and who wanted a limited monarchy and the preservation of the existing framework of the Church. Their attitudes were set out in the King's *Answer to the XIX Propositions* of June 1642 drawn up by Culpeper and Viscount Falkland. Also included in this grouping were Edward Sackville, Earl of Dorset, and the Duke of Richmond and Lennox, who were also in close attendance on the King during the First Civil War and similarly urged him to reach an accommodation with Parliament.[41] The absence of these two peers from their estates at Knole and Cobham in Kent during much of the 1640s inevitably meant the weakening of royalist leadership within the county.

In the wake of Charles I's attempt to arrest John Pym and other leading parliamentarians in January 1642, Dering too began to distance himself from their cause. In that month he published his speeches on religion in order to demonstrate that he had advocated only moderate reforms of episcopacy and not its abolition. Dering had introduced the 'Root and Branch' bill calling for the abolition of episcopacy into the House of Commons in May 1641 and his apparent change of heart about the issue has been ascribed by Derek Hirst to the information that Dering received about the activities of religious radicals from Kent parishes. There was no automatic right to report proceedings in Parliament

---

[39] *Sir Iohn Culpeper His Speech in Parliament,* London 1641.

[40] *Proceedings, Principally in the County of Kent, in Connection with the Parliaments Called in 1640 and Especially with the Committee of Religion Appointed in that Year,* ed. L.B. Larking, Camden Society, vol. 80, London 1862, pp. 27–39.

[41] D.L. Smith, *Constitutional Royalism and the Search for Settlement, c.1640–1649,* Cambridge 1994, *passim.*

and Dering's actions in doing so, and in identifying other speakers in his book, were regarded as breaches of parliamentary privilege. He was immediately disabled from sitting in the House and briefly imprisoned in the Tower of London. Before the end of the summer Dering also joined the King's entourage.[42]

On his release from the Tower Dering travelled first to Kent where he was active in moves to counter two pro-parliamentarian petitions delivered to the Lords and Commons in February 1642 by Sir Michael Livesey and other Kent gentlemen under the sponsorship of Sir Thomas Walsingham, MP for Rochester. These petitions endorsed both the recent militia bill and the bill to prevent bishops from sitting in the House of Lords and they marked a growing split between parliamentarian and royalist opinion in the county. They described the King as being 'seduced' by the malevolent advice of a party of 'malignants and cavaliers' and were presented on behalf of the 'knights, gentlemen, ministers and freeholders' of Kent.[43]

Dering helped to draw up the counter-petition formulated at the March 1642 assizes in Maidstone along with his fellow justice of the peace, Sir George Strode. This was the most famed of the Kent petitions of the early 1640s and it supported the established Church, requested Parliament to reach an accommodation with the King and, most pointedly, condemned the militia ordinance of 5 March 1642 as the exercise of 'arbitrary power', as it unilaterally gave control of the militia to Parliament. This was a crucial constitutional point since, unlike statutes, parliamentary ordinances did not carry the consent of the King and their use was interpreted by the growing body of royalist opinion as a tyrannical usurpation of the power of the Crown. The petition was circulated for signatures in the county and printed copies were rapidly produced in London. Its contents have been described as moderate by modern historians, but Parliament and its supporters in Kent took a different view. The House of Commons was informed at once about the events at the assizes by one of the justices, Thomas Blount, who would soon prove to be one of the most active parliamentarians in the county. The leading promoters of the petition were ordered to attend Parliament as delinquents, printed copies were publicly burnt by the hangman at Westminster, Smithfield and Cheapside, and when the petition was presented to the Commons by a party of Kent gentlemen two of them, Richard Lovelace, the cavalier poet, and Sir William Butler, were arrested and later bailed. Meanwhile Blount proceeded to circulate a pro-parliamentarian petition in the county and within a fortnight claimed to have collected over 6,000 names.[44]

---

42 In May 1641 Culpeper supported the execution of the Earl of Strafford. For biographical details of Culpeper and Dering see *DNB*; for Culpeper see also Smith, *Constitutional Royalism*, *passim*; for Dering see Hirst, *op. cit.*, and S.P. Salt, 'The Origins of Sir Edward Dering's Attack on the Ecclesiastical Hierarchy c.1625–1640', *Historical Journal*, xxx (1987), pp. 21–52.

43 *LJ*, IV, 570; *CJ*, II, 420–1.

44 Woods, *Prelude to Civil War, 1642: Mr Justice Malet and the Kentish Petitions, passim*; *The Petition of the Gentry, Ministers, and Commonalty of Kent. Agreed upon at the Generall Assizes . . . March 28. 1642*, London 1642.

The mass collection of signatures raises questions about how well the wider population of Kent was informed about political developments at Westminster. Certainly there was no lack of information about the disputes between King and Parliament in the county. Parliamentary speeches, petitions, tracts and newsbooks were produced both in print and in manuscript in order to serve a ready and growing market in the 1640s and 1650s. They included dozens of items specifically about Kent or written by its denizens. The letters of Henry Oxinden of Barham show, for example, that from the start of the Long Parliament he was keen to obtain pamphlets and other news from his correspondents in London, who included Sir Thomas Peyton, MP for Sandwich, who was disabled from sitting in the Commons in February 1644. By the summer of 1642 the news that Oxinden had received had persuaded him to support the parliamentarian cause and he informed his cousin, Henry Oxinden of Deane, that in the east of the county only half of the gentry and a few freeholders would obey the royal commission of array. Although he marched with the Kent trained bands to take part in the siege of Arundel in December 1643, Henry Oxinden of Barham's experience of bloodshed dampened his enthusiasm for the parliamentarian cause and in a letter written in early February 1644 to Peyton he described his grief 'to see men of the same Religion, of the same Nation, so eagerlie engaged one against the other'. Oxinden was also increasingly alarmed by the more extreme manifestations of religious radicalism and feared that the presbyterianism of the leading parliamentarian activists would 'equalize men of meane condition with the gentrie'.[45]

Oxinden was a bibliophile and was able to build up a considerable collection of newsbooks and other sources of printed information, but he was by no means atypical in his desire for news.[46] A court deposition taken in Sandwich in January 1645 described a group of men in a shoemaker's shop discussing a book, 'wherein there was men[n]con of the Scotch', with some vehemence. The incident illustrates the point of contact between printed news and its oral discussion for, despite the existence of the printing press, early modern Englishmen and women continued to rely on word of mouth as an important source of information. In the early 1640s rumours that Charles I was in the grip of a catholic plot, which centred on his French wife Henrietta Maria, were widely disseminated and were reinforced by news of the Irish catholic rebellion in November 1641. These issues were discussed in Kent and at the assizes held in March 1642 one Edward Fairbrother, a glasier of Gravesend, was accused of having 'said, published and in a loud voice pronounced these malicious and

---

45 *The Oxinden Letters, 1607–1642*, ed. D. Gardiner, pp. 186,189, 198, 313; *The Oxinden Letters, 1642–1670*, ed. D. Gardiner, pp. 42, 37.

46 For the circulation of news see R. Cust, 'News and Politics in Early Seventeenth-Century England', *Past and Present*, cxii (1986), pp. 60–90; Oxinden's library later formed the basis of the Elham parish library, which is the subject of current doctoral research by Sheila Hingley, Canterbury Cathedral Librarian. I am grateful to Mrs Hingley for information about Oxinden's bibliographic interests.

seditious words following . . . King Charles . . . is a papist', for which he was fined £40 and imprisoned at the King's pleasure.[47]

One of the most important formal arenas for the oral transmission of information was the pulpit. In January 1642 the House of Commons took exception to a sermon preached in Canterbury Cathedral by the sub-dean, Thomas Paske, in which he declared that 'the people were departed from the King. That they must come as Benhadad's servants did with halters about their necks.' The cathedral was naturally a centre of royalist resistance to Parliament and Paske and the Dean, Isaac Bargrave, had previously tried to secure support in Canterbury for a petition in favour of episcopacy, but according to Henry Oxinden of Barham 'although some set their hands to it, others refuse[d]'.[48] The parish clergy of Kent were also well aware of the importance of their role in interpreting the conflict to their auditors. In a strongly anti-episcopal and pro-Scots sermon addressed to the House of Commons on 28 September 1642, Thomas Wilson of Otham described ministers as 'the strength of a land, the chariots of Israel and horsemen thereof'. Wilson argued that the bishops were 'idolatrous' and that 'prelacy root and branch shall be taken away', because 'there is no *jus divinum* to plead for it'. Wilson not only found a platform in addressing members of Parliament, he also wielded a considerable influence over puritan sentiment in his parish and in neighbouring Maidstone, the home of his patron, alderman Robert Swinnock. During the 1630s a number of the town's worthies, including Swinnock and his wife, had been prosecuted in the church courts for deserting the ministry of Robert Barrell at their parish church of All Saints in preference for Wilson's preaching in Otham. In May 1641 Swinnock and other Maidstone inhabitants had sent Sir Edward Dering a petition against Barrell, who stood accused of negligence and over-enthusiastic acceptance of Laudian 'innovations', including railing the altar at the east end of the parish church. The signatories included nine former and future mayors of the town and amongst them was Andrew Broughton, who later served as mayor of Maidstone in 1648 and 1659 and was the clerk of the court which tried Charles I in 1649. He was attainted of high treason with the other surviving regicides in 1660, but fled abroad.[49]

Barrell too played his part in the war of words from the pulpit and on 24 July 1642 he preached an assize sermon at Maidstone aimed against the Parliament and its Scots allies, in which he endorsed the legality of the royalist commission of array. Dering's papers demonstrate that sermons in favour of railed altars or

47 British Library, hereafter BL, Add. MS 29,624, f. 174r; *Calendar of Assize Records, Kent Indictments, Charles I, 1625–1649*, ed. J.S. Cockburn, London 1995, p. 424.

48 *The Private Journals of the Long Parliament 3 January to 5 March 1642*, ed. W.H. Coates, A.S. Steele and V.F. Snow, New Haven 1982, pp. 222–3; *The Oxinden Letters, 1607–1642*, ed. D. Gardiner, p. 232.

49 T. Wilson, *Jerichoes Down-Fall*, London 1643, pp. 2, 6, 10; Lambeth Palace Library, VG4/22, ff. 5r–7r, 80v; Larking, *op. cit.*, pp. 202–5; G. Aylmer, *The State's Servants: The Civil Service of the English Republic, 1649–1660*, London 1973, pp. 277, 419; *The Statutes of the Realm*, vol. v, London 1819, pp. 288–9.

against the Scots were regarded as particularly contentious in the county before the outbreak of civil war and Barrell was called before the House of Commons later that summer. His living was sequestrated by order of Parliament in the following year.[50] The conflict played out at parish level between Barrell and his puritan parishioners was duplicated in other parishes in the county. In the Wealden parish of Cranbrook, where there was a tradition of puritanism going back to the mid-1570s, the moderate episcopalian minister Robert Abbot was challenged by a group of separatists who wished to place authority in the hands of the entire congregation, 'both men and women'. Abbot complained to Dering in 1641 that the Cranbrook radicals opposed both the Church hierarchy and his use of the prayer book. During the 1640s and 1650s Cranbrook and neighbouring Wealden parishes continued to maintain a reputation as a centre of religious independency. The link between radical religious beliefs and parliamentarianism is highlighted by the fact that in August 1642 many of the inhabitants of the Kentish Weald petitioned Parliament to be allowed to train as volunteers under the command of Thomas Plumer. Their support for Parliament was well known in the county and during the armed revolt of July 1643 the rebels in Tonbridge were frightened that the 'Cranbrook roundheads' would descend on them along with parliamentarian soldiers, but by then Abbot had already left Cranbrook for a more congenial living in Hampshire.[51]

The assizes at which Barrell preached provided the scene for a power struggle between parliamentarians and royalists in late July 1642. Before the assize court met, the House of Commons had instructed a committee of seventeen of its members with Kent seats or connections to attend in order to prevent the spread of 'rumours to the scandal of Parliament'. They were unable to obtain permission from judge Thomas Malet to address the court, but in response to their presence a group of royalists drew up a petition to the King and an address to Parliament. Referring to the possibility of civil war, the address demanded that Parliament should surrender the magazine held by Sir John Hotham at Hull to the King, refrain from mustering the militia, restore the navy to the command of the King and adjourn Parliament to a place safe from the tumultous assemblies of the London crowds. According to Sir Roger Twysden's memoirs, these documents were carried to the King by a deputation consisting of Sir John Mayney, Paul Richaut, Edward Filmer, Sir Thomas Bosville and Sir William Clerke. They were subsequently printed in early August with Charles I's reply by Robert Barker, the royal printer in London, and the King ordered them to be read in all churches and chapels in Kent.[52]

---

50 Matthews, *Walker Revised*, p. 211.
51 P. Collinson, 'Cranbrook and the Fletchers: Popular and Unpopular Religion in the Kentish Weald', in *Godly People: Essays on English Protestantism and Puritanism*, ed. P. Collinson, London 1983, pp. 399–428; BL, Stowe MS 184, ff. 27–9; *CJ*, II, 714; *Papers Relating to Proceedings in the County of Kent, A.D.1642–A.D.1646*, ed. R. Almack, Camden Society 61, London 1855, p. 32; Matthews, *Walker Revised*, p. 209.
52 Woods, *op. cit.*, pp. 95–118; the petition and address are reproduced with the King's answer on pp. 153–7.

Following the return of the committee of MPs to Westminster, the Kent deputy-lieutenants, including Edwin Sandys, were ordered by Parliament to prevent the organisation of armed support for the King in Kent. Their initial target was Knole where, in the absence of the Earl of Dorset, the Earl's kinsman Sir John Sackville was arrested and taken to London along with five wagon loads of arms. At Cobham Hall and Hothfield the arms of the Duke of Richmond and John Tufton, the Earl of Thanet were taken and the houses of Sir Edward Dering, Sir William Butler and Sir Robert Filmer were ransacked. Particular attention was paid to the homes of catholic families including the Darrells, Ropers, and Finches. At Rochester and Canterbury Cathedrals the soldiers broke the altar rails and destroyed prayer books.[53] This was the first occasion on which the parliamentarians had turned their attention to the fabric of churches in Kent and their actions should not be regarded simply as mindless vandalism. The reformation of church buildings had been a central demand of the puritan agenda since the Elizabethan Settlement and was justified by reference to the second commandment against the worship of idols. Further attacks on images took place in Kent churches in response to the two parliamentary ordinances of August 1643 and May 1644.[54] In December 1643 Richard Culmer achieved notoriety for breaking stained glass depicting Thomas Becket in Canterbury Cathedral, when he described himself in an oft-quoted phrase as 'ratling down proud Beckets glassy bones'. Parts of the Edward IV window in the north-west transept of the cathedral representing the saints and the Virgin Mary were also destroyed at the same time, as were an image of the Archangel Michael and the image of Christ over the Christ Church gate. Culmer was acting officially in response to the earlier parliamentary ordinance, but the tensions that his actions caused in the cathedral precincts were reflected by the fact that the parliamentarian mayor of Canterbury, John Lade, provided a guard of soldiers to protect the iconoclasts. William Cooke, a Canterbury cordwainer was one of those who resisted the destruction in the cathedral and at the Restoration he petitioned the Dean and Chapter for compensation for the 'most violent blowes' dealt to him by Culmer and 'his company', which had subsequently prevented him from following his trade. Cooke described himself as 'a most loyall subiect' both to 'the late King' and to Charles II.[55]

At the Reformation the removal of church images and stained glass had been promoted by the Crown, but the iconoclasm of the 1640s was entirely different

---

[53] Pro-parliamentarian accounts of the activities of the deputy-lieutenants are contained in *A Perfect Diurnall of the Severall Passages in our Late Journey into Kent*, London 1642, and *A True Relation of the Late Expedition into Kent*, London 2 September 1642. An anti-parliamentarian account is to be found in *The Copy of a Letter Sent to an Honourable Lord by Doctor Paske, Subdean of Canterbury*, London 9 September 1642. The original letter from Paske to the Earl of Holland, dated 30 August 1642, is in the House of Lords Records Office, Main Papers Series, along with a second letter of 1 September 1642, in which Paske states that Sir Michael Livesey apologised for the excesses of the soldiers in Canterbury Cathedral.

[54] Firth and Rait, *Acts and Ordinances*, I, pp. 265–6, 425–6.

[55] R. Culmer, *Cathedrall Newes from Canterbury*, London 1644, pp. 20–4; Canterbury Cathedral Archives, DCC Petitions 232.

in that it was aimed at a royal regime which had seemingly condoned the rein-troduction of catholic altars and imagery in the 1630s. Image-breaking in the civil war period was not therefore solely a religious phenomenon, it was also a powerful challenge to the political power of the King.[56] One of the key fears of the parliamentarian party was that Charles I intended to rule as an absolute monarch, rather than in co-operation with Parliament and the classes it repre-sented. This explains in part why Sir Robert Filmer of East Sutton was repeat-edly under suspicion as a royalist despite the claims of his wife that he had no dealings with either party in 'deeds or so much as words'. Filmer was the author of *Patriarcha*, an extreme absolutist tract, in which he argued that the power of the King was analogous to the power of fathers over their families. Royal power was derived from divine right without the consent of the people and it could neither be shared with Parliament nor could it be opposed. This work was not published until 1680, when it was answered by John Locke and Algernon Sidney, but it may have been written as early as the late 1620s, when there were widespread complaints in Kent about the billeting of troops on local communi-ties. *Patriarcha* was reworked by Filmer in the 1630s and 1640s and it is most probable that his high royalist views were known in the county. Filmer was in his mid-50s when war broke out and he claimed to be too infirm to join the fighting, but in the mid-1640s he continued to write works upholding the absolute power of the Crown and published *The Free-Holders Grand Inquest*, *The Anarchy of a Limited or Mixed Monarchy* and *The Necessity of the Absolute Power of all Kings* at the time of the Second Civil War in 1648.[57]

(4) The County Committees

During the mid-1640s Filmer and other suspected royalists, including Sir Roger Twysden and the Earl of Thanet, were subjected to continual financial harrassment by the numerous parliamentarian committees set up in the county.[58] The committee system set up by Parliament in 1642 marked a significant depar-ture from traditional county government; nevertheless, the authority of the committee-men was based not just on their commissions from Parliament, but also on their more familiar powers as deputy lieutenants and justices of the peace. The chief county committee was concerned with the raising of taxation and the provision of armed forces, but its membership overlapped considerably

---

[56] J. Eales, 'Iconoclasm, Iconography and the Altar in the English Civil War', *The Church and the Arts*, Studies in Church History 28, ed. D. Wood, Oxford 1992, pp. 313–27.

[57] E. Melling, *Kent Sources, II. Kent and the Civil War*, Maidstone 1960, pp. 18–22; it has been sug-gested that Sir Robert Holborne wrote *The Free-Holders Grand Inquest* but Filmer's most recent editor argues that the weight of evidence favours Filmer as its author, see *Filmer: Patriarcha and Other Writings*, ed. J.P. Sommerville, Cambridge 1991.

[58] The passages that follow concerning the county committees are based on A.M. Everitt, *The County Committee of Kent in the Civil War*, University of Leicester, Department of English Local History, Occasional Papers No. 9 (1957).

with the sequestration committee set up in March 1643 to seize the estates of royalists and catholics. In 1644 an accounts committee was established with separate membership in order to audit the accounts of the first two committees. Separate committees were also established in Canterbury and Rochester and by the mid-1640s some twenty or so committees or sub-committees were operating in the county, towns and lathes of Kent in a direct parallel with the development of the committee system by which the Long Parliament governed from Westminster. The various committees and their membership were reorganised in the wake of the 1648 rising in Kent in order to ensure the loyalty of their personnel to Parliament. According to Everitt by 1660 some 274 men had served on the chief county committee, although he noted that only eight of them did so continuously – Richard Beale, Thomas Blount, Thomas Broadnax, Lambarde Godfrey, William James, Sir Michael Livesey, Thomas Plumer senior, and Augustine Skinner, who had replaced Dering as knight of the shire in 1642.[59] The turnover in personnel on the committee was paralleled in town administrations and in the parish livings of the county as central policies became more radical, and royalists, moderates and neutrals were ousted or resigned from positions of influence.

The main sources of committee revenue were the national assessment and the fines imposed on the royalists, which in practice included the cavaliers, who were in arms for the King, and also those who were either unwilling or slow to help Parliament. The national assessment was introduced by Parliament in February 1643 and Kent, Norfolk and Suffolk were the counties which were most heavily assessed at the weekly sum of £1,250. This was a reflection of Kent's position amongst the top three or four English counties in terms of both taxable wealth and population.[60] It has been estimated by Everitt that the total assessed on the county between 1643 and 1648 was £391,000, most of which was collected. A third of this sum was to be retained for expenditure in the county and the rest was to be sent to London. Receipts from the sequestration of royalists' estates have been estimated at no more than £70,000 between 1643 and 1649, of which £23,065 was sent to London. Revenue from composition, whereby sequestrated 'delinquents' could pay a fine and regain their estates, may have realised a total of £105,597 from the county in these years.[61] The highest composition fines in Kent were the sum of £9,000 imposed on the Earl of Thanet in 1644 and the sum of £9,810 imposed on the Duke of Richmond in December 1646.[62] Parliament also resorted to the introduction of an excise tax in July 1643 on tobacco, alcohol and imported luxury goods. More items were added in 1644 including meat and salt, but despite the unpopularity of the excise it was indispensable to the parliamentarian and Interregnum governments.

59 A. Everitt, 'Kent and its Gentry, 1640–60: A Political Study', London Ph.D. 1957, pp. 190, 500–4.

60 Firth and Rait, *Acts and Ordinances*, I, pp. 85–100; Clark, *English Provincial Society*, p. xiii.

61 Everitt, *The County Committee of Kent*, pp. 18, 32–5.

62 F. Hull (ed.), 'The Tufton Sequestration Papers, 1644–7', *Kent Records: A Seventeenth Century Miscellany*, pp. 35–67; Smith, *Constitutional Royalism*, pp. 203–4, 206–7, 263.

Under the Protectorate it was extended in 1654 to become almost a universal sales tax in order to pay for the maintainenance of the armed forces and for Cromwell's foreign wars.[63] The taxation raised in Kent in the 1640s and 1650s far outweighed the amounts imposed on the county by Charles I in the late 1630s when, for example, a total of £34,750 was demanded in ship money for the years 1635 to 1639.[64]

Most of the money retained by the central Kent committee was used for military purposes. In the eighteen months from January 1644 to June 1645 £45,530 was spent on the four main Kentish regiments in the field outside the county, Sir Michael Livesey's horse, Colonel Ralph Weldon's foot, Colonel Samuel Birch's foot in the south-west and Sir William Springate's foot at the siege of Arundel, while seventeen other troops and companies received lesser amounts. In the same period the sum of £13,880 was spent on arms and ammunition and a further £6,984 on military activity inside the county, including the garrisoning of Tonbridge castle and a guard for the committee.[65] The sequestrations and composition fines imposed on suspected royalists, the high level of parliamentary taxation needed to pay for the armed forces and the impressment of men to serve outside the county borders were all deeply resented in some quarters and during the 1640s the powers of the parliamentarian administration and its chairman Weldon came to be seen as oppressive. It was, however, largely external events rather than any direct action of the committee that sparked the first widespread armed resistance to Parliament in Kent in mid-1643.

(5) The First Civil War, 1642–46

The indecisive military events of the opening phase of civil war in late 1642 included the battle of Edgehill in October and the halting of the King's march on London at Turnham Green in November. By the summer of 1643, however, royalist fortunes were reviving and in May 1643 the discovery of Waller's Plot revealed evidence of royalist activity in London. Members of Parliament were now swiftly required to swear an oath of loyalty to Parliament and its forces.[66] In Kent the parish clergy were ordered to impose the oath on their parishioners, but at Ightham the minister, John Grimes, refused either to take it or tender it to his flock. Grimes' resistance was the rallying point for revolt and in mid-July armed men began to gather in the area around Ightham. News of this spread rapidly and three rebel camps were established at Sevenoaks, Aylesford and Faversham. Contemporary estimates suggested that the camps contained between 4,000 and

[63] J.P. Kenyon, *The Stuart Constitution*, Cambridge 1966, pp. 272–3.
[64] M.D. Gordon, 'The Collection of Ship-Money in the Reign of Charles I', *Transactions of the Royal Historical Society*, 3rd ser. iv (1910), pp. 141–62.
[65] Everitt, *The County Committee of Kent*, pp. 35–8.
[66] Firth and Rait, *Acts and Ordinances*, I, pp. 175–6.

6,000 men.[67] They were doubtless emboldened by news of the series of royalist victories in late June and early July in the north at Adwalton Moor and in the west at Lansdowne and Roundway Down. Sir Henry Vane, the elder, and two members of the county committee, William James of Ightham and Sir Isaac Sedley, acted as negotiators for Parliament, but were briefly held prisoner by the rebels. A detachment of parliamentarian troops commanded by Colonel Richard Browne was then ordered to advance on the camp at Sevenoaks, but found that most of their adversaries had fled. Browne's men drove the remaining stalwarts, whom he numbered at 500–600, towards Tonbridge where, urged on by some of the townspeople, they turned to face their pursuers. In his despatch to Parliament Browne described the 'very hot fight' on 24 July 1643 at Tonbridge where he claimed to have taken about 200 prisoners and killed more than a dozen of his opponents.[68] Tonbridge had already been described by the committee-man William James as 'wavering' in December 1642 and, although there was what he called a 'well-affected party' there, they were clearly in the minority. Thomas Weller, one of the most active parliamentarian officials in the town and also a captain of a trained band, wrote a description of conditions inside Tonbridge during the revolt, when his house was plundered three times by insurgents and he was repeatedly threatened as a 'roundheaded rogue' and 'Parliament dog'. As the fighting raged, Weller prayed for the success of Parliament's forces with 'divers well affected of my neighbours'.[69]

Fines were subsequently imposed on 197 known rebels, which allows some conclusions to be drawn about popular allegiances in Kent at this point in the war. George Hornby's research into allegiance in West Kent during the First Civil War of 1642–6 suggests that the rebels were not gentry led, but were independent minded yeomen, husbandmen and craftsmen, many of whom came from the Upper Medway Valley around Tonbridge, the Wrotham Chartlands, Maidstone and Greenwich. Although the rebels did not issue a manifesto, their central demands included their desire for the continued use of the *Book of Common Prayer*, hostility to puritan ministers intruded into parishes by Parliament and the refusal to take the oath imposed in the wake of Waller's Plot. It is difficult to say whether the rebels were motivated by royalist convictions or simply by anti-parliamentarian feeling, but as Hornby argues their royalism was implicit in their refusal to take an oath to support Parliament against the King. The importance of the rebels' religious demands is underscored by the fact that a number of ministers were punished by sequestration for amongst other things encouraging the rebellion, including Edward Ashburnham of Tonbridge, Richard Chase of Chislehurst and Stone, John Grimes of Ightham, Daniel

67 My account here follows George Hornby's important unpublished research, 'Allegiance in West Kent During the First Civil War, 1642–1646'. I am grateful to Mr Hornby for allowing me to make use of this work. See also Everitt, *The Community of Kent*, pp. 187–200.

68 Almack, *op. cit.*, pp. 26–34; *Fifth Report of the Royal Commission of Historical Manuscripts*, Part 1, London 1876, p. 97; see also *CJ*, III, 181.

69 Almack, *op. cit.*, pp. 6, 26–34.

Horsmonden of Ulcombe, where Horsmonden's brother-in-law, the royalist Sir Anthony St Leger, was patron of the living, John Jefferys of Faversham and Ticehurst, John Rowland of Foots Cray, and Edward Wallis of Tudeley.[70]

In the aftermath of the revolt in Kent and in the light of the royalist victories in mid-1643, it was clear to the parliamentarian leadership that if the King was to be defeated then more decisive military measures would need to be taken. In September 1643 Parliament forged a formal alliance with the Scots, the price of which was the Covenant, an oath imposed throughout the English parishes calling for uniformity in religion between Scotland, England and Ireland. While the Scots saw this as an agreement to abolish episcopacy and introduce a presbyterian system into England, many Englishmen took it with degrees of mental reservation. Scottish troops subsequently took part in the major parliamentarian victory at Marston Moor in 1644. Early in 1644 Parliament offered an amnesty to all 'malignants', who were to take the Covenant and compound for their support for the King. Sir Edward Dering was amongst the first to take this opportunity to return to his family and Kent estates. His action was understandably treated as a desertion by the royalist party, but Dering was already fatally ill and may possibly have been suffering from a brain tumour. He died in June and the agreed composition of £1,000 was waived by Parliament. The Earl of Thanet also took advantage of the amnesty in that year.[71]

At the end of 1643 Parliament restructured its military forces and an association was formed between Kent, Surrey, Sussex and Hampshire under the command of General Sir William Waller. This was to lead to complaints from the county committee about Waller's powers, especially as Parliament was now forced to rely more heavily on impressment and the use of the county militia to supply forces outside the county. In July 1644 Sir Michael Livesey marched his troops away from Waller's command at Abingdon amidst complaints of the general's maladministration, while the county committee justified Livesey's action and claimed that the forces were needed for the protection of the county. This claim was seemingly borne out when a royalist plot to seize Dover castle and to foment revolt in Sevenoaks and Rochester was uncovered later in the year and some eight conspirators were apprehended.[72]

In order to overcome objections to the deployment of local troops outside their county, the pro-war party in Parliament took measures in February 1645 to create a national force in the form of the New Model Army. The existing armies led by Waller and the Earls of Essex and Manchester were united and were to be joined by conscripts from London, and southern and eastern counties. Kent was to contribute 1,000 conscripts, but in early April approximately half of them

---

[70] Hornby, 'Allegiance in West Kent during the First Civil War, 1642–1646', pp. 58–9, 63–80, 97–101, 240–50; J. White, *The First Century of Scandalous Malignant Priests*, London 1643, p. 23; Matthews, *Walker Revised*, pp. 209–10, 213–14, 217, 219, 220, 224, 227.

[71] Larking, *op. cit.*, pp. l–li; Hull, 'Tufton Sequestration Papers', pp. 35–9.

[72] *CSPD, 1644*, pp. 370, 377.

rebelled at Wrotham Heath and a separate rising broke out around the Darent Valley. Parliamentarian forces commanded by Colonel Thomas Blount joined with the Kent trained bands to march on the rebels and took 50 prisoners, but simultaneously Sir Michael Livesey's regiment of horse was reported to be mutinous for lack of pay. Lady Isabella Twysden recorded in her diary that the rising was 'presently laid being but a few' and that Livesey's troops 'were sent back with promises of there paye'. Livesey's men eventually rejoined Fairfax's command in early May and fought at Naseby in June, where the parliamentarian victory finally destroyed the royalists hopes of winning the war.[73]

(6) The Second Civil War, 1648

Charles I did not formally surrender until May 1646, when it was widely believed that an accommodation would finally be reached. Despite his military defeat, however, the King refused to alienate any further powers of the Crown and he also hoped for the renewal of armed support. He therefore entered into separate negotiations with Parliament, the New Model Army leaders and the Scots in order to play for time. Charles's erstwhile opponents were unable to impose a settlement on him, because they themselves were deeply divided about what form it should take. Members of Parliament were now split between a majority, who wanted a national presbyterian church settlement, and a smaller number, who favoured an independent solution giving individual congregations greater toleration. Many of the latter finally endorsed the revolutionary solution of regicide.

Episcopacy was abolished by parliamentary ordinance in October 1646, thus opening the way for the sale of Church lands, and for the setting up of a presbyterian system in some counties. In Kent the county committee consulted twenty ministers and twenty gentlemen about the division of the county into presbyteries early in 1646. There is no evidence that a formal presbyterian organisation was ever in operation in the county, although there were a number of influential presbyterian ministers in Kent, such as Thomas Wilson and Richard Culmer. There was also considerable support for the various religious sects in Kent and by 1646 Samuel Fisher, the later Quaker convert, had already established himself as a baptist preacher with a considerable following at Lydd. In 1646 John Durant and John Davis were respectively accepted as pastors of the congregational churches in Canterbury and Dover and independent congregations also existed in Sandwich, as well as in a number of parishes in East Kent and the Weald.[74] The strength of these and other gathered churches may have persuaded

[73] I. Gentles, *The New Model Army in England, Ireland and Scotland, 1645–1653*, Oxford 1992, p. 32; F.D. Johns, 'The Royalist Rising and Parliamentary Mutinies of 1645 in West Kent', *Archaeologia Cantiana*, cx (1992), pp. 1–15; F.W. Bennitt, 'The Diary of Isabella, Wife of Sir Roger Twysden, Baronet, of Royden Hall, East Peckham 1645–1651', *Archaeologia Cantiana*, li (1940), p. 117.

[74] Firth and Rait, *Acts and Ordinances*, I, pp. 879–83; W.A. Shaw, *A History of the English Church,*

the county committee not to press ahead with Parliament's plans for a national presbyterian organisation.

The military were also important players in the negotiations with the King, since the fear of renewed royalist or anti-Parliament unrest meant that Parliament could not disband the armed forces before Charles agreed to terms. The continuance, however, of high levels of parliamentary taxation to meet the soldiers' wages and arrears of pay served to compound the antagonism felt in the provinces towards the politicians at Westminster. Moreover, the spread of radical religious beliefs within the army also meant that the generals were opposed to a purely presbyterian Church. In order to ensure that any settlement took their demands into account, the army seized Charles from the custody of Parliament in June 1647. Nevertheless, the King continued his various negotiations and in December he signed the Engagement with the Scots by which he agreed to accept a presbyterian system in England for three years in exchange for military aid against Parliament. Under the command of James, Duke of Hamilton a force of 20,000 Scots crossed into England at the height of the Second Civil War in July 1648 only to be defeated by Cromwell at Preston in the following month. In England localised fighting took place in the summer of 1648 in Wales, Kent and Essex, when groups of royalists were joined by malcontents, who resented high levels of taxation and feared a standing army. Initially the Kent insurgents looked to local figures to lead them, including the Earl of Thanet and Edward Hales the younger, although overall command was eventually vested in the hands of George Goring, Earl of Norwich.[75] The disparate revolts of 1648 were uncoordinated and there was very little chance that Parliament's forces led by Fairfax and Cromwell could be defeated.

In Kent anti-parliamentarian and anti-puritan sentiment had already led to unrest late in 1647 when William Bridges, the mayor of Canterbury, tried to enforce Parliament's orders against the celebration of Christmas Day. There were to be no special prayers or sermons in churches on 25 December, which that year coincided with the town's weekly Saturday market, but a disturbance ensued when market traders were forced to shut their stalls by an increasingly angry crowd and armed men stood guard at St Andrew's church to ensure that a sermon could be preached unhindered. Attempts to restore order provoked open violence against the mayor as an 'excise-man' and a number of arrests were made. Over the next few days the number of dissidents in the town was increased by outsiders encouraged by the news that the King had escaped from Carisbrooke Castle on 29 December. The rioters released their companions from prison, took command of the city magazine and closed the city gates against the troops sent to regain control by the county committee. A group of moderate aldermen and committee-men led by Sir William Mann, Avery Sabine,

1640–1660, vol. II (1900), pp. 372–3; Acheson, 'The Development of Religious Separatism in the Diocese of Canterbury, 1590–1660'; for Fisher see *DNB* and for Durant and Davis see *Calamy Revised*, ed. A.G. Matthews, Oxford 1988, pp. 158–9, 173.

75 R. Ashton, *Counter Revolution: The Second Civil War and its Origins, 1646–8*, London 1994, *passim*.

Vespasian Harris, and Francis Lovelace, a former recorder of the town, negotiated a truce and on 4 January the forces of the county committee were peacefully admitted to the town. The committee then ordered that the city walls should be slighted and the city gates destroyed. The most prominent rioters were imprisoned in Leeds Castle along with the moderate leaders Mann, Lovelace and Sabine.[76]

A special commission of oyer and terminer was held at Canterbury on 10 May 1648 to try the prisoners, but the grand jury returned a verdict of 'ignoramus', which allowed the accused to go free. The next day a petition was framed to Parliament from the county and signed by members of the grand jury which demanded a religious and political settlement that acknowledged the rights of both King and Parliament. The petitioners called for the payment of the army's arrears and its disbandment, for government by the 'established laws of this kingdon' and an end to Parliamentary taxation, especially the excise. The petition was circulated in the county and plans were made for copies to be brought in to Rochester on the 29th of the month and delivered to Parliament from Blackheath the next day.[77]

At Minster in Thanet Richard Culmer persuaded many of his parishioners not to subscribe the petition by arguing for the necessity of taxes and that the army was a protection from 'bloody wolves in Ireland, Papists, Atheists etc'. Culmer had been intruded into the living in 1645 in the place of Meric Casaubon, one of the canons of Canterbury Cathedral. He was now opposed by a group of local Thanet men (some of whom were soon to be active participants in the imminent rising), who disliked his refusal to use the *Book of Common Prayer*.[78] The petition proved to be a rallying point for resurgent royalist feeling in the county, though willingness to sign it needs to be distinguished from the activities of those men, many of whom had served in the King's army in the First Civil War, who now set about arming themselves in preparation for a violent confrontation with the Parliamentary forces. They were encouraged by news of the revolt of the Downs fleet, which was rumoured to be sailing to the Isle of Wight in order to rescue the King and take him to Kent. Chief amongst the royalist activists were the cavaliers Sir Anthony St Leger, Sir John Mayney, Richard Thornhill, and Sir John Boys of Bonnington, all of whom had previously been in arms for the King. They were joined by Sir Richard Hardres, who had served on the county committee in the early 1640s and who in late May set about securing strongholds for the rebels. After laying siege to Dover castle, Hardres took

[76] Firth and Rait, *Acts and Ordinances*, I, p. 954; Ashton, *Counter-Revolution*, pp. 359–61; Everitt, *County Community*, pp. 231–40; M.V. Jones, 'The Political History of the Parliamentary Boroughs of Kent', pp. 102–5; A.B., *A Letter from a Gentleman in Kent Giving Satisfaction to a Friend in London*, London 1648, p. 3; see also *Canterbury Christmas: or a True Relation of the Insurrection in Canterbury on Christmas Day Last. Written by a Citizen There*, London 1648.

[77] *CJ*, V, 422, 444; *The Humble Petition of the Knights, Gentry, Clergy, and Commonalty of the County of Kent*, London May 1648.

[78] Culmer, *Parish looking-Glasse*, pp. 30–1; for Culmer's career see *Calamy Revised*, ed. A.G. Matthews, Oxford, 1988, p. 154.

control of the castles of Deal and Walmer and left troops at Sandwich and Canterbury before moving on to Rochester where the insurgents had declared for the King. By the end of May there were some 11,000 men in arms in the county, whose numbers included not only local men, but also London apprentices, and sailors and royalist soldiers from outside Kent.[79]

On 1 June Sir Thomas Fairfax's parliamentarian forces engaged with those of Sir John Mayney and Sir William Brockman at Maidstone and, although a parliamentarian eye-witness estimated that Fairfax commanded some 7,000 troops, it is more likely that he had 4,000 men at his disposal. Nevertheless, his opponents numbered no more than 2,000 and despite a fierce defence the rebel troops were overcome. The Earl of Norwich, who had set out to relieve Mayney and Brockman, now turned his troops towards Rochester, where he decided to join the insurgents in Essex. By the time his men reached Greenwich, Norwich led an increasingly dwindling band of no more than 3,000. From there they crossed into Essex and joined the unsuccessful defence of Colchester. Most of the remaining rebels in Kent had already dispersed to their homes, but a remnant of no more than 1,300 joined Sir Richard Hardres at Canterbury. They were overcome by the troops of Fairfax who advanced from the west and colonels Hewson and Rich who advanced from the south.[80] Dover and Walmer castles surrendered to Parliament within days, although Deal and Sandown did not capitulate until after the defeat of the Scots at Preston.[81] In October Parliament ordered the sequestration of the estates of all those who had been in arms against Parliament or who had otherwise aided the rebellion and, according to Everitt, moderate fines were hastily imposed on some 280 families. Parliament also tightened security by billeting increased numbers of troops in Dover and Sandwich. The garrisoning of soldiers in Kent towns, including Maidstone and Rochester, continued to be a source of tension throughout the 1650s.[82]

(7) The Interregnum

The suppression of the Second Civil War in 1648 was the prelude to the execution of Charles I. In early December 1648 the army purged members of Parliament who were unlikely to endorse the trial of the King; they included six men with Kent constituencies – John Boys of Betteshanger (Kent), Sir Norton

---

[79] The most detailed descriptions of the 1648 rising in Kent are to be found in Ashton, *Counter-Revolution*, and Everitt, *Community of Kent*, pp. 231–70; see also Gentles, *New Model Army*, pp. 247–9. First-hand accounts are contained in R. L'Estrange, *L'Estrange His Vindication to Kent*, London 1649, and M. Carter, *A Most True and Exact Relation of that as Honourable as Unfortunate Expedition of Kent, Essex and Colchester*, London 1650.

[80] Gentles, *New Model Army*, pp. 247–9, 511 n. 61; R.K.G. Temple, 'Discovery of a Manuscript Eye-Witness Account of the Battle of Maidstone', *Archaeologia Cantiana*, xcvii (1982), pp. 209–20; B. Lyndon, 'Essex and the King's Cause in 1648', *Historical Journal*, xxix (1986), pp. 17–39.

[81] Ashton, *Counter-Revolution*, pp. 425–9.

[82] Firth and Rait, *Acts and Ordinances*, I, pp. 1, 222–3; Everitt, *County Community*, pp. 274–5; M.V. Jones, 'The Political History of the Parliamentary Boroughs of Kent', pp. 374–88.

Knatchbull (New Romney), Sir Edward Partherich (Sandwich), Charles Rich (Sandwich), Sir Humphrey Tufton (Maidstone) and Thomas Twisden (Maidstone). Three more, Sir Henry Heyman (Hythe), Richard Lee (Rochester) and Thomas Westrow (Hythe) were not formally secluded, but avoided sitting in the House until after the King's execution. Four others, John Nutt (Canterbury), Augustine Skinner (Kent), Sir Thomas Walsingham (Rochester) and Benjamin Weston (Dover) continued to sit, but avoided committing themselves in December and January. They accepted the *status quo* in February 1649 when the House of Commons abolished both the monarchy and the House of Lords, and declared England to be a Commonwealth. The regicides, John Dixwell (Dover), Augustine Garland (Queenborough) and Sir Michael Livesey (Queenborough), were known radicals, who were allowed to take their seats in the House of Commons and openly committed themselves to the revolution.[83]

Although public opinion in Kent has been depicted as strongly anti-Parliament in the aftermath of the Second Civil War, a radical petition calling for the trial and execution of the King was circulated in the county early in January 1649. It attracted 1,135 signatures including some of the town councillors of Canterbury, Sandwich and Hythe and members of independent church congregations. Their names were headed by William Kenwricke of Boughton under Blean, who was one of the five representatives from Kent to the Nominated or Barebones Parliament of 1653.[84] No major gentry families were represented amongst the signatories, nor were any of them women. Although Everitt argues that 'it is doubtful if the lengthy lists of signatures . . . are genuine' but he gives no convincing evidence for this opinion. It is reasonable, therefore, to conclude that the petition demonstrates the expression of public opinion that was a hallmark of the civil war period and that there was active, but limited, support for the regicide in Kent.[85] The reception of the petition was undoubtedly an important factor in persuading the radicals in the army and in Parliament that there was sufficient support in the localities for the regicide to go ahead.

After the execution of the King, some of the county's active royalists withdrew from political life. The Earl of Dorset retired to his London house and died there in 1652, leaving his son in considerable debt as the result of the sequestration of his estates in Kent and Sussex. Similarly the Duke of Richmond resided quietly at Cobham Hall, where he rejected attempts to engage him in royalist conspiracies, but was closely watched by the government until his death in

---

[83] Heyman, Knatchbull, Lee, Nutt, Partherich, Tufton and Walsingham had all been elected in 1640, the others were recruiter MPs who had been elected to replace disabled or deceased members, see Underdown, *Pride's Purge*, pp. 366–90; for John Boys see also D. Underdown, 'The Parliamentary Diary of John Boys, 1647–8', *Bulletin of the Institute of Historical Research*, xxxix (1966), pp. 141–64.

[84] Bodleian Library, Tanner MS 57b and Rawlinson MS A298; Acheson, 'The Development of Religious Separatism in the Diocese of Canterbury, 1590–1660', p. 214. For Kenwricke see A. Woolrych, *Commonwealth to Protectorate*, Oxford 1982, pp. 420–1, and R. Greaves, *Deliver Us From Evil: The Radical Underground in Britain, 1660–1663*, Oxford 1986, pp. 71, 117, 122–4, 172, 250.

[85] Everitt, *County Community*, pp. 271–2.

1655.[86] The constant fear of counter-revolution in the late 1640s and 1650s led to the reorganisation of the system of county committees. At the end of 1648 the accounts committee in Kent was abolished and this was followed by the abolition of the sequestration committee in February 1650. The powers of the general county committee were eclipsed by the creation of two new bodies, the militia committee and the committee of assessment with headquarters at Maidstone, whose members were largely minor gentry.[87]

The eleven years from 1649 until the Restoration of Charles II in 1660 constituted a period of republican experiment in which a series of *ad hoc* governmental forms were established and abandoned. The Rump of the Long Parliament remained in session until 1653 when it was dismissed and replaced by a nominated assembly summoned by Cromwell as Commander-in-Chief of the army. The men who represented Kent in this short-lived body were Thomas Blount, Andrew Broughton, William Cullen the mayor of Dover, William Kenwricke, and Philip Sidney, Lord Lisle.[88] Later in 1653 Cromwell accepted the office of Lord Protector under the terms of the Instrument of Government, but he was opposed not only by monarchists, but also by republicans such as Algernon Sidney, who wanted power to rest with a wider ruling body. Cromwell's death in 1658 inevitably precipitated a political crisis to which the return of the Stuart monarchy seemed to offer the most widely acceptable solution.[89]

Throughout the Interregnum Kent was regarded as one of the main centres of potential opposition to the series of *de facto* governments because of the relative ease of communication between the county and the royalist exiles in France and the Netherlands. In the early 1650s Richard Thornhill and Sir Thomas Peyton emerged as the most influential royalist agents in the county. In 1650 Thornhill had proposed a plan to seize Dover castle for Charles II, which proved unsuccessful, and in 1651 Peyton and a number of other Kent suspects were arrested amidst fears of renewed agitation in the county. In 1655 Peyton and Thornhill were both members of the royalist Action Party's high command, when a revolt in the county was planned to coincide with Penruddock's rising in Wiltshire. The failure of the 1655 rising led to Peyton's confinement in the Tower of London, the arrest of the Earl of Thanet and the flight of other conspirators.[90]

As a reaction to Penruddock's rising the control of central government was extended by the brief establishment of the rule of the major-generals, which was introduced in October 1655 in order to suppress rebellion and disarm former royalist forces. The major-generals were also ordered to promote godliness by enforcing the laws against drunkenness, profanity and breaking the sabbath.[91]

---

[86] Smith, *Constitutional Royalism*, pp. 259–64.
[87] Everitt, *Community of Kent*, pp. 288–92.
[88] Woolrych, *Commonwealth to Protectorate*, pp. 410–33.
[89] Scott, *Algernon Sidney and the English Republic, 1623–1677*, pp. 113–23.
[90] Underdown, *Royalist Conspiracy*, pp. 37, 47, 109–11; *The Oxinden Letters, 1642–1670*, ed. D. Gardiner, pp. 210–13.
[91] C. Durston, 'The Fall of Cromwell's Major-Generals', *English Historical Review*, cxiii (1998), pp. 18–37.

The expenses of this regime were to be met by a 10% tax on the estates of royalists, the decimation tax, which in Kent raised a total of £3,936 4s. 2d. in the eighteen months for which it was collected. As major-general for Kent, Thomas Kelsey headed a commission to impose the tax in the county, the most active members of which were army commanders including Sir Michael Livesey and captains Charles Bowles, John Browne and Martin Pyke. The names of nearly 400 suspected royalists who were investigated by the commission have survived and it is clear that the commissioners concentrated their attentions on royalist activity in areas which had been involved in the 1648 revolt, particularly the north-west of the county around Bromley and Dartford and in the east around Canterbury. Amongst those suspected royalists summoned by the commission between November 1655 and January 1657 were the Earl of Thanet, Edward Hales the younger, Sir John Boys of Bonnington, Richard Thornhill, Sir Thomas Peyton, Sir John Mayney, Sir Richard Hardres and Sir Roger Twysden.[92]

Kelsey was also responsible for policing the religious beliefs of the population and in 1655 he arrested the itinerant preacher Richard Coppin after a disputation in Rochester cathedral with two local ministers, Walter Rosewell of Chatham and Daniel French of Strood. Kelsey accused Coppin of preaching blasphemous tenets including that 'Christ's humane nature was defiled with sinne . . . [and] all men showld be saved'. Kelsey believed that not only the townsfolk, but also the soldiers in Rochester had been tainted with these opinions and feared Coppin's followers would demand liberty of conscience and 'say it's persecution wors than in the bishops time'.[93] Kelsey's power as major-general lapsed early in 1657 when Parliament refused to pass a bill for the permanent establishment of the decimation tax, but he remained a key figure on local commissions. There was, however, already evidence of strong dislike for the Protectorate in Kent by this date. At the assizes held in March 1656 Isaac Atkinson of Wichling was accused of seditious words for calling Cromwell 'a rogue, a robber and a thief' and for saying that 'within a year and a half he will have a bullet in his arse'. A year later Thomas Bennett of Hoo was accused of saying that 'the land is governed now by none but rogues, knaves and thieves for want of a king'.[94] Under the terms of the Instrument of Government royalists were specifically excluded from standing for parliamentary elections or from voting.[95] Nevertheless, at the Maidstone elections held in August 1656, Kelsey informed Cromwell that the royalists and the presbyterians were acting together 'against you and the government, and the spirit is generally bitter against swordsmen, decimators, courtiers etc'. He noted that most of those elected as

[92] J.T. Cliffe, 'The Cromwellian Decimation Tax of 1655: The Assessment Lists', *Seventeenth-Century Political and Financial Papers*, Camden 5th ser. vii (1996), pp. 407–77; Bloomfield, *op. cit.*

[93] *A Collection of the State Papers of John Thurloe*, ed. T. Birch, London 1742, vol. iv, p. 486; for Coppin see *DNB*.

[94] *Calendar of Assize Records, Kent Indictments, 1649–1659*, ed. J.S. Cockburn, London 1989, pp. 242, 281.

[95] M.V. Jones, 'Political History of the Parliamentary Boroughs of Kent', p. 503; Kenyon, *The Stuart Constitution*, p. 334.

MPs were of the 'same spirit' and 'give out that they will down with the majors-general, the decimators and the new militia'. Kelsey recommended that such men should be excluded from sitting in Parliament.[96] Eight Kent MPs were duly excluded as being hostile to the Protectorate – Richard Beale, John Boys of Betteshanger, Lambarde Godfrey, William James, John Seyliard, Daniel Shetterden and Sir Thomas Style, who were all elected to serve for the county, and James Thurbarne, MP for Sandwich.[97]

The final three years of the Interregnum saw an intensification of political tension following Cromwell's decision in May 1657 to accept the Humble Petition and Advice, by which the Protectorate became an hereditary office. The accession of Richard Cromwell as Protector in September 1658 on the death of his father prompted splits in the army between his supporters and those who wanted to limit his powers. Under the aegis of the army leaders the Rump of the Long Parliament was recalled in early May 1659 and Richard Cromwell abdicated later that month. Kelsey's position in the county now reflected the vagaries of central politics. In August he was employed in quashing a royalist revolt in Kent co-ordinated by Sir Thomas Peyton, Sir John Boys of Bonnington and Sir Anthony Aucher of Bishopsbourne, when fifty or so activists were arrested. In October, however, Kelsey was deprived of his military commission by Parliament for his part in circulating a petition calling for the greater independence of the army from civil government. He was associated with major-general Lambert in the subsequent dismissal of the Rump, but when its members were restored in December, Kelsey was ousted once again and fled into exile at the Restoration.[98]

(8) The Restoration

In response to the instability of central government the leading Kent royalists drew up a *Declaration* in January 1660 calling for the recall to the Rump of the members of the Long Parliament, who had been secluded at Pride's Purge and for free elections to fill the vacant seats of MPs who had died.[99] The *Declaration* was one of many such documents presented by the counties in early 1660 to the Rump and to Colonel Monck, the newly appointed commander in chief of the army. Under Monck's influence the fully restored Long Parliament finally ordered its own dissolution and new elections were held.[100] On this occasion royalists were once again able to vote and it was reported that at the county election held at Maidstone 'all the royalists and moderate men in the county' agreed

96   *CSPD 1656–7*, pp. 87–8.
97   Everitt, *County Community*, p. 295 n. 2.
98   R. Hutton, *The Restoration: A Political and Religious History of England and Wales, 1657–1667*, Oxford 1985, pp. 3–84; for Kelsey see *DNB* and *CJ*, VII, 669, 723, 749, 796, 806, 812.
99   *The Declaration of the Nobility, Gentry, Ministry, and Commonalty of the County of Kent*, London 1660.
100 Everitt, *County Community*, pp. 306–9.

to return Sir Edward Dering, son of Sir Edward, first baronet, and Sir John Tufton, cousin of the Earl of Thanet, both of whom had played little part in the politics of the 1640s and 1650s. Dering recorded that the supporters of their republican opponents, Colonel Ralph Weldon and John Boys of Betteshanger, were 'not one thousand and our party judged to be 6,000 [so] that it was yielded without polling'.[101]

In April 1660 the Convention Parliament met in order to oversee the return of the monarchy and in May Charles II arrived at Dover to claim his kingdom. Contemporary accounts of the King's reception at Dover, Canterbury, Rochester and Chatham record the loyal addresses made by the members of the town corporations and the celebrations of the many crowds who thronged his route through Kent to London.[102] Despite such displays of unity, dissent would continue to be a major factor in Restoration politics, and the county and urban elites of Kent were subjected to further purges in the 1660s and 1670s. Some 63 incumbents were also ejected from their livings in Kent under the terms of the Act for Confirming and Restoring of Ministers of 1660 and the Act of Uniformity of 1662. Religious nonconformity continued to have a particularly strong hold in towns such as Canterbury, Maidstone, Dover and Sandwich as well as in certain rural areas of the county.[103]

Despite the Restoration anti-monarchical sympathies were not entirely extinguished. Few republicans were as outspoken, however, as Simon Oldfield a shoemaker of Canterbury, who reputedly stated at the end of 1660 that he had always been against 'kingly government' and that Charles I had had a 'fair and legal trial'. Nor were most anti-royalist statements made so dramatically as that of the Deal woman, who was later accused of declaring, when her hands were covered in pig's blood, 'oh that my hands were in that regall bloude [of] Charles Stewart'.[104]

These words, spoken by an artisan and by a woman, are a reminder that political and religious debate was not a preserve of the elite in the early modern period. There has been a tendency amongst some historians to portray the population of Kent as gentry-led, insular and locally minded in the seventeenth century, but this should not be exaggerated. Political and religious beliefs divided not only the gentry, but also the wider population who often saw the clergy, and even lay preachers, as their mentors and spokesmen. The circulation of national news in the county and the mass petitioning campaigns there of the 1640s demonstrate both that the expression of public opinion was regarded as an important factor in the political process and that politicians were not immune to

---

[101] *The History of Parliament: The House of Commons, 1660–1690*, ed. B.D. Henning, vol. 1, London 1983, p. 275.

[102] Everitt, *County Community*, pp. 312–18.

[103] Nuttall, *op. cit.*, p. 175. For the later history of nonconformity in Kent see Yates, Hume and Hastings, *Religion and Society in Kent, 1640–1914*, Woodbridge 1994, pp. 14–17, 40–4.

[104] *Calendar of Assize Records: Kent Indictments Charles II, 1660–1675*, ed. J.S. Cockburn, London 1995, pp. 23–4; cited in Acheson, 'The Development of Religious Separatism in the Diocese of Canterbury, 1590–1660', p. 129.

popular pressure. In Kent some men were prepared to go further in demonstrating their ideological beliefs by volunteering to fight for King or Parliament, and the risings of 1643, 1645 and 1648 also indicate that there was strong support for the royalist cause amongst the county population. Such powerful evidence of royalism should not lead, however, to the assumption that opposition to the Crown was insignificant in Kent, for a broad spectrum of public opinion was to be found there in the 1640s and 1650s. During the civil war period, therefore, the county cannot accurately be described as predominantly royalist, parliamentarian, republican or even moderate, for what is significant about Kent is that all of these opinions were strongly represented in the county. This diversity was an outcome of the geographical, strategical and administrative importance of Kent, which rested on its various relationships with the capital, its key defensive role and the presence of the archbishopric of Canterbury within its borders. The demands that this placed upon the inhabitants of the county were well understood by contemporaries and they were expressed in terms of national issues, as well as in terms of local and personal grievances. It was not simply local concerns, but the balance between central and provincial affairs, which lay at the heart of county politics in Kent, not only during the years of civil war, but throughout the early modern period.[105]

[105] I am grateful to Richard Cust, Christopher Durston, Richard Eales, Kenneth Fincham, George Hornby, Fred Lansberry, John Morrill, Stephen Roberts and Conrad Russell for their advice in the preparation of this chapter. I am also indebted to Sheila Hingley and Michael Stansfield, and their staffs at the Canterbury Cathedral Library and Archives, for their help in meeting my various requests for information.

2

'Tempered Despotism'?:
The Government of the County

FREDERICK LANSBERRY

(1) The Restoration in Kent

In January 1660 after the fall of Richard Cromwell, but before the King had been restored to the throne, the nobility, gentry, ministry and commonalty of Kent, with Canterbury, Rochester and the ports in the county issued a declaration to the Speaker of the House of Commons and 'to the present great arbitrator of the nation's peace and happiness, General Monk'

> We must publish our resentment of our present calamities; our friendlessness abroad and divisions at home; the loud and heart-piercing cries of the poor; the disability of the better sort to relieve them; the total decay of trade; the loss of the nation's reputation; and the apparent hazard of the Gospel, through the prodigious growth of blasphemies, heresies and schism, all threatening universal ruin.[1]

These claims, patterned on similar declarations by other counties, were generated by Kentish Royalists headed by Sir John Boys, a committed Cavalier, Thomas Engeham and Sir William Mann, both at one time members of the County Committee, William Somner, Canterbury's antiquarian, and Mr Masters, whose father, Sir Edward Masters, Member of Parliament for Canterbury, had been excluded in Pride's Purge. The Council of State ordered John Dixwell, Governor of Dover Castle, to send a party of horse to round them up and imprison them in Dover and Deal castles.[2] The calamities they complained of were exaggerated but continuance of the same political regime after the fall of Richard Cromwell was no longer acceptable in Kent or elsewhere. In the end, therefore, there emerged a compromise: a monarchy stripped of its feudal trappings – feudal taxes and land holding were not restored – and a monarchy freed from the attempts at deification of the first two Stuarts. The Declaration Charles issued at Breda offered a general pardon for past offences (except those here-

---

[1] *CSPD, 1659–1660*, p. 340.
[2] A. Everitt, *The Community of Kent and the Great Rebellion, 1640–1660*, Leicester 1966, p. 307; *CSPD 1659–60*, p. 330.

after excepted by Parliament) and a respect for the *status quo* of the kingdom and its officers as he might find it. He hoped for 'the quiet and peaceable possession of that our right' and 'that all our subjects may enjoy what by law is theirs'. In particular Charles declared a liberty to tender consciences and 'that no man shall be disquieted or called in question for differences of opinion in matter of religion which do not disturb the peace of the kingdom'. These statements which raised issues sufficient to start another conflict were not analysed and 'moderation and prudence silenced the voices of the realists who might have insisted on immediate answers to awkward questions'.[3]

Charles landed at Dover on Friday, 25 May 1660. Samuel Pepys, who had sailed with the royal party, entered in his diary: 'Infinite the croud of people and the gallantry of the horsemen, citizens, and noblemen of all sorts. The Mayor of the town came and gave him his white staffe, the badge of his place, which the King did give him again. The Mayor also presented him from the town a very rich Bible, which he took and said it was the thing that he loved above all things in the world.'[4] The Cinque Ports Brotherhood sent an address of loyalty to Charles in which they claimed to 'have faithfully reteyned (though forced to be hidden in their own ashes) those livelie sparkes of loialtie love and affection towards your Majestie'.[5] During a four day triumphal and emotional progress through Kent, Charles was presented with pieces of gold and silver-gilt plate by the corporations of Canterbury and Rochester.

Addresses of congratulation poured in to the King, including one from the Kent gentry with numerous signatures. For men like Sir Richard Hardres of Great Hardres, who claimed to have set on foot the Kentish petition of 1648, led 2,300 horse to capture Sandwich, hazarded his life for the royal cause, suffered three long imprisonments and the loss of £7000, the return of Charles appeared to be the moment for retribution not reconciliation.[6] Scores of petitions quickly followed from Royalists reminding Charles of their sacrifices on his behalf and asking for places of profit or influence. Alderman Richard May of Canterbury, 'ever loyal and instrumental in promoting the late Kentish declaration for a full and free Parliament for which he would have been sequestered but for the Restoration', asked for the offices of Water Bailiff and Verger of Dover and Sandwich. Thomas Brewer, whose father 'was murdered in his own house in Kent and his estate plundered for an attempt to restore the late King in 1648', asked to be recommended to the Mayor of Maidstone for the place of Recorder.[7]

Not all Royalists turned out to cheer Charles. Sir Roger Twysden, who, like

3 Joan Thirsk, *The Restoration*, London 1976, pp. xxii–xxiv, xxxiii.
4 *The Diary of Samuel Pepys*, ed. R. Latham and W. Matthews, London 1970, vol. 1, p. 158. Fastened with gold clasps, the Bible has not survived in the royal collections. It was presented not by the mayor, Thomas Broome, but by the chaplain to the corporation, John Reading, minister of St Marys, an aged loyalist and onetime chaplain to Charles I. *Ibid.*, n. 2.
5 *A Calendar of the White and Black Books of the Cinque Ports*, ed. Felix Hull, Kent Records vol. 19, Maidstone 1966, pp. 510–11.
6 *CSPD, 1660–61*, pp. 4, 332.
7 *CSPD, 1660–61*, pp. 137, 138, 246.

many of the Kentish gentry had lost large but affordable sums through seques-tration, nevertheless had reservations about the constitution and the monarchy and did not leave East Peckham although Charles passed within two hours' ride of his estate.[8] As the Earl of Clarendon later admitted, the Restoration was brought about 'by a union of contradictions, by a concurrence of causes' which 'never desired the same effects'. The monarchy had been restored; but the country was deeply divided and continued so for much of Charles's reign.[9]

No doubt for a major part of the community of Kent the Restoration came as a relief from an overbearing, centralised regime. But there were some, a few committed Republicans, for whom the Restoration was anathema. Sir Henry Vane, the Younger, whose family owned the estate of Fairlawn in Shipbourne, had been one of the most notable Commonwealthmen and Parliamentarians. Although a republican, he had not supported the call for Charles I's execution. But his ability was such that it was grudgingly admired and feared. Clarendon described him as 'a man of extraordinary parts, a pleasant wit, a great under-standing, which pierced into and discerned the purposes of other men with wonderful sagacity' yet 'a man above ordinances, unlimited and unrestrained by any rules or bounds prescribed to other men, by reason of his perfection'.[10] Vane had been one of those excluded from the general amnesty. At his trial for treason in 1662 he maintained that it was no treason to obey a government in power; if it were there were others, General Monk, newly created Duke of Albemarle, for instance, who were equally guilty. Although Charles had given his word that he would grant a pardon if Vane was found guilty, Vane's belief that the supreme power in England lay in Parliament made him 'too dangerous a man to let live, if we can honestly put him out of the way'.[11]

Vane's execution in June 1662 convinced his one time near neighbour, Algernon Sidney, that England was no safe place for committed republicans and he was to become Kent's most notorious republican and later the first martyr of the Whigs. Algernon, the second son of Robert, second Earl of Leicester and of Dorothy Percy a daughter of Henry, ninth Earl of Northumberland was born at Penshurst in 1622. He was, therefore the scion of two ambitious, aristocratic families. He was trained by his father for office. When he was ten he ac-companied his elder brother Philip and his father, who had been made ambas-sador, to the court of Christian IV in Denmark. Four years later he went with his father, who was again ambassador, to Paris and to Rome. When Leicester returned to England he was given the post of Lord Deputy of Ireland in succes-sion to the executed Strafford. Algernon, and his elder brother Philip, were given commissions in their father's regiment in Ireland. When they returned to England in 1643 they were retained by the Parliamentary Commissioners and

---

8 F.W. Jessup, *Sir Roger Twysden 1597–1672*, London 1965, p. 103.
9 Tim Harris, *Politics under the Later Stuarts: Party Conflict in a Divided Society 1660–1715*, London 1993, pp. 26, 47.
10 G. Huehns, *Clarendon*, Oxford 1978, pp. 147–51.
11 W. Cobbett, *Complete Collection of State Trials*, London 1809–26, vi, pp. 187–8, Charles II to Clar-endon.

sent to London. By spring of the following year Algernon had joined the parliamentary forces and was made a captain of horse in the Eastern Association, then
under the command of his cousin, the Earl of Manchester. Shortly after he was
promoted to Lieutenant Colonel he charged at the head of his regiment at the
battle of Marston Moor receiving many wounds. He virtually retired from active
service at the age of 22 but kept the title of colonel, which he obviously valued,
and an admiration for the spartan qualities of the New Model Army.[12] Henceforth his duties were administrative but his ambitions were political. In July
1646 he was sent to Ireland, where his brother was Lord Lieutenant, and made
governor of Dublin. In October 1648 he was made governor of Dover Castle. He
was nominated as one of the commissioners to try Charles I but took no part in
the trial, in fact, he is alleged to have maintained that the king could be tried by
no court, and from Penshurst he objected to the sentence of death.[13]

Sidney was not popular with the officers of the garrison and in 1651 was
replaced as governor of Dover. He was keenly aware of his patrician origins; the
family crest of a porcupine made an appropriate device. But by 1651 Sidney was
far more interested in politics than in military administration. He became a
member of the Rump Parliament and in November 1652 was elected to the
Council of State. He opposed Cromwell's usurpation of power and was turned
out by Cromwell and his musketeers with the rest of the Rump in April 1653. He
retired to Penshurst and kept aloof from public affairs until the restoration of the
Long Parliament in 1659 when he again took his seat and was placed on the
Council of State. When Charles landed at Dover Sidney was abroad acting as a
parliamentary commissioner. Although, as he believed, innocent of the charge
of regicide, Sidney was totally opposed to monarchical rule and passionately
rejected the suggestion that he might live under such a regime.

> Shall I renounce all my old Principles, learn the vile Court Arts, and make my
> Peace by bribing some of them? shall their Corruption and Vice be my safety?
> Ah! no; better is a Life among Strangers, than in my own Country upon such
> Conditions . . . I hope I shall die in the same Principles in which I have liv'd;
> and will live no longer then they can preserve me.[14]

He began a long exile on the Continent settling first in Hamburg where he wrote
the letter vindicating his conduct, later published in Somer's *Tracts*. From
Germany he went to Italy and it was while he was in Rome that he learned of Sir
Henry Vane's execution. Vane, like Sidney, had opposed arbitrary power,
whether it be by Charles or Cromwell, and his execution transformed Sidney
into an active conspirator, one of the small band on the Continent headed by the

---

[12] J. Scott, *op. cit.*, p. 24.

[13] Brigid Haydon, 'Algernon Sidney, 1623–1683', *Archaeologia Cantiana*, lxxvi (1961), p. 117.

[14] 'The Honourable Algernon Sidney's LETTER against Bribery and Arbitrary Government, written to
his Friend, in answer to theirs, perswading his Return to *England*', in *Somer's Second Collection of
Tracts*, London 1750, vol. III, p. 81.

regicide General Edmund Ludlow.[15] It was at this time that Sidney wrote his encomium of his friend, *A Character of Sir Henry Vane.*

Republican opposition to the Restoration came also from the opposite end of the social spectrum. George Keddell who had urged his Kentish neighbours to bring Charles to trial 'declared himself ready to shed his own blood rather than see monarchy triumph'. The execution of ten of the regicides after October 1660 merely confirmed some republican sentiment. A Canterbury shoemaker maintained that Charles I had a fair and legal trial and that the regicides had suffered wrongfully.[16]

But the most significant centres of opposition to the monarchy and to the re-established Anglican Church came from the non-conforming sects. Indeed it has been claimed that all forms of radicalism in early modern England had a religious origin and that the agency of the State which confronted the subversive in men's everyday life was not Parliament where 'elections were infrequent, contests were less frequent still, the franchise restricted, and access to MPs minimal for most electors. The ubiquitous agency of the State was the Church, quartering the land not into a few hundred constituencies but into ten thousand parishes, impinging on the daily concerns of the great majority, supporting its black-coated army of clerical intelligentsia, bidding for a monoply of education, piety and political acceptability.'[17]

The religious settlement imposed by the Cavalier Parliament paid scant attention to Charles's offer of toleration and comprehension and re-established a High Anglican church. Furthermore a series of acts created a code which harshly penalised those who failed to conform. The Clarendon Code, i.e. the Corporation Act of 1661, the Act of Uniformity of 1662, the Conventicle Act of 1664 and the Five Mile Act of 1665 passed by the Cavalier Parliament were framed to impede and discourage non-conformist worship and to strengthen the authority of the Church of England. The Act of Uniformity (14 Car.II, c.4) in fact created two societies: those who accepted the revised Book of Common Prayer and those who did not – the non-conformists or Dissenters. The Conventicle Act (16 Car.II, c.4), forbad meetings of five or more 'under colour or pretence of any exercise of religion'. For a first offence the punishment was a fine of £5 or three months' imprisonment, for a second offence, £10 or six months, for a third, £100 or transportation for seven years. The Five Mile Act (17 Car.IIc.2) forbad any preacher or teacher who had not subscribed to the Act of Uniformity and did not swear that it was unlawful to take up arms against the King to come within five miles of any city or corporate town which returned members to Parliament or any parish or place in which he or she had previously preached in unlawful conventicles and assemblies. Non-conformists especially resented the implementation of the acts, invariably executed through the

---

15 J. Carswell, *The Porcupine: The Life of Algernon Sidney,* London 1989, p. 134.

16 R.L. Greaves, *Deliver us from Evil: The Redical Underground in Britain 1660–1663,* Oxford 1986, pp. 24, 32.

17 J.C.D. Clark, *English Society 1688–1832,* Cambridge 1985, p. 277.

authority of an Anglican magistrate and, in the case of the Conventicle act, summarily, without the normal procedure of trial by jury. Liberty for tender consciences was at an end and continued so until the end of Charles' reign. Fifty-nine persons, mostly artisans, but including a sprinkling of gentlemen, were indicted for recusancy in February and March 1685 and a widow of Felborough hundred was indicted for allowing religious conventicles to meet in her house in March 1685.[18]

The Quakers and the Baptists were particularly harried. The Quakers' pacifist stance exemplified by George Fox was of fairly recent adoption;[19] but their own codes of conduct undermined the social fabric and infuriated their superiors and persecutors. Professor Stone has noted that: 'the peculiar ferocity with which the Quakers were treated can only be explained if we realise how shattering a psychological blow to the conceptual framework of society was their quiet refusal to remove their headgear'.[20] The parish of St Mary's, Sandwich had ' "many sectaryes and enemies to ye late King, some subscribers to his death"; and Northbourne was full of Anabaptists and Quakers, or so it was alleged'.[21] At Lee a conventicle was attended by ex-parliamentary Colonels Blount and Thompson and a congregation of more than a hundred which the informer, Edward Potter, thought would 'prove as Dangerous to the government of England as any if They are not sudenly prevented'. The size of the conventicles was particularly alarming. At Reculver 500 men had met and marched out in a warlike manner. Egerton, on the edge of the Weald, was said to have had a large meeting of 800 foot and 200 horse.[22] When Thomas Palmer, an ejected minister, was arrested at Egerton with thirty of his followers some 170 others escaped.[23]

The Weald of Kent was one of the centres of Baptist beliefs. At Cranbrook two hundred or more Baptists met every Sunday, among them 'many strange faces'. In particular the Weald had been influenced by the scholarly teaching and preaching of Samuel Fisher, onetime pastor of a large congregation at Ashford and later a Quaker. While at Ashford Fisher had engaged in a lively debate about the validity of infant baptism,[24] and had published a weighty tome *Baby Baptism meer Babism*. But the most radical part of Fisher's teaching was his criticism of the Bible. He maintained that it was not the word of God but simply 'a bulk of heterogeneous writings compiled together by men taking what they could find of the several sorts of writings that are therein, and . . . crowding

---

[18] *Calendar of Assize Records: Kent Indictments Charles II, 1676–1688*, ed. J.S. Cockburn, pp. 235, 236.

[19] 'The mighty day of the Lord is coming . . . a day of slaughter is coming to you who have made war against the Lamb . . . The sword you cannot escape, and it shall be upon you ere long.' C. Hill, *The Experience of Defeat*, New York 1984, pp. 153–63.

[20] Lawrence Stone, *The Crisis of the Aristocracy 1558–1640*, Oxford 1979, p. 35.

[21] N. Yates, R. Hume and P. Hastings, *Religion and Society in Kent, 1640–1914*, Woodbridge 1994, p. 15.

[22] *CSPD, 1663–4*, p. 177.

[23] Greaves, *op. cit.*, pp. 63, 98, 106.

[24] *Infants Baptism mainteined: or, a True Account of the disputation between [S. Fisher and others] held at Ashford in Kent Julie 27 1649.*

them into a canon'.[25] Fisher's book could have ended an 'epoch of protestant
Bibliolatry' and 'the authority of the Book'. More generally interpreted it
simply spelt the end of hierarchical authority.[26] How far had these beliefs
become current, thus giving grounds for those who composed the Declaration in
January 1660 that there was indeed a prodigious growth of blasphemies, here-
sies and schism which threatened universal ruin? By the end of the seventeenth
century lack of personal professions of belief had caused one Kentish rector to
appeal to his readers, 'let your Will be so composed, so framed and worded in
the commendatory Part, as to declare yourself a Christian'.[27]

Disaffection with a Church of England dominated by high churchmen, and
with the monarchy, was widespread, but serious plotting against the regime was
ineffectual. The Tong Plot to cause an insurrection in 1662 to assassinate the
king and chief ministers was inept and puffed up by hearsay but it did have some
Kentish involvement. Colonel William Kenrick, who had been arrested in
connection with the Presbyterian Plot of the previous year, was said to be the
leader of the Kentish dissidents about Canterbury who were 'very high and insolent, and threattin all persons that have been any way loyall'.[28] The castles at
Deal and Dover were to be surprised and captured. Colonel Thomas Culpeper,
with parties of horse, chased around East Kent searching for Kenrick and
General Edmund Ludlow, the alleged leader of the insurrection, who, it was
said, intended to 'fall upon Kent and kill man, woman and child of the king's
party'.[29] In fact, Ludlow had not left his exile in Switzerland.

(2) A Seat in the Country

The Restoration restored not only the monarchy but also the traditional ruling
élite, whose power was largely based upon landed wealth. By 1640 it was the
gentry who owned the greatest proportion of the land in Kent. By purchase of
one-time monastic lands, former crown lands and nearly two-thirds of the lands
of the older nobility, the gentry owned as many as 1,100 out of the 1,350 greater
properties.[30] Furthermore, it was the older gentry families who not only were

---

25 S. Fisher, *The Testimony of Truth exalted by the collected labours of S.F. etc.*, London 1679, pp. 396,
   400, 403, 420, 435; C. Hill, *Some Intellectual Consequences of the English Revolution*, London 1980,
   p. 81.

26 C. Hill, *The World turned upside down: Radical ideas during the English Revolution*, Harmondsworth
   1974, pp. 259–68. In May 1659 Fisher, with others, was holding meetings in Dunkirk of some hundreds of officers and soldiers. See *This to thee O King and thy Council* [signed by S. Fisher and
   others, 1660].

27 William Assheton, *A Theological Discourse of Last Wills and Testaments*, London 1696, pp. 18–19,
   quoted by Christopher Marsh, 'In the name of God? Will-making and Faith in Early Modern England', in *The Records of the Nation*, ed. G.H. Martin and Peter Spufford, Woodbridge 1990, pp.
   221–2.

28 *CSPD, 1663–4*, pp. 117, 122–3.

29 *Ibid.*, p. 72.

30 C.W. Chalklin, *Seventeenth Century Kent*, London 1965, p. 196.

restored but who actually increased their power base. Professor Everitt has noted that

> The older gentry who formed the backbone of the moderate party proved far more capable of weathering the economic storm of the period than the new. Not a single family of importance was established in the county as a result of the Restoration settlement. Of the families who had established themselves in Kent since 1603, only 29% retained their hold till 1688; whereas 87% of the gentry of medieval stock survived into the eighteenth century. More than two thirds of the properties sold by the newer families, moreover, were now purchased by those who had been established in the county before the Tudor period.[31]

The growth of a powerful resident gentry between 1560 and 1660 and the concurrent expansion in the functions of the justice of the peace have been termed the greatest revolution in social control ever to have occurred in rural England.[32] The symbol of that control was the country house and its surrounding estate. From the dissolution of the monasteries in the mid-sixteenth century until the building of the barracks for the Napoleonic wars at the end of the eighteenth century, country houses were the largest buildings constructed in England. Look at any of the thirty or so depictions of Kentish country seats in John Harris's *History of Kent*, published in 1719, and one is presented with a series of self-sufficient, self-governing institutions.[33] The great house, with stables, stockyards, dovecotes and dairies attached, is surrounded by formal and kitchen gardens, orchards, fish ponds, parks containing deer and woodlands containing game. These birds-eye views, drawn by Thomas Badeslade, a practical estate surveyor and engraved by John Kip around 1715, are precise but drawn in a way to impress and impose. In particular the treeplanting in single and double avenues, the massing of trees in carefully contrived wildernesses bisected by sightlines, enhanced the owners' feelings that they were lords of all they surveyed. It has been claimed that 'most forms of aristocratic tree-planting were deliberate assertions of ownership',[34] and the same may be said of the gentry's estates. Compared to the views of some of the same houses in Edward Hasted's *The History and Topographical Survey of Kent*,[35] published half a century later, after the iconoclasts Launcelot Brown and Humphrey Repton had worked their worst, these estates are the epitome of order and control.[36]

---

[31] Everitt, *Community of Kent*, p. 324.

[32] L. Stone and J.C. Fawtier Stone, *An Open Elite? England 1540–1880*, Oxford 1986, p. 202.

[33] John Harris, *History of Kent*, London 1719. See plate 3a.

[34] K. Thomas, *Man and the Natural World: Changing Attitudes in England 1500–1800*, London 1983, p. 208.

[35] Edward Hasted, *The History and Topographical Survey of Kent*, Canterbury 1774. See plate 3b.

[36] Leonard Knyff and John Kip had drawn and engraved birds-eye views of the seats of. royalty and nobility which were later collected and published as *Britannia Illustrata*, see John Harris, *The Artist and the Country House*, London 1979, p. 155; see also H. Chapelle, *Thirty Six Different Views of Noblemen and Gentlemens's Seats; in the County of Kent. All Designed upon the Spot. By the late T. Badeslade, Esq: Surveyor*, c.1750

In the seventeenth century the greatest houses in Kent belonged to members of the aristocracy. Knole, acquired by the father of newly ennobled Thomas Sackville, was a vast, amorphous pile of Kentish ragstone, which apart from the curved gables on its west front looked more like a Tudor village than a mansion. Penshurst, the seat of the Sidneys, eulogised by Ben Jonson, presented an altogether more mellow and civilised aspect, in spite of its medieval core. Cobham, brick with stone trimmings, intended as a prodigy house for Elizabeth's galumphings, stood unfinished until 1660, owing to the alleged treason of Lord Cobham.[37]

In the second flight, Somerhill, built for the Earl of Clanricarde, to a plan by John Thorpe, and Chilham, built for the Master of the Rolls, Sir Dudley Digges, in the second decade of the century, were, apart from the eccentric pentagonal plan of Chilham, conservative, gabled country houses. Chevening, built for Lord Dacre, before 1630 and Lees Court, built for Sir George Sondes around mid-century, are the most notable houses in Kent which exhibit classical, Inigo Jonesian, aspects, and show the owners' connections with the court or the City. But many other houses, such as St Clere, Surrenden Dering, Godinton, Groombridge Place, Broome Park and Bridge Place, built or enlarged in the seventeenth century, some even in the period of the Interregnum, are evidences of the increasing wealth and sophisticated taste of the gentry.[38] How did Sir Basil Dixwell conceive the design of Broome Park, the finest example of brick *bravura* in Kent? We know the Continental sources for much of the interior decoration of Knole,[39] but little of the carvers and panellers who decorated Godinton.

The life and entertainment in one of these houses was described by William Schellinks, a Dutch topographical artist, who visited Sir Arnold Braemes at Bridge Place in September 1661. Braemes, a wealthy merchant trading through Dover, was an active royalist who had joined Prince Rupert's fleet with his own ship. Braemes married three times and with increasing advantage: firstly Joan, the daughter of Walter Septvans, an ancient Kentish family; secondly, Elizabeth, the daughter of Sir Dudley Digges of Chilham Castle; and thirdly Margaret, daughter of Sir Thomas Palmer, first Baronet, of Wingham.[40] He bought the manor of Blackmanbury near Bridge and built in brick a large mansion. Braemes was a generous host and Schellinks, invited to stay for as long as he wished, stayed for three months, during which he described this Kentish Elysium:

37 Esmé Wingfield-Stratford, *The Lords of Cobham Hall*, London 1959, pp. 76–83, 111–18.

38 John Newman, introductory essay to *The Buildings of England: North and East Kent* and *West Kent and the Weald*, Harmondsworth 1969, pp. 83–7.

39 Anthony Wells-Cole, *Art and Decoration in Elizabethan and Jacobean England*, Yale 1997, pp. 64, 75, 88, 127, 172, 211–12.

40 *Visitation of the County of Kent 1663–1668*, ed. G.J. Armytage, Harleian Society vol. 54, London 1906, p. 24.

The estate of Sir Arnold Braems lies in a valley of outstanding beauty; it contains in addition to his own fine residence, a large number of rooms, chambers, halls and other good apartments; there is also a large deer park with many deer and does, woods, a rabbit warren in the hills, and very beautiful well kept pleasure grounds with fruit trees, well watered by a fast flowing, fresh sparkling stream of wonderfully clear sweet water. This splits up into several branches and rivulets, also some fishponds, in which a certain kind of fish called trout is bred, which is very similar to a large carp, and, prepared in the English manner, tastes very delicious. There are also some vineyards round the house and gardens, producing yearly two or three hogsheads of wine. There is a dovecot like a chapel, in which are at all times so many young pigeons that throughout the whole summer and longer 12 to 14 dozen can be taken out every week to put into pies or prepared otherwise. His people go out hunting every day and catch a lot of partridges and pheasants, which we had every day on the table, besides a choice of other delicate food, all with the most delicious English sauces; there is an ample supply of drinks, different kinds of wines and perry, which is made from pears. He also has his own brewery, bakery, wine press, hop garden, barns, stables, oxen, cows, sheep, pigs, geese, ducks, corn and fruit, everything that one can desire in such an establishment. And because he is, with all this, so kind and hospitable and keeps such a princely table, he has so many visits from noblemen, gentlemen and ladies, so that his table is always surrounded by his own people and outside guests. The church stands not far from his house and he has the right to nominate a minister of his choice for it. He has planted a fine avenue of lime trees from his house to the church, under which one is protected from rain and sun.[41]

Such princely living brought ruin and Braemes' heirs were forced to sell the estate in 1704 to John Taylor of Bifrons, who pulled down the greater part of it but was still left with a gentleman's residence.[42] The painting of Bridge Place, c.1670, attributed to Adriaen Ocker, shows the hip roofed, pink brick house of two and a half stories with dormer windows in the roof. In the foreground a hunting party departs.[43] This is more than a piece of elegant staffage, for it embodies the game act of 1671, which, according to Addison's Tory squire, was the only good law passed since the Revolution.[44]

(3) The Gentry as the Medium of Social Control

Historians of widely differing political persuasions are agreed upon the significance of the preservation of game and its extraordinary influence upon the exercise of political and judicial power. 'For many generations to come, grave social

---

41 *The Journal of William Schellinks' Travels in England 1661–1663*, ed. M. Exwood and H.L. Lehman, Camden 5th ser. i, London 1993, p. 64.
42 Hasted, *op. cit.*, 2nd edn Canterbury 1800, vol. 9, p. 288.
43 See John Harris, *The Artist and the Country House*, p. 48.
44 G.M. Trevelyan, *England under Queen Anne: Blenheim*, London 1930, p. 24.

consequences were to flow from the excessive eagerness of the country gentlemen about the preservation of game.'[45] After studying 'The Black Act', the most ferocious piece of anti-poaching legislation of an early Hanoverian parliament, which created over fifty offences threatening capital punishment, E.P. Thompson concluded that

> the hegemony of the eighteenth century gentry and aristocracy was expressed, above all, not in military force, not in the mystifications of a priesthood or of the press, not even in economic coercion, but in the rituals of the study of the Justices of the Peace, in the quarter sessions, in the pomp of Assizes and in the theatre of Tyburn.[46]

In his *Commentaries upon the Laws of England*, William Blackstone condemned the game laws as a bastard slip of the obsolete forest laws, 'both founded upon the same unreasonable notions of permanent property in wild creatures; and both productive of the same tyranny to the commons: but with this difference; that the forest laws established only one mighty hunter through-out the land, the game laws have raised a little Nimrod in every manor'.[47]

Restrictions on the taking of game have a long history. In 1389 a statute of Richard II[48] established most of the principles, which were repeated later, by declaring that none shall hunt but they which have sufficient living. It identified potential trouble makers as artificers, labourers, servants, grooms and idle priests. A property qualification of forty shillings a year was required for a man to keep a greyhound or other hunting dog. Ferrets, heys, nets, harepipes and other engines were made illegal. Justices of the peace had power to identify and punish offenders with one year's imprisonment for the offence of taking 'gentle-man's game'. In 1495 any person of whatever condition was forbidden to take pheasants and partridges upon the freehold of any other person without permis-sion.[49] In 1540 it was made illegal to buy partridges or pheasants, or to sell them except to officers of the royal household.[50] Restrictions on the seasons when one could take pheasants and partridges were introduced in Elizabeth's reign[51] and from 1604[52] it was illegal for anyone to shoot either with gun or bow at any feathered game or at hares. The game act of 1671[53] declared that disorderly persons laying aside their lawful trades do betake themselves to taking game, to the great damage of this realm and prejudice of noblemen, gentlemen and lords

---

45 *Ibid.*, p. 23.
46 E.P. Thompson, *Whigs and Hunters: The Origin of the Black Act*, London 1975, p. 262.
47 William Blackstone, *Commentaries upon the Laws of England*, Oxford 1773, 'though the forest laws are now mitigated, and by degrees grown intirely obsolete, yet from this root has sprung a bastard slip, known by the name of the game law, now arrived to and. wantoning in its highest vigour', pp. 415–16.
48 13 Ric. II cap.13.
49 11 Hen. VII c. 17.
50 32 Hen. VIII c. 8.
51 23 Eliz. c. 10.
52 1 Jac. I c. 27.
53 22/23 Car. II c. 25.

of manors. The act restricted the keeping of guns, dogs and nets to those, or their wives, having an estate of the annual value of £100. It allowed lords of manors, not under the degree of esquire, to appoint gamekeepers with power to search houses of those suspected of keeping hunting dogs.

Indictment at Assizes was used more frequently in the seventeenth century to deter poachers. In 1677, labourers at Rainham and Ashford were indicted for taking hares, pheasants and partridges using a hare pipe and setting dog and for taking trout from the river at Ashford with a trammel net. Yeomen of Elmstone and Stone and a clerk and farmer of Elmstone were charged with keeping greyhounds to course deer and spaniels, as well as snares and guns, with the intention of killing deer, hares, pheasants and partridges.[54]

Further game acts were passed in the eighteenth century, which carried penalties of fines, imprisonment and whipping. However, the full rigour of the law was rarely applied for it would have required a jury trial at either Quarter Sessions or Assizes. By the middle of the eighteenth century prosecutors preferred the more speedy process before one or two justices of the peace sitting in petty sessions even though only fines could be imposed.[55] William Emmett's diary, listing his activities as a justice in Bromley between July 1711 and April 1737, shows the use of the warrant and mittimus, i.e. a precept committing the offender to gaol, until a fine is paid; search warrants granted to constables and borsholders to discover guns, dogs and nets for the destruction of game; confessions of poaching and undertakings not to poach, hunt or ferret, nor fish upon his own manor.[56] Poaching game was endemic in the countryside and by many not considered a crime. 'The more laws, the more evasion,' exclaimed John Byng. 'Go where you will, everyone is a sporter, alias poacher; every market place is overrun by greyhounds and pointers.'[57]

The sale of game had been illegal since Tudor times, but by the early nineteenth century, when pheasants were being preserved in their thousands to be shot in battues, i.e. driven to standing sportsmen with improved shotguns,[58] the surplus game was sold in London's Leadenhall market and provided plentiful supplies for London's middle classes.[59] As only one game act was ever repealed until 1831 the game laws became a perverse legal minefield. In *The Justice of the Peace and Parish Officer*, John Burn in the section on the game laws commented that

---

54 *Calendar of Assize Records*, pp. 42, 234.
55 P.B. Munsche, *Gentlemen and Poachers: The English Game Laws 1671–1831*, Cambridge 1981, pp. 77–8; Norma Landau, *The Justices of the Peace 1679–1760*, California 1984, pp. 24–5, has a table showing far more cases taken to judgement in petty sessions for evasion of excise duty than for offences against the game laws.
56 CKS, U.310, O14, ff. 15, 21, 22, 23, 27.
57 Quoted in G.E. Mingay, *English Landed Society in the Eighteenth Century*, London 1963, p. 249.
58 Lord Eldon complained in the House of Lords in 1827 that 'every plantation was turned into a poultry yard, and a sportsman was thought nothing of unless he could kill his thousand birds a day'. Spencer Walpole, *A History of England from the Conclusion of the Great War in 1815 to 1858*, London 1913, vol. 1, p. 138.
59 Munsche, *op. cit.*, pp. 55–62.

the statutes relating to this title are very numerous, and the sense sometimes a little perplexed, so that perhaps upon a view of the whole, it may seem that about four or five new acts, comprehending the several heads here undermentioned, and repealing all the preceding ones, would conduce to render this branch of our laws more intelligible and useful.[60]

The game acts were perhaps the most obvious example where there was a conflict of interest between the magistrate, invariably a member of the country gentry with game to preserve, and the judicial ideal of the patriarchal patrician, ruling impartially his local flock. The acts created a class, firmly based upon landed property, of those who were qualified to take what originally had been *ferae naturae*, i.e. wild animals, which by their very nature defied ownership, and those who were not qualified. After 1671 the qualification for taking game was fifty times that required for voting in a county election. 'Even more than politics, partridges caused squire and yeoman to look at one another askance'.[61]

It was generally accepted by the country gentry that all members of the local élite, men of a certain status and property, should be magistrates regardless of party or factional allegiances.[62] However, because justices wielded political influence and because the appointment to the commission was made by the Lord Chancellor, usually on the recommendation of the county's lord lieutenant at the beginning of each new monarch's reign, the composition of the commission was politically sensitive and could lead to exclusion from the commission. In March 1678 four of Kent's gentry, two of whom, Sir Vere Fane and Sir John Tufton were MPs, were put out by the order of Charles II because they were listed as exclusionists, i.e. they had sided with Lord Shaftesbury in his attempts to exclude James, Duke of York, a known Roman Catholic, from succession to the throne.[63] Between 1711 and 1713 the Tories were in the majority in every one of Kent's fourteen petty sessional divisions: after the lord lieutenant had reviewed the commission on the accession of George I the Tory predominance was reduced to just two divisions. So, during the reigns of the first two Georges 'few Tories were justices and still fewer acted, meetings of petty sessions were local conferences of Whig governors'.[64]

The great and the not-so-good of the country and the county were uniformly included in the commission regardless of whether they intended to act. The justices listed for the 1676 Assizes began with the archbishop of Canterbury and included the dukes of Buckingham and Monmouth, Samuel Pepys and over one hundred members of the Kent gentry.[65] On average only about 25% of those appointed to the commissions of Kent, Hampshire, Bedfordshire, Oxfordshire, Herefordshire, Cambridgeshire and Gloucestershire between 1738 and 1760

60 J. Burn, *The Justice of the Peace and Parish Officer*, London 1797, vol. ii, pp. 359–462, 'Game'.
61 Trevelyan, *op. cit.*, p. 23.
62 F. Heal and C. Holmes, *The Gentry of England and Wales 1500–1700*, London 1994, pp. 238–9.
63 L.K.J. Glassey, *Politics and the Appointment of Justices of the Peace 1675–1720*, Oxford 1979, p. 34.
64 Landau, *op. cit.*, p. 234.
65 *Calendar of Assize Records*, Maidstone Assizes 1676, pp. 1, 2.

took out their *dedimus*, which authorised the justice to take the oaths of office.[66] Thus the commission of the peace was a social register for the county as well as an instrument of empowerment. 'To gentry below the first rank promotion to the bench meant the first step on a ladder which could lead in the next generation to social parity and a seat at Westminster.'[67] But the commission was not equally attractive in all parts of Kent, especially in urban areas near to London where the crime rate was much higher than in rural areas. As early as 1666 John Evelyn refused to act as justice because of the perpetual trouble in the parishes around his home of Sayes Court, Deptford. By the mid-eighteenth century by far the largest number of cases involving commitment to gaol before the Assizes was in Blackheath and of the 66 cases in Kent referred in 1748–9 only five were in East Kent.[68]

Justices acted singly in cases of petty misdemeanor and could extract recognizances, i.e. a bond to appear before further proceedings, or to keep the peace and be of good behaviour. In petty sessions, two or more justices could make nearly all the administrative decisions for their area, often affecting their own property, e.g. an adjustment of the rates. At quarter sessions, sometimes held more or less often than four times a year, their powers were judicial and administrative and, from the Restoration to the nineteenth century, their administrative powers were constantly being increased by statute law.

By the seventeenth century quarter sessions had acquired the powers of the moribund hundred courts and the manorial leet courts, so that no local courts challenged their jurisdiction. Quarter sessions were the most august and powerful category of local authority – an exclusive and very priveleged group, with enormous power in the countryside. 'They constituted in a very real sense a ruling class.'[69] If attendance is a guide, Quarter Sessions took on an increasing importance when compared with the Assizes. 'In the 1670s between 40 and 50 JPs (at least half of those active on the commission) were present at any one Kentish Assizes; by the last decade of Anne's reign there were only about 20.'[70] Owing to multiple arraignment, trials at Assizes were falling into disrepute. Cases were discharged swiftly with little or no time for meaningful deliberation by the jury. Increasingly the foreman exercised an extraordinary degree of control over the jury's deliberations and verdicts. There were signs that the position of foreman became institutionalised. Bernard Ellis, a Darenth yeoman, between 1640 and 1663, was sworn to at least 50 juries on 41 of which he was foreman. Robert Day serving as an assize juror for thirteen years in the 1630s and 1640s took part in at least 118 trials, 111 of them as foreman. In fact, it has been claimed that 'serial service for rank and file jurymen brought an unprece-

---

[66] Landau, *op. cit.*, p. 140.

[67] J.S. Cockburn, *A History of English Assizes 1558–1714*, Cambridge 1972, p. 156.

[68] *Ibid.*, pp. 181, 202–3.

[69] B. Keith-Lucas, *English Local Government in the Eighteenth and Nineteenth Centuries*, London 1977, p. 7.

[70] Landau, *op. cit.*, p. 39.

dented degree of stability to the Kent trial jury in the second half of the seventeenth century'. As a consequence experienced juries initiated a form of plea bargaining in which charge reductions were exchanged for guilty pleas, usurping the discretionary powers of judge and sovereign.[71] Magistrates were expected to arbitrate in local disputes before matters reached their courts through indictment. Lambard maintained that the justice of the peace should 'step in betwixt those that be at variance, as (by reason of his learning, wisdom, authority and wealth) he is like to prevail more, by his mediation and entreaty than is another man'.[72] By preferring the warrant to appear before them for possible arbitration, to the recognizance which required the accused to appear at Quarter Sessions and possible indictment, it has been argued that some justices, particularly the urban justices, acted as a compounder as well as a commissioner of the peace.[73] However, the notebooks of the Brockman family show that the rural population became increasingly disinclined to request judicial aid in the resolution of their disputes.[74]

(4) A Seat at Westminster

From 1711, when membership of the House of Commons was restricted to those having a real estate of £600 a year for county MPs and £300 a year for borough MPs, 'representatives' were drawn from a stratum which contained at most 0.5% of the population. This ' "permanent fixed interest" in the country combined to create, in the Revolution Settlement [of 1688], government of the property owners, for the property owners, by the property owners'. Three quarters of all MPs, including the majority of borough MPs, were country gentlemen.[75] With the exception of Edward Dering, the son of a baronet, and Sir Vere Fane, the son of an earl, all the members of parliament returned for the county of Kent in the reign of Charles II were baronets. This superior title of knighthood, created by James I in 1611, was limited to 200 applicants who could prove that their family had been armigerous for at least three generations. This criterion, rapidly eroded, went some way to establishing a pecking order in the burgeoning Kentish gentry, where it was not unusual to produce families of sixteen and seventeen children.[76] Initially a baronetcy cost £1095, allegedly to defray the

---

71 *Twelve Good Men and True: The Criminal Trial Jury in England 1200–1800*, ed. J.S. Cockburn and T.A. Green, Princeton 1988, pp. 168, 169, 172.
72 Quoted in C.B. Herrup, *The Common Peace: Participation and the Common Law in Seventeenth Century England*, Cambridge 1987, p. 54.
73 Landau, *op. cit.*, pp. 174–208.
74 *Ibid.*, pp. 194–5.
75 W.A. Speck, *Tory and Whig: The Struggle in the Constituencies, 1701–1715*, London 1970, pp. 3–4; B.D. Henning, *The House of Commons, 1660–90*, London 1983, vol. 1, p. 59.
76 E.g. the Derings, Twysdens and Honeywoods. The implications of Mary Honeywood's prolificity – she had 367 descendants at her death, Everitt, *Community of Kent*, p. 36 – gave real meaning to the saying 'Kentish cousins', and problems for the College of Arms, which attempted to uphold a measure of exclusivity to its clients.

cost of maintaining thirty soldiers for three years in the plantation of Ulster, but with James I's propensity to lavishly distribute honours, it rapidly fell to £700 in 1619 and to £220 in 1622.[77] In matters of precedence the baronets were placed above the knightage but below the baronage. The case was passionately argued before James I in the Privy Council by two Kentish knights, Sir Moyle Finch and his son-in-law, Sir William Twysden, both created baronets on 29 June 1611.[78] The order subsequently became debased, but its earlier recipients clearly regarded themselves as superior gentry, and in economic terms they were. Between 1640 and 1660 the average income of thirty-one baronets was £1,405, for fifty knights it was £873 and for 750 squires and gentlemen £270.[79]

Although the gentry thought that to be a member of Parliament for the county was the most prestigious post, they represented only one part of the Kentish electorate. Before the Reform Act of 1832 the parliamentary representation of Kent comprised two MPs for the county and two MPs from each of the corporate boroughs of Maidstone, Rochester and Queenborough. Canterbury, a city and a county in its own right, also returned two MPs. The Cinque Ports of Dover, Sandwich, Hythe and Romney, which were placed cartographically within the borders of Kent, but which claimed to have no governmental or administrative connection with the county, also each returned two MPs.[80] Thus, that part of Kent west of the Medway, shared with east Kent, the representation of the two county MPs. Kent east of the Medway shared the county MPs, eight MPs from the corporate boroughs and eight MPs from the Cinque Ports on its south eastern periphery. The county electorate made up of about 7,000 free-holders elected two MPs: the corporate boroughs with an electorate of just over 4,000 freemen, elected sixteen MPs. The arrangement was medieval and reflected an assessment of the importance of East Kent, which by the second half of the seventeenth century no longer held true. At least half the ports were either moribund or much diminished in importance. But, for a monarch who might wish to influence the composition of the House of Commons, four fifths of which were borough MPs, this medieval prospect was intriguing, for the rights exercised by the corporate boroughs, in many cases, had been granted by royal charter.

(5) Management of the Boroughs

All the parliamentary boroughs of Kent, Canterbury and the Cinque Ports returned members to parliament by freeman franchise. The number of freemen voters varied considerably. Queenborough had 30 voters, Rochester 300 and

[77] Stone, *The Crisis of the Aristocracy*, p. 93.
[78] G.E. Cokayne, *The Complete Baronetage*, Exeter 1900, vol. 1, pp. 35, 74; Stone, *Crisis of the Aristocracy*, pp. 82–97.
[79] Everitt, *Community of Kent*, p. 41.
[80] In the volumes of *The History of Parliament* the Cinque Ports constituencies are listed after Yorkshire and before Wales.

Canterbury 700 in 1688, whilst Maidstone had 400 in 1681.[81] Of the Cinque Ports, New Romney had 16 voters, Hythe 30 and Sandwich 230 in 1690 and Dover over 300.[82] However, this did not mean that New Romney was easier to manage than Canterbury. Family in-fighting within the corporation of New Romney meant that the borough required constant and careful attention by the neighbouring gentry. The creation of even a few new freemen could lead to a crop of actions in King's Bench.[83] The Lord Warden managed the Cinque Ports for the government, but it was not an easy task. Explaining why William III did not want to give the Lord Wardenship to the Earl of Winchelsea, Heneage Finch, Earl of Nottingham wrote, '[the king] chooses rather to show his esteem of you by doing something which may be more beneficial to you and yet leave you more at liberty to attend his service as Lord Lieutenant and Custos Rotulorum of Kent than you could be if diverted by the necessary but vexatious business of the government of the Cinque Ports'.[84] Although it was alleged that the Lord Warden had a right to nominate one member for each of the ports this was often contested. In the elections to the Cavalier Parliament in 1660 the Lord Warden, the Duke of York, placed five nominees but was only successful in half the twelve subsequent by-elections.[85]

Between 1689 and 1715 no fewer than twelve general elections were called, more than have been held in any 25 year period before or since. Elections were strongly contested in the boroughs.

The factious and sectarian nature of borough government precludes any simple assessment of national party affiliation. The members returned to parliament might answer to Tory or Whig divisions in the House, but this was little reflection of the political awareness of their constituencies. Non-conformists tended to favour the Whigs, but when James II attempted to relax the penal laws in order to free Roman Catholic worship, and incidentally the worship of the Dissenters, he was strongly supported by the boroughs. The connection of an MP with his constituency tended to be local and personal. He might have an interest in foreign affairs and in foreign trade but that was not the reason the electors sent him to the Commons. Thomas Papillon, a very successful merchant of Hugenot extraction, MP for Dover from 1673 to 1681 and from 1689 to 1695, a director and in 1681 a Deputy Governor of the East India Company, strove to limit the commercial power of France. In his address to the electors of Dover on his re-election in February 1679, he claimed to be 'a sincere Protestant, a loyal subject, a true Englishman, and a Freeman of Dover . . . and under the strictest of repeated kindness to endeavour the welfare of this Corporation and of every

---

81 Maidstone's electorate doubled in the fifty years after 1681, P. Clark and L. Murfin, *History of Maidstone*, Stroud 1995, p. 99.

82 Henning, *op. cit.*, vol. 1, pp. 276 and 498.

83 *The History of Parliament: The House of Commons 1715–1754*, ed. R. Sedgwick, London 1970, vol. 1, p. 367.

84 *Historical Manuscripts Commission, Finch MSS*, London 1913, vol. ii, p. 222.

85 Henning, *op. cit.*, vol. 1, pp. 67–8.

Table 1

Contested Elections in Kent, 1701–15a

Constituency	1701	1705	1708	1710	1713	1715
Kent county	x	x	x	x	x	x
Canterbury			x	x	x	x
Maidstone	x	x	x	x		x
Queenboro		x		x	x	x
Rochester	x	x	x			x
Cinque Ports:						
Dover	xb				x	
Hythe			x	x	x	x
Romney				x		
Sandwich	x	x	x	x		x

a Derived from Speck, *Tory and Whig*, p. 104.
b Marked with a ? by M. Horwitz, *Parliament, Policy and Politics in the Reign of William III*, Manchester 1977, p. 333, because there is evidence of a canvas but not of a poll, and later accepted by Speck in *The Birth of Britain*, Oxford 1994, p. 29 n. 26.

member thereof'.[86] In the following century, members of parliament became more and more involved in obtaining local acts creating statutory authorities to such a degree that Horace Walpole complained that 'the House of Commons is become a meer quarter sessions, where nothing is transacted but turnpikes and poor rates'.[87] Of the 2779 acts passed between 1715 and 1754 2009 were introduced on petition as private bills.[88]

Management of 'interest' was more important than policies as far as corporations were concerned. No matter how important the government's nominee, it was useless to try to move a stubborn corporate bench. Secretary of State, Sir Charles Hedges, failed to keep his seat at Dover in the 1701 election because he did not acknowledge his supporters in the corporation. John Mackay, the local agent, writing to John Ellis, under-secretary of state, complained

about Mr Secretary's election here, you may depend upon not only the freemen in the pacquetboats but all the other Interest that I can make, but I am afraid that all will not doe, for the whole corporation is disgusted that since the last election he never came or sent amongst them to thank them, and that Interest on which his last Election was founded is entirely fallen off from him

[86] Henning, *The House of Commons 1660–1690*, vol. 3, pp. 202–4; David Ormrod, 'Puritanism and Patriarchy: The Career and Spiritual Writings of Thomas Papillon, 1623–1702', in *Studies in Modern Kentish History*, ed. A. Detsicas and N. Yates, Maidstone 1983, pp. 125–30; A.F.W. Papillon, *Memoirs of Thomas Papillon*, Reading 1887, p. 146.
[87] *Historical Manuscripts Commission, Dropmore MSS*, London 1892, vol. i, p. 139.
[88] Sedgwick, *op. cit.*, p. 10.

... They have trumpt up odd Characters upon him; they say Mr Aylmer and he did not Vote the same way, but the general objection is his neglect.[89]

Similarly, the Lord Lieutenant, the Earl of Winchilsea, writing from Dover to the Secretary of State, complained:

endeavouring to make an interest for Sir Charles Hedges I find there reigns such a spirit of obstinacy among the Bench they will not admit of any application to remove either of the old members, tho the most probabler means has been used to perswade them. They do not regard their own interest in setting up such men as they must know will be obnoxious, and can do them no service; but all arguments are out of reason with them whilst they are under the power of their benefactors and Mr Wivill continues in such an influencing employment as Victualler to the Port.[90]

Later in the eighteenth century a much more effective way of controlling a borough emerged. William Oldfield, in his *History of the Boroughs* written in 1792, noted:

Sir Edward Dering has, by a very simple method, possessed himself of an influence in this port not easily to be rendered insecure. His property in the neighbourhood is tenanted out *without lease* at *very easy* rents to the electors; who, feeling that gratitude which never fails to inspire those immediately interested in the present possession of a good thing, could not be so ungenerous as to oppose the inclination of a passive landlord in so trifling a concern as the election of a Member of Parliament.[91]

(6) The Politics of the Gentry

To be chosen for the county was a matter for family pride rather than party persuasion. Sir Edward Dering claimed that

since of the last five legal elections for our county our family hath succeeded in four ... I think it is now time to set down in quiet and leave other gentlemen to take their turn, few having in our county the honour to be chosen twice knight of the shire and no young man, that I know of, during his father's life, but only my son.[92]

Dering had succeeded his father, the first Baronet, and to his sequestered estates, in 1644. Although living in reduced financial circumstances during the Interregnum he refused office and was in fact like so many of the Kent gentry, a

89 BL, Add. MS 28887, f. 374, J. Mackay to J. Ellis, 16 Nov. 1701.
90 BL, Add. MSS 29588, Earl of Winchilsea to Nottingham, 12 July 1702.
91 *The History of Parliament: The House of Commons 1754–1790*, ed. Lewis Namier and John Brooke, London 1964, vol. 1, p. 452.
92 Henning, *The House of Commons 1660–1690*, vol. 1, p. 275.

latent royalist. At the Restoration he contested a county seat and was returned to the Convention Parliament. He did not stand in 1661 preferring to let his finances recuperate. In 1662 he was appointed one of the Commissioners to Ireland to adminster the Act of Settlement, an office which restored his finances and made him henceforth a supporter of the court. Returned for East Retford in 1670 he became from then on a very active member of the Commons, serving on over two hundred committees and making over seventy speeches. His parliamentary diaries reveal his close attention to procedure in the House.[93] Dering was of the court party, he identified with court and country in his diaries, and he was also a strong supporter of the Church of England. In a speech in the Commons in 1675 he identified the papists as 'the greatest danger and most formidable enemie'.[94] He died the year before James II's accession and thus avoided the Tories' dilemma of a Roman Catholic monarch. His son, yet another Edward, was a fervant Whig supporter, suspected of being involved in the Rye House Plot, and 'contributed more than any man in Kent towards bringing about the Revolution'.[95] Political loyalties were not always based upon family alliances.

Although at times the county's electorate of forty shilling freeholders might cast their votes they did not normally elect the county's members; that was done by the county's gentry. Only two of the seven general elections for the county held between the Restoration and the accession of William and Mary went to a poll; and even then, on the first occasion in February 1679, it was suggested by Sir William Twysden, that the matter be settled by drawing lots. Before the second poll, in September 1679,

> it was agreed by Sir William Twysden and the rest of the gentry present that for avoiding the trouble of a poll there should be two gentlemen on each side and the high sheriff to be umpire to determine the election upon a view between these two. Whereupon both parties drew up several times and it seemed to appear that the number on Colonel Dering's side was far greater . . . However, some gentlemen on the other party, being not well satisfied, demanded the poll, which continued until almost nine o'clock at the county court upon the heath, and was from thence adjourned by consent to the Town Hall in Maidstone on Tuesday morning.[96]

'Both parties drew up several times' conveys the character of the proceedings, for the horsemen were drawn up like troops for a battle. At the first election of 1679 two horsemen were wounded when over one hundred mounted supporters of Dering and Twysden, jostled for position before the hustings in an

---

[93] *The Parliamentary Diary of Sir Edward Dering 1670–1673*, ed. B.D. Henning, New Haven 1940, pp. ix–xvi.

[94] *The Diaries and Papers of Sir Edward Dering, Second Baronet, 1644 to 1684*, ed. Maurice F. Bond, London 1976, p. 62.

[95] Henning, *The House of Commons, 1660–1690*, vol. 2, pp. 207–8.

[96] *Loc. cit.*

attempt to vote first.[97] Penenden, or Pickenden, Heath was the traditional assembly place before the elections for the county's MPs, which were held at the ancient shire hall or court house on the heath, which provided ample space for the mounted gentry to manoeuvre, show off their followings, and cry up their leaders.

To follow the convolutions of party allegiances would mean unravelling a tangled skein. From 1679 until 1685 the county had been represented by Sir Vere Fane and Edward Dering, who were classed as Whigs because they had supported Shaftesbury's attempts to exclude James, Duke of York, a known Roman Catholic, from the succession. In 1685 the Whigs did not field candidates and Sir William Twysden and John, later Sir John, Knatchbull, both nominally Tories, were returned without a contest. Twysden was a constitutional legitimist and supported the Court. Knatchbull had not been impressed by James II's conduct when he met him at Faversham during the king's first unsuccessful attempt to flee the country, and he recorded in his diary,

> December 14 Friday When we came in he turned from the window and seeing Sir Basil [Dixwell, colonel in the Kent militia and James's escort back to London] come towards him I observed a smile in his face of an Extraordinary size and sort, so forced, awkward and unpleasant to look upon, that I can truly say I never saw anything like itt; he took no notice of me, tho I was just bending my knee to kiss his hand and he immediatly turned to Sir Basil[98]

Sir John later joined the Association formed to support William of Orange. Twysden was less nimble-footed. Although he declared 'he was as much for the Prince of Orange and Protestant Religion as anybody and that he had no dislike to the Association, yet he thought it was a base thing to be frightened into it for the sake of an Election'.[99] His prevarication cost him the seat.[100]

Dering, Knatchbull and Twysden were old gentry; their families established for at least two centuries, Knatchbull's account illustrates the posturing sensibilities that underlay the simple affiliations of party:

> Saturday the 12th [Jan. 1689] We went in Sir Edward's [Dering's] coach to Pickenden Heath, who I observed took noe care of calling on the freeholders in his parts . . . When we came to Bersted we gott on horseback, & when we came to the Heath I believe we had not a hundred in our party though we came through soe many parishes; it was between nine and ten when we came on the heath, but we found nobody there, so we rid all loosly about the field, & within half an hour Sir Thomas Roberts came in – Sir Edward went presently up to him & discoursed with him privately for some time. Soon after Sr Vere Fane, Sir Stephen Leonard, & that party came in, & then they all wispered, &

97 J.R. Twisden, *The Family of Twysden and Twisden*, London 1939, p. 278.
98 BL, Add. MSS 52924, f. 21.
99 *Ibid.*, f. 27v.
100 J.H. Plumb, 'The Elections to the Convention Parliament of 1689', *The Cambridge Historical Journal*, v (1935–7), p. 252.

most of the rest of the Gentlemen joined them. I took notice of it but did not intrude myselfe but rid about by my Selfe, in this time I suppose it was agreed between Sr Vere, Sr Stephen & Sir Thomas who should be set up against Sr William in case he refused to sign the Association: about halfe an hour after Sr William Twysden came in . . . I saluted Sr William and bid him good morrow & quickly perceiv'd an unusual coldnes in him . . . I think him a man of great virtue and worth yet I had observed at those 2 visits I gave him about the first report of the Prince of Orange's coming, that he would stick at the mark & not think well of this Invasion as he called itt.[101]

The occasion illustrates the dilemma faced by Tories and erstwhile monarchists. They were supporters of monarchy; but even more so supporters of the Church of England. The ghastly smile on the face of James II at Faversham was that of a man who had totally misread his supporters. The Tory position that English monarchs ruled by divine right, strengthened by the publication of Robert Filmer's *Patriarcha* in 1680, had some popular support. Shaftesbury and the Whigs had been defeated in their attempt to exclude James from the succession by the simple expedient of Charles' dissolution of Parliament. Charles' explanatory Declaration in April 1681 brought a flood of loyal addresses from grand juries and borough corporations. There were a few expressions of popular support for the Duke of Monmouth. Nicholas Wraight of Charing, collar maker, was indicted for seditiously saying 'The Duke of Monmouth is now in the North with forty thousand men, and if I were with him I would spend the best blood in my body with him and for him.' Martha Tickner of Deptford, also charged with seditious words said, 'I hope the Duke of Monmouth will gett the better of the King. And if he doth, I will hang twenty of you.'[102] However, the Rye House plot and the failure of Monmouth's rebellion enhanced the monarchy's standing in spite of the bloody persecutions of Judge George Jeffreys. Furthermore Charles' and James' measures to pack the corporations with their own supporters were highly successful. When James called his first Parliament in May 1685 there were only 51 Whigs among the 513 MPs, so that 'few English monarchs have come to the throne in as strong a position'. Yet James threw away his advantages because he misjudged his supporters' priorities, for, 'rather than seeing the Tories as royal absolutists it is better to see them as conservative legal-constitutionalists, deeply committed to the rule of law and the Anglican church'. Sir William Twysden was their epitome.[103]

Although the Whigs encouraged the idea of a populist vision of government, the ways in which political opinions might be expressed were somewhat limited and were in any case orchestrated by the parties' leaders. In 1682, Lord Russell, various nonconformist ministers and several citizens of London were active in the area of Tunbridge Wells 'in suggesting to the people fears and jealousies of popery and arbitrary government, printed papers being daily sent them which

---

[101] BL, Add. MSS 52924, f. 27.
[102] *Calendar of Assize Records*, pp. 236, 237.
[103] Harris, *Politics under the Later Stuarts*, pp. 119–21; Twisden, *op. cit.*, pp. 280–4.

speak evil of our present government'.[104] The press certainly reinforced political awareness. It played a large part in the election campaigns of both parties in 1710 and by arousing popular feelings over the issues of war with the French and over Henry Sacheverell's defence of the Church of England and attack upon the dissenters.[105] But newspaper circulation was small. By Anne's reign it has been estimated that the average daily sale of newspapers was 7300. Of these the *London Gazette* printed 6000 and Defoe's *Review* only 400. After the Stamp Act of 1712 which imposed a tax of one penny on each sheet, newspapers became relatively expensive. Towards the end of Anne's reign, when every newspaper was on the payroll of the government or of members of the opposition, the earl of Jersey noted that in Kent 'Postboys, Examiners, etc., [both Tory periodicals] are the usual entertainments of the country gentry'.[106]

The device of the petition also could be used to bring the pressure of popular opinion upon parliament. The Petition of Right of 1628 maintained the right of the subject to petition the monarch, a right which Charles I had reluctantly accepted. In spite of an Act of 1664 which attempted to control petitioning in the interests of public order, the House of Lords in 1669 had resolved that 'it is the inherent right of every Commoner of England, to prepare and present petitions to the House of Commons, in case of grievance'.[107] It was a recognised means to embarrass the government of the day. Algernon Sidney had been involved in the monster London petition of 1680.[108] Thomas Papillon, MP for Dover in 1678, drafted a 'aggressive' petition to parliament alleging that for many years there had been a popish plot to destroy protestantism and the established government. Kent's grand jury had been one of those to renounce such petitioning.[109] Nevertheless, it was believed that the meeting of quarter sessions, with its attendant grand jury, constituted one of the few quasi-political assemblies which could rightly petition for the redress of grievances.

At the General Quarter Sessions at Maidstone begun on 29 April 1701, some of the principal freeholders expressed dissatisfaction with the prosecution of the war against the French. The Chairman of Quarter Sessions, William Colepeper, advised that 'it was the proper work of the Grand Jury to present the grievances of the country'.[110] The Grand Jury asked the Chairman to draw up the petition and this was done. The petition was then signed by all 21 members of the Grand

---

104 Tim Harris, 'The Parties and the People: The Press, the Crowd and Politics "Out-of-doors" in Restoration England', in Glassey, *op. cit.*, p. 128.

105 Mary Ransome, 'The Press in the General Election of 1710', *The Cambridge Historical Journal*, v (1935–7), pp. 209–21.

106 R.D. Altick, *The English Common Reader*, Chicago 1957, pp. 47–9; Harris, *Politics under the later Stuarts*, p. 186.

107 W.C. Costin and J.S. Watson, *The Law and Working of the Constitution: Documents 1660–1914*, London 1952, vol. 1, p. 160.

108 Mark Knights, 'Petitioning and the Political Theorists: John Locke, Algernon Sidney and London's Monster Petition of 1680', *Past and Present*, cxxxix (1993), pp. 94–111.

109 Mark Knights, *Politics and Opinion in Crisis, 1678–81*, Cambridge 1994, pp. 272–3.

110 Daniel Defoe, 'The History of the Kentish Petition', in *A Second Collection of Scarce and Valuable Tracts*, ed. Somers, London 1750, vol. iv, p. 302.

Jury and by all 23 members of the bench of magistrates. It was entitled 'the humble petition of the Gentlemen, Justices of the Peace, Grand Jury and other Freeholders, at their General Quarter Sessions of the Peace holden at Maidston in Kent, the 29th day of April, in the 13th year of our Sovereign Lord King William the Third' and it set forth,

> that they, deeply concerned at the dangerous estate of this kingdom, and of all Europe; and considering that the fate of them, and their posterity, depends on the wisdom of their representatives in Parliament . . . And praying that this House will have regard to the Voice of the People; that our Religion and Safety may be effectually provided for; that the loyal Addresses of this House may be turned into Bills of Supply; and that his Majesty may be enabled powerfully to assist his Allies, before it is too late.[111]

The Petition, possibly encouraged by Junto Whigs and designed to embarrass the Tory administration, was presented by William Colepeper. The House resolved that the Petition 'is scandalous, insolent, and seditious; tending to destroy the Constitution of Parliaments, and subvert the established government of this realm'. In spite of clause 4 of the Bill of Rights of 1689, that it is the right of subjects to petition the King and all commitments and prosecutions for such petitioning are illegal,[112] the promoter of the Petition, William Colepeper, and Thomas Colepeper, David Polhill, Justinian Champneys and William Hamilton who accompanied him were placed in the custody of the Serjeant at Arms.[113] The terms of the Petition were moderate and, in fact, the following day the House resolved to support the King's allies 'in maintaining the liberties of Europe' but this was followed by Daniel Defoe's Legion Memorial – Legion, for we are many – which was a much more comprehensive catalogue of the Commons' shortcomings, and alleging that the Commons had no power to imprison persons other than their own members. If the Commons betrayed their trust, it was the right of the people to call them to account and proceed against them as traitors.[114] The House of Commons was now on the defensive and the Petitioners were national heroes, given a celebratory dinner in Mercers Hall on their release. The Kentish Petition was still a piece of gentry politics: the magistrates who engineered it, the Grand Jury, hand-picked by the Sheriff, and most of the signatories were the country gentlemen on horseback, in no way to be compared to Christopher Wyvill's Association and its petitions in the 1780s or the more popular petitioning movements later in the century. The five year period ending in 1789 produced 880 petitions to parliament. By 1831 the figure had risen to 24,492, by which time petitioning had become a recognised and

111 Costin and Watson, *op. cit.*, vol. i, pp. 191–2.
112 E.N. Williams, *The Eighteenth Century Constitution 1688–1815*, Cambridge 1970, pp. 28, 408.
113 Defoe, *op. cit.*, p. 306. Two were placed in a garret and two in a cellar, without their night-gowns and necessaries.
114 Speck, *The Birth of Britain*, p. 27; David Ogg, *England in the Reigns of James II and William III*, Cambridge 1984, p. 463.

standardised form of political expression, used to gain hearing and support for the campaigns for parliamentary reform and the abolition of the slave trade.[115]

After 1707 a member who accepted a place under the crown was required to vacate his seat and stand for re-election. The requirement eventually changed the political allegiance of Sir Edward Knatchbull, 'a pretty warm Tory' during the reign of Queen Anne. Knatchbull was returned for Rochester in 1702 and for the county in 1713 but he lost his seat in 1715. He was returned for the county in 1722 and is remembered chiefly for the act of 1723 which allowed separate parishes to establish workhouses. But he realised that in the reign of the Hanoverians there was no governing future for a Tory member of parliament and increasingly became a supporter and admirer of Sir Robert Walpole. With the onset of the 1727 election Knatchbull found that his Tory friends in Kent were naturally shy of his growing admiration for Walpole. For the general election of 1727 Knatchbull found that the Whigs would only support men who had been staunch party supporters and not turncoats. However, using the Whig Duke of Dorset as a go-between, he applied to Walpole on account of his 'zeal for the public service and my particular attachment to you' and was brought in for Lostwithiel, Cornwall, from which time he supported the administration.[116]

It was difficult for Tories under the first two Georges to remain true to their traditional loyalties and yet avoid the charge of Jacobitism, but there was a 'country platform', capable of appealing to Whig and Tory alike. When William, first Viscount Vane, an opposition Whig, and Sir Edward Dering, the leader of the East Kent Tories, stood for the county in 1734, they were able to claim

> These are candidates untainted in their principles, and uncorrupt in their practice, who have always shown their inclination to maintain liberty and Property, their zeal in opposing that badge of Slavery an Excise and the Instrument of Arbitrary power a standing Army.

Of the 4,441 Kentish freeholders who are recorded in the pollbook as having voted for Dering, 3,993 split their votes between him and Vane; only 26 were sufficiently purist to plump for the Tory alone.[117] Dering had been returned for the county in 1733 on the death of Sir Robert Furnese of Waldershare, who 'went off delirious, roaring against the excise . . . not having been sober for ten days before he was taken ill'.[118] In his epitaph Dering claimed that he had 'honourably and successfully maintained the independence of the county of Kent in the first four Parliaments of George II.[119]

There was another alternative; retirement into a lofty disdain. Percyvall Hart, a knight of the shire in the last two parliaments of Queen Anne, found that the

115 Williams, *op. cit.*, p. 408.
116 *The House of Commons 1715–1754*, ed. R. Sedgwick, vol. ii, p. 191.
117 L. Colley, *In Defiance of Oligarchy: The Tory Party 1714–60*, Cambridge 1982, p. 217.
118 Sedgwick, *op. cit.*, ii, pp. 56–7.
119 *Ibid.*, i. p. 611.

expense of contesting county elections had become too costly and had inscribed on his tomb in his church at Lullingstone his 'strong attachment to the OLD ENGLISH CONSTITUTION . . . abhorring all venality, and scorning to buy the Peoples Voices as to sell his own' which he maintained disqualified him from parliamentary service.[120]

Treating, which gradually shaded into bribery, was an acknowledged consequence of electioneering. William Glanville of St Clere, near Sevenoaks, who represented Hythe for nearly forty years, wrote to his patron, the Duke of Dorset, Lord Warden of the Cinque Ports, on 28 September 1733, 'when I have got as many as by Drink and good words I shall then go to work with half guineas under your pretence of horse hire and expenses'.[121] However, the expense of electioneering was of particular concern to Charles Stanhope, Viscount Mahon, the second son of the second Earl Stanhope of Chevening. Mahon, began his political career as a radical. Some of his radicalism may have been acquired while he served on the council of two hundred of the city state of Geneva.[122] On returning to this country in 1774 he stood unsuccessfully as a Wilkesite candidate for Westminster. In 1777 he contested Maidstone but withdrew before the poll. He refused an invitation to stand again for Westminster apparently because of the expense of the former occasion.[123] Soon afterwards he joined Christopher Wyvill's associating movement for economic parliamentary reform and became chairman of the Kent corresponding committee. Wyvill's Yorkshire association was generated by the failure of Lord North's administration to cope with the war against the American colonists, increasing taxation, and the influence that the administration was able to wield in the Commons through places and patronage. Reducing taxation became less important to Wyvill's programme once he realised that Yorkshire and the North was less heavily taxed than the South, and some of the wilder demands of some of his supporters, such as annual parliaments and adult male suffrage, were dropped by Wyvill, but the other plank of his programme, an increase in the number of relatively independent county MPs and a reduction in the venal borough representatives, was one which could appeal to the gentry country-wide. Mahon energetically pressed for more county members of the Commons and for the county poll to be taken at various places throughout the county, thus reducing the expense of getting electors to the poll, which provided an opportunity for bribery and treating by the candidate.[124] After he succeeded his father as third Earl Stanhope in March 1786, he continued to work for the reform of county elections by introducing four bills in the Lords to register county electors and to reduce bribery.[125]

---

[120] Heal and Holmes, *op. cit.*, p. 236.
[121] CKS, U269/C148, quoted in Peter L. Humphries, 'Public Opinion and Radicalism in Kentish Politics 1768–84', Kent MA 1979, p. 40.
[122] A. Newman, *The Stanhopes of Chevening*, London 1969, p. 132.
[123] Namier and Brooke, *op. cit.*, vol. 3, p. 462.
[124] I.R. Christie, *Wilkes, Wyvill and Reform*, London 1962, pp. 91–5.
[125] G.M. Ditchfield, 'The House of Lords and Parliamentary Reform in the Seventeen-Eighties', in

As the century progressed the arrangements for polling the county became more and more elaborate and burdensome. Angus Greenland, the under-sheriff of Kent in 1790, whose job it was to organise the poll, breathed a sigh of relief when it was all over and expressed the fervent hope that it would not soon happen again. In a preface to the printed poll book for the election he described in detail the manner in which the poll booth was constructed on Penenden Heath and the way in which the poll was taken. The booth, constructed by a carpenter to Greenland's own design, was 106 feet wide, 25 feet deep and 12 feet high. A rail 3 feet 6 inches high and 7 feet from the front of the booth kept back horsemen. The booth was divided into 14 boxes or polling places which matched the number of magistracy divisions of the county. Above each box were the names of the parishes within the division. The freeholders stood on a step one foot high to give their votes; they had two. Before them sat the sheriff's poll clerks, behind them sat the check clerks of the candidates, behind them, yet more elevated, sat the inspectors for the candidates with a rail to lean on when they wished to scrutinise the clerks' books before them. At the pinnacle of the booth was a box for the High Sheriff to oversee the whole proceedings. Also in the booth were tables where the clerks could eat and drink. At the back were two narrow entrances to admit those freeholders too infirm to hazard the boisterous reception at the front. These entrances were guarded by four bailiffs and ten 'Javelin men'. Carpenters were on hand to make running repairs should the need arise.[126]

(7) The End of the *Ancien Regime*?

England was the only major country in Europe to emerge from the Napoleonic era with its *Ancien Regime* virtually intact, i.e. with its monarchy, aristocracy and established church constitutionally unchanged from that of the previous century. The Reform Act of 1832 redistributed some seats; the county increased its MPs from two to four – two for East Kent and two for West Kent, New Romney and Queenborough lost their seats and Hythe was reduced to one seat. Chatham was given one seat. Thus Kent returned 16 MPs to Parliament after 1832 compared to 18 MPs before 1832. The franchise was extended to include the £10 householder in the boroughs and excluded non-resident freemen; in the counties the 40 shilling freeholder was joined by the £10 copyholder. But the old habits of venality died hard. Charles Greville noted in his diary that at Maidstone 'the one prevailing object among the whole community is to make money of their votes, and though . . . there are some exceptions, they are very

Peers, Politics and Power: The House of Lords 1603–1911, ed. C. Jones and D.L. Jones, London 1986, pp. 327–38.

126 *The Poll for Knights of the Shire, Kent, Penenden Heath on Monday, Tuesday, Wednesday, 28, 29, 30 June 1790*, Rochester 1790. In the county election of 1640 the walls of the Shire House were broken down in the anxiety of electors 'to put through the names of the freeholders for their friends to be written down', Everitt, *Community of Kent*, pp. 82–3.

few indeed'. As for the new electors they were if possible worse than the old: 'The people are generally alive to public affairs – look into the votes and speeches of members, give their opinions – but are universally corrupt.'[127] Dover, Hythe and Sandwich were still subject to government influence at elections. Chatham, which had been created a parliamentary borough by the Reform Act, was formally recommended for disfranchisement twenty years later by a parliamentary committee of enquiry which noted that on no single occasion had its electors failed to return a candidate recommended to them by the government.[128]

Richard Cobden, the leader of the middle-class Anti-Corn Law League which had campaigned against the landed classes was forced to admit in 1857: 'During my experience the higher classes never stood so high in relative social and political rank, as compared with the other classes, as at present.'[129] Kent remained a county dominated by gentry. Compared to the great landowners of the Midlands and the North, such as the Spencers and the Dukes of Buccleugh, the estates of the Kentish aristocracy and former aristocracy were comparitively modest. At Knole, Lord Sackville owned 8,550 acres with a gross annual value of £11,250, but less than 2,000 acres lay in Kent. Lord De L'Isle and Dudley at Penshurst, owned 9,250 acres of which about half lay in Kent. Viscount Holmesdale of Linton Park, Maidstone, with 18,000 acres had 16,000 acres in Kent. Earl Stanhope of Chevening held 14,200 acres 4,300 of which were in Kent.[130] The gentry still occupied a considerable proportion of the large number of landed estates in the county. Over 20% of the total area of Kent was occupied by the greater gentry with estates of between 3,000 and 10,000 acres. A further 13% was occupied by lesser gentry with estates of between 1,000 and 3,000 acres.[131] Many of the older gentry families occupied the seats they had acquired three or four centuries before. Sir Edward Dering, MP for Romney and East Kent, at Surrenden Dering, Pluckley, owned over 7,000 acres wholly in Kent and Sir Wyndham Knatchbull, MP for East Kent, at Mersham Hatch, had 4,600 acres wholly in Kent. The Brockmans were still at Beachborough with 3,800 acres.

The established church, 'far too important a part of the political and social structure of the country for any man of property . . . lightly to abandon',[132] also survived remarkably intact. At first it was believed that the Church was crucial to the integrity of the state. As Lord Eldon, the Lord Chancellor, pointed out, the Establishment was founded upon tolerant Anglicanism. But that toleration went only so far as religious worship for some non-conformists. It could not tolerate non-Anglicans in the seats of power. For 'the Establishment' he said, 'is

---

[127] Norman Gash, *Politics in the Age of Peel*, Hassocks 1977, pp. 123, 125.

[128] *Ibid.*, p. 337.

[129] Geoffrey Best, *Mid-Victorian Britain, 1851–75*, London 1971, p. 239.

[130] John Bateman, *The Great Landowners of Great Britain and Ireland*, London 1883, pp. 126, 224, 392.

[131] F.M.L. Thompson, *English Landed Society in the Nineteenth Century*, London 1963, pp. 114–15.

[132] G.F.A. Best, *Temporal Pillars: Queen Anne's Bounty, the Ecclesiastical Commissioners, and the Church of England*, Cambridge 1964, p. 3.

formed, not for the purpose of making the Church political, but for the purpose of making the State religious'[133] Tories in the 1820s found themselves repeating Filmer's assertions made almost two centuries previously. The true foundation of every Christian monarchy rests upon the principle that 'the powers which be are ordained of God' and that the king is Christ's vicegerent. Thus 'the [democratic] principle is a principle of rebellion: and dissent or schism may not inaptly be termed spiritual republicanism'.[134] The repeal of the Test and Corporation Acts and Roman Catholic emancipation, it was feared, would herald the end of Anglican supremacy. In fact, the majority of churchgoers in Kent in the nineteenth century remained loyal to the Church of England. This was partly due to rebuilding and refurbishment, which offered more seats for religious posteriors to sit on. Anglican churches in Kent offered 65% of the total 'sittings' for worshippers.[135] Non-conformists did not swamp the Anglicans and the Roman Catholics were a tiny minority.[136]

The collection of tithe in kind, i.e. the tenth sheaf, the tenth bushel of hops or the tenth lamb, was an ancient and perennial problem.[137] Also, it was claimed by John Boys that tithes seriously deterred agricultural improvement in Kent.[138] The passing of the Tithe Redemption Act of 1836, by which payment of tithes in kind was converted into an annual money charge based upon the price of grain crops, allowed the Church of England to side-step the knock-out blow of the total abolition of tithe, that some radicals had intended.[139] 'The Act of 1836 was followed, not by uproar and despair, but by calmness and relaxation, as if a great weight had been taken off the clergy's minds and a bone of contention removed from their society.'[140]

[133] Quoted in Clark, *op. cit.*, pp. 351–2.
[134] *Ibid.*, p. 351.
[135] *Religious Worship in Kent: The Census of 1851*, ed. Margaret Roake, Kent Records XXVII, Maidstone 1999, p. xxvi.
[136] Yates, Hume and Hastings, *op. cit.*, p. 53.
[137] Frederick Lansberry, 'Improper Impropriators and *Autiel Petit Choses*', in *Studies in Modern Kentish History*, pp. 103–9.
[138] John Boys, *General View of the Agriculture of the County of Kent*, 2nd edn London 1805, pp. 39–43.
[139] Elie Halévy, *The Triumph of Reform*, London 1961, pp. 201–3.
[140] Best, *Temporal Pillars*, p. 466.

3

Old Corruption: Government in the Boroughs

BRYAN KEITH-LUCAS† and FREDERICK LANSBERRY

(1) Incorporation

Municipal corporations were usually created by the royal grant of a charter of special and exclusive privileges to burgesses who usually, but not always, represented the merchant community of the town; or, as in the case of Gravesend, whose first charter of incorporation allowed 'The rights and profits of the ancient water passage or "Long Ferry" between London and Gravesend to the "Men of Gravesend" '.[1] Along with trading went fiscal privileges; the right to tax 'foreigners' allowed to trade in the town, and freedom from certain taxes for the freemen trading outside the borough's boundaries. With these rights went courts of enforcement, such as courts of record and market courts. Most importantly, the chief officer or officers, such as the mayor or portreeve, were granted the powers of a magistrate and the members of the commonalty[2] of the borough were granted the right of pleading in their own courts. The Webbs have made the grant of the magistracy the defining criteria of a municipal corporation.[3]

The grant of a charter of incorporation was greatly to be desired, not only for its trading, fiscal and judicial privileges but for the right to exclude 'foreign' agents of government, even royal. This right was taken seriously. On 14 August 1300 the mayor, town clerk and some of the men of Sandwich assaulted the king's itinerent justices, refusing to let them enter the town's liberty, 'and cut open the pouch with the king's rolls and break the bows and arrows of the men of the aforesaid justices'.[4] In the case of the Cinque Ports the authority of the king's county representative, the Lord Lieutenant, was specifically excepted in the terms of the commission issued to Heneage Finch, Earl of Winchilsea, at the Restoration.[5] The Liberty of the Cinque Ports has been described by the Webbs as 'the most remarkable example of a Municipal Hierarchy – an example unique

---

†   Section (7) Improvement Commissioners, was written by Professor Bryan Keith-Lucas.
1   R.P. Cruden, *Gravesend*, Pickering 1843, p. 189.
2   The governing body and freemen or burgesses, but in the Corporation of Romney Marsh it comprised every resident householder of full age within the limits of the Marsh.
3   S. and B. Webb, *English Local Government: The Manor and the Borough*, London 1963, p. 275.
4   Justin Croft, 'An assault on the royal justices at Ash and the making of the Sandwich custumal', *Archaeologia Cantiana*, cxvii (1997), pp. 13–32.
5   *The Twysden Lieutenancy Papers, 1583–1668*, ed. G. Scott Thomson, Kent Records vol. x, 1926, pp. 29–33.

in England and Wales'.[6] This uniqueness was the Ports' claim to exclude all other government authorities and was a reflection of their belief that they were a confederation of little republics.[7] Municipal corporations, then, were enclaves of exclusivity and speciality within the normal framework of county administration.

Although there were some boroughs who claimed their rights by prescription, i.e. from time immemorial, the majority were of royal creation. Fears that their charters were in some way inadequate, or that royal favour might change, led to frequent inspections and confirmations. Canterbury could exhibit some twenty-seven charters granted between the reigns of Henry II and George III. The monarch's more punitive method of examination was through the use of the royal writ of *quo warranto*, which allowed him to question the exercise of their privileges. It was a tempting tool but, as Edmund Burke was later to point out, 'Corporations, which have a perpetual succession and a hereditary noblesse . . . are the guardians of monarchical succession.' In other words, they were in the same constitutional category as the house of lords, the monarchy, the established church and freehold tenure of office.[8] When the Municipal Corporations Amendment Bill was being debated in Parliament, it was Lord Lyndhurst, leader of the House of Lords, who put up the most stubborn defence of corporate rights.

(2) Loyal Corporations

Corporations were in some senses the creations of the monarch; but they were by no means his creatures. Towns had histories before they were corporations. Inextricably woven into those histories were ancient customs and common practices, sometimes manorial in origin, which the inhabitants might recall when faced with oligarchic government. Furthermore, the arena for radicalism in early-modern England has been identified as religion and the battleground was the Church of England;[9] the cockpits of this contest were often within the municipal corporations.

The provisions of the Corporation Act (13 Car. II c. 1) were foreshadowed in a royal warrant of 7 May 1661 which stated 'that in drawing up all future charters for boroughs or corporations, there be express reservation to the Crown of the first nomination of aldermen, recorders and town clerks; the filling up of places in the Common Council with persons nominated by the borough and the future nomination of all recorders and town clerks; also that there is a proviso

6 Webb, *op. cit.*, p. 372.
7 Montague Burrows, *Cinque Ports*, London 1895, pp. 201–2: 'Sandwich, like the rest of the Ports, was both before and after the Conquest, a sort of republic.'
8 Webb, *op. cit.*, p. 703.
9 J.C.D. Clark, *English Society, 1688–1832*, Cambridge 1985, pp. 277–8.

for elections for Parliament to be made by the Common Council only'.[10] In remoulding corporation charters Charles II was following Commonwealth precedents: 'Cromwell, like Charles II after him, employed the same method of altering the electorate by obtaining a voluntary surrender of borough charters, and issued new charters framing the constitution on a more oligarchic model.' There is a notice of the charter of Sandwich having been called in by the Committee for Corporations in 1652.[11]

The Corporation Act of 1661 was part of royal and Cavalier Parliament policy to regulate the constitution of the governing bodies of the corporations, many of which had been dominated by dissenters during the Interregnum. The Act contained oaths of Allegiance and Supremacy 'to the end that the succession in such Corporations may be most probably perpetuated in the hands of persons well affected to His Majesty and the established Government'. It also specified that all future officers and common councilmen of the corporations, including those of the Cinque Ports, should take the sacrament according to the rites of the Church of England.[12]

Commissioners were appointed to visit all corporate towns, including the Cinque Ports, to extract from all mayors, aldermen, common councilmen and officers the Oaths of Allegiance and Supremacy and a declaration that it was unlawful upon any pretence whatsoever to take up arms against the King and a further declaration that they were not bound by the oath of the Solemn League and Covenant. All who refused were to be removed from office and their offices and places were to be void 'as if the said respective persons so refusing were naturally dead'. The act was a comprehensive attempt to make the municipal corporations creatures of the king. There were many who were unable to forswear their recent past. At Canterbury five aldermen and five councillors were removed by the king's command; a further three aldermen, five councillors and the town clerk were removed by the commissioners. At Rochester the corporation was drastically purged in 1662 with no fewer than ten aldermen and almost one hundred freemen removed. At Maidstone six jurats and sixteen common councillors were deprived.[13] Sandwich, which had been controlled by Presbyterians and Independents, suffered the severest pruning. With the exception of the mayor, all the jurats were dismissed and out of the common council of twenty-two only nine survived. Even some who took the oath were dismissed. The aim was to remove from the corporations all those who were disaffected to royal government and this included freemen, who were disenfranchised.[14] The purge was too much for one of the commissioners, Sir Roger Twisden, a strict

---

10 *CSPD, 1660–61*, p. 582.
11 B.L.K. Henderson, 'The Commonwealth Charters', *Transactions of the Royal Historical Society*, 3rd ser. vi (1912), pp. 134–5; *HMC 5th Report*, London 1876, p. 571.
12 W.C. Costin and J.S. Watson, *The Law and Working of the Constitution: Documents 1660–1914*, London 1952, vol. 1, p. 15.
13 *The House of Commons 1660–1690*, ed. B.D. Henning, vol. 1, pp. 276, 281; P. Clark and L. Murfin, *History of Maidstone*, Stroud 1995, p. 97.
14 M.V. Jones, 'The Political History of the Parliamentary Boroughs of Kent 1642–1662', pp. 194–239.

constitutionalist and presently a judge. A precise man when it came to points of law, he objected to the removal of Lake, the Recorder of Maidstone, on the grounds that he had been appointed to office since the passing of the act. He withdrew from the commission condemning the source of its powers as 'a very arbitrary byll'. The attempt to instal four gentlemen as jurats of Maidstone failed because the sitting jurats would not waive their precedence to the newcomers.[15] However, the majority of the commissioners were staunch royalists and episcopalians and this allowed the Anglican gentry to control the boroughs for a short time. The powers of the commissioners lapsed in 1663 and over the next few years even the most ardent royalist members of corporations had to compromise. Many of those evicted were able to ease themselves back into office through the simple expedient of not taking the oath. John Strode, the Lieutenant Governor of Dover Castle reported in 1680 that at Sandwich the oath had not been tendered since 1662.[16]

(3) Non-Conformity and the Corporations

Throughout the reigns of Charles II and James II the most persistent disputes in the boroughs related to the re-emergence of corporations controlled by non-conformists or 'Phanaticks'. The surrender of the charters of Dover, Canterbury and Sandwich in 1684 has been shown to have come not so much from royal initiative but rather from pressure exerted by royalists or loyalists within the corporations.[17] At Dover, the mayor, Nicholas Cullen, a Dissenter who had been turned out in 1662, but had returned to office without taking the sacrament or subscribing the oaths, was challenged by a self-styled loyalist, Warham Jemmett, a local brewer. Jemmett alleged that the deputy mayor, William Stokes, another Dissenter, had refused to grant a licence to any alehouse selling Jemmett's beer. Also, it was claimed, that both Cullen and Stokes refused to prosecute Dissenters who were charged with holding conventicles. Disputes between Anglicans and Dissenters at Dover led to two mayors being elected in 1682 and being sworn in by their respective supporters.

In Canterbury, too, there were prolonged battles between non-conformists and the 'Cathedral party'. The large congregation of John Durant, an inflamatory Independent minister, who had preached in the cathedral during the Interregnum, was influential in municipal politics. Durant had been dubbed 'the most seditious conventicle preacher in the county . . . the Belweather of the Independent faction' and 'a leading Rebell from his cradle'.[18] After the Declaration

---

[15] F.W. Jessup, *Sir Roger Twysden 1597–1672*, London 1965, p. 172.

[16] Tim Harris, *Politics under the Later Stuarts*, Cambridge 1993, p. 39; Jones, *op. cit.*, p. 236.

[17] Colin Lee, ' "Fanatic Magistrates": Religious and Political Conflict in Three Kent Boroughs, 1680–1684', *The Historical Journal*, xxxv (1991), pp. 43–63.

[18] M.V. Jones, 'The Divine Durant: A Seventeenth-Century Independent', *Archaeologia Cantiana*, lxxxiii (1968), p. 203.

of Indulgence in 1672 his congregation was said to have increased in numbers and 'taking advantage of the late Indulgence, have worked themselves so into power that they are now the majority of the aldermen and common council, admitting none to be livery men or sheriffs but their own party, all juries and constables being of the same stamp'.[19]

In 1675 the corporation resolved to remove their recorder, Thomas Hardres, from office, which they were entitled to do by the terms of their charter. Hardres, though a somewhat inactive member of parliament for the city from 1664 to 1681, was a government supporter and his removal was treated as an infringment of parliamentary privilege. The mayor and aldermen and the re-placement recorder were placed in custody until Hardres was re-instated. Sir Edward Dering clearly disagreed with the action of the Commons and recorded in his Diary on Friday 30 April 1675

> Then we had the Mayor Canterbury before us and five of his brethren upon their knees at the barr. They had been sent for in custody upon a complaint of breach of priviledge by Serjeant Hardress, their Recorder, and now upon their submission after a week's imprisonment they are discharged, paying their fees and restoring the Recorder to his place. Now that is a high straine of our priviledge, it being plain that the Recorder is an officer of the corporacion's, and by expresse words in their charter removeable at pleasure, and that they may chuse another. Yet it seemes the sense of the house that no possession of a parliament man, how unjustly got soever, or how arbitrarily possest, shall be removed during time of priviledge[20]

To the end of his life Hardres was chivied by Canterbury's non-conformists causing him to complain 'If I must not only spend my time in his Majesty's service without any recompense, but be hectored out of my reason to comply with a fiery pretender to Reformation, I must quit that service unless I receive better encouragement.'[21]

The mayor of Sandwich, Bartholomew Coombes, excommunicated by the Church of England and 'a great friend and protector of Phanaticks', abated assessments to the poor rate made on meeting houses and on houses of some known Dissenters and also took no action when given notice of conventicles. The Anglicans of the town were led by the vicar of St Clement's church, Alexander Mills. When, in 1682, there was a mayorial election which was held in St Clement's church, Coombes' supporters 'brought in half a dozen bottles of wine, clapped them on the communion table and there sat as at an alehouse bench, smoked tobacco and drank and committed other filthy things'. When Coombes' opponents called for a poll they were shouted down by the roisterers and Coombes was elected 'by most voices'.[22] The king's mild reprimand to

---

19 *CSPD, 1680–81*, p. 505, quoted in Lee, *op. cit.*, p. 49.
20 *The Diaries and Papers of Sir Edward Dering*, ed. M.F. Bond, London 1976, pp. 74–5.
21 *The House of Commons 1660–1690*, ed. Henning, vol. 2, p. 491.
22 Lee, *op. cit.*, p. 57.

these contraventions of the laws passed against non-conformists can be understood only in the light of Charles' and James' determination to form an alliance
with the Dissenters to achieve the repeal of the Test Acts and ease the way for
Roman Catholics to office.

(4) Corporation Officers

The governing body of the larger municipal corporations was usually divided
between an inner court or bench, often of twelve aldermen or jurats, and a more
numerous common council, often twenty-four assistants as at Canterbury, Sandwich, Hythe and Faversham. Dover had thirty-six members on its common
council, Maidstone at one time had forty. Rochester had eleven aldermen and
twelve assistants. On the smaller corporations, such as Lydd, the governing
body was the bailiff and twelve jurats and an indefinite number of freemen.
Even smaller was Queenborough which had a mayor, four jurats and two
bailiffs. At Tenterden the freemen were accounted the common council, but
there were less than twenty.[23]

The mayor, portreeve or, as at Lydd, the bailiff, headed the governing body,
usually chosen from amongst the aldermen or jurats by the common council, but
at Queenborough the selection of the mayor was made by and from the seven
persons who made up the mayor, jurats and bailiffs. Although the office was
considered prestigious and carried considerable ceremonial, the office in the
larger boroughs could be onerous. At Dover and its surrounding liberties, the
mayor found it a full-time job, attending the council hall or town clerk's office
nearly every day.[24] However, in his evidence before the Parliamentary Select
Committee on 16 April 1833, the then mayor, W. Knocker, esq., said that the
duties of the mayor were 'very little more than that of a jurat, though the mayor
is considered during his time the most active character'.[25] The mayor of Canterbury was engaged on corporation business for three or four hours every day
during winter months. In addition to being a magistrate, chairing the petty and
sometimes the quarter sessions of the borough, the mayor might preside over the
Court of Record, if there was one, and be Clerk of the Court of the Market. If the
borough returned members to parliament, the mayor could be returning officer
for the writ. At Dover the mayor was also coroner within the liberties. The
mayor of Rochester was an admiral within the city's liberties, which included
part of the Medway estuary, even to the exclusion of the Admiral of England.

---

[23] Except where otherwise indicated, information about the constitution and officers of corporations is
taken from the Report from the Select Committee on Municipal Corporations, which contains evidence from the mayors and town clerks of Dover and Gravesend, and the First Report of the Commissioners on Municipal Corporations of England and Wales.

[24] *British Parliamentary Papers: Appendix [Part II] to the First Report of the Commissioners on the
Municipal Corporations of England and Wales 1835*, Dublin 1969, vol. 3, p. 945.

[25] *British Parliamentary Papers: Report from the Select Committee on Municipal Corporations with the
Minutes of Evidence taken before them*, Dublin 1969, vol. 1, p. 275, question 6336.

The mayors of Maidstone and Faversham were governors of the grammar schools. During the eighteenth century mayors were usually ex-officio commissioners of the statutory authorities which applied to the borough, and frequently chaired these bodies.

The expenses of office were generally acknowledged to exceed the salary, if there was one. The mayor of Dover had a salary of £100 and 13s 4d from every inquest in the town and three bushels of coals from every foreign vessel delivering coals in Dover. The mayor of Queenborough had a salary of £80 a year, the right of pasturing twenty-four sheep and three cows upon the green and oysters for his own table from Queenborough's fishery. Only £5 was allowed to the mayor at Maidstone although by the early nineteenth century his expenses averaged between £100 and £200, a large part of which was made up by providing a breakfast for all the respectable inhabitants of the town on the day he went out of office. It is not surprising that some at Maidstone employed bribery to avoid being mayor. At Tenterden the mayor's salary was nil, but his expenses were nil. In smaller boroughs the office of mayor might become a cosy sinecure – almost an inherited post in some families. In Fordwich, for example, members of the Jennings family were mayors for forty years between 1688 and 1829.[26]

Not quite such a factotum, but possibly more influential, was the town clerk. He was usually a practicing attorney who might draw a small salary from the corporation, but this was more in the nature of a retainer, for his chief income came from fees charged in the borough's courts. If the borough had retained residual manorial functions, he might preside at the courts baron and leet. Again the office could run in a family, as at Dover, where three generations of the Wellard family served as town clerk between 1705 and 1763 and in addition served the office of mayor on two occasions.[27]

The larger corporations had recorders, usually stipulated in the charters to be 'a man learned in the law', in practice, a barrister. He was elected by the mayor and aldermen and held office during their pleasure. On occasion he might be used to give an opinion on the corporation's rights, particularly when it came to the creation of freemen. The recorders of Dover and Faversham always conducted the general sessions, although they were not magistrates for the towns. At Sandwich the recorder was a magistrate of the town but only acted as such during general sessions. The recorder of Canterbury had a house in the city where he resided during general sessions. In other towns the recorder, who usually lived in London, was allowed to appoint a deputy; at Maidstone, from the middle of the eighteenth century, this was the town clerk.

In addition to these officers there was a swarm of minor officials, some of whose posts were created by charter, such as the sheriff, chamberlain, coroner, sword bearer, serjeants-at-mace, gaol keeper and tollenger at Canterbury, and others, such as, the two constables, eight borsholders, two searchers and sealers

26 C.E. Woodruff, *A History of the Town and Port of Fordwich*, Canterbury 1895, pp. 75–7.
27 J.B. Jones, *Annals of Dover*, Dover 1938, pp. 368–9.

of leather, the ten water bailiffs, the town crier, beadle and pound-keeper at Rochester, who were appointed by the corporation to carry out duties connected with their various courts.

(5) Courts of the Corporation

Each corporation held, or had the right to hold, criminal, civil and administrative courts and some had courts of special jurisdiction, such as Rochester's Court of Admiralty. In all boroughs, except Queenborough, this right excluded the county's jurisdiction. The General or Quarter Sessions held by the boroughs were similar to those held by the county except that the pool of magistrates of mayor and jurats was much smaller than that of the county commission of the peace, with consequent delays in gaol delivery. Some sessions, such as those at Canterbury, Dover, Faversham, Sandwich and Rochester, could try felonies.[28] At such trials the recorder, usually a barrister, was present. Executions were rare but were still being carried out in the early decades of the nineteenth century. Even a small corporation such as Tenterden, tried, found guilty and hanged two burglars in 1785,[29] but by 1833 felonies had been transferred to the county for trial at the assizes. Weekly petty sessions were held in all the larger boroughs, usually before the mayor. At Rochester petty sessions were held twice a week, and it was noted that there were not enough magistrates for the liberty. However, 'the administration of justice was universally admitted to have been perfectly pure: this admission was readily, and indeed eagerly, made by the parties most bitterly opposed to the present system of the corporation'.[30]

Every corporation possessed a court for debts, real, personal and mixed, i.e. involving lands, money or both. Usually entitled the Courts of Record, they were also known as the Courts of Portmote, as at Rochester and Faversham, or the Courts of Pleas, as at Canterbury and Maidstone, or, in the case of Fordwich, the Hundred Court. Sometimes, as at Dover and Faversham, there was no upper limit on the amount of the pleas. Because court fees and lawyers' fees were relatively high these courts tended to fall into disuse during the eigtheenth century, to be succeeded by the Courts of Requests. However, at Sandwich the Court of Record was still being used in 1833 when seven writs were sued out of it, one for over £200.[31]

The Court Leet, originally a manorial court, was a court of minor misdemeanor. Sometimes a view of frankpledge – a listing of the resiants or freeholders – was taken and small fines exacted for non-attendance at the leet. After

---

28 Canterbury's gallows were moved in 1660 to another place in the Castle ditch: *Kentish Sources: Crime and Punishment*, ed. E. Melling, Maidstone 1969, p. 163.

29 *Ibid.*, pp. 140–2.

30 BPP: *Report of the Royal Commission on Municipal Corporations* [hereafter *RCMC*] *1835*, vol. 3, p. 857.

31 *Ibid.*, vol. 3, p. 1050.

the leet jury had toured the borough and 'presented' nuisances there followed the leet dinner paid for from the corporation's funds. By 1833, in most cases the proceedings were *pro forma* with officers and jury being chosen and a formal presentment that there was nothing to present being returned.[32] Queenborough provides an excellent example of the way in which manorial courts became marginalised in the seventeenth century and eventually ossified in the nineteenth. The Webbs, quoting from the First Report of the Royal Commission on Municipal Corporations, noted that between 1661 and 1728

> almost the whole affairs of the Corporation seem to have been transacted at the Court Leet. This court is held before the Mayor. At a Court Leet, held the 21st October 1661, Freemen were created; orders were made respecting dredging and fishing; a Deputy Mayor and a Justice of the Peace were elected; and victuallers were licensed . . . During these years, in fact, the management of the affairs of this corporation was sometimes in the hands of the Court Leet, sometimes in those of the Mayor, Jurats, and Bailiffs, and sometimes, as in 1716 and 1717, in those of 'the Court of Burghmote' at which all the burgesses may have had the right to be present. Eventually, the Close Body of the Mayor, Jurats and Bailiffs got the whole business; the Court of Burghmote was not summoned; and though the Court Leet continued to be held, its proceedings gradually became only formal.[33]

The process by which a select few became the governing body is well exemplified by what happened at Queenborough, but something similar happened to most of the corporations. The Bailiff of the Liberty of Romney Marsh became the appointee of the Lords of the Marsh and in 1604 it was resolved that twenty-four of the freeholders should henceforth 'be instead of the whole commonalty, and no other of the commonalty to intermeddle under pain of five pounds'.[34] The horns which once had called all the burgesses to burghmote or commonhall gathered dust, while the mayor conducted business with his cronies behind the closed doors of his court. Only at Sandwich was the constitution still 'of the most popular nature'. The commissioner was able to report that 'No inconvenience has been ever experienced from the share which freemen take in all the affairs of the corporation.' There, indeed, the freemen were informed by the blowing of the horn round the town early on the morning of the common assembly.[35]

---

32 *Loc. cit.*
33 Webb, *op. cit.*, pp. 347–8.
34 *BPP: RCMC*, vol. 3, p. 1025; Webb, *op. cit.*, p. 361.
35 *BPP: RCMC*, vol. 3, p. 1047.

(6) The Freemen

In origin, no doubt, the freemen were chiefly tradesmen and artisans who gained their freedom because they lived and traded in the town. The only charter possessed by Fordwich is a grant of gild merchant to the men of Fordwich, but its custumal closely follows that of Sandwich, from which its corporate status may have been assumed.[36] The first charter of Queenborough granted by Edward III, was framed in expansive and generous terms – 'the town should be a perpetual and free borough, and the men of it be burgesses, and have all the liberties and free customs belonging to a free borough'.[37] With the freedom might go the right to common pasture as at Fordwich,[38] or, as at Canterbury, the right to hunt in one of the city's parks.[39] The freemen of Queenborough had the monopoly of the town's oyster fishery.

Freedom of a borough had been a very valuable political, economic and social privilege. The first freedom of the medieval freemen of Canterbury was to speak and be heard in the city's Council. This right to have a voice in the government of their town was gradually whittled away over time. At Maidstone, the oligarchy which dominated the bench of jurats repeatedly attempted to reduce the voting rights of the common council and of the freemen in the eighteenth and nineteenth centuries.[40] The governing body at Queenborough comprised seven men, i.e. the mayor, four jurats and two bailiffs. Attempts by the free burgesses to get a voice in the running of the town and, more importantly, the regulation of the valuable oyster fishery, were steadily opposed throughout the eighteenth and early nineteenth centuries. Cases brought by the burgesses for their recognition were repeatedly referred to the court of King's Bench which occasioned great expense. Between £11,000 and £12,000 were taken from the funds of the fishery, which was entirely neglected during this period, to pay for actions in King's Bench and Chancery to counter the burgesses' claims.[41] Canterbury freemen could trade without the agreement of the Chamber; they were free of prises or taxes upon wine in every other port in England; they could not be forced to trial by battle; for offences within the city they had to be tried within the city.[42] These and other rights made the freedom of the city well worth having.

Usually one obtained the freedom of a corporation in one of five ways; by birth, marriage, apprenticeship, gift or purchase. At Canterbury every son of a freeman born within the liberties of the city was entitled to claim his freedom at the age of twenty-one. Marriage to the daughter of a freeman entitled the husband to his freedom when he was twenty-one. Apprenticeship for seven

---

36 Woodruff, *op. cit.*, pp. 49–53.
37 *BPP: RCMC*, vol. 3, p. 823.
38 Woodruff, *op. cit.*, p. 65, although this had been lost by 1835.
39 BL, Stowe MS 850, f. 19, 'also fremen of Caunterbury shall have ther huntyng and disport within their bounds of ther prevylege'.
40 Clark and Murfin, *op. cit.*, pp. 98–9.
41 *BPP: RCMC*, vol. 3, p. 837.
42 BL, Stowe MS 850, f. 19.

years to a resident freeman entitled the apprentice to his freedom when he was twenty-one. Freedom by gift was sometimes conferred as an honour, usually for political purposes. For instance, when Heneage Finch, solicitor-general and MP for the city in 1660, was given his freedom the city is said to have 'showered freedoms on royalists' when it returned Finch and Sir Anthony Aucher to the Convention Parliament.[43] On payment of £20 a person might be admitted to his freedom. In the seventeenth century this was sometimes done by surgeons or apothecaries who had acquired their training outside of the city. By the early nineteenth century, when being a freeman was still the sole qualification for the parliamentary franchise, freedom by redemption or purchase became increasingly common.[44] Purchase money provided a useful source of income for the corporation. 281 bought their freedom between 1824 and 1834. Sandwich had an unusual entitlement called the Frank Tenement. An inhabitant householder who, for a year and a day, held an estate within the town valued at £5 which was not subject to quit rent or fee-farm was entitled to his freedom.

Small fees were payable on admission, which at Canterbury, in the cases of birth, marriage and apprenticeship averaged around £1 15s, of which £1 was stamp duty and the remaining shillings were divided between the town clerk, chamberlain and minor officers of the Chamber, such as the serjeants-at-mace. At Sandwich too the fees were small; 8d for admission by birth and 9s 10d for admission by marriage, apprenticeship and gift.

(7) Improvement Commissioners

The old unreformed municipal corporations were not created to provide services which are now regarded as essential to a modern town. If they had acquired manorial rights and held a court leet, a jury might be summoned to annually perambulate the town to indentify and present nuisances, which might be heaps of garbage, unsafe spoutings, open cellars and encroachments upon the highway. They might pass bye-laws regulating the markets, creating the job of scavenger to clear offal from the butchers' shambles and, as at Canterbury, make it an offence to pollute the River Stour. But it was not their job to pave and light the streets, provide a sewerage system or generally look to the welfare of the inhabitants of the town. Nevertheless an increasing population, particularly in those towns which laid claim to lead county society, led to a variety of improvements being undertaken. Maidstone, aping the *bon ton* at The Wells at Tonbridge, laid out tree lined walks and repaired and extended the Tudor water supply to the town.[45]

For whatever purpose, it was found that local acts of parliament creating a

---

[43] Jones, *op. cit.*, p. 204.

[44] *The Freemen of Canterbury 1800–1835*, ed. Stella Corpe and Anne M. Oakley, Canterbury 1990, p. ix.

[45] Clark and Murfin, *op. cit.*, p. 105.

body of commissioners or trustees, with statutory powers to levy a rate for a specific purpose, were the most desirable form of authority. From the early eighteenth century promoters petitioned parliament for an ever increasing number of these enabling acts until Burke exclaimed that Parliament had become nothing more than a bustle of local agency. In some towns it was the corporation that realised the need for improvement and petitioned Parliament for a paving and lighting act, but in other towns the corporation opposed any such action. For example, in 1768 the inhabitants of Rochester and Strood jointly petitioned for a paving act in order to widen and improve the streets, but the corporation of Rochester submitted a counter petition, complaining that the commissioners to be appointed if the bill were passed would have powers in conflict with those of the mayor, aldermen and assistants of the city. The Sandwich bill of 1787 proposed that the cost of improvements should be met out of the proceeds of a duty to be levied on coal coming into Sandwich harbour; the people of Canterbury and neighbouring villages, whose coal normally came by ship into Sandwich harbour, resented this, as it would increase the price of coal, and only the inhabitants of Sandwich would get any benefit from the proposed improvements. A petition was prepared and advertisements placed in the local papers, urging people to sign it at the office of the mayor of Canterbury.[46] The bill was duly amended. So too a bill for improvements in Maidstone in 1791 included a provision for the erection of gates at the entrances to the town, where tolls would be levied on all cattle, horses and vehicles entering the town. The neighbouring farmers and squires submitted a counter petition, and the clause was struck out by the parliamentary committee.

All the boroughs of Kent obtained improvement acts during the eighteenth or early nineteenth centuries, and most of them found it necessary to have not one but two or more acts, each explaining or extending its predecessors. Thus Canterbury obtained its principal act in 1787, but further acts were passed in 1791, 1801, 1802, 1804, 1822, 1824, 1825, 1842 and 1844. The complications and costs of promoting all these bills was out of proportion to the benefits, and the passing in 1846 of the national Public Health Act, together with the clauses act of 1847, made the traditional parliamentary procedure less necessary, but not obsolete. Most of the local acts for the Kentish towns and boroughs were repealed by the County of Kent Act 1981.[47]

The purposes of this mass of legislation were wide and various. Most important, perhaps, was the sanitary problem arising from the increasing population in ancient towns which had neither drains nor sewers, where the streets in winter

---

[46] *KG*, 16 and 27 March 1787.

[47] Before the passing of the Municipal Corporations Act of 1835 the boroughs obtained their first improvement acts as follows.

Rochester and Strood	1769	Faversham	1789
Gravesend	1773	Deal	1791
Dover	1778	Maidstone	1791
Canterbury	1787	Folkestone	1796
Sandwich	1787	Hythe	1798

were ankle-deep in mud, mixed with horse manure and other ordure. But there were other problems such as the enforcement of law and order, for which the traditional constables proved quite inadequate. Lighting the streets at night was another purpose of these acts, particularly after the introduction of gas in the early years of the nineteenth century. Some acts contained sections dealing with markets, with widening the streets, with the prohibition and removal of encroachments in the streets and of overhanging upper storeys of houses. Some provided for numbering the houses and naming the streets of the town.

The general form of the acts was standardised. They began with the 'preamble', which paraphrased the petition, defining the reasons for the act. The Dover Paving Act of 1778 (18 Geo. III c. 76) used the standard form

> whereas the Streets and Lanes within the Town and Port of Dover, in the County of Kent, and in the several Parishes of St Mary the Virgin and St James the Apostle in the said Town and Port and County, are very ill paved, and not sufficiently cleansed, lighted and watched and by Annoyances and Incroachments therein are rendered incommodious and dangerous.
> And whereas it would tend greatly to the Benefit, Convenience and Safety of the Inhabitants of the said Town and Port and Parishes, and of all persons resorting to and travelling through the same, if the said Streets and Lanes were properly paved, cleansed, lighted and free from Annoyances and Incroachments, but as the same cannot be effected without the Aid and Authority of Parliament,
> May it therefore please your MAJESTY . . .

Then follow the operative sections, the first of which appoints the commissioners for putting the act into execution. These would be the principal citizens of the town specified by name and other people of standing and influence. In Gravesend the list starts with the seneschal or high steward of Gravesend and Milton, the subseneschal or recorder, the governor and deputy governor of the forts of Gravesend and Tilbury (all ex-officio) and thirty other inhabitants, including the rector of Milton. In Canterbury 225 commissioners were appointed, including the members of parliament for the city, the mayor, recorder and justices of the city, the dean and vice-dean of the Cathedral and eleven other clergymen. In 1844 however an amending act (7 & 8 Vic. c. 53) excluded all the ex-officio commissioners. In Rochester and Strood the list included Lord North (then Chancellor of the Exchequer), Lord George Sackville (the Secretary of State for the Colonies), fourteen Kentish baronets and one hundred and eighty others. In Maidstone the commissioners included the members of parliament for the town and for the county, the mayor, recorder, justices, the lord of the manor and all the inhabitants qualified by property (real estate of £10 annual value, or rated for the poor law at £15 or more), but the effective power was lodged in a committee of seven, who were to meet every three weeks.

Next would come the sections dealing with the choice of new commissioners as vacancies occurred. In most cases the procedure was one of cooption rather than election – the existing trustees could appoint whomever they would, provided he had the necessary property qualification. In Canterbury however the act of 1787 provided that vacancies were to be filled by ballots in the courts leet. This apparently implied a secret ballot – a method of election expressly forbidden by the privy council in 1637.[48] This provision was repealed in 1844 in favour of a system of rotation of office, under which one third of the trustees were to be elected annually by the ratepayers of the city assembled at the Guildhall. In Deal the commissioners were to be elected by a system of plural voting, similar to that introduced in parishes under the Sturges Bourne's Act of 1818, giving the richer ratepayers up to six votes each. In all the towns there was a property qualification for all the members of the commission, except the ex-officio members. This varied from the occupation of property worth £20 a year or ownership of property worth £500 in Dover to occupation of property worth £50 a year or ownership of property worth £1,000 in Strood.

Next would come the financial provisions, authorising the levying of rates. The rate in the pound would commonly vary from one part of the town to another according to the benefit which it was assumed the inhabitants would receive, or according to the rent of the property. In Faversham there was a complicated scale of rates, varying from 9d to 1s 9d in the pound according to the rent. Arable, hop and marsh ground was totally exempt. In Gravesend payment of the rate (based on the poor law assessments) carried with it exemption from the duty for statute labour on the roads. In Canterbury and Deal public buildings were to pay a rate based on the length of the frontage to the street.

In addition to money raised by the rates, the acts commonly provided for tolls on horses, carts, coaches, etc., collected at the principal entrances into the town. This was much resented in some towns, such as Canterbury and Maidstone. Exemptions from payment of these tolls were provided, as in the turnpike acts, for funerals, people going to church, electors going to vote in parliamentary elections, and for parsons visiting the sick. In Gravesend the capital needed for the proposed improvements was to be raised by the granting of annuities for the lives of the subscribers. As the subscribers died, the local rates were to be reduced *pro rata*.

The clauses dealing with the functions of the commissions followed a standard pattern, with some variations; power to purchase land, to pave and light the streets and footpaths; prohibition of nuisances such as cock-throwing, showing stallions in the streets, riding or driving furiously in the streets, letting off guns or fireworks, and beating carpets in the streets. They commonly included power to employ watchmen; in Dover these were to replace the traditional duties of watch and ward; in Canterbury they were to work with the petty constables who were still appointed by the courts leet. In Deal there were special penalties for publicans who allowed the watchmen when on duty to spend the time in the public house.

One particular problem was the removal of soil from the 'necessary houses' at

48 *CSPD, 1637*, 17 September 1637, p. 420.

the backs of dwelling houses. This was done by specially appointed scavengers who were to give notice of their approach by ringing a bell. The collected piles of 'ashes, dust, muck, dung or manure' belonged to the scavengers, and were a valuable property, for which farmers would pay a good price. The Golden Dustman in Dickens' *Our Mutual Friend* had grown rich on this business, and it was in some towns a punishable offence for anyone else to appropriate the spoil; in 1834 the Sandwich commissioners served notice on two townsmen, warning them 'not to collect the manure in the parish of St Mary the Virgin to the injury of the appointed scavengers'.[49] In Deal it was provided that necessary houses, privy cess pools, slaughter houses and dung holes were not to be emptied except between the hours of 11p.m. and 5a.m.

After the act had been passed the commissioners had to put it into force. The act commonly laid it down where and when they were to hold their first meeting. In Dover it was provided that the mayor should take the chair as 'President'; elsewhere the chairman was to be chosen by the commissioners. The first meeting was commonly well attended; at Canterbury in 1787 both the members of parliament – Charles Robinson and George Gipps – were there, together with the vice-dean of the cathedral, eight other clergymen, ten magistrates and 131 other commissioners.[50] The commissioners chose Gilbert Knowles as chairman, and James Simmons as treasurer – these being the two members of the corporation who had played the leading part in getting the act on to the statute book.[51]

At the second meeting, which was held on the next day, they made a rate of 1s 6d in the pound and of one shilling a yard for every yard running of public buildings; they arranged for temporary lights to be put up in the streets, and appointed toll collectors.[52] For the first two weeks of their existence they met very nearly every day to discuss the business of the city; they appointed committees and officers, entered into contracts, bought equipment for the watchmen, dealt with a combination of journeymen carpenters demanding higher wages, and received reports from the courts leet of obstructions and nuisances. In 1806 Alderman Simmons was himself presented for an 'eve drop' in Mill Lane.[53]

As the months passed attendance dropped until on 6 April 1789 only two commissioners attended. The same falling off of enthusiasm occurred in other towns; at Deal no quorum was achieved at six successive meetings in 1795,[54] and the position was much the same twenty-five years later. At Sandwich in 1831 a succession of meetings had to be cancelled for lack of a quorum.[55] The Faversham commissioners resolved in 1836 to abandon their monthly meetings and thereafter to meet only once a quarter.[56] Similar problems arose in

49 CKS, Sa AUp 1, 27 May 1834.
50 Canterbury Cathedral Archives (CCA), CC/Q/PC/D1, 9 April 1787.
51 F.H. Panton, 'James Simmons: A Canterbury Tycoon', *Archaeologia Cantiana*, cv (1988), pp. 221–6.
52 CCA, CC/Q/PC/D1, 10 April 1787.
53 CCA, CC/JA, Northgate Court Leet, 7 October 1806.
54 CKS, De AUp l/1, 20 January 1795 *et seq.*
55 CKS, Sa AUp l, 16 August 1831 *et seq.*
56 CKS, Fa AUp/l, 6 December 1836.

Maidstone,[57] and in Dover also there was difficulty in getting a quorum at the meetings.[58]

After the first flush of enthusiasm inhabitants began to realise to their cost the extent of the powers wielded by the commissioners. In Dover the commissioners' energetic action in ordering the removal of numerous bow windows and penthouses led to considerable opposition, and in one case to an action in the King's Bench. Owners naturally resented the expense and inconvenience of having to make structural alterations to their houses; the commissioners at Sandwich were particularly ruthless in their demands.[59] The implementation of the acts made a great difference to the appearance of the towns – a difference which may perhaps now be deplored. Many roads were widened, and new roads were made. The picturesque but old-fashioned projecting upper storeys were removed as possible fire hazards. Houses were refronted, rising perpendicularly from the foundations. Many of those thus brought up to date with the fashionable 'Georgian' faces were clad in the 'mathematical tiles' that were then becoming popular. The ancient conduit which stood in the middle of the High Street of Maidstone was destroyed; all but one of the medieval city gates of Canterbury were pulled down because they obstructed the traffic.

At the time the changes were generally welcomed and acclaimed. William Gostling, who lived in the Precincts of Canterbury, wrote

> In 1787 an act of Parliament was passed, for paving, lighting, watching and otherwise improving this ancient city; under which, in the space of two years the whole was new paved, the carriage ways of the principal streets with Guernsey pebbles, the footpaths, in all, with Yorkshire squared stone, defended by a strong kerb, of Scotch granite. The streets now, instead of being dark and dirty, and encumbered with signs, bulks, posts, spouts and other encroachments and annoyances, are open, and airy, clean swept, and nightly guarded by able watchmen.[60]

In 1835 the Royal Commission on Municipal Corporations presented its monumental report. In this it recorded the progress or failure of some of the Kentish improvement trusts. The Deal commissioners had incurred substantial debts; they did not exercise their power to license porters, because of the violence it had caused among the boatmen and others who acted as porters.[61] In Hythe there was complaint about the system of self-election of the commissioners. In Dover the elections had become intensely party political, on account of the patronage in the hands of the commissioners.[62] At Faversham the Royal Commission found that the improvement commissioners were managing their affairs efficiently, and that 'it seemed to be agreed on all hands that the watching

57 CKS, Md UPal/1, 9 September 1857 *et seq.*
58 CKS, Do UP/Am 1, 15 June 1780.
59 *Ibid.*, 2 June 1780. Cf. plates 6 and 7.
60 W. Gostling, *Walk in and about the City of Canterbury*, Canterbury 1825, pp. 87–8.
61 *BPP: RCMC*, vol. 3, pp. 935–6.
62 *Ibid.*, p. 949.

was sufficient, and that the state of the town was very quiet and orderly'.[63] On the other hand they found at Folkestone that 'the town is not lighted, and the Paving Act is in many respects defective; among others in excepting inhabitants from the rate where their dwelling happens not to abut on the pavement'.[64] In Canterbury they found that 'a meeting is held every month, nine commissioners are a quorum; meetings are frequently adjourned for lack of that number, but not so often as to cause any material inconvenience . . . the act is well administered; but all parties concurred in the opinion that it was a very injudicious one, and inefficient. The district which it includes does not take in nearly the whole of the town.'[65]

In the subsequent Municipal Corporations Act it was provided that the improvement commissioners might transfer their powers to the new town councils which replaced the old corporations, and that the town councils should also take over the management of the police in the borough. Thus the improvement commissioners up and down the county were absorbed into the town councils, not all at once, but one by one. In Sandwich the commissioners survived until 1864, in Deal until 1874.

(8) Courts of Requests

Corporations might be criticised for the decline in use of some of their many courts; in particular the courts which were intended to deal with actions for debt, both real and personal. Once regarded as a valuable privilege, because they allowed actions to be made and tried locally, by the middle of the eighteenth century most of these courts were either moribund or being called for purely formal functions. They were known by a variety of names: the most usual one was the Court of Record, as at Sandwich, Queenborough, Deal, Dover, Hythe and Folkestone; at Rochester and Faversham they were the Courts of Portmote; at Maidstone it was the Court of Pleas, at Canterbury it was the Mayor's Court and at Fordwich the Hundred Court. Only at Sandwich was there a Court of Record still in effective use. There seven writs were sued out of it as late as 1833, one of them for the large sum between £200 and £300. Execution was given against goods or, when there were insufficient goods, against the person – presumably the debtor was held in the newly built gaol at Sandwich which could accomodate various categories of prisoners.[66] At Dover, where 'The practice of the Court is not accurately known even by officers of the court' and at Canterbury, actions might be begun in the Court of Record or Mayors Court but then were removed to superior courts, such as King's Bench.[67] At Deal the Court of

---

63 *Ibid.*, pp. 971–2.
64 *Ibid.*, pp. 982–3.
65 *Ibid.*, p. 710.
66 *Ibid.*, pp. 1050 and 1052.
67 *Ibid.*, pp. 948 and 700.

Record met, but only to swear the officers. When these courts for debt had been operative the fees claimed by the attorneys were high and the procedures complicated and dilatory.

Tradesmen of the towns needed a quick and cheap means of collecting small debts. Courts of Requests, which were Tudor in origin, fitted the bill and were a popular piece of local legislation in the eighteenth century. Most of the courts dealt with debts of between two and forty shillings; Sandwich and Dover had an upper limit of £5. The qualifications of the commissioners of the courts varied. No officer of the corporation of Faversham was included in its Court of Requests although the mayor and jurats were included by name. At Dover commissioners had to have a property qualification valued at £30 in real property or £500 in personal property. At Canterbury the mayor and aldermen were to assemble every quarter to nominate two aldermen, five common councillors and one householder, not being an alderman or a councillor, from each parish within the boundaries of the court's jurisdiction, to serve for three months. There was some rotation of office but even so the process of selection was nominative. However, the courts were well used: at Rochester the Court of Requests dealt with over 900 cases a year on average between 1822 and 1832; at Canterbury there were 545 suits in 1826; Dover dealt with thirty cases a month and at Sandwich there were an average of 300 cases annually between 1830 and 1832.[68] Usually the actions were against the goods of the defendant, but sometimes there were no goods and then the plaintiff might bring an action against the person and obtain an imprisonment. But at Dover and Faversham the plaintiff had to provide 3d. a day for the keep of the debtor. When added to the court costs it was apparent that long imprisonments were not practical for a debt of 40 shillings. Nevertheless, at Faversham and Sandwich the courts were reportedly 'efficient and useful'. Court fees were kept to a few shillings; even so, it was estimated that the clerk's fees in the busy court at Rochester amounted to £200 a year.[69]

There was some opposition to the growth of the courts from the legal profession. Sir William Blackstone described the courts as 'a petty tyranny in a set of standing commissioners'. They were not popular with lawyers because they lost business by them. At Dover professional lawyers were not allowed to practice in the Court of Requests. In 1846, by the County Courts Act (9 & 10 Vic. c. 95) courts of requests were replaced by the new county courts with a barrister acting as judge.

---

[68] Ibid., pp. 701, 950 and 1051.
[69] Ibid., p. 859.

(9) The Royal Commission

Although with the aid of the statutory authorities, such as the paving and lighting commissioners, government of the boroughs had been greatly improved in the early nineteenth century, reform of the boroughs was hastened by political exigencies. The Reform Act of 1832 had given the vote to the £10 householder in the towns and had increased a section of the electorate which, the Whigs hoped, would strengthen their support. Some of the smaller boroughs, such as New Romney and Queenborough, lost their parliamentary representatives, but the boroughs still returned the majority of MPs and corporations were able to in-fluence their return. In spite of the repeal of the Test and Corporation Acts in 1828 non-conformists still felt excluded by unrepresentative oligarchies. Benthamite radicals under the shibboleth of 'utility' spearheaded the attack upon the boroughs and called for reform. A Select Committee was appointed on 14 February 1833 to enquire into municipal corporations in England and Wales and report to the House any defects, and what measures should be taken for their remedy. Among the evidence collected in this limited investigation was that of William Knocker and William Ledger, mayor and town clerk of Dover, and of William Eagle, mayor of Gravesend.[70] The Committee reported that 'Corpora-tions as now constituted are not adapted to the present state of society' and it recommended the appointment of a Royal Commission to carry out a full scale enquiry. The need for such a Commission was set forth trenchantly in *The Times* on 25 June 1833

> The most active spring of election bribery and villainy everywhere is known to be the corporation system. The members of corporations throughout England are for the most part self-elected, and wholly irresponsible but to themselves alone . . . The fact is, that Parliamentary Reform, if it were not to include corporation reform likewise, would have been literally a dead letter, except in so far as the county representation be concerned.[71]

The Commission was appointed in July 1833 and its members, mostly of the legal profession and personal radical friends of Joseph Parkes, the secretary of the Commission,[72] were urged to make the report speedily.

Three commissioners, D. Maude, P. Bingham and T.F. Ellis, shared the work of investigating the sixteen Kentish corporations. The commissioners had no powers to compel persons to submit to examination and they were more strongly defied in Kent than in any other part of England and Wales. Of the five towns which refused all information, three of them were in Kent – Dover, Maidstone and New Romney; Rochester was one of the four towns which refused to answer

---

[70] *BPP: Report from the Select Committee on Municipal Corporations Session 1833*, Dublin 1969, vol. 1, pp. 195–205 and 274–290. Although Dover Corporation felt unable to answer the questions of the Royal Commissioners, the mayor and town clerk answered over 350 questions of the House of Commons Select Committee.

[71] G.B.A.M. Finlayson, 'The Municipal Corporation Commission and Report, 1833–35', *Bulletin of the Institute of Historical Research*, xxxvi (1963), pp. 37–8.

[72] B. Keith-Lucas, *The English Local Government Franchise*, Oxford 1952, p. 49.

parts of the enquiry. The mayor and town clerk of Dover had fully cooperated in the inquiry of the Select Committee but at a Common Assembly of the Mayor, Jurats and Commonalty held in the Guildhall, Dover, on 14 December 1833 it was resolved that the 'Municipal Commission, as at present constituted has no legal authority to require such investigation . . . this assembly considers it would be compromising its own dignity and be guilty of a violation of its public trust, if it permitted its records to be produced, or its officers examined before such Commission'.[73] The town clerk of Maidstone, acting in his capacity of deputy recorder and legal adviser to the corporation, had no hesitation in stating that the Commission was contrary both to the common law and statute law of the realm.[74] New Romney sturdily repeated this defiance; it too, on high authority, questioned the legality of the commissioner, Peregrine Bingham, and secured the distinction of being the only Kentish corporation which successfully withheld its charters and records and for which there is no information entered in the report.

According to the *Kentish Gazette* even in those towns that did cooperate the information was partial and selective.

> The commission of inquiry into the state of the Corporation of the City of Canterbury was yesterday opened at the Guildhall. We have in former numbers expressed our opinion of the absolute ineffectiveness of the commission for the object proposed and one days attendance at the court convinces us that such opinion was most correctly founded. The very fact of the commissioner being obliged to sit powerlessly and hear persons refuse but to give him only just so much information as they pleased, and withhold that which he required to make out his case, places the whole affair in a truly ludicrous point of view.[75]

However, the commissioners unearthed and collated a massive amount of information or evidence which makes up the appendices to parts 1 and 2 of the report.[76]

The reports of each of the boroughs are entered in a standard pattern. Firstly, the physical boundaries of the corporation's authority are set out in some detail. The commissioners appear to have followed the maps of the Boundary Commissioners, because at Dover the commissioner noted that there was a slight error in the town's boundaries in that Charlton church and a few houses adjoining were not within the boundaries of the town and port.[77] Then follow the charters of incorporation, twenty-eight in the case of Canterbury, a list of the officers named in the charters, other officers, the freemen, a description of the governing

73 *BPP: RCMC*, vol. 3, p. 941.
74 *Ibid.*, p. 751.
75 *KG*, 7 January 1834.
76 *Report of the Royal Commission to Enquire into Municipal Corporations* (1835), pp. xxiii–xxvi. Reissued by the Irish University Press, Dublin, reprints series but with renumbered volumes. The Kent boroughs and Cinque Ports are listed in the South-Eastern Circuit; Gravesend is in the Home Circuit.
77 *BPP: RCMC*, vol. 3, p. 941.

body and its committees, the functions of the officers, the extent of the jurisdiction of the corporation, an account of corporate property, what fairs and markets are held, the revenues and payments of the various bodies, a brief note of the state of the town and an abstract of population totals from the decennial censuses taken since 1801, and a list of local parliamentary acts and sometimes assorted documents and accounts which the commissioner had acquired in the course of his investigation. The accumulated mass of detail, far from offering a ludicrous point of view, is a monument to 'thorough' even before the heyday of Victorian parliamentary reports and papers.

Criticisms of the Kent corporations fell into three broad categories; corruption, political partiality and financial mismanagement. At Canterbury fairly small sums of money were offered during elections of the mayor. It was alleged that on occasion the Town Crier, a corporation servant, proclaimed that 2s.6d. and a pint of ale would be given to every freeman who voted for a certain candidate, but not until after the election so that it should not be considered bribery.[78] The sheriff was considered a political appointee because he could propose a freeman for election to common council. The city, being a county in and of itself, could impose a county rate, which was first done in 1773. Certain precincts, such as Eastbridge Hospital, White Friars and the Old Castle, which were within the city boundaries but outside the city's jurisdiction, escaped rating. The extension of the old gaol at Westgate had been financed by a county rate, although previously the charges of the old gaol had been found from corporation funds. The commissioner recommended that all the precincts within the city should come under the same municipal jurisdiction as the city, and that the parliamentary boundary should form the limits of the city (Map 1).[79] On the whole, Canterbury escaped severe censure.

Two commissioners investigated Maidstone (Map 2) and they acknowledged that their report was deficient because they were refused access to the best sources of information. Nevertheless, they produced a damning indictment: 'it is not easy to imagine a greater perversion of municipal institutions, than a system under which bribes are given for the purpose of escaping from the highest office, and under which that office is inflicted as a measure of hostility'. They identified the cause as 'purely the effects of political party spirit, which prevails with the utmost rancour and bitterness of feeling. Both parties go to the contest with the object only of showing their strength and annoying their opponents.'[80] In their remarks upon the constitution of the corporation the commissioners revealed their middle class predilections and distrust of the lower class voter: 'it is scarcely to be expected that the proceedings of a body, composed as the freemen are, would be regulated by considerations of the well-being of the town.

---

[78] *Ibid.*, p. 689.
[79] *Ibid.*, p. 702. The Boundary Commission reports, *Reports of the Commissioners upon the Boundaries of Certain Boroughs and Corporate Towns* (1837) contain maps of 178 towns, including the newly enfranchised towns such as Chatham.
[80] *BPP: RCMC*, vol. 3, p. 755.

The result has been that, where the decision of a question is not influenced by bribery, the issue most commonly depends upon the popular feeling prevalent among the lowest classes at the time, and is independent of the merits.'[81]

Rochester (Map 3) also experienced party strife. One of the chief criticisms was that the governing body was completely self-elected – a subject of 'bitter complaint on the part of many of the freemen' who were chiefly members of the opposing political party. Election to the common council brought financial advantages. Whenever work was to be done for the corporation, tradesmen who were members of the common council had preference. The corporation could also be charged with secrecy in that it declined to produce the most recent accounts for 1830, 1831 and 1832 and ordered the chamberlain, who was at variance with the majority of the common council, not to show his books to the inquiry. The town clerk's suggestion that the corporation considered themselves 'the guardians of public and vested rights, and that, consistently with their duty as such guardians, they cannot produce or allow the inspection of the documents required' was scornfully dismissed by the commissioner.[82]

The main issue at Queenborough was that the governing body of the mayor, two bailiffs and four jurats, controlled the valuable oyster fishery and denied the freemen any rights in its management. The receipts from oysters in 1832–3 totalled £12,852; expenditure on seed oysters, their laying, catching and sale amounted to £10,000. All freemen or burgesses had a right to dredge for the oysters but as there were about ninety this right was stinted and they earned about £25 a year catching and another £1 laying the oysters in the spring. This left the tiny corporation with a very handsome profit, a large part of which was used in expensive court actions to defeat the claims of the freemen.[83] The commissioner recommended that the management of the fishery be vested in a select body, as at Faversham.

(10) The Cinque Ports

Hastings, Romney, Hythe, Dover and Sandwich were the original Cinque Ports to which were later added the two ancient towns of Winchelsea and Rye. The speciality and idiosyncrasies of their rights and privileges clearly intrigued the commissioner, D. Maude, and they were given a separate introductory report. He noted that 'For all, except one or two municipal purposes, each of the Cinque Ports and corporate Towns possesses all the jurisdiction and arrangements of a separate county. For no purposes whatever are they connected with any county, except so far as the Act 51 Geo.III c.36 has placed three of the unincorporated members under the county jurisdiction.'[84] Although Sandwich was one of the

---

81 *Ibid.*, p. 760.
82 *Ibid.*, p. 851.
83 *Ibid.*, p. 836.
84 *Ibid.*, p. 925.

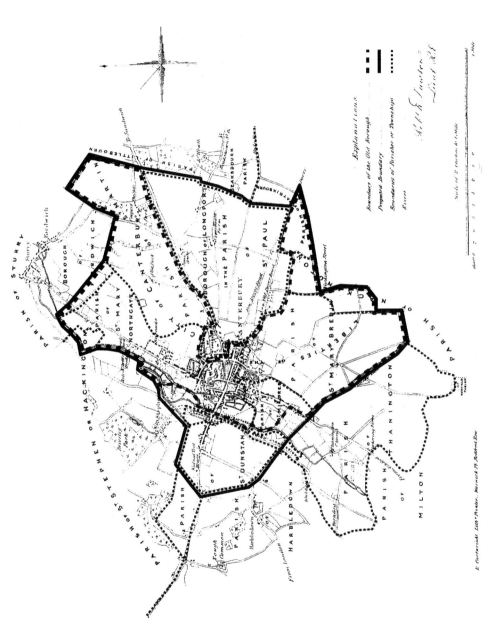

Map 1. Proposed municipal boundaries of Canterbury, 1835

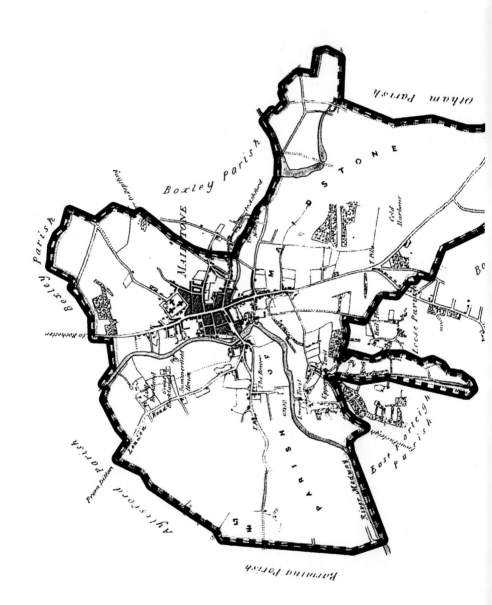

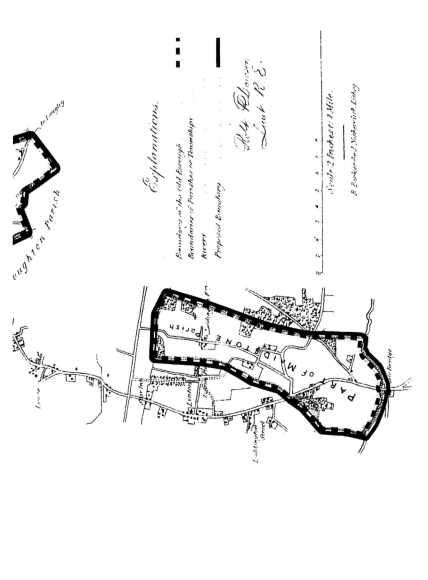

Map 2. Proposed municipal boundaries of Maidstone, 1835

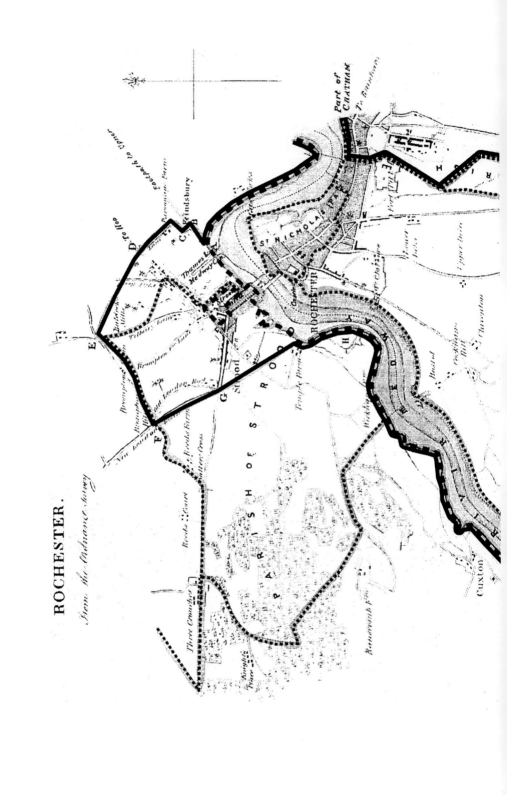

ROCHESTER.

from the Ordnance Survey.

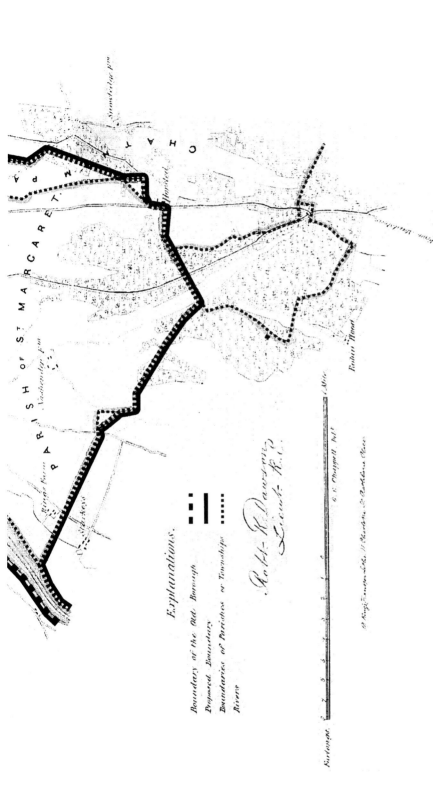

Map 3. Proposed municipal boundaries of Rochester, 1835

official ports of embarkation for the American plantations and vessels of 200 tons were still able to dock there in 1634,[85] the ports had declined greatly in importance. Some no longer had effective harbours, and the reason for their original privileges was no longer apparent, yet they clung to the belief that their rights were inviolate. By the early seventeenth century the ports could no longer provide ship service,[86] but this did not stop them claiming exemption from taxation – an exemption granted in return for ship service. The minutes of the meetings of the Brodhull or General Brotherhood of the Ports, which was more of an administrative than a judicial court, at which petitions were presented of grievances,[87] make it clear that combarons, i.e. freemen of the ports, were taking their cases to superior courts in London rather than their local courts.

Confronted with the rumblings of reform, the ports trusted in their unique constitutional position in the country. At a meeting of the General Brotherhood and Guestling on 22 July 1828, they were urged by Robert Cruden, Secretary of the Municipal Society, to help form a union of all corporations for preserving their rights and liberties, but the mayor of Hastings 'evinced the impolicy of such a combination asserting that this assembly is itself a body for the Ports abundantly sufficient for its own protection. That the Cinque Ports . . . formed a separate class of corporations. Their privileges, rights and charters are distinct and superior to those of other corporate bodies and that therefore it would be impolitic for them to unite with any other society.' The Brotherhood agreed.[88]

The jurisdiction of the ports extended from Birchington, north-east of Margate, along the whole of the Kentish coast to Seaford in Sussex, a corporate limb of Hastings. All the Cinque Ports and the town of Rye had unincorporated limbs or members and all the ports except Hythe and the town of Winchelsea had corporate members. In Kent the corporate members were Lydd, a limb of New Romney; Folkestone and Faversham, limbs of Dover; Fordwich and Deal, limbs of Sandwich; and Tenterden, a limb of Rye. Except in the case of Deal, which obtained a late charter of incorporation from William III which gave it a jurisdiction of its own, each incorporated member had within its liberty the same jurisdiction and municipal functions as the port of which it was a member. Except in the case of Deal and Sandwich, where Sandwich held a concurrent jurisdiction with Deal, the ports had no power or right of interference with their members. While there were obvious advantages for the corporate limbs to have their own independent jurisdiction, there appear to have been positive disadvan-

---

85 *Sandwich Guildhall 1579–1979*, Sandwich Local History Society, New Series no.1, Sandwich 1979, p. 11.

86 In 1634 the ports were unable to provide an 800 ton ship or the 260 men to man it: *A Calendar of the White and Black Books of the Cinque Ports*, ed. Felix Hull, Kent Records vol. xix (1966), p. xxvi.

87 A grievance repeated in the seventeenth, eighteenth and nineteenth centuries was that the French were fishing too close inshore and using nets of too fine mesh. Not only were fishing families in danger of being ruined, 'they interfere with the Portsmen and being as many as a thousand in number gain an equal knowledge of the soundings on your Majesty's said coasts': Hull, *op. cit.*, p. 563. See also, pp. 554, 573.

88 *Ibid.*, p. 574.

tages to being a non-corporate member particularly in the case of Margate which was twenty-one miles from its head port of Dover. The mayor of Dover, acting in his capacity as coroner, was the only person who could conduct an inquest at Margate; similarly, only Dover magistrates could license publicans at Margate. By the early nineteenth century the population of Margate was beginning to overtake that of Dover and, as there was more crime in Margate than in Dover, some jurymen recruited in Margate had to attend the Court of Sessions held at Dover.

There was much that was historical and traditional but little that was practical and useful to hold the Cinque Ports together, and the commissioners were bound to the precepts of utility. The picture painted was one of decay. Deal was 'in a very depressed state'; and Dover, while it 'presents the appearance of a good deal of traffic, and was stated to be upon the whole in a thriving state' yet 'there is great poverty and want of employment in the old parts of the town amongst the class of the population which depends upon the shipping'; Hythe had long since ceased to function as a port and significantly, part of the corporation's property was 500 acres of shingle; Sandwich was 'very dull and has little or no trade of any kind.[89] The best houses let for £35 and many of them are uninhabited . . . A project has long been entertained of making a harbour near the mouth of the river, and shortening the navigation to Canterbury by means of canals. This would benefit Sandwich greatly, but there seems to be no probability of its being carried into execution.'[90] The Cinque Ports were dead,[91] but would not lie down. The Liberty of the Cinque Ports continued to exist as an administrative unit until the Local Government Act of 1888, 51 & 52 Vic. c. 41, merged them into the newly created county councils of Kent and Sussex. Only Dover, by constant dredging, had a future as a port.

(11) Reform

When the report was presented to parliament it was condemned by the Duke of Wellington because it was not based on its own information – he refused to call it evidence. Lord Lyndhurst in the Lords declared 'a political measure more base . . . had never been thought of. It was a Whig measure – Whig in principle, Whig in its character, and Whig in its object.'[92] The Webbs confirmed this opinion and

---

[89] Earlier the Boundary Commissioners had noted that 'Sandwich is a dull, deserted Town, with little prospect of improving its decayed condition.' *Parliamentary Reports, Reports from the Commissioners on the Proposed Division of Counties and Boundaries of Boroughs*, 1832, vol. 2, part 1, p. 15.

[90] *BPP: RCMC*, vol. 3, pp. 936, 954–5, 1008, 1055.

[91] At a meeting of the Brotherhood and Guestling on 29 October 1857, the Speaker noted that although it had been resolved in 1828 that no more than seven years elapse between meetings, in fact twenty-nine years had elapsed. In 1925 the charter of Charles II lost in 1903 was rediscovered in an accumulation of old papers at Lydd. The flag of the ports was in a deplorable state. Hull, *op. cit.*, pp. 578, 616.

[92] Finlayson, *op. cit.*, p. 51.

condemned it as a 'bad case of a violent political pamphlet being, to serve Party ends, issued as a judicial report'.[93] The report concluded that 'the existing municipal corporations of England and Wales neither possess nor deserve the confidence and respect of Your Majesty's subjects, and that a thorough reform must be effected before they can become, what we humbly submit to Your Majesty they ought to be, useful and efficient instruments of local government'.[94]

The Municipal Corporations Amendment Act, 5 & 6 Will. IV c. 76, embodied parts of the hostile report which the commissioners delivered. It was generally regarded as a political measure. Thomas Creevey wrote, 'Municipal Reform marshalls all the middle classes in all the Towns of England in the ranks of Reform . . . I consider it a much greater blow to Toryism than the Reform Bill itself.'[95] R.W. Greaves, writing of the corporation of Leicester concurred: 'The reform of the municipal corporations was, as the case of Leicester particularly clearly shows, the most complete of the triumphs of the middle class.'[96] In one sense the reform was revolutionary for it confiscated private property rights, which Lord Eldon, the former Lord Chancellor, maintained were the same as those exercised by individuals, and it transferred those moneys derived from the sale of corporation property into a borough fund to be used for the 'public benefit of the inhabitants and the improvement of the borough'.[97] The principles of public election and public accountability which the act embodied dominated the whole field of English local government for the next century. They were applied to county councils by the Local Government Act of 1888 and to district councils in 1875 and 1894.[98] But 1835 was not a complete revolution. The act did not apply to the City of London, one of the greatest and richest corporations in the land, nor to the city companies. The powers of the new councils were few and needed to be extended either by local acts of parliament or by the use of general enabling acts.[99] The act affected 178 corporations in England and Wales, replacing the old bodies with councils consisting of mayor, aldermen, and councillors, who were to be elected by the burgesses, the inhabitant rate-payers of the borough. Election replaced co-option and a measure of middle class, democratic control was deemed, naively, a remedy for corruption.

At Canterbury the municipal electors were the resident householders living in or within seven miles of the borough who had paid rates for two and a half years. In the municipal elections of December 1835 and January 1836 a large Liberal/Radical majority was returned. *The Kent Herald* of 4 February 1836 was jubilant: 'The Town Council have done away with all the paraphernalia of office

---

[93] Webb, *op. cit.*, p. 721.
[94] *A Century of Municipal Progress: The Last Hundred Years*, ed H.J. Laski, W.I. Jennings and W.A. Robson, London 1935, p. 57.
[95] Quoted by Keith-Lucas, *op. cit.*, p. 56.
[96] R.W. Greaves, *The Corporation of Leicester 1689–1836*, Oxford 1939, p. 143.
[97] Laski *et al.*, *op. cit.*, pp. 55, 63.
[98] *Ibid.*, p. 61.
[99] The act needed sixteen amending acts before 1844: Keith-Lucas, *op. cit.*, p. 52 n. 5.

– no sword – no mace or other gegaws or foolery pertaining to the late corporation being allowed – this is business-like and gentlemen-like.'[100] Eight from the old council were included in the new 24-man council. J. Nutt, clerk of the old corporation since 1820 was elected town clerk and clerk of the peace. A Watch Committee was set up in January 1836 to take over the watching and policing functions of the Improvement Commissioners. Inherited debts of £15,000 were partly reduced by the sale of corporate property. The Assembly Rooms and the Canterbury Bank building were sold to Hammonds, bankers.[101]

The most serious problem facing the new councils was the dangers to public health caused by bad sanitation and an inadequate fresh water supply. The reports of Edwin Chadwick to parliament revealed that although the improvement commissioners may have given a face lift to parts of towns the real problems lay with lack of drainage and an expanding population crammed into appalling housing. In the six months between 1 July and 31 December 1837 over 130 died of typhus and diarrhoea in the unions of Medway, Thanet, Maidstone, Tonbridge and Sevenoaks.[102] In working class housing in Bromley where sanitation was non-existent the medical officer of the union said that malaria was endemic.[103]

At Canterbury a general rate of one shilling in the pound was levied on the city in March 1836 but this was not sufficient to deal with sanitation. Parts of Canterbury, particularly in the area of St Peter's parish, were very unhealthy. The River Stour was kept artificially high by the requirements of Abbot's Mill, the largest mill in the city, constructed by Alderman James Simmons to John Smeaton's design. Adjacent cesspits and wells were frequently inundated and the wells, used for drinking water, contaminated. George Rigden, surgeon to the Canterbury Dispensary published details of illnesses treated in the Dispensary[104] but the Council were reluctant to increase the rate to improve the drainage, even after the cholera outbreak of 1848–9. During the epidemic 675 people were treated as out-patients in the Kent and Canterbury Hospital.[105] The central board of health set up in 1848 had powers to enforce local boards of health where the death rate was above 23 per thousand head of the population: Canterbury's was 23 per thousand. The average life span was thirty-four years. Not until 1865 did the Council adopt the enabling Local Government Act of 1858 which constituted the Council as a board of health with powers to levy a separate rate.

---

100 J.A. Young, 'Aspects of Local Government in Canterbury c.1820 to c.1870', Kent MA thesis, 1985, pp. 93–4.
101 *Ibid.*, p. 96.
102 *BPP, Sessions 1837–42, Health General, Chadwick Report*, vol. 3, Dublin 1971, pp. 98–9.
103 *Ibid.*, pp. 154–5.
104 George Rigden, *The Sanitory Condition of Canterbury, with a Nosological Table of the diseases for which poor patients have applied for admission to the Benefits of the Canterbury Dispensary*, Canterbury 1847.
105 F.M. Hall, R.S. Stevens and J. Whyman, *The Kent and Canterbury Hospital 1790–1987*, Canterbury 1987, pp. 69–70.

Similar problems were experienced with the River Len at Maidstone which was described as 'one complete series of cesspools'.[106] The wealthy middle class inhabitants showed considerable reluctance to pay for improvements in poorer quarters and it needed intervention from central government to provide the stimulus to tackle the problems of public health, which led Clark and Murfin to conclude

> The municipal history of Maidstone illustrates the *ad hoc* way that councils in medium sized county towns acquired new responsibilities in the nineteenth century. In this community late-Victorian pride in municipal achievement was relatively low key, compared with some of the larger cities in the country, but there is evidence of a growing sense of civic ambition as manifested in the work of new committees, particularly in the education field.[107]

The new councils still were seen as trustees of property, albeit public property, rather than as providers of public services, and still they were preserved as enclaves of separate administration entirely divorced from the surrounding countryside.[108] The concept of the chartered privilege, i.e. an exclusive right granted to a select body which could excercise its powers to its own advantage, remained an attractive one.

---

[106] Clark and Murfin, *op. cit.*, p. 152.

[107] *Ibid.*, p. 175.

[108] Bryan Keith-Lucas, *English Local Government in the Nineteenth and Twentieth Centuries*, London 1977, p. 11.

4

Radical Movements and Workers' Protests to c.1850

PAUL HASTINGS

(1) Dearths and their Consequences

'The people will never listen to reason on the subject of dear bread.'[1] The remark was made in Paris, but the fact remained universal. The trinity of grain, flour and bread dominated the well-being of the majority of society. Scarcity and plenty were governed by many factors. It was not until the middle of the eighteenth century that more than ten grains of wheat could be garnered from each grain sown in England. Wheat production was labour intensive. Jethro Tull recommended repeated tilling as well as manuring for a plentiful crop. A string of bad harvests as in 1659–62 and 1692–9 in Kent led to high prices for wheat and great shortages of bread. Perhaps one third of the rural population of Kent at this time were living on subsistence level, so that high prices or fluctuations in supply spelt hardship if not famine.[2] Most of the riots of the eighteenth century occurred when there was a shortage or a sudden rise in the price of food. 'In England . . . the bulk of the population were small consumers dependent upon the cheap and plentiful supply of bread. When harvests were bad, when wartime needs imposed a heavy strain on stocks, or when wheat was exported abroad in times of growing shortage, prices rose and . . . the fear of famine provoked disturbance.'[3] Food riots, rather than wage strikes, were the typical form of social protest. The majority of these riots took place in the chief exporting areas of the north and west of the country rather than in the corn growing areas of the south and east. From the beginning of the Napoleonic wars to the middle of the nineteenth century cyclical and technological unemployment and fluctuations in domestic harvests and high food prices led to social and political unrest.[4]

All these factors at times applied to Kent. In 1605 rioting in the Medway

1   Fernand Braudel, *Civilization and Capitalism, 15th–18th Centuries, Vol. 1, The Structures of Every-day Life*, London 1981, p. 143.
2   *Ibid.*, pp. 104–45. C.W. Chalklin, *Seventeenth Century Kent*, London 1965, pp. 253–5.
3   G. Rudé, *The Crowd in History*, London 1964, pp. 36–7.
4   W.W. Rostow, *British Economy of the Nineteenth Century*, Oxford 1948, p. 109.

ports stemmed from large scale purchase of grain for export to Spain. Similar concerns were expressed by Kentish food rioters in 1631.[5] As poverty became increasingly acute Kent experienced renewed social and economic disorder in the 1640s with the continued siphoning off of local grain to feed the capital. Movement of grain from the area brought higher prices locally particularly in time of scarcity. So, too, did forestalling and regrating. In 1768, a year of food riots nationally, notices posted on Tenterden and neighbouring church doors threatened farmers who refused to sell their wheat at £10 a load and local millers who paid more. The poor were urged 'to raise a mob at Woodchurch Green'. Those refusing would have their right arms broken.[6]

During the French Wars of 1793–1815 the great dearths of 1795–6 and 1799–1801 coincided with the threat of French invasion and the naval mutiny at the Nore in 1797. Rising prices and food shortage saw strikes and disturbances among Kent urban workers in Maidstone and the Medway towns who, at the same time, were increasingly influenced by the radical teachings of the London Corresponding Society. In the winter of 1794–5 the *Charleston* of Baltimore was found disabled by Dover boatmen with eleven of her crew suffering from frostbite. At Margate the sea was frozen 'to a greater extent than ever known' with the ice continuing to Whitstable and Sheppey. The 'Great Snow' of January 1795 brought falls of up to three feet in East Kent followed by a sudden thaw and hard frost which left roads blocked by ice.[7]

The deficient crop in 1794 had already enabled one Ham Street farmer to sell his wheat at 123 shillings per quarter.[8] As prices escalated threatening letters were sent to local figures such as the Revd Thomas Morphett of Rolvenden.

> This is to acquaint you that if you don't order your Pereishenners to Lower the price of Wheate to 12 pounds per load . . . murder will soon be done amongst you all for we are above 15000 strong . . . We don't mind your Horse . . . Consider our Strength to your 30 Horse . . .[9]

In the countryside the authorities were quick to react both from humanitarian motives and to prevent distress from turning into social disaffection. Against the background of the French Revolution, the London Treason Trials, the massive rally at Copenhagen fields, and the 'Two Acts' of 1795–6, parish and urban authorities responded promptly. Beckenham vestry, using a public subscription, ordered that wheat should be bought, ground and sold to the poor at 9d a loaf.

5   P. Clark, *English Provincial Society from the Reformation to the Revolution: Religion, Politics and Society in Kent 1500–1640*, Hassocks 1977, p. 250; *An Atlas of Rural Protest in Britain 1548–1900*, ed. A. Charlesworth, London 1983, pp. 74, 76.
6   *Gentleman's Magazine*, May 1768. See also John Stevenson, 'Bread or Blood' in *The Unquiet Countryside*, ed. G.E. Mingay, London 1989, p. 23–4.
7   Gerald G. Davey, 'The Great Snow of 1795', *Bygone Kent*, vol. 7, no. 5, p. 267.
8   *KE*, 2.12.1916.
9   PRO, HO 42/36. Published in Richard Grover, 'Social Discontent during the Napoleonic Wars', *Cantium* (Winter 1974), p. 72.

Meopham in 1795 bought flour in bulk and retailed it cheaply to 53 families.[10] At Eltham a subscription was spent on the distribution of bread, meat, cheese, and flour to counter 'the present dearness of bread and almost every other necessity of life'.[11] £500 subscribed at Canterbury relieved 'near 3,000 persons in bread and flour'. Chatham spent £180 on bread and coals while Maidstone supplied over 3,000 people with cheap flour.[12] When heavy rains brought a second great dearth in 1799–1801 the price of wheat rose to over 60 shillings a quarter at Faversham and 115 shillings a quarter at Ham Street.[13] An Act of 1801 prohibited the sale of bread which had not been baked six hours 'since people can eat a smaller quantity of stale bread than new'.[14] Potatoes, potato flour and rice became unpopular substitutes for wheat. Subscriptions were again hastily raised. The vicar of Christ Church, Canterbury, organised a subscription and ran a daily soup kitchen because of the 'present scarcity'.[15] Birchington overseers sold subsidised rough meal, wheaten bread and wheat as they had done in 1795. More importantly the crisis brought in many Kent parishes the introduction of the child allowance.[16] John Boys, writing in 1803, was quick to defend the farmer:

> Nothing could be more unjust . . . than the clamour that was raised against farmers, millers and merchants during the great scarcities of 1795 and 1800. It was said that farmers hoarded their corn, that millers monopolised it and that merchants destroyed whole vessel loads . . . to keep up prices . . . Had importation not taken place bread could not have been found for the people. The cause of this scarcity is to be traced to the severe winters and dry summers preceding the harvests of those years.[17]

Even so Kent was fortunate to avoid greater social disturbance. In 1794, as yeomanry were raised throughout the county, David Masters and three labourers from Warehorne and Orlestone were convicted of inciting farm workers in neighbouring parishes to join the French if invasion came and to seize the coastal batteries. An attack on Lamberhurst and other mills in 1795 was largely ignored by the Kent bench.[18] Six agricultural labourers were charged in February with riot at Eton Bridge (Edenbridge) 'in order to have their wages

---

10 Robert Borrowman, *Beckenham Past and Present*, Beckenham 1910, p. 44; C.H. Golding Bird, *The History of Meopham*, London 1934, p. 185.
11 A.E. Newman, 'The Old Poor Law in East Kent 1606–1834', Kent Ph.D. 1979, p. 163; Davey, *op. cit.*, p. 268.
12 Davey, *loc. cit.*
13 *KE*, 2.12.1916; F. Giraud and Charles E. Doure, *Visitors Guide to Faversham*, Faversham 1876, p. 40.
14 A.J. Dunkin, *History of the County of Kent: Blackheath Hundred*, London 1855, p. 246.
15 Newman, *op. cit.*, p. 127; Giraud and Doure, *op. cit.*, p. 40.
16 J.P. Barrett, *History of the Ville of Birchington*, Margate 1893, pp. 154, 167; see Paul Hastings, 'The Old Poor Law 1640–1834', in N. Yates, R. Hume and P. Hastings, *Religion and Society in Kent 1640–1914*, Woodbridge 1994, p. 126.
17 John Boys, *A General View of the Agriculture of the County of Kent*, 2nd edn, London 1805, pp. 196–7.
18 *KE*, 26.2.1870; Roger Wells, *Wretched Faces: Famine in Wartime England 1793–1801*, Gloucester 1988, p. 101.

raised, the price of flour lowered and for divers other dangerous purposes . . .'[19] At Chatham, in March, the poor forced butchers to lower prices and burned bad meat.[20] In Canterbury mutinous militiamen helped to impose similar price controls. There were further disturbances in early May although Sir Hugh Dalrymple, commanding officer at Chatham, expressed the view that 'we have hitherto had tumults of a very gentle and mitigated Nature'.[21]

The famine of 1799–1801 produced a more violent reaction. In September 1800 there was rioting in Dover Court House over the price of butter. By December hunger and discontent had evoked the traditional response of rick burning. John Boghurst of Delce had his rick fired on 15 December 1800. In return he circulated a handbill offering fifty guineas reward. The London insurance companies doubled this reward for the successful conviction of incendiaries.[22] Even before bakers began selling brown bread North Kent labourers had conspired 'to take up Arms against the Government'.[23]

(2) Early Trade Unionism

The Royal Dockyard at Chatham, the largest industrial enterprise in the county employing over 1,500 artisans and labourers, had undergone some industrial disturbance during the eighteenth century. There was no trade union organisation. Workers had to choose their time carefully to strike, ensuring that their shipbuilding skills were urgently needed nationally, thus forcing the Navy Board to submit. The yard was dominated by the shipwrights, the elite responsible for all work upon ships under construction or repair.[24] In March 1795, at a crucial stage in the French Wars, the shipwrights decided to strike against the use of house carpenters on the vessel *Melpomene*. They addressed the first of a number of petitions to the admiralty which promptly sacked the shipwrights' quartermen and began a hunt for the ringleaders of the strike. The dispute lasted until May with the government using the shortage of shipwrights and the national emergency as an excuse. Ultimately a compromise allowed the limited use of house carpenters under shipwright supervision.[25]

Maidstone papermakers, equally undeterred by dearth or war, won a substantial pay increase in March 1796, a month in which dockyard ropemakers also

[19] *MJ*, 17.2.1795.
[20] *MJ*, 31.3.1795. I am indebted to Bruce Aubry for this reference.
[21] Wells, *op. cit.*, pp. 101, 105.
[22] Newman, *op. cit.*, p. 106; Grover, *op. cit.*, p. 72. A Westerham yeoman was severely punished for incendiarism as early as 1545. See Clark, *op. cit.*, p. 45; see also *Annals of Agriculture*, xxxiv (1800), pp. 113, 601–7.
[23] Wells, *op. cit.*, p. 152.
[24] P. MacDougall, 'The Early Industrial Dispute: Chatham Dockyard during the 18th Century', *Bygone Kent*, vol. 1, no. 5, May 1980, pp. 265–7.
[25] *MJ*, 24.3.1795, 31.3.1795, 7.4.1795, 21.4.1795, 5.5.1795, 12.5.1795.

struck successfully against the amount of hemp they were required to spin.[26] Afterwards, despite legal pressure from the Master Paper Makers' Associations locally and nationally, the illegal journeymen's union, the Original Society of Papermakers, remained strong and well-organised in Kent. Apprenticeship was strictly controlled. Help was given by the society to members who struck to avoid wage reductions. A further wage increase was secured in 1801 and in 1815 the union headquarters moved from St Paul's Cray to Maidstone.[27] By 1825 Kent's thousand members represented about a third of the union's total strength.[28] In 1832 Assistant Poor Law Commissioner Majendie blamed the closed shop, high wages and restrictive practices of the paperworkers' combination in Maidstone district for unemployment and the movement towards the use of machinery. Nevertheless the union continued to play an influential role in one of the few industries in an essentially rural county.[29]

There were also signs of increasing trade union activity in the Kent building trades. The earliest instance of a combination among bricklayers is to be found in the creation at Maidstone of the United Friendly Society of Bricklayers in March 1810.[30] Repeal of the Combination Acts in 1825 brought further trade union activity. Even before repeal a general strike among Maidstone building workers, caused by the rising cost of living, brought wage increases for mechanics, carpenters, plumbers and bricklayers.[31] Their example was followed by boot and shoe makers in Rochester and Chatham as prices continued to increase in the mid 1820s.[32]

In Kent's dockyards, however, the position was reversed. The eighteenth century had seen a number of disputes. In the following century the workforce was much more quiescent, particularly after the dispute of 1801 brought the widespread dismissal of ringleaders by the Navy Board and prosecution of men at Sheerness for 'riots'. Thereafter dockyard workers only indicated their displeasure by petition to the Admiralty showing an almost total dependence on the goodwill of their employers. Long term job security, pensions and sickness benefits combined with the period of peace between 1815 and 1852 to encourage acceptance of lower wages.[33]

26 *MJ*, 1.3.1796, 22.3.1796.
27 *MJ*, 1.3.1796; Michael McNay, *Portrait of a Kentish Village: East Malling*, London 1980, pp. 97–8; D.C. Coleman, *The British Paper Industry 1495–1860*, Oxford 1958, pp. 263–9, 272.
28 Coleman, *op. cit.*, p. 267.
29 *BPP* 1834, xxviii, Appendix A, Part 1, pp. 215–16.
30 *VCH*, iii, p. 395.
31 *MG*, 1.3.1825.
32 *MG*, 9.8.1825.
33 P. MacDougall, *The Changing Nature of the Dockyard Dispute*, typescript n.d., pp. 1–16.

(3) Co-operation

This quiescence was reflected in the establishment of some of the earliest co-operative ventures in Kent's dockyards. Associated trading was adopted at Woolwich as early as 1806. Ten years later, during 'the dearth and great deficiency' of 1816, the Sheerness Economical Society was created by the officers and workmen of HM Dockyard, Ordnance and New Works at Sheerness to obtain for themselves and their families a supply of wheaten bread, flour and butchers' meat. James Mockett, a dockyard joiner, was the society's first chairman and F. Venables, a local solicitor, its first secretary. The remaining founder members were also dockyard workers such as smiths, shipwrights and joiners. The society began as a protest against the adulteration, short weight and high prices of local bakers. Before long it had not only established a well-conducted bakery but was selling eight sacks of flour weekly together with butchers' meat. Since Sheerness' polluted water was 'far more dangerous than industrial discontent' the society also took the unusual step of selling pure water at a halfpenny a pail from a well which it had developed.[34] Membership was confined to the dockyardmen with every class of worker represented. It cost five shillings. The committee met every Monday evening 'the hour of assembly being determined by the time of ceasing work'. Each member had a ticket upon which was written the weekly quantity of bread to which he was entitled, a rationing system being developed so that the bakery's exact output was always known. Meat was sold at contract price while management expenses were met by a subscription of a penny a week. Bread was carefully regulated as to ingredients and weight.[35] The society, which preceded that at Toad Lane, Rochdale, by a generation, also benefited non-members by restraining the prices of local shopkeepers.[36] Shipwrights at Chatham dockyard also began to slaughter beasts in 1817 to secure cheaper meat but there is no evidence of the further development of this embryonic form of co-operation as happened at Sheerness.[37]

(4) Political Agitation in the Late Eighteenth Century

In November 1792 a small reform society at Rochester addressed the French Convention deploring Grenville's failure to recognise the new French republic. The Loyalist backlash was immediate. On 10 December a meeting at Rochester Guildhall established an Association for Defending Liberty and Property and a persecution of reformers began. Little more was heard of the Rochester reformers until in October 1795 the London Corresponding Society received a

---

[34] W. Henry Brown, *A Century of Co-operation at Sheerness*, Manchester 1919, pp. 8, 14, 18–19, 21, 28; *MG*, 9.10.1838.

[35] Brown, *op. cit.*, pp. 21–2, 24, 26.

[36] *Ibid.*, p. 33.

[37] *MG*, 25.2.1817.

request for help from those societies working for parliamentary reform in mid and north Kent. The London society duly despatched a Deputy, 'Citizen' John Gale Jones, surgeon and apothecary, to visit the Kent societies in February 1796. His mission was to enquire into their situation in the wake of Pitt's 'Two Acts' and forge links with the London radicals.[38]

Harassed by loyalist spies and *agents provocateurs* he met bitter patriotic hostility to radicals and dissenters. He also found a deeply divided community. Rochester's postmaster sought permission to open his mail and called upon the mayor to 'suppress these seditious societies'. On the other hand Bishop Horsley of Rochester had been recently burned in effigy for pronouncing that 'the people have nothing to do with the laws but obey them'. Much popular hostility existed towards the officers of the garrison in the Medway towns. At Maidstone 'party ran so high that many . . . would not traffic with those of opposite opinion . . . Going into a tavern frequented by different parties might subject a man to . . . being turned out . . .'[39] While the Castle Inn was reputedly a venue for Jacobins the Star Coffee House was a rendezvous for their opponents. 'Near seventeen hundred workmen' at Chatham Dockyard had refused to sign a loyal address to the king. Instead they had unanimously petitioned against the Convention Bills.[40] Radical support was undoubtedly helped by the current economic climate. At Luton, Jones noted 'the bread was very brown' and the landlord observed that soon there 'might be no bread at all'. At Rochester the inhabitants were 'in a bustle' since 'bread had been raised' and the displeasure of the soldiers 'strongly excited' by the increased cost of meat.[41] 'Provisions are now so dear', stated one of Jones's travelling companions, 'that a poor family can scarcely live.'[42]

During his tour Jones addressed 'numerously attended meetings' at Rochester, Chatham, Brompton, Gillingham, Luton, Gravesend and Maidstone. The societies were organised into 'divisions' along Wesleyan lines where political reform was discussed. He attended the formation of a new division at Gillingham and on 22 February saw a meeting of the United Corresponding Societies of Rochester, Chatham and Brompton resolve to act in concert with the London Corresponding Society. If his account is to be believed enthusiasm for 'Universal Suffrage and Annual Parliaments' was strong in north and mid Kent with their expanding economic activity, and proximity to London. Although the Rochester Society had been 'diminished from the timid apprehensions of some . . . of its members' Jones concluded that 'the inhabitants in general were attached to the Whig interest and the London Corresponding Society'.[43] Chatham, Gravesend and Maidstone also had 'many friends of reform'.

---

38 John Gale Jones, *Sketch of a Political Tour through Rochester, Chatham, Maidstone, Gravesend etc.*, London 1796, p. 1.
39 *Ibid.*, pp. 10–16, 29–30, 39, 71, 79, 81–2.
40 *Ibid.*, pp. 61, 81; *MJ*, 24.11.1795.
41 Jones, *op. cit.*, pp. 75, 89–90.
42 *Ibid.*, p. 92.
43 *Ibid.*, pp. 8, 27, 31–2, 38, 56, 61, 72, 83, 112.

The latter included Clement Taylor, papermaker and MP, and a second Maidstone papermaker all of whose workers were 'citizens' since 'their wages were less and the price of provisions greater than ever'. Among the other men of liberal mind, that Jones was so surprised to meet outside London, were doctors, millers and farmers of considerable substance.[44] While his claim to have 'awakened the whole county . . . to . . . a determination to assert its Rights' was exaggerated there is little doubt that 'the general sentiments' of much of the area that he visited were decidedly against 'the present Ministers and the War'. Convinced that both were responsible for their misery many found the idea of reform attractive. Jones also encountered a Gillingham farmer, 'a strong Democrat and . . . something more than a Reformer' who was representative of many who felt 'it is now too late for Reform'.[45]

E.P. Thompson has suggested that the visits paid by London Corresponding Society members to naval dockyards 'may be one among the threads which link the Jacobins to the naval mutinies at Spithead and the Nore in 1797'.[46] When the Nore fleet, centred upon Sheerness, mutinied on 12 May 1797 it seemed as if north Kent and the Medway towns had become a centre of insurrection. Reinforced by vessels from the Downs, Gravesend and Yarmouth Roads, the mutineers turned their cannon on the port and threatened to bombard it. Initially their organisation was impressive. Large numbers landed daily at Sheerness. Waving red flags they marched through the streets and under the leadership of Richard Parker, an ex-schoolmaster and quota man from Leith, held delegate meetings in the Sheerness taverns. Their initial grievances were low pay; arrears of wages; absence of shore leave; poor quality and short weight food; overcrowding and the brutal discipline allowed by the Articles of War. On 2 June the mutineers blockaded the Thames. Over 100 ships lay idle at anchor. A further 100 vessels at Tilbury were kept in port lest their capture should provide the mutineers with supplies. Sheppey and the Isle of Grain were raided by the seamen for sheep and cattle. Others marched unopposed through the dockyards and entered the barracks to enlist the sympathy of the garrison.[47] Some sailors were members of corresponding societies: others, particularly aboard the *Inflexible*, belonged to the revolutionary Society of United Irishmen. Some undoubtedly tried to turn the situation to their advantage. The mutiny arose, however, largely from the recruitment practices used to man a grossly-expanded wartime navy. These brought together criminals, pressed men, and Irish prisoners with professional sailors and better educated quota men. There is insufficient hard evidence of any widespread and systematic attempt by a politically conscious minority to turn a seamen's strike into an agenda for revolution or a movement for peace.[48]

44 *Ibid.*, pp. 19, 32, 39, 41, 85.
45 *Ibid.*, pp. 32, 57, 110.
46 E.P. Thompson, *The Making of the English Working Class*, Harmondsworth 1968, p. 162.
47 C. Gill, *The Naval Mutinies of 1797*, Manchester 1913, pp. 111–12.
48 Gill, *op. cit.*, pp. 320, 324–5, 329, 357; G.E. Manwaring and B. Dobree, *The Floating Republic*, London 1935, pp. 132, 150, 248. R. Wells, *Insurrection: The British Experience 1795–1803*, Gloucester 1983, esp. pp. 79–109, 253–65 argues the insurrectionary case. But see also H.T. Dickinson,

Even so, in the midst of a French war, there was widespread panic. While wealthy Sheerness residents fled to Chatham 'with their most valuable effects' and Faversham formed an armed association to defend the town, Henry Fellowes, a London Corresponding Society contact, distributed handbills among soldiers at Maidstone paid for by the local corresponding society. Further handbills were circulated to soldiers and marines at Chatham and to the West Kent militia.[49]

> Why is every regiment harassed with long marches but to keep them strangers to the people and to each other . . . We have two choices either to submit to the present impositions or to demand the treatment proper for men . . . The regiment which sends you this are willing to do their part . . . They . . . will make their demands as soon as they know you will not draw the trigger against them . . .[50]

North Kent garrisons were reinforced. An infantry regiment and mortar battery were stationed in sight of the Nore and navigational buoys removed from the Thames. There was widespread fear that the fleet would desert to the French. The mutineers, however, were fatally divided from the outset and any danger disappeared with the mutiny's collapse on 15 June. Parker and 28 others were executed. The Corresponding Societies' Act 1799 completed the suppression of the London and other corresponding societies.[51]

(5) The 1830s and 1840s: More Turbulence: The Swing Riots

The Swing Riots (Figures 1 and 2),[52] a massive outbreak of arson, machine breaking and wage rioting, began in Kent in June 1830 spreading to Hampshire, Wiltshire, Buckinghamshire, Sussex and Surrey and to a lesser extent into the remaining English counties. The North, Midlands and South-West suffered much less severely than the South and East. The riots took place against a background of parliamentary reform in England and revolution in France and Belgium. Consequently there was a strong temptation for contemporaries to look for political causes. Mrs Arbuthnot believed that the labourers' rising in Kent 'was a mere imitation of France and Belgium'. 'The factor which turned

British Radicalism and the French Revolution 1789–1815, Oxford 1985, pp. 56–7, E. Royle, *Revolutionary Britannia?*, Manchester 2000, pp. 27–9. J. Archer, *Social Unrest and Popular Protest in England 1780–1840*, Cambridge 2000, pp. 90–1.

49 Giraud and Doure, *op. cit.*, p. 40; *MJ*, 23.5.1797, 30.5.1797, 13.6.1797. I am indebted for these references to Bruce Aubry.

50 National Army Museum, Acc. No. 6807–370–30. Seditious handbill addressed to the British army found at Chatham barracks, 21 May 1797.

51 See papers circulated or read by Philip MacDougall, Christopher Doorne *et al.*, at the bicentenary conference of the Nore Mutiny, 'Mutiny and the Navy', Chatham Dockyard, 5 July 1997.

52 Swing was a *nom de guerre* and not a person. The derivation of the term Swing is still a matter of debate. To rural contemporaries it was the term for a leader of a party of haymakers. It was also the swinging staff attached to a flail which may have had punitive associations for the loss of winter work.

THE LIFE

AND

HISTORY OF SWING,

THE

KENT RICK-BURNER.

WRITTEN BY HIMSELF.

See page 21.

LONDON:
PRINTED AND PUBLISHED BY R. CARLILE,
62, FLEET-STREET.
1830.

Price Threepence.

Figure 1. Title-page of *The Life and History of Swing, the Kent Rick Burner,* 1830

the scale was the example of France' wrote Halevy: 'two years earlier the peasantry of Picardy and the district around Boulogne had burned the mills. After
the July Revolution it seemed natural to the Kentish labourers to imitate their
French comrades.'[53] Thomas Pile, a Cranbrook farmer, wrote in his journal of
'Great thoughts of a revolution taking place in England'.[54] There were reports of
labourers hoisting the tricolour on several occasions. It was brandished by the
mob which stormed a Newington vestry meeting on 25 October 1830 but radical
meetings at Benenden, Cranbrook and Maidstone staged to 'congratulate the
French people on their glorious triumph . . .', were attended by few English
labourers.[55]

A minority of labourers were undoubtedly influenced by the radical political
thinking of the day which they obtained from the radical press in the beer shops.
'Much harm was done by the press, by the writings of the Cobbetts and Carlyles
which were taken at all the ale and beer houses where they were read and
commented on by the lower classes . . .' stated George Moore, vicar of
Wrotham.[56] The most widely circulated radical handbill was 'Nice Pickings'
often quoted by labourers' leaders. This pointed out the enormous annual
incomes of peers, archbishops and bishops of the United Kingdom and the colonies suggesting that they would maintain 92,224 families allowing £50 per year
to each.[57] Such thoughts inevitably had their effect. At a meeting of labourers
addressed by the High Sheriff in October 1830 one labourer remarked 'we will
destroy the corn stacks and threshing machines this year. Next year we will take
a turn with the parsons and then we will make war on statesmen.'[58] When a
magistrate told Stephen Eves, leader of the Goudhurst labourers, that farmers
would not pay higher taxes he responded 'then let us have the land'.[59]

Many contemporaries saw the riots as demands for reform if not revolution.
Cobbett alleged that there was 'infinite corruption' in Kent.[60] Certainly the
government had a strong electoral influence in the county. The Treasury, repre-
sented by the Lord Warden of the Cinque Ports, had considerable power in
Dover. The Admiralty was strong at Rochester and Sandwich. The
Queenborough electorate was virtually owned by the Ordnance while the
Derings nominated all candidates in their rotten borough of New Romney.[61]
Nonconformist and political radicals were mostly found in Kent's seven major
towns. At Maidstone over 600 ratepayers and property owners were disenfran-

---

53 *Journal of Mrs Arbuthnot*, London 1950, vol. 2, p. 396; E. Halevy, *A History of the English People in the 19th Century*, vol. 2, London 1961, p. 8.
54 CKS, U683 A2, Diary of Thomas Pile, 29.10.1830.
55 *KG*, 29.10.1830; *MJ*, 21.9.1830, 5.10.1830.
56 *PP* 1834, xxxiv, Appendix B1 to First Report from Poor Law Commissioners, Part V, Answers to Rural Queries, p. 256c.
57 PRO, HO 52/8, Englishmen Read! Nice Pickings.
58 *MG*, 19.10.1830; *KH*, 21.10.1830.
59 CKS, QS/BW 124.
60 William Cobbett, *Rural Rides*, vol. 1, London 1830, p. 41.
61 J.H. Andrews, 'Political Issues in the County of Kent 1820–1846', London M.Phil. 1967, pp. 10–11.

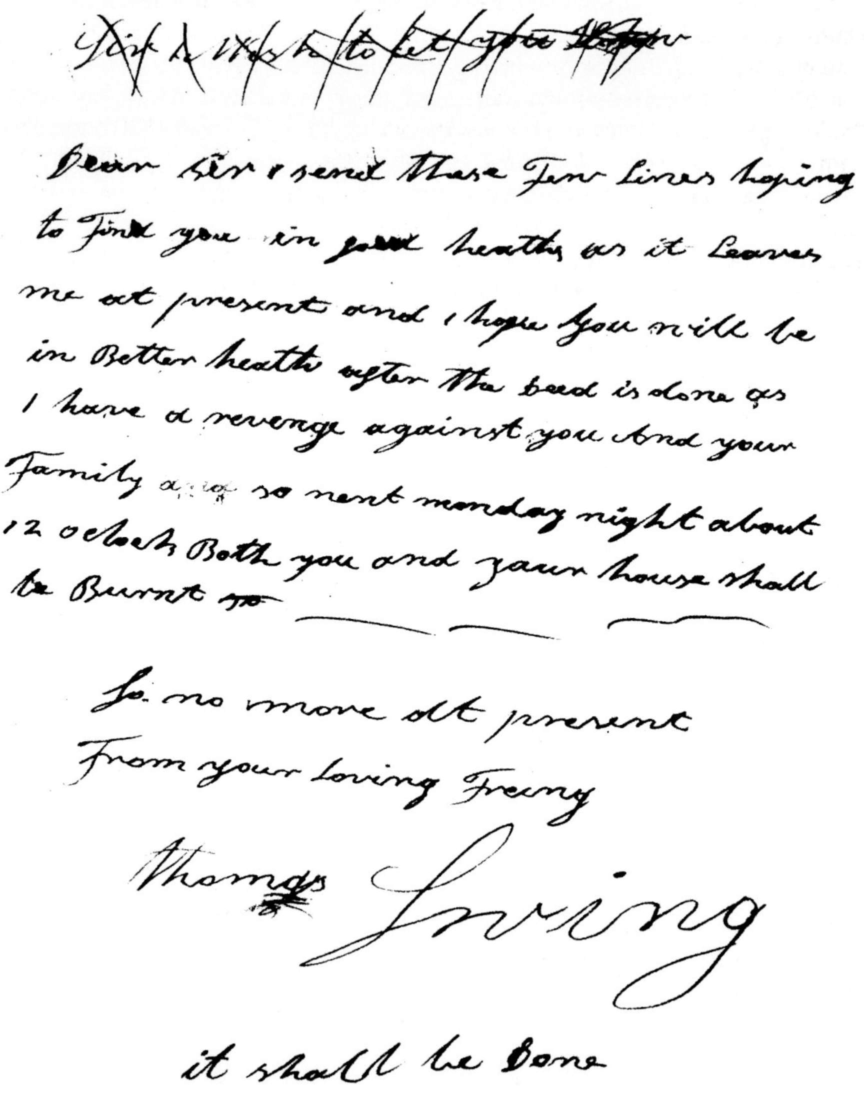

~~Sir I Wish to let you Know~~

Dear Sir i send these Few lines hoping
to Find you in good heath as it Leaves
me at present and i hope You will be
in Better heath after the deed is done as
I have a revenge against you And your
Family and so next monday night about
12 oclock Both you and your house shall
be Burnt so

So no more at present
From your Loving Freny

Thomas Swing

it shall be Done

Figure 2. Swing letter, c.1830–1

chised. Not surprisingly the town was 'infested with radicals' prepared to take any opportunity to carry their message of radical parliamentary reform to the countryside. John Adams and Patman, radical Maidstone shoemakers, and Halliwell, a Maidstone journeyman tailor, were spokesmen for the 600 labourers who marched on Maidstone in October 1830.[62] At Langley, Adams informed the son of the local rector that if they were not granted their rights they would 'bedew the country with blood . . . pull down the house . . . and build up the New with honest materials'. At Boughton Monchelsea he told magistrates, who blocked the way with armed soldiers, that 'these people want bread, not powder and shot; we blame not the farmers. They are oppressed with enormous taxes and cannot pay the labourer. We want the removal of taxation and abuses.' A similar message was delivered to Sir John Filmer at East Sutton Park.[63] Stephen Crawte, a relative of Cobbett and another Maidstone radical, again urged upon a mass meeting of labourers at Penenden Heath on 31 October 1830 the merits of parliamentary reform while Robert Price, a leader of wage rioters in the Sittingbourne, Faversham, East Malling and Maidstone areas was evidently a Jacobin and Republican naval deserter.[64]

While the London radicals undoubtedly welcomed demonstrations so close to the capital many Kent reformers were frightened by the scale and intensity of the labourers' movement. Major Charles Wayth of Thurnham, a leading Kent radical, promised his workmen that '. . . thorough Reform and Vote by Ballot would eventually redress their grievances (want of employment, inadequate wages and cruel taxation) . . . The present tumultuous proceedings . . . can only harm . . . the cause we advocate . . .'[65] Nor was there any sinister involvement of foreign agents as was often alleged at the time. The mysterious carriages sometimes reported in the vicinity of fires were figments of the imagination or members of the metropolitan police.[66] Some Kent labourers may have seen political reform as a prerequisite to improvement of their conditions, but the basic motivating force behind the rioting was the increasing pauperisation of the labourer resulting in sheer destitution. 'The origin of these . . . outrages is . . . from no political feeling', wrote the *Kentish Gazette*, 'but great and dire distress . . .'[67]

Unemployment and underemployment had been increasing at an alarming rate since the post-war depression of 1815.[68] They peaked when the bad harvest

62 *Ibid.*, p. 5; E.J. Hobsbawm and George Rudé, *Captain Swing*, Harmondsworth 1973, pp. 46, 58, 184–5.

63 *Ibid.*, p. 185; letter dated 6 November 1830, cited in Monju Dutt, 'The Agricultural Labourers' Revolt of 1830 in Kent, Surrey and Sussex', London Ph.D. 1966, pp. 155–6.

64 *MG*, 2.11.1830; CKS, QS/BW 124, Statement of Charlotte Stacey of Hill Garden House, Stockbury.

65 *MG*, 2.11.1830.

66 *MG*, 26.10.1830, 9.11.1830, 19.11.1830, 14.12.1830.

67 *KG*, 8.10.1830. Roland Quinault, 'The French Revolution of 1830 and Parliamentary Reform', *History*, lxxix (1994), pp. 389–91, still argues the belief of contemporary and subsequent historians that the riots were triggered by the French Revolution and helped cause the fall of Wellington's government.

68 See Hastings, *op. cit.*, pp. 112–18.

of 1829 combined with the severe winter of 1829–30. A wet summer followed
and the hop crop failed. Winter unemployment was already a regular feature
resulting from the disappearance of the annual hirings. Thirty-one of thirty-three
Kent parishes responding to the Poor Law Commissioners in 1832 admitted
substantial winter unemployment. Sixteen of these also had large numbers of
summer unemployed as well.[69] In 1826 Thomas Hodges of Benenden stated to
the Select Committee on Emigration that in the Weald of Kent every parish 'for
some years past' had suffered from surplus population. Since 1823, he maintained, pauperism had extended to about half the population of the Cranbrook
division including 682 labourers for whom no work could be found 'in any part
of the year'. Even at harvest time they were unable to get work due to competition from Irish labourers.[70] Not surprisingly these parishes were seriously
affected by the rioting of 1830. Minster-in-Sheppey 'had almost always for the
last ten years 60 labourers out of work and the convicts were a great deal better
off than our labouring class of poor'.[71] Henry Boyce complained of a great
number of unemployed labourers in the parishes of Ash and Woodnesborough in
1828 while failure of the hop gardens brought further unemployment in 1830.
Next year in Benenden between thirty and eighty able bodied labourers were
reported to be unemployed at all times of the year, and a similar situation existed
at Lenham.[72] In 1830 the Earl of Winchelsea, supported by Lord Camden, told
Parliament of widespread unemployment in the Kentish Weald while the
Radical, Francis Place, corroborated the fact that there was a large number of
Kentish labourers wishing to work but for whom no profitable work could be
found.[73] 'Undoubtedly great distress prevails and while want of employment is
added how can the effects be wondered at?', wrote the Kent magistrate Henry
Tylden to Sir Edward Knatchbull, the MP for East Kent.[74]

In March 1830 a County Meeting, attended by some 7,000 people, was called
to petition the King on the county's distress. Three months later a deputation
from twenty-one mid-Kent and Wealden parishes memorialised the Lords of the
Treasury stating that there was insufficient corn to feed their inhabitants and
ratepayers were unable to pay poor rates.[75] While Kent's aristocrats and resident
gentry expressed deep concern at the distressed state of the county they were
unable to turn their concerns into political action. In June 1833 a petition to the
Commons from Rolvenden's agricultural labourers still emphasised

---

[69] *BPP, Report of Royal Commission on Poor Laws (1834)*, Appendix B, pp. 235a–268c.
[70] *BPP, Report of Select Committee on Emigration (1826)*, IV, I, p. 133.
[71] *BPP, Report of Select Committee on the Poor Laws (1828)*, IV, pp. 13, 15.
[72] *Ibid.*, p. 20; *BPP, Report of Select Committee on the Poor Laws (1831)*, VIII, pp. 14, 89–90.
[73] Francis Place, *Essay on the State of the Country*, London 1831, p. 3; Dutt, *op. cit.*, p. 53.
[74] *Ibid.*, p. 286.
[75] *MG*, 16.3.1830, 1.6.1830; *KG*, 3.6.1830.

that the cause of the distress . . . as in almost all other parishes in agricultural counties, arises from the want of employment and suitable remuneration for their labour to enable them to obtain the necessaries of life.[76]

Parochial attempts to deal with unemployment or underemployment only compounded the difficulties.[77] In many instances the poor were distributed among the farmers at a low rate of wages through a Roundsman system or Labour Rate. The difference between the wage and the 'allowance' to which an unemployed labourer was entitled in accordance with the price of bread and the size of his family was paid out of the poor rate. In some places, such as Ash-next-Sandwich, pauper labour was auctioned weekly to the highest bidder. Consequently farmers, who were the principal ratepayers, discharged regular hands in order to hire them back at auction or employ 'ticketed' men at a cheap rate.[78] In many Kent parishes it was alleged that farmers did not attempt to give their own poor regular work knowing that whenever they needed hands they could be supplied by the parish overseers at 1s 0d a day.[79] In the Wingham Division the lowest wage paid in one parish was 6d a day; in four parishes 8d a day; in a further eleven parishes 1s 6d; in four parishes 2s 0d; and in most other parishes 1s 0d a day.[80]

In proportion to the number of applicants the amount of productive work was small. Most surplus hands were employed on the parish roads or in the stone and gravel pits.[81] Henry Boyce reported to the Select Committee on the Poor Laws in 1828 that in Ash-next-Sandwich and Woodnesborough he had seen '30 or 40 young men, degraded in their estimation as well as that of their beholders, hooked to carts or wheelbarrows dragging stone to the highway because they could not get employment elsewhere'. A similar 'horrible and disgusting sight' was witnessed by T.L. Hodges in a parish between Maidstone and Ashford.[82] Of 43 respondent parishes to the Poor Law Commissioners in 1832 39% gave unemployment as a cause of the Swing Riots and 35% low wages.[83] 'The poor in . . . Kent have been greatly ground down . . . by the Poor Laws', wrote a magistrate for Kent and Sussex to the Home Office: 'instead of helping peasants they have made miserable and sour-tempered paupers. Every parish has its peculiar system . . . executed with more or less severity and harshness.'[84] It is small wonder that when the riots began many of Swing's victims were overseers and other parish officers. 'Your petitioners', stated the Rolvenden labourers, 'are

---

[76] *MG*, 25.6.1833.

[77] See Hastings, *op. cit.*, pp. 112–37.

[78] BPP, *Report of Select Committee on the Poor Laws (1828)*, IV, p. 21; *Report of Select Committee on Labourers Wages (1824)*, VI, pp. 42–3.

[79] Dutt, *op. cit.*, p. 56.

[80] BPP, *Report of Select Committee on Labourers' Wages (1824)*, VI, p. 5.

[81] See Hastings, *op. cit.*, pp. 134–5.

[82] BPP, *Report of Select Committee on the Poor Laws (1828)*, IV, p. 20; *Report of Select Committee on the Poor Laws (1831)*, VIII, p. 18.

[83] BPP, *Report of Royal Commission on Poor Laws (1834)*, XXX–XXXIV, Appendix B, pp. 235a–268c.

[84] Dutt, *op. cit.*, p. 286.

often obliged to subsist on a small parochial allowance while they are willing to work for their bread.'[85]

The labourers' distress was aggravated by three further factors: the use of threshing machines; the employment of Irish labourers; and the effect of tithes. The immediately explosive issue was the threshing machine which, by 1830, was used in several parts of the county but particularly in East Kent. The rioters, helped by those farmers who voluntarily destroyed machines they had hired, did the job so thoroughly that it is difficult to know what the machines in question looked like. On some big farms they were fixed horse or water-powered installations. Most, however, seem to have been cheap, horse-powered machines which could be hired and set up in a barn or field.[86] The *Kent Herald* maintained that the 'infernal machine did as much work in three days as would employ a man during the winter' while Cobbett suggested that one machine took the wages from ten men.[87] Barham vestry recommended their disuse, 'there being a great many able men with large families out of employ'. Eastry parish officers similarly acknowledged that 'the use of threshing machines made employ still more scarce than before'.[88] The labourers wreaked a terrible revenge on the machines which had robbed them of their only winter living especially in the bitter winter of 1829–30 (Figure 3).

The increased employment of Irish labourers also depressed wages during the corn, hay and hop harvests and left many Kent labourers unemployed. West Kent incendiarism in particular was closely connected with employment of the Irish. 'I think the greatest impediment in the country . . . is the universal immigration of Irish labourers who fill the places in which surplus population has been hitherto employed', stated T.L. Hodges, MP for West Kent.[89] A West Wickham witness felt that the Irish 'had almost driven our poor out of harvest work' while *The Times* reported that at the height of the rioting 'every man who had ever employed an Irishman was in constant dread of arson'.[90]

'The chief cause of the evil (disturbances) is the want of employment and the chief cause of that want of employment is the tithe system', wrote a correspondent to the *Kent Herald*. Tithes were believed to prevent the improvement of the land. Consequently many small farmers made common cause with the labourers in the hope that the rioting would lead to reductions in rents, tithes and taxation.[91] General Dalbiac, sent to command the troops in Kent and Sussex, reported that:

85 *MG*, 25.6.1833.
86 J.C. Loudon, *Encyclopaedia of Agriculture*, London 1831, pp. 436–9; J. Ransome, *The Implements of Agriculture*, London 1843, pp. 152–3; G.E. Mingay, 'Rural War: the Life and Times of Captain Swing', in *The Unquiet Countryside*, ed. G.E. Mingay, London 1989, p. 47, suggests that it may have been the appearance of cheap machines in the south, putting machine threshing within reach of every small producer of corn, that triggered the rioting.
87 Dutt, *op. cit.*, p. 83; *KH* 30.9.1830.
88 *BPP, Report of Royal Commission on Poor Laws (1834)*, XXXIV, pp. 237e, 243e.
89 *BPP, Report of Select Committee on Poor Laws (1831)*, VIII, pp. 23–4.
90 *BPP, Report of Royal Commission on Poor Laws (1834)*, XXX, p. 266a; *The Times*, 8.11.1830.
91 *KH*, 25.11.1830; see Dutt, *op. cit.*, p. 88.

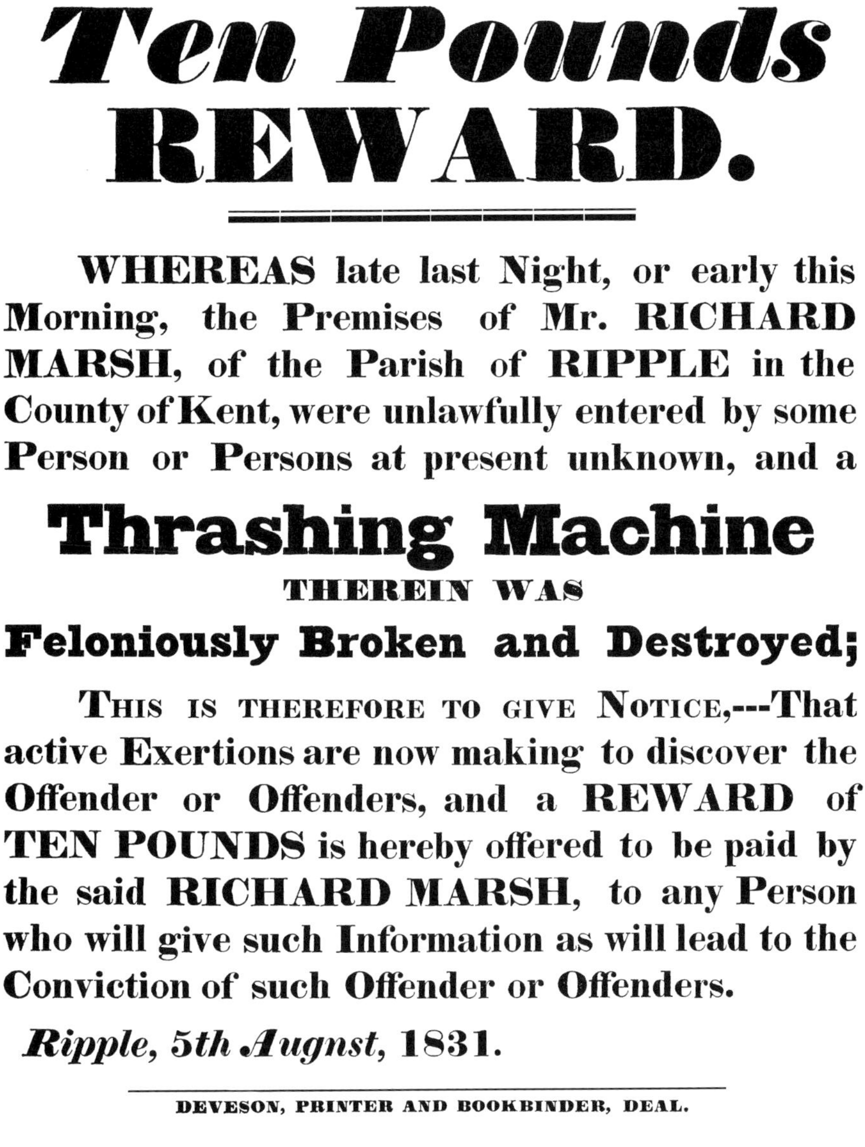

Ten Pounds REWARD.

WHEREAS late last Night, or early this Morning, the Premises of Mr. **RICHARD MARSH**, of the Parish of **RIPPLE** in the County of Kent, were unlawfully entered by some Person or Persons at present unknown, and a

Thrashing Machine

THEREIN WAS

Feloniously Broken and Destroyed;

THIS IS THEREFORE TO GIVE NOTICE,---That active Exertions are now making to discover the Offender or Offenders, and a **REWARD** of **TEN POUNDS** is hereby offered to be paid by the said **RICHARD MARSH**, to any Person who will give such Information as will lead to the Conviction of such Offender or Offenders.

Ripple, 5th Augnst, **1831.**

DEVESON, PRINTER AND BOOKBINDER, DEAL.

Figure 3. Printed notice about damage to agricultural machinery, 1831

> In many places the demands for increase of wages have been submitted to . . .
> The farmers have shown little or no disposition to resist their demands . . .
> under the hope that the present clamours . . . may finally lead to a reduction of
> Rent, Tithes and Taxes.[92]

The farmers 'in too many instances encourage the labourers and in none
endeavour to repress them' complained a Kent magistrate.[93] Cobbett, who in
October 1830 began a lecture tour of Kent, Sussex and Hampshire against the
background of the riots, advised farmers to explain their difficulties to their
labourers.

> Let every farmer . . . call the labourers together . . . explain to them the cause
> of his own poverty; that he is poor as well as themselves and that it is not his
> wish to oppose them but that he was not able to pay them as he desires.[94]

Within a short time labourers were campaigning for reduced rates, tithes and
taxes as a pre-condition of raising their own wages. Mr Wildash, a Wrotham
farmer who pressed the Revd George Moore to reduce his tithes during the
Wrotham wage riot, was described by the Treasury Solicitor as 'an aider and
abettor if not a ringleader of the rioters'. Two of his labourers, James Buss and
William Harding, in fact led the riot. Harding's bail was paid by Wildash and
another farmer while Wildash also testified on behalf of Buss.[95] At Chilham
small farmers encouraged rioters to destroy threshing machines 'which enabled
the opulent farmer to avail himself of every rise in the market' while the small
farmer, threshing with the flail, was always too late.[96] This unlikely alliance of
small farmer and labourer was a constant and interesting feature of the riots and
had serious repercussions on attempts by the authorities to suppress them.

It has recently been suggested that the impulse towards united action shown
by the rioters was 'in line with the developing theories of trade unionism of the
first third of the nineteenth century'.[97] Labourers at Marsh Gate Farm, Coolinge
struck for higher wages in October 1830 and refused to work even when brought
before the magistrates.[98] In a second strike at Ash married men refused to work
for less than 2s 6d a day. When farmers resisted they threatened to destroy their
ploughs.[99] There had been a similar strike at Eastry, a short time before Richard
Dixon allegedly fired the barn of James Hatfield, a local vestryman. Dixon and
his associates had met 'to devise some scheme compelling the farmers to raise

[92] Dutt, *op. cit.*, p. 94.
[93] *Loc. cit.*
[94] *Ibid.*, p. 100.
[95] *MG*, 4.1.1831; *KG*, 14.1.1831.
[96] *BPP, Report of Royal Commission on Poor Laws (1834)*, XXXIV, p. 241e.
[97] Shirley Burgoyne Black, 'Swing: The Years 1827–30 as Reflected in a West Kent Newspaper', *Archaeologia Cantiana*, cvii (1989), p. 105.
[98] *KG*, 5.11.1830.
[99] Dutt, *op. cit.*, p. 342.

their wages'.[100] A threatening letter, sent in 1831 to one of the largest employers of rural labour in Kent, was signed 'Swing Union'.[101] As late as 1835 panic-stricken parish officers from Wittersham reported that 'the union are in the habit of . . . meeting very frequently . . . in the neighbourhood . . . Two men stand on each side of the door with drawn swords . . . They that intend to be members are sworn in blindfolded . . . The man (informant) says they intend that the King should have less, the parsons less and the poor more to live on.'[102] This apart there is little evidence of any underground trade union activity. Local contemporaries were emphatic that 'there does not appear to be anything like an organised system established . . . nor is there evidence of any such conspiracy existing among the agricultural labourers'.[103] Despite press statements about 'evil combinations' Alderman Atkins, at a meeting of Sevenoaks proprietors to discuss protection from incendiarism, denied there existed any 'compact amongst persons setting fire to property . . . but that the fires were kindled by a vindictive spirit of a private nature and were not the results of a formidable combination'.[104]

Rick burning and anonymous threatening letters were not new to Kent.[105] Nor was the discontent which erupted so violently in the summer of 1830 unexpected. The immense increase in the criminal calendar, which had more than doubled in 1825–31 compared with 1811–17, is a clear indication of the mounting hardship and social tension. At West Kent Quarter Sessions in January 1830 the chairman partly attributed the increase in crime to the unprecedented distress and urged all who could to employ the poor.[106] Theft of corn and livestock and highway robbery were among the most frequent crimes. From at least 1827 incendiarism and the destruction of threshing machines had also featured.[107]

In Kent, where the Swing Riots not only began but persisted the longest, the disturbances may be basically divided into five phases. June and July 1830 saw the first of a series of 'alarming fires' in the vicinity of Bromley, Orpington, Brasted and Sevenoaks. One of the first victims, an Orpington farmer named Voules, had pulled down a cottage and evicted the occupants on a neighbouring common. Two other victims, Masters and Thompson, were magistrates prominent in suppressing local smuggling and poaching gangs. Thompson's various properties were fired four times. The fires here are terrible reported the *Maidstone Gazette*.

100 *MG*, 20.12.1831, 27.12.1831.
101 *MG*, 1.2.1831.
102 Sir Francis Bond Head, 'English Charity', *Quarterly Review* (1835), pp. 487–8.
103 *MG*, 28.9.1830, 5.10.1830, 30.10.1830.
104 *MG*, 28.9.1830, 11.12.1832.
105 See Clark, *op. cit.*, p. 67, and Grover, *op. cit.*, p. 72.
106 *MG*, 19.1.1830.
107 See *MG*, 5.1.1830 to 23.3.1830; Black, *op. cit.*, pp. 91–6.

Scarcely a night passes without some farmer having a cornstack or barn set fire to . . . Our town engine as well as Lord Stanhope's and Mr Nourraile's was there but to very little purpose . . . The pipes were so cut that they could not be used . . . The expressions of the mob are dreadful . . . Damnit . . . let it burn . . . I wish it was a house . . . we only want some potatoes; there is a nice fire to cook them by.[108]

The fires were accompanied by 'Swing' letters threatening murder, arson and assault to unpopular owners and occupiers.[109] [See Figure 2]

At the end of August, while the fires continued in north-west Kent despite the formation of an association for the protection of property, a second and totally different phase began with the nightly destruction of hired threshing machines by gangs, 'in some instances armed', in East Kent.[110] On 28 August a mob of nearly 400 labourers from Elham, Lyminge and Stelling destroyed machines at Lower Hardres and Lyminge. Magistrates called in dragoons from Canterbury but the work of destruction continued throughout September despite a reward of £500 for capture of the ringleaders and the swearing in of special constables. By the end of October, when the disturbances reached a terrifying scale, some 100 machines were reported destroyed in Kent at places as far apart as Sturry, . . . Folkestone and Dover.[111] Along the dead walls of Dover and for some miles along the road to Canterbury ran the significant word 'Swing'. Some farmers, on receipt of 'Swing' letters, placed their hired machines in the fields to await destruction.[112]

Initially there was considerable sympathy for the rioters. 'We doubt not that many of the infatuated men who have been engaged in . . . destruction of threshing machines were . . . satisfied in their own minds that they were justified in their desperate deeds', wrote the editor of the *Kentish Gazette*.[113] At a meeting of magistrates Sir Edward Knatchbull stated that 'he would wish to see as little violence used in suppressing the disorders as possible'.[114] Others urged discontinuation of the use of threshing machines and implementation of a labour rate for the unemployed. The Court of Guardians of Canterbury workhouse decided to use the surplus monies of the Poor Priest's Hospital to build cottages for rural paupers.[115] Thus encouraged the rioters finally destroyed the last machine hired out by Mr Barton, a Ewell millwright: 'so intent were the

---

[108] Hobsbawm and Rudé, *op. cit.*, pp. 71–82; *MG*, 6.11.1830, 3.8.1830, 10.8.1830, 17.8.1830, 21.9.1830; *KG*, 10.9.1830.
[109] *MG*, 21.9.1830; *KG*, 8.10.1830, 15.10.1830.
[110] *MG*, 7.9.1830, 14.9.1830, 28.9.1830, 5.10.1830; *KG*, 3.9.1830.
[111] *KG*, 3.9.1830; *MG*, 7.9.1830, 28.9.1830; *The Times*, 25.10.1830; *KH*, 21.10.1830. The figure of 100 machines was almost certainly an exaggeration at this stage.
[112] *KG*, 8.10.1830, 15.10.1830.
[113] *KG*, 28.9.1830.
[114] *MG*, 5.10.1830. See also Mingay, *op. cit.*, p. 45.
[115] *KG*, 12.10.1830, 15.10.1830.

labourers on the demolition of the machine that not a fragment was left more than a foot long'. Its owner was ironically obliged to seek parish relief.[116]

Late in October, as fires swept through East and West Kent and rioters in Sittingbourne district smashed machines in broad daylight, discharging guns when the work was complete, large bodies of labourers also began to march from parish to parish pressing others to join them. They visited farmers; stormed vestry meetings, tithe audits and rent dinners; and demanded sustenance from the wealthy. Their demands included 2s 3d a day in winter and 2s 6d a day in summer; reductions in rent and the price of fuel; constant employment for all and increased parish allowances for each child after the second.[117]

Terrified farmers and vestries usually conceded. 'Parish after parish rises and parish after parish will rise', reported Collingwood: 'the farmers say the government has scorned . . . them and talk of civil war. If with the whole of the agricultural classes the manufacturers . . . rise, what will be the outcome?' 'We are at this moment under mob law and have no efficient means of protecting our property or even our lives' confirmed a Sandwich magistrate.[118]

One large mob marched to Lenham, Hollingbourne, East Sutton and Langley. A second, led by Robert Price and preceded by a tricolour, gathered at Stockbury going from thence to Newington, Wormshill, Frinsted, Hartlip and Rainham. Almost every village within a seven mile radius of Maidstone was visited.[119] At Hollingbourne labourers had printed cards stuck in their hats saying 'Starving at 1s.6d. per day'. All carried bludgeons.[120] The process culminated at the 'Battle of Boughton Quarries' where 500–600 labourers, led by the Maidstone radicals, who had visited the Cornwallis and Rider estates, were dispersed by soldiers and magistrates before they could continue their march to the county town. Their leaders were arrested.[121]

In early November wage riots and machine breaking began in West Kent, reaching into the Sussex Weald. East Malling, West Peckham, Yalding, Hawkhurst, Rolvenden, Marden, Staplehurst, Headcorn, Goudhurst, Benenden, Tenterden and Wrotham, where the mob raised the old cry of 'Bread or Blood', also saw serious disturbances. The authorities were powerless and obliged to

---

[116] *KG*, 1.10.1830, 5.10.1830; *MG*, 12.10.1830.

[117] *KG*, 29.10.1830; Dutt, *op. cit.*, pp. 357–9. Mingay, *op. cit.*, pp. 36–7, argues that many outbreaks can be traced as developing along the network of main roads and that imitation was important in the spread of Swing incidents. James Huzel, 'Aspects of the Old Poor Law, Population and Agrarian Protest in Early 19th Century England with particular reference to the county of Kent', Kent Ph.D. 1975, produced a profile of Kent parishes most likely to take Swing action based on the Answers to Rural Queries, *Report of Royal Commission on the Poor Laws (1834)*, XXXIV. He included in his profile parishes which were rural, remote from London, but situated on turnpikes or main coach routes; in addition he listed parishes which were inland rather than coastal, and parishes which had workhouses, assistant overseers or select vestries and no child allowances or allowances in aid of wages. He also included parishes which had surplus labour problems; declining farming capital; and an above average population of craftsmen and shopkeepers but no allotments for labourers.

[118] Dutt, *op. cit.*, pp. 293–4.

[119] *MG*, 2.12.1830; *KG*, 5.11.1830; CKS, QS/BW 124; Dutt, *op. cit.*, p. 146.

[120] *KG*, 5.11.1830.

[121] *MG*, 2.11.1830; Dutt, *op. cit.*, p. 150.

make temporary concessions regarding wages and poor relief while throughout the county magistrates tried to force farmers to submit to a labour rate. At the same time a petition to both Houses of Parliament from Ightham warned that the distress of the poor had reached 'a height beyond control because many contributors to the poor rate are themselves bordering on pauperism'. At High Halden tithe audit on 15 November a 'violent paper' was distributed throughout the parish warning farmers to boycott the audit or 'beware of fire'.[122]

After mid-November came a further round of fires, wage riots and machine breaking county-wide with serious disturbances at Ruckinge.[123] 'Society is now completely unhinged', wrote the *Kentish Gazette*, 'almost every town and village in Kent having been visited by . . . the labouring classes . . . They not only demand a regulation of wages but extra money for sustenance wherever they go.'[124] According to the Hammonds the labourers were masters over almost all the triangle 'of which Maidstone is the apex and Hythe and Brighton the bases'.[125] This was despite the presence by this time of metropolitan police, troops, the Treasury Solicitor, artillery and Bow Street Runners. When the wage riots died down at the close of November there was further arson and machine breaking in East Kent and Romney Marsh in 1831 and smaller amounts of arson, largely to the west, in 1832. A handful of fires in 1833 were mostly associated with a return to former wage levels.[126]

There was a recurrence of fires in 1835–6 during the anti-Poor-Law Riots. Victims included John Wells, the former Maidstone MP, who sustained damage worth £10,000, having employed haymakers from 'the sister country'.[127] Arson revived yet again in the 'hungry forties' culminating in a second Swing outbreak coinciding with the re-introduction of threshing machines in 1849–50.[128] A third but smaller outbreak seems to have taken place during the farmers' retrenchment in the agricultural depression of the late nineteenth century.

Not only did the disturbances of the 1830s last longer in Kent than has sometimes been stated. They were also on a greater scale than previously calculated. Hobsbawm and Rudé in their excellent analysis of the riots estimate that between 1 January 1830 and 3 September 1832 there were 37 instances of machine breaking, 61 cases of incendiarism, 41 examples of wage and other riots and 11 Swing letters. These figures are derived largely from Home Office Papers and *The Times*. If they are combined with figures from the county press the number of incidents is substantially greater. There were some 141 instances of arson; 81 examples of machine breaking; and 60 outbreaks of riot. Swing

---

[122] *MG*, 9.11.1830, 16.11.1830, 23.11.1830, 30.11.1830; *The Times*, 18.11.1830; *KG*, 19.11.1830; CKS, QS/BW 124; Dutt, *loc. cit.*

[123] *MG*, 16.11.1830, 23.11.1830, 30.11.1830, 7.12.1830, 14.12.1830, 21.12.1830.

[124] *KG*, 19.11.1830.

[125] J.L. and B. Hammond, *The Village Labourer 1760–1832*, London 1927, p. 181.

[126] See Maps 4 and 5.

[127] *MG*, 18.8.1835.

[128] *MG*, 16.3.1841, 24.8.1841, 17.2.1846, 16.2.1847, 27.11.1847, 8.8.1848, 29.5.1849, 11.9.1849, 2.10.1849, 1.1.1850.

incidents were recorded in 154 Kent parishes out of a total of 433. These are the minimum figures because not all events were reported. Nevertheless some 35.5% of all Kent parishes were directly affected by one or often more Swing episodes.[129]

The initial sympathy of many in authority was reflected in the trial of the first machine breakers in late October 1830. Convicted on the statements of two of their number, who had turned King's evidence, Sir Edward Knatchbull, to the concern of the Home Secretary and the amazement of Lord Camden, discharged them with a three-day prison sentence and a caution.[130] When the 'kindness and moderation' of the magistrates produced a continuation of arson and machine breaking on an alarming scale attitudes hardened. After the destruction of Thomas Knight's farmhouse and barn at Borden with a loss of £1,200–£1,400, Revd John Poore, a Sittingbourne magistrate, procured a troop of the 7th Dragoons from Canterbury to try to calm the terrified farmers and Lord Harris's estate at Belmont was placed under permanent guard 'since no one who has property considers himself safe'.[131] In early November, as the disturbances continued, a detachment of the 81st Regiment marched from Chatham to Maidstone. On the same day a Royal Artillery detachment arrived at Chatham from Woolwich. Colonel Middleton, the local commander, convinced after Boughton Quarries that the situation was out of control, persuaded the Home Secretary to send a cavalry detachment and two field guns to Maidstone. The latter also sent the Treasury Solicitor and five police officers to assist the magistrates in detecting 'the wicked incendiaries'.[132]

With the outbreak of the wage riots the Home Secretary appointed General Dalbiac, 'a most active and intelligent officer' to take control of the troops throughout Kent and Sussex. He quickly arranged for the 7th Dragoon Guards, based at Canterbury, to police East Kent, and the 2nd Dragoon Guards, with their headquarters at Maidstone and a squadron at Chatham, to police Sittingbourne, Cranbrook and mid-Kent. The 5th Dragoon Guards, based at Tunbridge Wells, were to police West Kent and Sussex. Magistrates were to seek aid from the nearest garrison.[133] At Ramsgate the authorities were strengthened by 'blockade men'. When the second set of machine breakers from Stour Valley

---

129 Hobsbawm and Rudé, *op. cit.*, Appendix 1. The authors in their introduction to their Penguin edition (1973) state that 'they underestimated the extent of the movement in certain areas' (p. xii). The total of eleven Swing letters is certainly an underestimate since many went unreported to the authorities and were not usually reported in the press. In a rare exception, *The Times*, 25.11.1830, stated that letters had been sent to farmers in almost every village around Canterbury threatening destruction if they yielded to the demands of the tithe collectors. Arson was a much greater cause of financial loss than the destruction of machines. See Mingay, *op. cit.*, pp. 47–8.

130 *KG*, 26.10.1830; *MG*, 26.10.1830; Dutt, *op. cit.*, p. 140.

131 *KG*, 29.10.1830, 5.11.1830; *MG*, 26.10.1830, 9.11.1830.

132 *MG*, 26.10.1830; Dutt, *op. cit.*, pp. 151–2.

133 *MG*, 7.12.1830; Dutt, *op. cit.*, pp. 160–1; CKS, U840, memorandum showing stations of troops in Kent and Sussex.

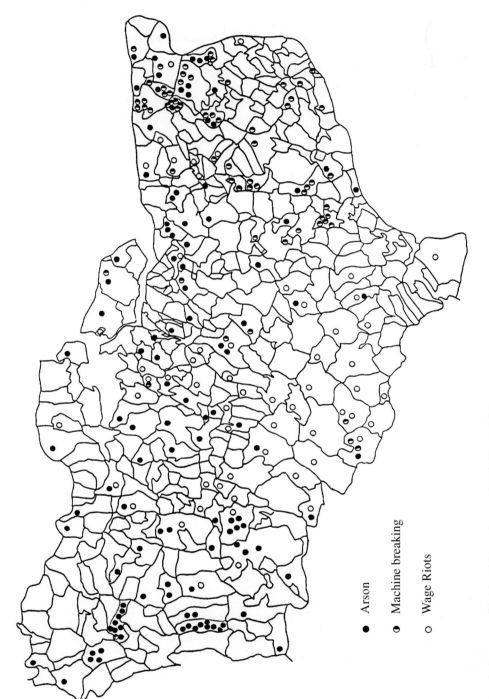

Map 4. Arson, machine breaking and wage riots in Kent, 1830

Arson ●

Machine breaking ◑

Wage Riots ○

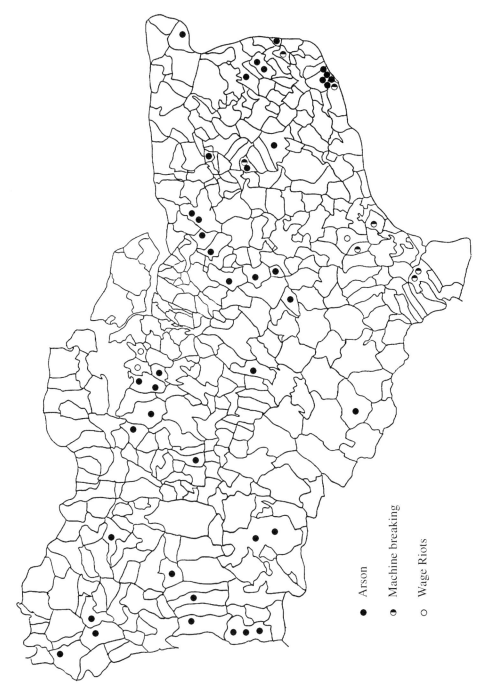

Map 5. Arson, machine breaking and wage riots in Kent, 1831–2

Arson ●

Machine breaking ◑

Wage Riots ○

appeared before the same Sir Edward Knatchbull at a special sessions in November one man was transported for life and six for seven years.[134]

In addition to a substantial military presence some urban and a few rural parishes organised their own patrols. Twenty gentlemen and tradesmen kept watch at Sandwich from 9.00p.m. to 5.00a.m. All farming premises were watched day and night at Faversham and three men were placed each night on the church tower. Regular patrols also took place at Ashford, New Romney, Chislet and Hoath. A subscription at Ospringe for paying the nightly watch included £50 from Lord Harris. Some individuals such as Thomas Rider of Boughton Monchelsea Place also hired watchmen to look after their own premises.[135]

The reluctance of many farmers to enlist as special constables caused great concern. Only 40 of 300 gentry and farmers, who met at the Bull Inn, Maidstone, on 29 October, enrolled because they did not wish to become 'marked men'.[136] Colonel Middleton confided privately to the Home Secretary that the disturbances had reached such a serious state owing to the inactivity and lack of co-operation among the local gentry and magistrates.[137] Many small farmers declared openly that they considered the cause of the rioters their own. At Tonbridge only 52 of 300 took the oath. The rest complained of the burden of taxation and government inattention to their distress. The majority of persons summoned from Marden, Staplehurst, Cranbrook, Woodchurch, Frittenden, Chilham and Ashford also refused to be sworn in.[138] Farmers also objected to an attempt by Lord Darnley to re-establish the Cobham Yeomanry cavalry originally created for internal security during the French Wars. Sixty Faversham farmers attended a similar meeting but only 10 or 12 enrolled:[139] 'there was a silent consciousness that it was not the thing required, that it would not render farmers more able to pay their landlords or their labourers'.[140] On the other hand there was a full complement of volunteers at Tunbridge Wells.[141]

The riots reflected clearly 'the continual state of warfare between employers and labourers'.[142] At Otford, labourers not only refused to firefight but surrounded the burning stacks smoking their pipes. When a threshing machine caught fire they gave three cheers. There was similar behaviour at Salutation Farm, near Sandwich, Cobham and Selling Court. At Fisher, near Tonbridge, labourers cut the hoses of the fire engine, a stratagem practised elsewhere.[143]

---

134 *MG*, 30.11.1830.
135 *MG*, 2.11.1830, 9.11.1830, 7.12.1830, 14.12.1830; *KG*, 9.11.1830, 12.11.1830, 23.11.1830.
136 *KH*, 4.11.1830.
137 Dutt, *op. cit.*, pp. 151–2.
138 *MG*, 9.11.1830, 23.11.1830; *KG*, 26.11.1830.
139 *KG*, 26.11.1830.
140 *KG*, 19.11.1830.
141 *MG*, 11.1.1831.
142 *KG*, 9.9.1831.
143 *MG*, 26.10.1830, 2.11.1830, 9.11.1830; *KG*, 22.10.1830, 29.10.1830; *KH*, 28.10.1830.

Stockbury labourers scoffed at those who fought a fire then paraded through the village carrying a black flag.[144]

With such deep class divisions it is surprising that the riots brought no deaths. In March 1830 a shot was fired at a Benenden overseer attending a vestry meeting at the Bull Inn. Two men on patrol at Herne were also fired on in November, while at Boughton Aluph an incendiary discharged a pistol at the owner's mansion before departing.[145] Among fifty labourers from Newington, who destroyed a threshing machine at Hartlip, were some smugglers 'having their faces blackened' and armed with pistols. Smugglers were not only 'natural rebels' whose trade was becoming increasingly depressed by the vigilance of the preventive service, but smuggling also accustomed agricultural labourers to working in large groups in resistance to authority.[146] Some incidents were acts of revenge. The corn stacks of Revd Ralph Price of Lyminge, a magistrate who had played a leading role in apprehending the Elham Valley machine breakers, were fired in October. Alland Farm, Thanet, the property of George Hannon, a Cinque Ports magistrate, was attacked three times. Clare Park House, near Maidstone, where a stack was fired in June 1831, was the seat of yet another magistrate.[147]

Unpopular parish officers were also common targets. The Revd G.R. Gleig, vicar of the troubled parish of Ash, near Wingham, who describes in his novel, *Chronicles of Waltham*, the horrors of the farm fire of overseer Amos, was describing the fire at Golstone Farm, Ash. The blaze, which could be seen all over Thanet, cost £3,000. Golstone Farm was the property of Ash overseer, Michael Becker, who had reduced wages on the parish farm and forced an unemployed shepherd to walk daily the thirteen miles from Margate to collect his dole until after nine weeks he collapsed.[148] Thomas Knight of Borden was another overseer who suffered similarly. J. Oliver, a Hollingbourne farmer and overseer, was called 'a damned bad one' for having starved the poor in the winter of 1829–30 but escaped more lightly. The overseers of Lamberhurst and Benenden fled their parishes during the wage riots in November. The Wrotham assistant overseer was dragged by the mob over the parish boundary in a cart, failing to use the brace of pistols he had boasted he possessed.[149] A lodge belonging to the assistant overseer at Sundridge was destroyed in December 1832. In 1833 Richard Whitehead, a Stockbury pauper, slashed 500 hop bines on the grounds of Mr Dawson, the Stockbury overseer who had had him imprisoned.[150] Mr Dodds of Shotley Court, near Wingham, whose two farmyards were destroyed in February 1834, was 'an active member of the vestry' which had

---

144 *MG*, 26.10.1830.
145 *MG*, 2.3.1830, 23.10.1830; *KG*, 5.3.1830, 16.4.1830, 23.11.1830.
146 Dutt, *op. cit.*, pp. 79–80, 142; CKS, U957 C177/35; *PP* 1834, xxviii, p. 197A.
147 *MG*, 12.10.1830, 21.12.1830, 21.6.1831.
148 G.R. Gleig, *Chronicles of Waltham*, Paris 1835, vol. 2, pp. 18–25; *MG*, 12.10.1830; *KG*, 8.10.1830.
149 *MG*, 21.12.1830, 30.11.1831.
150 *MG*, 4.12.1832, 23.7.1833, 30.7.1833.

reduced relief by 1s 6d a week.[151] The 'terrific and destructive fire' on the farm of J. Smith of Hoo was 'no doubt the work of some secret villain whom he had offended in his capacity of overseer'.[152]

Although Captain Swing was a mythical figure, his fellow leaders such a 'Captain' Revell at Ash and 'General' Moore, the 22-year-old Garlinge labourer who led the machine breakers of Thanet, were more real.[153] Horton, another labourer who wore a white hat for identification, was leader of the Stour Valley machine breakers. Most local leaders, however, seem to have come from the ranks of the small craftsmen. Stephen Eves and William Standen, the labourers' spokesmen at Goudhurst, were a sawyer and glover respectively. Two of the Maidstone radicals who led the labourers to Boughton Quarries were shoe-makers. The third was a tailor. The Wrotham ringleader, George Ayling, was also a shoemaker as was Taylor of Bridge. Unable to get full employment he had turned occasionally to agricultural labouring. Of the leaders of the Hawkhurst district, Jack Ballard, labourer, was 'a notorious smuggler', John Tickman was a journeyman bricklayer, G. Berrow was a journeyman carpenter, and W. Crisford a tailor's apprentice. One of the leading Elham machine breakers was a black-smith and another a butcher.[154] Those who followed them were mostly labourers although the Thanet machine breakers included ploughmen, threshers, waggoners, shoemakers and a brickmaker, all from different parishes.[155] Most were members of the local community who knew their victims well. John Dike, who fired the property of Michael Stokes of Bearsted and Mr Ashurst of Thurnham, had been refused poor relief by Stokes and held Ashurst responsible for a friend's transportation. Similarly Jack Seman, indicted for burning a straw stack at Otford, had been dismissed by the farmer, Isaac Jordan.[156]

Richard Dixon, 35-year-old father of five children, who was executed for destroying the barn of Eastry overseer, John Hatfield, was described as 'a man of stern, determined appearance and Herculean frame of body'. A thatcher, he had been 'on the parish' a considerable time and had been employed on the high-ways. He lived in the same cottage as Richard Devison and his wife. Devison had been refused relief by Hatfield when he went to the vestry because he had once left Hatfield's employment. When Dixon was charged, his wife went mad and was confined as a lunatic in Eastry workhouse when her husband was executed at Maidstone in December 1831. On the night of his execution a barn containing 70 quarters of wheat and a quantity of oats belonging to the chairman of Ulcombe vestry, ten miles from Maidstone, was fired as a tribute and an act of revenge.[157]

The Swing Riots were 'the greatest machine breaking episode in English

[151] MG, 25.2.1834, 18.3.1834.
[152] MG, 4.11.1834.
[153] Hobsbawm and Rudé, op. cit., p. 174; MG, 23.12.1830.
[154] MG, 16.11.1830, 30.11.1830, 21.12.1830.
[155] Dutt, op. cit., p. 178.
[156] MG, 31.1.1830, 21.12.1830.
[157] MG, 13.12.1831, 20.12.1831, 27.12.1831.

history and by far the most successful'.[158] In Kent the hated threshing machines were temporarily abandoned. The Earl of Guildford ordered his tenants to discontinue their use. Barham's Guardian of the Poor reported in 1832 that 'the Farmers have never used any Threshing Machines since'.[159] *The Times* noted that

> the farmers whose threshing machines have been broken do not intend to renew them. So far, therefore, the object of the riots will be answered. Farmers do not consider threshing machines of much advantage . . . They throw the labourers out of work and on the parish.[160]

In 1845 Buckland records them present only in Sheppey. Elsewhere 'threshing is still done in most cases by the flail'.[161] By 1848, however, they were returning, increasingly precipitating further, but less successful, outbreaks of arson.[162]

Repression of the Kent rioters was severe. By 1832, 102 prisoners had been tried of whom 25 had been acquitted. Four were executed for arson; 48 were imprisoned and 52 transported, mostly for machine breaking.[163] When it is considered that only four out of a minimum of 141 incidents of arson brought convictions, the detection rate was exceedingly low despite the ultimate presence of dragoons, artillery, police, and Bow Street runners who infiltrated the beer shops.[164] Rewards offered ranged from £100 to £600 – fortunes for an agricultural labourer – but like the northern Luddites 'not one of the miserable beings availed themselves of becoming rich'.[165] Offenders remained undetected although undoubtedly known to many.

A slogan painted on a wall near Thomas Knight's house at Borden threatened 'Death to informists' but a *Kent Herald* reporter who attended the fire at Shotling Court noted among the many onlookers that 'the prevailing feeling seemed to be a remarkable guardedness, a kind of repressed thinking'.[166] Juries were reluctant to convict for capital offences. When James Whales, suspected of two other acts of incendiarism, was cleared of firing a vestryman's barn at Wingham, the verdict was met 'with such a . . . clapping of hands that silence was with difficulty restored'. A number of farm labourers had testified in his defence.[167]

The roving bands of rural rioters 'remained rioters rather than rebels'. They did not establish links with Kent's small minority of industrial workers including the scattered but well-organised local paperworkers. A strike of

[158] Hobsbawm and Rudé, *op. cit.*, p. xxiii.
[159] *BPP, Report of Royal Commission on the Poor Laws (1834)*, XXXIV, p. 237e.
[160] Hobsbawm and Rudé, *op. cit.*, p. 74; *The Times*, 14.10.1830.
[161] George Buckland, *On the Farming of Kent*, London 1846, pp. 258, 269.
[162] *MG*, 17.2.1846, 22.11.1847, 8.8.1848, 11.9.1849, 2.10.1849, 1.1.1850, 4.8.1850.
[163] Hobsbawm and Rudé, *op. cit.*, Appendix 1 and p. 223.
[164] Dutt, *op. cit.*, p. 342.
[165] *MG*, 9.11.1830.
[166] *MG*, 25.2.1834.
[167] *MG*, 10.8.1830, 21.12.1830, 15.2.1831, 4.3.1834, 11.3.1834.

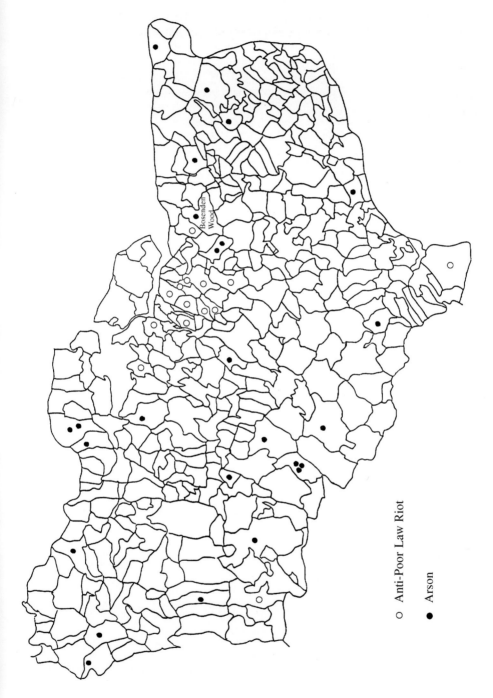

Map 6. Arson and anti-Poor Law rioting in Kent, 1835

○ Anti-Poor Law Riot

● Arson

Chatham labourers in December 1830 passed unnoticed.[168] Threats were made to blow up the Dartford gunpowder mills. Swing letters were sent to the principal factories of Greenwich and Deptford threatening that 700 men would march from Sevenoaks to destroy the machinery. The only outcome was the appointment of special constables. A visit by rioters to the paper mill at East Malling also failed to persuade the paperworkers to join them.[169] Nevertheless W. Baker of the paperworkers' union, who helped to establish the Kent and Sussex Labourers' Union in April 1872, recounted at its inaugural meeting how he, as a young man, had taken part in one of the wage riots of 1830.[170] A letter sent to the Duke of Richmond at Goodwood (Sussex) in December 1830 threatened to destroy his estate and the property of all magistrates and constables unless sentences on the Kent machine breakers were reduced but inter-county co-operation among Swing's followers was rare.[171]

(6) The Last Revolt of the Agricultural Labourers: The Courtenay Rising of 1838

The defeat of 1830–2 did not end the labourers' agitation which merged into the Kent anti-Poor Law riots of 1835. When Assistant Poor Law Commissioner, Sir Francis Head, came to Kent to establish the new poor law unions he found the Kent landowners in fear of their labourers and an 'Association' already forming among the 'peasantry' to resist the Poor Law Amendment Act.[172] As the poor law unions were created the landowners' fears were justified when the Swale villages rioted and incendiarism rose again to the level of 1831.[173] Popular protest terminated with the 'Last Rising of the Agricultural Labourers' on 31 May 1838 in which the self-styled Sir William Courtenay and nine of the ill-armed labourers who followed him were killed in a day-long battle against an overwhelming force of soldiers and special constables in Bosenden Wood. The brother-in-law of a constable sent illegally to arrest him and a lieutenant of the 45th Regiment were also despatched by Courtenay himself.[174]

Courtenay, an exotic and popular demagogue who claimed supernatural and messianic powers, was a former maltster from Cornwall named John Nicholls Tom. A champion of the poor, who had probably been a Spencean socialist, he stood unsuccessfully as a parliamentary candidate for both Canterbury and East Kent. He also won local notoriety for committing perjury in defence of smugglers before his certification as a lunatic in October 1833. Returning to the

---

168 *MG*, 14.12.1830.
169 *MG*, 9.11.1830; *KG*, 30.11.1830, 7.12.1830.
170 *KM*, 24.4.1872.
171 West Sussex Record Office, Goodwood MS 1446, g18.
172 Head, *op. cit.*, p. 487; see also Hastings, *op. cit.*, pp. 160–2; John Lowerson, 'Anti-Poor Law Movements and Rural Trade Unionism in the South East 1835', in Charlesworth, *op. cit.*, pp. 155–8.
173 See Map 6 opposite, and Figure 7 below.
174 Barry Reay, *The Last Rising of the Agricultural Labourers*, Oxford 1990.

Boughton-under-Blean area four years later he gathered around him a devoted following. The 'most desperate affray' in Bosenden Wood was the culmination of two days of recruitment marching through an area which had been prominent in the Swing Riots and had provided two of their martyrs.[175]

It was no coincidence that the poverty-stricken parishes within a ten mile radius of Hernhill through which Courtenay rode, with a brace of pistols and a naked cutlass, preceded by a loaf on a pitchfork dipped in blood, had also seen widespread anti-Poor Law rioting in 1835.[176] While the local press and frightened local farmers noted Courtenay's violent denunciations of the New Poor Law and rumours that he and his band intended to blow up the 'Blean Bastille' (Blean Union workhouse), the official view was that his followers were largely 'the victims of fanaticism, imposture and superstition'. This view was supported by the barrister, Frederick Liardet, who, in his report for the Central Society of Education, denied that poverty was a major factor in the rising.[177] Lord Chief Justice Denman also emphasised at the Summer Assizes that the New Poor Law 'which extends relief so largely to the poorer and more unfortunate classes' carried no blame for the disturbances and urged the magistrates and gentry of Kent 'to improve the minds of their peasantry'.[178] Only the Chartist national leaders, Bronterre O'Brien and G.J. Harney, raised pertinent questions about the legality of the whole affair, demanding a parliamentary enquiry and accusing the justices of 'magisterial murder' which 'had grown out of the New Poor Law ... with its victims driven almost to madness by the workhouse system'.[179]

When P.G. Rogers published his *Battle in Bosenden Wood* in 1961 he continued to concentrate on Courtenay himself rather than upon the local context of his activities, concluding once again that he said little of the New Poor Law and that the main motive of his followers was not economic but 'religious fanaticism born of ignorance and boredom'.[180] He failed also to appreciate that, mad or otherwise, Courtenay's dangerous social doctrines were extremely attractive to the contemporary rural and urban poor. Courtenay's electoral programme of December 1832 included not only the old radical commitment to reform the Commons, abolish tithes and transfer the burden of taxation from the poor to the rich but anticipated in other ways the People's Charter.[181] In defence of smugglers he argued that smuggling was created only by the distress of the time while exploitation of factory children would disappear only when reduced taxes and abolition of tithes enabled manufacturers to pay their fathers a living wage for a ten-hour day. In the countryside his talk of 'the war of the poor against the rich' and his Spencean proposals for land redistribution, and the destruction of

175　*Ibid.*, pp. 76–7, 88, 110–29.
176　See Map 6; also Hastings, *op. cit.*, pp. 162–3; Thompson, *op. cit.*, p. 880.
177　*The Globe*, 1.6.1838; *MG*, 31.7.1838; Anon., *A Canterbury Tale Fifty Years Ago*, London 1896, p. 28; Reay, *op. cit.*, pp. 88, 137–41.
178　P.G. Rogers, *Battle in Bosenden Wood*, Oxford 1961, pp. 184, 215–17, 219.
179　*NS*, 9.6.1838, 16.6.1838; A.R. Schoyen, *The Chartist Challenge*, London 1958, pp. 32–4.
180　Rogers, *op. cit.*, pp. 216–17; *MG*, 7.8.1838.
181　Rogers, *op. cit.*, p. 20; *A Canterbury Tale*, pp. 3–5.

private property in land,[182] also found ready listeners since, as the *Maidstone Gazette* admitted, 'this feeling is deeper seated among the agricultural population than many are dispelled to believe'.[183] During his imprisonment in 1833 a detachment of soldiers guarded Canterbury gaol to prevent his liberation by the mob.[184]

An early attempt to make some sense of Rogers' 'strange story of Sir William Courtenay' was made by Beverley Robinson in 1980. More recently Barry Reay has successfully produced a detailed case study of the motivation and mobilisation of Courtenay's followers arguing strongly that Bosenden Wood was not only the last revolt against the New Poor Law and England's last millenarian uprising but also the last rising of English agricultural labourers rather than the Swing Riots.[185] He also shows clearly how class tension between farmers and labourers, falling wages, pressure of population and the harsh winter of 1838 combined to produce an abortive insurrection under a messianic leader. Contemporary and later denials of the role of the New Poor Law in mobilising the labourers are shown to be untrue. In fact protest against the sudden and painful changes wrought by the 1834 Act was of considerable significance.[186]

Some magistrates claimed that men from other parishes arrived too late to join an insurrection that had already been defeated. 'Had the madman been allowed to go about the county for a day or two longer', wrote Rev. John Poore, a Murston magistrate, to Lord John Russsell, 'the consequences would have been still more lamentable.'[187] A death roll as high as Peterloo in the 'The New Poor Law Battle' contrasted starkly with the absence of mortality during the Swing and anti-Poor Law riots.[188] Within a week the gentry and farmers were said to be 'boasting of the salutary effect the massacre . . . already had on the deluded peasantry'. While Poore hoped 'the terrible Example . . . would prevent any further Disturbance', Assistant Poor Law Commissioner Tufnell rejoiced that 'the worst gang in the county has been . . . thoroughly annihilated'.[189] These pronouncements marry significantly with O'Brien's verdict that 'The object in view was to strike terror into the hearts of the peasantry that without further resistance they may submit to the infamous Poor Law.'[190] Courtenay would, perhaps, have been surprised to find himself hailed as a typical 'physical force', anti-Poor-Law leader and 'Tomism' compared with Chartism.[191] The outcome of the 'Kent Massacre', four years after Tolpuddle, was to ensure that the Chartist

---

182 'We must destroy not only personal and hereditary Lordship, but the cause of them, which is Private Property in land.' Quoted in E.P. Thompson, *The Making of the English Working Class*, p. 177.
183 *MG*, 12.3.1833; *KG*, 5.6.1838.
184 *MG*, 2.4.1833.
185 Beverley Robinson, *The Red Lion*, Gravesend 1980; Reay, *op. cit.*, p. 175.
186 Reay, *op. cit.*, 78–9, 81, 104, 139–41.
187 PRO, HO 40/36. Letter from Revd John Poore to Lord John Russell 31.5.1838; Reay, *op. cit.*, pp. 103, 108.
188 Reay, *op. cit.*, p. 99; *Northern Liberator*, 9.6.1838.
189 *MG*, 5.6.1838; Reay, *op. cit.*, p. 153.
190 Schoyen, *op. cit.*, p. 33.
191 *Ibid.*, p. 34; *MG*, 19.11.1839.

movement did not link up with the anti-Poor-Law movement and secured no foothold in rural Kent as it did briefly in neighbouring Sussex, Essex and Suffolk. Instead the Kent labourer returned, until the coming of rural trade unionism in the 1870s, to the muted protest of incendiarism, cattle maiming, sheep stealing and the slashing of hop bines. Even then there were no branches of the Kent and Sussex Labourers' union at Hernhill or Dunkirk. The 45th Regiment, the victors of Bosenden Wood, went on to account for the deaths of twenty Chartists at Newport a year later.[192]

(7) Kent Chartism

Reformers in Kent, led by the West Kent Liberals Thomas Rider, T.L. Hodges and Major Wayth of Thurnham, had been active in their pressure for parliamentary reform both before and after the Reform Act of 1832. Canterbury reformers in 1832 recommended resistance to taxes and the stoppage of supplies. Reform meetings at Chatham, Sittingbourne, Blackheath, Hythe and Tonbridge attracted large audiences. Political unions emerged at such places as Maidstone, Sevenoaks, Gravesend and Milton but Kent's experience of radical politics dating from the 1790s was not easily transformed into support for Chartism. Chartism had little impact on Kent for a variety of reasons. The Chartist artisans and craftsmen of Canterbury, Chatham, Sheerness and Tonbridge had no mass of industrial workers either in the decaying craft industries or the new factories to whom they could make their appeal. While Sussex Chartism was quickly espoused by Shoreham dockyard workers, Chatham and Sheerness dockyard workers seemingly held back. The Wealden iron industry had all but vanished by the end of the seventeenth century. The Wealden cloth industry had died in the eighteenth century. The early nineteenth century saw the demise of the Canterbury silk industry and the Maidstone linen thread industry. 'The manufacture of woollens and silks, which formerly gave employment to a number of hands in the county, have gone to those parts of the Kingdom where coal is plentiful and where inanimate power can be fully employed in every department of manufactures', wrote Samuel Bagshaw in 1847.[193]

The 1831 census listed only twelve weavers, thirteen woolcombers, two worsted makers and one stocking maker in Canterbury. 'There are no manufactures in this City', reported the Canterbury overseers in 1832, a statement echoed at Folkestone, Gravesend, Ramsgate and Chatham. Rochester, 'although situated on one of the finest rivers in Europe', did not enjoy the benefit of any

---

[192] Reay, *op. cit.*, pp. 99, 172; see also A.F.J. Brown, *Chartism in Essex and Suffolk*, Chelmsford and Ipswich 1982; Hugh Fearn, 'Chartism in Suffolk', in *Chartist Studies*, ed. Asa Briggs, London 1967; and M. Kemnitz, 'Chartism in Brighton', Sussex D.Phil. 1969.

[193] Samuel Bagshaw, *History, Gazeteer and Directory of Kent*, Sheffield 1847, vol. 1, p. 32; *MG*, 22.5.1832, 29.5.1832, 3.7.1832, 28.8.1832, 11.9.1832, 16.7.1833, 23.7.1833.

industry and its commercial prosperity was largely dependent on the naval and military establishments at Chatham. At the river port of Tonbridge the only manufacture of any consequence was Tonbridge ware. In Kentish London, Greenwich although 'a place of but few manufactures' had several iron foundries and steam boiler establishments, a ropery and a tannery, giving employment to a considerable number of men. Woolwich had its dockyard and arsenal, Lewisham an extensive silk mill and Deptford a chemical works and shipbuilding apart from the Royal Dockyard which employed between 1,000 and 1,500 men in time of war. These provided a basis for Chartism in Kentish London but elsewhere in Kent the only factory industry was papermaking. Dartford possessed several extensive paper mills. Six mills in the vicinity of Maidstone employed 800 hands, excluding Springfield Mill where William Balston had over 200 workers. There were other more isolated rural paper mills at places like Hollingbourne, Great Chart, East Malling and Ashurst. The Chartists seem to have made no attempt to win the paperworkers. There remained only the fishermen of the ports. While fishermen made excellent smugglers they played no regular part in politics or public life. Chartism, therefore, even if it was a national movement, lacked any economic base in the agricultural communities of Kent which were dominated by great landowners and the established church. Kent Chartism was too weak to get its message into the countryside where, in any event, agricultural labourers remained cowed by the Courtenay massacre until the 1870s.[194]

A Canterbury Radical Association, formed in July 1837, stood for household suffrage, triennial parliaments, vote by ballot and alteration of the Poor Law Amendment Act of 1834. Meeting fortnightly at the Carpenters Arms it adopted the Charter and National Petition in October 1838.[195] A Tonbridge Reform Association, established in September 1837, also adopted the Charter in January 1839 at a packed meeting attended by 'a large proportion of agricultural labourers and influential tradesmen'. Before adoption the Charter was explained by Henry Hetherington and Robert Hartwell of the London Working Men's Association, who were strongly supported by Mr Whiting, editor of the *Maidstone Gazette*. The Association was 'principally composed of working men although several tradesmen and some few voters had recently joined it'. The subscription was 1d. a week with which the association bought 'books and pamphlets for diffusing sound political knowledge among the members'.[196]

It was only in Kentish London that Chartism established any substantial or lasting presence. Here Chartism differed yet again. Kentish London lacked any clear tradition of Radical organisation. A third of all the localities in London were tied to a single craft or trade, but there were no such specialised groups in Kentish London on which Chartism could focus. At a local level class conflict

194 *BPP, Reports and Accounts (1834)*, XXXV–XXXVI, Answers to Urban Queries; 1831 Census; Bagshaw, *op. cit.*, vol. 1, p. 32.
195 *MG*, 11.7.1837, 16.10.1838.
196 *MG*, 4.9.1838, 22.1.1839.

was lacking. The dominant trades were not cabinet making, silk weaving, shoe-making and tailoring, trades that lay at the heart of Chartism elsewhere, since they were threatened by mechanisation and organisational change. Consequently the Radicalism of Kentish London was that of the small employer rather than the worker. It concentrated its attacks on the traditional political structure and the landed privilege that sustained it; on the Tory Party, the established church and the landed aristocracy. Its main strategy was to break those corrupt forces by the achievement of political democracy. Little attention was paid to industrial wealth for the issue was not the poor against the rich or employer against employee but that of the people against the parasitic elite. Radicalism in Kentish London was not concerned, therefore, with basic social change.[197]

A Reform Association was established at Greenwich in 1839 and Democratic Associations set up at Deptford and Old Kent Road. The first Chartist branch did not appear until May 1841 in Deptford and grew throughout that summer to become a joint Deptford and Greenwich Association. Woolwich lagged behind. It was not until July 1842 that the Chartist movement emphatically emerged with a massive open-air demonstration in Deptford Broadway. There was general inactivity in 1843 and 1844 and some revival created around the Land Company in 1845. The final stage was the new Chartist Campaign launched in October 1847, which continued until the march from Kennington Common and ended with the arrest of the national leaders.[198]

Chartism in Kentish London was an intermittent movement without a continuous leadership, lacking drive and direction when compared with the Midlands and the North. Far from hostility between the Deptford and Greenwich middle class and the Chartists there was a willingness among Chartists to work with middle class Liberals. Despite this picture of general weakness Chartism could mobilise considerable support on big occasions. Some 2,000 were at Deptford Broadway in July 1842 and twice that number on Blackheath next day to greet the Chartist orator, Peter McDouall. There were regular audiences of around 1,000 for Chartist lectures and meetings. True some Chartists were led into the Orange Tree Plot in 1848, but there were few activists for much of this time and no missionary forays into rural Kent such as were launched from Brighton and Ipswich into the rural hinterland, or by Darlington Chartists into the rural North Riding of Yorkshire.[199]

Nonetheless the movement in Kentish London was far more active than elsewhere in Kent. Not least significant was the presence of Woolwich Arsenal. On 6 May 1839 an Irish soldier asked for an organiser of the London Democratic Association to be sent to Woolwich to address the troops. A subsequent meeting

[197] Geoffrey Crossick, *An Artisan Elite in Victorian Society: Kentish London 1840–1880*, London 1978, pp. 200, 203.

[198] *Ibid.*, p. 201; Dorothy Thompson, *The Chartists*, London 1984, pp. 355–6.

[199] Crossick, *op. cit.*, pp. 202, 204, 209; Hastings, 'Chartism in South Durham and the North Riding of Yorkshire', *Durham County Local History Society Bulletin*, 22 November 1978, pp. 9–11; Kemnitz, *op. cit.*, pp. 155–6; Brown, *op. cit.*, pp. 50–3.

chaired by a sergeant with about 70 privates in attendance, declared that soldiers would not fight 'the people'. By 25 May Greenwich magistrates were seriously concerned at the regular Chartist meetings on Sundays on Blackheath. General Napier maintained that his men could obtain Chartist plans as they drank in the public houses of Woolwich. 'Thus', he said, 'I make spies of them despite themselves.' On the occasion of the first Chartist petition dockyards and churches were guarded but the authorities need not have bothered. There were only 382 signatories from the area, presumably largely from the Greenwich, Deptford and Old Kent Road Democratic Associations. Otherwise in 1838–9 things passed off quietly.[200]

In the remainder of Kent there was virtually no sign of Chartist activity at all. In February 1839 the Convention sent L. Pitkethly, the former Huddersfield weaver and J.B. O'Brien to Kent to collect signatures but nothing further was heard of them. There were 329 signatories from Wilmington, 461 from Tonbridge and 228 from Canterbury as opposed to 7,020 from Ipswich and 2,072 from Colchester. The existence of reform associations in Canterbury and Tonbridge undoubtedly helped in the collection of signatures there. Canterbury Radicals contributed £1 to the National Rent. Robert Owen terrified the authorities with a series of well-attended lectures on socialism at Rochester, Chatham and Maidstone. Otherwise little happened.[201] In February 1839 the superintendent, two inspectors and eighteen constables of Rochester's police force were authorised to help Chatham's constables in anticipation of 'riot'. The occasion was not a Chartist meeting but the public auction of goods distrained for non-payment of church rates which had produced rioting the previous year.[202] Five months later there were serious riots by Ramsgate fishermen. Houses were damaged and prisoners rescued only to be re-taken by the coastguard. 170 special constables were appointed before order was restored. The disturbance was wholly unconnected with Chartism and arose from the prohibition of fish hawking under the recent Ramsgate Improvement Act.[203] Eighty special constables, nominated for Kent and Surrey in February 1839, were appointed to deal with problems created by 'navvies' from the London and Croydon Railway. Yet more were appointed at Tonbridge in October 'from the fear of tumult . . . by reason of the number of labourers on the South Eastern Railway . . . within the . . . parish'.[204] The only Chartist excitement occurred in Canterbury when William Davis, a Chartist concerned in the Newport Rising, was arrested at the home of Revd William Davis, the Baptist minister. Both were charged with high

---

200 Thompson, *Making of the English Working Class*, p. 355; *The Democrat*, 6.5.1839; Barbara Ludlow, *Chartism in the Greenwich District*, Notes and References, Greenwich Local History Library.

201 Thompson, *Making of the English Working Class*, pp. 346, 366, 368; *NS*, 4.5.1839; *KH*, 14.2.1839; *MG*, 21.8.1838, 16.7.1839, 22.10.1839.

202 PRO HO/40/43, Special Sessions of Magistrates for Northern Division of the Lathe of Aylesford, 11.2.1839.

203 *Ibid.*, 10.7.1839.

204 *Ibid.*, 12.2.1839; HO 40/54, 10.10.1839.

205 *NS*, 30.11.1839.

treason.[205] A petition for a pardon for John Frost and the other Newport leaders secured 600 signatures in Canterbury and a further 300 'signed exclusively by females'. 'Considering the proverbial stupidity of a cathedral town', wrote the *Southern Star*, 'we think these numbers augur well for the promotion of Chartist principles.'[206] More significant perhaps was the fact that, although the *Southern Star* had agents in Darlington, Bishop Wearmouth, Birmingham, Newcastle and Merthyr Tydfil, its only Kent agent was W. Smith of Blackheath Hill.[207]

The remainder of the Kent Chartist story is a largely urban one. In Kentish London there were Chartist meetings in July 1842 but things were sufficiently quiet to enable troops to be sent from Woolwich to the disturbed districts of Yorkshire and Gosport. Conversely Chartism reached its peak in the rest of Kent in the first half of 1842. Branches of the National Charter Association had been established in Chatham and Tonbridge by late 1841. A smaller branch also met at the Ship Inn, Sittingbourne, under the leadership of J. Tright. It was probably members of the Chatham branch who were responsible in May 1841 for the circulation of the *English Chartist Circular*, which urged privates and non-commissioned officers not to act against the Chartists. An outraged James Smith of Rochester immediately sent a copy to the Home Secretary.[208]

The branches at Sittingbourne, Tonbridge and Chatham seem to have been initially weak since John Campbell, secretary of the National Charter Association, appealed in the *Northern Star* for contact from their respective sub-secretaries. 'This is but a dark and unenlightened part of the country yet . . . the People's Charter is making some little progress here', reported the Tonbridge Association on its fourth anniversary when it was again addressed by Hetherington. Led by B. Payne, 'a most staunch advocate of the rights of man', the association was composed principally of working men who still enjoyed the benefit of their own political library.[209]

Kent Chartism received some impetus from the missionary tour in 1842 of Peter McDouall. McDouall was a member of the National Charter Association executive and 'the most popular and exciting peripatetic orator in the provinces'.

> I would . . . have visited Chatham but the fog in the river prevented me from reaching that place in time . . . I visited Canterbury and lectured in the Town Hall to an audience who had never heard of the Charter except from prejudiced sources. The impression was good and an association was formed (presumably from the Canterbury Radical Association) in the priest-ridden city to whom I disposed of 50 cards.[210]

His visit seems to have had considerable short term impact.

---

206 *SS*, 9.2.1840.
207 *SS*, 1.3.1840.
208 *Kentish Mercury*, 20.8.1842; *NS*, 24.12.1841; PRO HO 45, 2410c, James Smith of Rochester to Marquess of Normanby, 6.5.1841.
209 *NS*, 11.9.1841, 24.12.1841, 5.2.1842; *MG*, 14.9.1841.
210 *NS*, 22.1.1842.

The Association has a strong and firm footing in Canterbury, reported the Northern Star . . . We have penetrated into one of the seats of State Church intolerance . . . The splendid lecture on Chartism delivered by the talented Mr McDouall is working great good . . . Our newly-formed Chartist Society is increasing weekly. We are now endeavouring to make arrangements with the Chartists in other localities in the Kent County for the engagement of a lecturer . . . to agitate the leading towns.[211]

Canterbury nominations to the General Council show that Chartism was rooted among the city's artisans . Of the thirteen persons nominated five were tailors. The remainder consisted of a shoemaker, newsagent, plumber, baker, bricklayer, turner, bookseller and carrier. George Cole, the secretary, was a painter. Of 62 petitioners who sought permission to use the Guildhall for further Chartist meetings, 42 were said to be registered electors. When permission was refused by the Mayor they hired the Concert Room instead to stage two more lectures by the London Chartist and Convention member, Edmund Stallwood. These meetings, chaired by Mr Burnfield, a working man, again attracted audiences of some six hundred and after the Petition had been read over 200 signatures were received.[212]

From Canterbury, attention shifted to Chatham, where in the same week Stallwood addressed two meetings at the Companions Tavern chaired by a local Chartist shoemaker named Clark. The Petition was again adopted and many signatures received.

All that is now required is the presence of Feargus O'Connor to make Chartism fashionable here. Then hoorah for the cause in the government borough of Chatham.[213]

At Chatham, like Canterbury, Chartist leadership was again drawn from artisans and craftsmen. Members nominated to the Council consisted of five shoemakers, a ropemaker, brushmaker and blacksmith. These came, however, from Rochester and Strood as well as Chatham. From Tonbridge, where the Chartists were receiving pamphlets and petition sheets from the Brighton Chartists, reports were much more favourable than the year before.[214]

The cause is progressing with wonderful rapidity in this part of the county. Many of the middle class are now coming out for the Charter. A meeting was held last Tuesday at the Chequers Inn for adopting the National Petition . . . This was the first public meeting held by the Chartists in which all speakers were members . . . There are many towns willing and waiting to be enrolled. The agricultural districts have been much neglected.[215]

211 *NS*, 29.1.1842.
212 *NS*, 29.1.1842, 5.2.1842.
213 *NS*, 5.2.1842.
214 *NS*, 16.4.1842.
215 *NS*, 5.2.1842.

In an effort to spread the Chartist message county-wide a delegate meeting of the Kent branches was held at Chatham on 28 February 1842. Significantly there was no delegate from Sittingbourne or Kentish London although a new branch at Sheerness was represented. The meeting decided to engage a lecturer to serve the whole county. A fund was created to meet the costs with each branch bearing its share of the expense. It was also decided to ask O'Connor to visit Kent. L. Snelling, a Tonbridge Chartist, was made secretary and treasurer of the lecturer's fund and empowered to levy the monies from branch secretaries.[216]

The Charter was accepted at Tunbridge Wells after another lecture by Snelling on 24 March. Petition sheets received from Canterbury and Chatham in May each contained 1,400 signatures according to the *Northern Star*. Chartists were still active in Sittingbourne, Sheerness, Tonbridge, Canterbury and Chatham in mid-June but with the failure of the Petition this short-lived burst of enthusiasm disappeared. In an open letter to the Chartists of Great Britain in the *Northern Star* in July, John Campbell bemoaned that Kent was 'one of the counties one hardly ever heard tell of' and that the five Kent branches were among those which had made no financial contribution to the central association in the last three months. A small subscription was sent to the National Chartist Association from a handful of working men in Dartford but there is no evidence that a branch existed there until 1848.[217]

In 1848, Kent Chartist activity was limited solely to Kentish London. A wave of Chartist meetings at the Greenwich Literary Institute, Blackheath and in the taverns of Greenwich and Deptford provoked a panic-stricken reaction on the part of the authorities. On 6 April workers in the Turners' and Painters' department of Woolwich Dockyard worked overtime making constables' staffs in preparation for the Chartist meetings at Blackheath on 9 April and Kennington Common on 10 April. A whole day was spent in the enrolment of special constables at the Arsenal, Woolwich and Deptford dockyards and the General Steam Navigation Company to protect them against the Chartists if confrontation came. Each tradesman sworn in as a special constable from Greenwich was provided with a staff costing 6d.[218]

By the time of the Chartist meeting at Kennington Common some 8,720 Chelsea and Greenwich pensioners had been enrolled to guard the bridges over the Thames and at the Mint, the Bank and the Tower. Not all were used in the Metropolis since the figure also included out-pensioners of the Chelsea and Greenwich hospitals. The Royal Artillery placed six additional permanent sentries at the roads leading to the barracks to prevent civilians 'from infusing the principles of the Chartists among the troops'. Double sentries were placed at the gates of the Arsenal.[219] When 10 April came tension ran high.

216 *NS*, 5.3.1842.
217 *NS*, 2.4.1842, 1.5.1842, 25.6.1842, 9.7.1842, 16.7.1842, 4.3.1848.
218 See Ludlow, *loc. cit.*
219 *Loc. cit.*

It is reported that there has been a riot in the borough and that the people have been fired on. A quarter past two. The Kennington number are all ordered off. The people have assembled to the amount of 150,000 on the Common. Artillery are on all the bridges. Five o'clock. All is quiet here and we hear that it has been so over the water. The reports are so various that no dependence is to be placed on them.

Thus wrote the Rev. Thomas Beeman, a nonconformist minister from Cranbrook, who next day was applying to the Magistrates to visit Charles Hubbard, a member of his congregation, arrested as a Chartist on Kennington Common.[220]

In Greenwich, the Wat Tyler Brigade of Chartists was broken up in August as a result of George Davis, a police spy and *agent provocateur* who delivered reports of their activities to Inspector Mark of R Division Police.[221] Davis's principal victim was Kent's Chartist export, William Cuffay (Figure 4). Cuffay, 'a little, middle aged, spritely and by no means ugly mulatto' with a keen sense of humour was the son of a West Indian slave who had been a labourer in the storekeeper's department at Chatham dockyard. Cuffay's sister was married to a mechanic at the dockyard. Cuffay had been apprenticed as a tailor and worked for a firm of Chatham tailors until he moved to London where he became a leader of the London Chartists. Physically deformed, like many tailors, Cuffay was a late convert to trade unionism and 46 years old before he became involved in radical politics in 1834. He was Westminster delegate to the Metropolitan Chartist Council; a member of the national executive of the National Charter Association in 1842 and, by 1848, acknowledged leader of London Chartism and a member of the National Convention. Turning to physical force he was involved in the Orange Tree conspiracy in 1848 and sentenced to 21 years' transportation to Tasmania. As a convict and ticket-of-leave man he again took up radical politics, dying in poverty in 1870 aged over eighty. His third wife, who had been a servant in the house of Richard Cobden, was sent by the Medway Guardians and the government to join him in 1853.[222]

In the rest of Kent the third Chartist phase had little impact. The East Kent Yeomanry assembled at Goodnestone Park and 'performed the usual field evolutions'. Special constables enrolled at the time were again intended to curb the depredations of navvies on the South Eastern Railway.[223] In some parts of Kent a handful of Chartists was moving belatedly in the direction of the Temperance movement and a joint meeting between the Friends of Total Abstinence and local Chartists was held at the Swan Inn, Sutton Valence in January 1848.[224] The

220 CKS, U1583 C14.
221 Crossick, *op. cit.*, p. 209; Ludlow, *loc. cit.*
222 Thompson, *Making of the English Working Class*, pp. 189–90; John Saville's entry for Cuffay in Joyce M. Bellamy and John Saville, *Dictionary of Labour Biography*, Basingstoke 1972, pp. 77–80; *Reynolds's Political Instructor*, 13.4.1850; *MG*, 18.4.1848, 16.5.1848,14.8.1849.
223 *MG*, 11.4.1848.
224 *NS*, 8.1.1848.

REYNOLDS'S
POLITICAL INSTRUCTOR.

EDITED BY GEORGE W. M. REYNOLDS,

AUTHOR OF THE FIRST AND SECOND SERIES OF "THE MYSTERIES OF LONDON," "THE MYSTERIES OF THE COURT OF LONDON," &c. &c.

No. 23.—Vol. 1.]   SATURDAY, APRIL 13, 1850.   [PRICE ONE PENNY.

MR. WILLIAM CUFFAY.

WILLIAM CUFFAY, loved by his own order, who knew him and appreciated his virtues, ridiculed and denounced by a press that knew him not, and had no sympathy with his class, and banished by a government that feared him, has achieved a celebrity that fully entitles him to a place in our Portrait Gallery. He was born in the year 1788, on board a merchant ship, homeward bound from the Island of St. Kitts, and is consequently sixty-two years old. Cradled on the vast Atlantic, he became by birth a citizen of the world, a character that, in after life, he well maintained. His father was a slave, born in the Island of St. Kitts; his grandfather was an African, dragged from his native valleys in the prime of his manhood. On arriving in England, himself and his parents became free, and during his services in the cause of Democracy, he, the stern man, has often shed genuine tears of gratitude for this boon, and declared that the sacrifice of his life and his liberty if needed, was due to the complete emancipation of that nation which had inscribed his name upon the list of free men, and this burst of generous feeling has been, as events have proved, no idle boast, nor has it fallen without producing its effect upon the hearts of his fellow toilers.

Soon after his arrival in England his father procured a berth as cook on board a man-of-war, and Cuffay spent the years of his childhood with his mother at Chatham: though of a very delicate constitution, he took great delight in all manly exercises. As he advanced toward manhood, he entered the ranks of the proletarians as a journeyman tailor, and was reckoned a superior workman. He was thrice married, but has left no issue: his only child, a boy, died in its youth. Scrupulously neat in his person, he carried a love of order and regularity even to excess in all his transactions, whether social or political, this characteristic procured him much esteem and adapted him to fill offices which men of greater talents sought for in vain; during his whole career, he occupied an active post in the ranks of his own trade and was never found wanting in any of the requisites essential to the maintenance of a character for sterling and unflinching integrity. In a letter written by one who has known him upwards of forty years, he says, "Cuffay was a good spirit in a little deformed case: I have known some thousands in the trade, and I never knew a man I would sooner confide in: and I believe this to be the feeling of thousands in the business to this day. It was always his great delight to take young men by the hand and instruct them, not only in the trade, but mentally." He disapproved of the Trades' Union movement in 1834, and was nearly the last of his society in joining the lodge; but ultimately he gave way, and struck with the general body, remaining out until the last, thereby losing a shop where he had worked for many years; since which time he has had but very partial employ. He early saw through the deception of the Reform Bill, and from 1839, when the struggle for the Charter commenced, until his banishment, dedicated his whole energies as a worker to the task of enfranchising the millions; in 1840 he was elected as a delegate from Westminster to the Metropolitan Delegate Council, an office which he ably discharged during the long and energetic existence of that body in 1842, when the Chartist Executive, with the exception of Morgan Williams, were arrested; he was elected by acclamation, together with Thomas Martin Wheeler, John George Drew, and James Knight, to supply that vacancy. In 1845 he was appointed one of the auditors of the National Land Company, which office he held until his arrest: he was a member of nearly every Convention which was called into existence during these exciting times, and fulfilled his duties with honour to himself and satisfaction to his constituents. Elected as one of the delegates for Westminster to the National Convention and Assembly of 1848, he allowed his enthusiasm to overcome his usual cool judgment, and was singled out by the press for ridicule and vituperation: he bore it unflinchingly, he even seemed to glory in it. As early as 1842 he had been especially singled out by the Times as a leader of the opposition in London to the Anti-Corn League, which facetiously denominated the Chartists as the "Black man and his Party." Entrapped by the infernal spy-system into an almost involuntary attendance at the so-called insurrectionary meetings in the autumn of 1848, he fell a victim, but he shrunk not: flight was open to him, but he refused to avail himself of it, and during his confinement, both prior and after his sentence, his spirits maintained their usual equilibrium.

Notwithstanding the Government punishment of transportation for twenty-one years, it has been intimated that on reaching his destination he will receive a ticket of leave giving him his freedom in the colony. We trust this is a fact; but whatever may be his after fate, whilst integrity in the midst of poverty, whilst honour in the midst of temptation are admired and venerated, so long will the name of William Cuffay, a scion of Affic's oppressed race, be preserved from oblivion.

Figure 4. Illustrated article on William Cuffay, published in *Reynolds' Practical Instructor*, 1850 (University of London Library, Goldsmith's Library of Economic Literature)

Maidstone portion of the Chartist petition bore 3,000 signatures but the *Maidstone Gazette* reported 'We do not believe there are 100 Chartists in the town . . . The names are undergoing strict scrutiny by some gentlemen whose names are said to be attached without their knowledge.'[225]

Undoubtedly convinced Chartists remained. Some attended the inaugural meeting of the essentially middle class 'New Reform Movement' at the County Assembly Room, Maidstone, in May 1848. One, G. Box, a Maidstone journeyman tailor, spoke bitterly of 'Tory tyranny and Whig hypocrisy'. A second, Mr Ferguson, as the leading Maidstone Chartist by 1847, told how he and three others had been prevented from reading the *Northern Star* to some Coxheath men. The group had been ejected from a Coxheath public house on the instructions of a magistrate who then lay in wait with six constables anticipating disorder.[226]

More significantly Ferguson also claimed that there were now 146 subscribers to O'Connor's Land Scheme in Maidstone and that O'Connor was expecting to purchase an estate in the neighbourhood.[227] If anything it was the Land Scheme of 1845 which appeared to capture the imaginations of surviving Kent Chartists and brought to light some pockets of Chartism which had hitherto passed unnoticed. Land Company branches were predictably established at Greenwich, New Kent Road, Woolwich, Sheerness, Tunbridge Wells, Maidstone and Rochester. Here there had been some Chartist activity. A meeting of members of the Land Company, which was supposed to be attended by O'Connor, was also advertised at Loose but failed to take place. Individual Land Company subscribers not surprisingly existed among Sittingbourne brickmakers, at Chatham, and at Strood. They were also to be found at Dartford, Gillingham and Penshurst, the rural seat of Lord De L'Isle. Roger Wells notes the presence of 61 subscribers to the Land Scheme in fifteen villages of the Maidstone district. Half of these were 'labourers' who paid their contributions through the town branch. There were certainly other rural Chartist adherents in villages like Speldhurst and Penshurst, near Tonbridge. The latter had had a branch of the National Charter Association in 1841. It is difficult to accept, however, the implication that 'there were Chartist supporters . . . in most country parishes' of southern England. Certainly their presence throughout rural Kent, on any significant scale, would be surprising.[228]

With the collapse of the Land Scheme some Kent Chartists moved towards Liberalism. G. Box was secretary of the Maidstone Working Men's Reform Association from 1848–56. When this became the Liberal organisation in Maidstone he continued as secretary. George Pattison of Chatham, one time

---

225 *MG*, 8.4.1848.
226 *MG*, 23.5.1848.
227 *Loc. cit.*
228 Thompson, *Making of the English Working Class*, pp. 345–7, 355–7, 362–6; *MG*, 23.5.1848; *MJ*, 12.9.1848; Roger Wells, 'Southern Chartism', in *Crime, Protest and Popular Politics in Southern England 1740–1850*, ed. John Rule and Roger Wells, London, pp. 146–7, 149, 151.

shoemaker and secretary to the Chatham Chartist Association, became paid deputy secretary to the Chatham Liberal Association in 1859. George Floyd, the Deptford Chartist baker, also took a leading role in the Advanced Liberal Association.[229] Apart from some fleeting contact in 1840 and 1842 with the Brighton Chartists, 'the leaders of agitation in the South', Kent Chartism remained isolated and ineffective. Its very weakness encouraged further neglect by the Convention which, in any event, directed its attention and limited resources towards the more firmly established, urban centres of the movement.[230]

In 1842 Edmund Stallwood had observed opimistically that 'could the Chartists raise sufficient funds they might effect great good in Kent. They had good localities at Greenwich, Chatham and Canterbury and he believed Tonbridge. . . .' Six years later when membership of the 'National Assembly' was under consideration, only 'Maidstone' and 'Brighton' were considered worthy of representation in Kent.[231]

[229] Crossick, op. cit., p. 203; CN, 2.7.1859, 4.6.1892; I am indebted to Bruce Aubry for this information.
[230] NS, 11.7.1840, 5.2.1842.
[231] NS, 23.4.1842, 18.4.1848.

5

Conservative and Liberal: National Politics in Kent from the Late 1820s to 1914

BRIAN ATKINSON

> I often think it's comical
> How nature always does contrive
> That every boy and every gal,
> That's born into this world alive,
> Is either a little Liberal
> Or else a little Conservative.

When W.S. Gilbert wrote these words for *Iolanthe*, first performed in 1882, it was a fair delineation of the political landscape of Britain, though, of course, the gals, even when grown up, were not allowed to vote in parliamentary elections until 1918. It was also true of Kent, though in reverse order, Conservative first.

The Conservatives had evolved from the Tory party, a process associated with Sir Robert Peel's response to the new situation created by the 1832 Reform Act. The Liberal party's formation is traditionally ascribed to a meeting in London in 1859 of Whigs, Liberals, Radicals and ex-conservative followers of the then dead Peel led by W.E. Gladstone. However such precision is illusory as the parties evolved from their predecessors and continued to evolve in ideology and practice in response to changes in society and the political system itself. Whig and Tory continued to play prominent roles through to the end of the nineteenth century and indeed beyond. Similarly the term liberal was in widespread use long before 1859.

(1) Whig, Liberal and the Struggle for Parliamentary Reform

Liberal in the political sense was a term first used on the Continent so given Kent's proximity thereto it is not surprising to see it present here long before 1859. The Canterbury-based Whig *Kent Herald* referred to 'the Liberals' in 1826[1] and in the election of that year welcomed the return of Charles Poulett

---

[1] *KH*, 20 April 1826.

Thompson 'the *Liberal Candidate*' at Dover.[2] The term was given wider currency in 1828 in the controversy over granting civil rights to Roman Catholics, Catholic Emancipation. The *Herald*'s account of the Kent County meeting of freeholders in October was freely sprinkled with liberals, Liberals, even 'the Liberal Party' but its tolerant condemnation of 'the refusal of political rights to a large class of your countrymen – for are not the Irish as well as the English Catholics your countrymen', while well grounded in the Whig tradition of Civil and Religious Liberty, failed to carry the majority of the 30,000 reported to be present.[3]

The passing of Catholic Emancipation in 1829 by the Tory government of the Duke of Wellington and Peel who had previously opposed it was highly unpopular and had immense consequences, not least in Kent. The *Herald* was quick to point the way forward: with the resolution of the Catholic issue, parliamentary reform now came to the fore. 'We hope the attention of the Liberals . . . will once more be directed to this all important subject.'[4]

It was not only Liberals who drew this conclusion. The prominent Kentish nobleman, the irascible Earl of Winchilsea, argued that the passing of Catholic Emancipation against the wishes of the people showed that government had been corrupted and that the House of Commons needed reform. Winchilsea and his fellow Ultra-Tories played a significant part in bringing down Wellington's government in November 1830. Winchilsea spoke against the Duke in the Lords on 4 November and Sir Edward Knatchbull, Bt, one of the two county MPs for Kent, voted in the majority against the government on 15 November, thus precipitating its downfall. It was replaced by a Whig administration led by Earl Grey, committed to reform.

There had been signs of pro-reform sentiment in Kent earlier in 1830. A county meeting on 12 March was generally held to have voted in favour but it was a confused affair and disappointed the *Herald*. Instead of a united Reforming Party, containing 'every grade of Whig, Radicals and Liberals' [an interesting anticipation of the composition of the future Liberal Party], 'the bond of union which in Kent has so long held tolerably well together the whole force of the Old Opposition or Blue Party [i.e. Whigs] was dissolved'. The Whig aristocracy and gentry seemed to be colluding with the Tories against 'the Liberals – the thorough-paced Reformers – composed chiefly of the middle and industrious classes'. However the *Herald* could console itself with the fact that Whigs, Liberals and Tories were all in favour of reform. Winchilsea, who had headed the list of notables calling the meeting, declared: 'I am a Reformer, but not a visionary one. I wish the people to have a just weight in the Commons House of Parliament.' He was rewarded with 'loud cheering'.[5]

In the 1830 general election Thompson held his seat at Dover (he was to

2   *KH*, 22 June 1826.
3   *KH*, 23 and 30 October 1828.
4   *KH*, 4 June 1829.
5   *KH*, 4 and 18 March 1830.

become Vice-President of the Board of Trade in Grey's government) and, as a further sign of the times, Canterbury returned two reformers. They had impeccable aristocratic credentials: the Hon. R. Watson's brother was Lord Sondes, Viscount Fordwich was the eldest son of Earl Cowper. The *Herald* lovingly described a sumptuous banquet given by Fordwich in London to Canterbury freemen resident there, at which 'wines of the best description' were consumed.[6]

A brief discussion of the unreformed political system in Kent is now appropriate. Four boroughs (Canterbury, Maidstone, Queenborough and Rochester) and four Cinque Ports (Dover, Hythe, New Romney and Sandwich) each returned two MPs. All except New Romney were freemen constituencies, i.e. the freemen constituted the electorate. Freemen did not have to be resident; indeed the London-based freemen of Kentish constituencies seem to have acted as ginger groups, benefiting from their position at the centre of political life. The *History of Parliament* considered Canterbury and Dover to be large constituencies by the standards of the time and indeed in 1830 Watson polled 1,334 votes, and Fordwich 1,101 to the defeated Tory's 731, while Thompson at Dover polled almost 1,000. Of the Canterbury voters, 354 resided in London.[7]

The most prestigious MPs from Kent were the two Knights of the Shire, elected by the forty shilling freeholders. Since these were relatively numerous, contested elections could be ruinously expensive and were therefore avoided. By convention, one Whig and one Tory were returned unopposed, one from East Kent, one from West. Thus in 1830 Knatchbull represented the Tories as he had since 1819 when he succeeded his father in the seat, Thomas Law Hodges the Whigs.

The outbreak of agricultural disturbances known as the Swing Riots (see chapter 4), which began near Canterbury in October 1830, gave Kent politicians cause for alarm. The rioters were motivated by distress, not politics, but those in authority worried that the farmers and lesser gentry were not rallying to the support of law and order. Winchilsea's speech on 4 November, mentioned above, was in support of his bill to provide for the maintenance of agricultural labourers. He argued that there was a need to redress popular grievances and relieve distress otherwise there would be no security for property. He went on to support Grey's views on moderate reform and attacked Wellington's intransigence.[8] Speaking a week later in the Commons in support of a petition from Tenterden 'recently the scene of very unpleasant transactions' (i.e. disturbances), Hodges claimed 'if a very great retrenchment were not made and very shortly the tranquility of England would be put to hazard'.[9] This was the classic Whig-Liberal position. Distress was the result of high taxation which meant farmers and employers could not pay adequate wages. Taxation was high

6   *KH*, 22 July 1830.
7   *KH*, 12 August 1830; *The History of Parliament: The House of Commons 1790–1820*, ed. R.G. Thorne, vol. 1, London 1986, pp. 359–60.
8   *Hansard's Parliamentary Debates*, 3rd ser., vol. 1, cols 195–9.
9   *Ibid.*, col. 383.

because of the need to support a bloated, antiquated establishment. Political reform of this establishment was necessary to allow for retrenchment, the reduction of public expenditure (and for the more extreme, the abolition of tithes) to enable taxes to be cut and the economy to prosper.

The introduction of the Grey government's Reform Bill on 1 March 1831 triggered over a year of bitter political strife. Throughout Kent meetings were held to petition for the bill including a county meeting at Maidstone on 24 March at which Winchilsea spoke warmly of Grey and expressed his support for the measure 'in the principles of which he fully concurred'.[10] The petition was approved unanimously according to Winchilsea when he presented it to the Lords but the attendance, at 4,000 in poor weather, compared unfavourably with that at the Catholic Emancipation meeting in 1828. Two days earlier the Commons had voted to approve the second reading of the bill by 302 to 301: among the majority were ten Kent MPs including Hodges, Watson, Fordwich and Thompson; Knatchbull was paired against. The defeat of the bill in Committee led Grey to call an election. In Kent as elsewhere the popular constituencies came out overwhelmingly in favour of reform. Hodges was joined by Thomas Rider as representatives of the cause, Knatchbull, after an attempt to portray himself as a reformer, though a moderate one, withdrawing without a contest. According to his Committee, the canvass suggested that he could not be returned against 'the torrent of public opinion which calls for "*the Bill, the whole Bill and nothing but the Bill*" '.[11]

At Canterbury, Watson and Fordwich were returned unopposed as were the reformers at Rochester. The Tory *Kentish Gazette* consoled itself by noting the spiritless nature of the chairing of the MPs at the latter return, which it attributed to the fact that 'the Liberals, anxious to be foremost in the ranks of Reform, had determined to discontinue the usual allowance of "heavy wet" ' to the disappointment of the freemen 'being naturally thirsty souls'.[12] Elsewhere there were contests but only at Queenborough and New Romney, which were scheduled to be disfranchised, were anti-reformers successful. The *Herald* waxed lyrical: 'The Tory power is broken down and trampled in the dust. The "*hereditary borough*" of the Knatchbulls' is emancipated and the emblem of Liberty, the old *Blue Banner of Reform* [note the use of the old terminology] floats victoriously from one end of the county to the other.'[13]

Reform was now secure in the Commons but that did not prevent the Lords rejecting the second bill in October 1831, Winchilsea having now changed sides deciding the measure was too extreme. While Kent did not experience the violent disturbances which occurred elsewhere, notably at Bristol, local committees were set up to support the bill, co-ordinated by a central committee in Maidstone, meetings were held and the Archbishop of Canterbury, who had

---

[10] *KH*, 31 March 1831.
[11] *KG*, 6 May 1831.
[12] *KG*, 3 May 1831.
[13] *KH*, 12 May 1831.

Plate 1. Sir Edward Dering, first Baronet (CKS, U1769 F7/2).

To the right Hono[ble] the [Knights] & others
of the Comittee for sequestracons /

The humble Petition of the Lady Dering /

Sheweth /

That notw[th]standing y[e] petitioner hath to her great
damage been formerly thrice distressed by souldiers, nevertheless
vpon the 22[th] of this instant May there came to number
of troopers [crossed out] and in a violent maner
entred y[e] petition[er] ground, driveing away all her Cattle
both horses, Bullocks and Sheepe, without shewing any one
by whose authority they did it, and in like maner entred
her house and tooke an Inventory of all her goods, and
with many threatning speeches charged her y[t] no part
thereof should be wanting when they came to seize
them, w[ch] should bee soddainely; and withall told her
that if shee had not been then in the house they
would have kept her out, and also then charged her
tenants vpon theire perills, not to pay her any Rents

Now forasmuch as y[e] petitioner doth not beleive
that it is the pleasure of the Parliam[t] y[t] any such
extreamitie should be vsed towards yo[r] pet[t] it tending
to the ruyne of her [selfe] and her children, without any
personall fault by her or them comitted in word
or action.

Yo[r] petitioner therefore in all humilitie be-
seecheth that yo[r] hono[r] will please to take into
yo[r] serious consideracon her miserable
condition, and for her releife and those that
depend vpon her, to give some present order
(they being [stripd] of all) for theire maintaynance
whereof otherwise must of necessitie [faile]

And yo[r] petitioner (as in duty
bound) shall pray. &c

Originall Gentes 29° Maij 1643 /

Plate 2. Petition of Lady Dering, 1643 (CKS, U1350 O13).

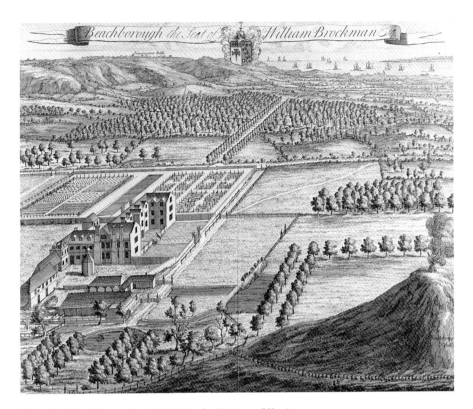

Plate 3a. Beachborough, c.1720 (Harris, *History of Kent*).

Plate 3b. Beachborough, c.1780 (Hasted, *History of Kent*).

Plate 4. Sir Edward Knatchbull, by Michael Dahl (from the Brabourne family portraits at County Hall, Maidstone).

Plate 5a. Mereworth Castle, built 1723 (CKS).

Plate 5b. Rick burning in Kent (*Radio Times* Hulton Picture Library).

Plate 6. Sandwich, Fish Market and St Peter's Church, c.1790 (Boys, *History of Sandwich*).

Plate 7a. Sir William Courtenay (Dawes Collection).

Plate 7b. The Battle of Bosenden Wood (National Army Museum).

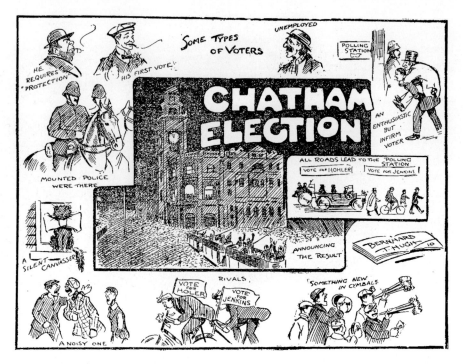

Plate 8a. Chatham election, 1910 (*CN*).

Plate 8b. The first County Council, 1889 (CKS, CC24/1).

voted against the bill in the Lords, was given a rough reception when he visited the city. Eventually after much tension especially in May 1832 when, after the third bill was defeated in the Lords, Grey resigned and Wellington tried but failed to form a Tory ministry, the bill was carried. Typically, when Grey successfully moved the third reading in the Lords on 4 June it was Winchilsea who spoke first against, in apocalyptic terms, claiming to be witnessing the downfall of his country, the closure of the Lords, the end of the Monarchy, revolution no less. In a final irony he praised the old Constitution for producing among other boons 'an illustrious Duke', namely the same Wellington he had so bitterly denounced less than two years earlier to help set in train the whole reform process.[14] The wheel had come full circle and in that sense a revolution had taken place, but in no other.

(2) The Reformed System and the Evolution of the Conservative and Liberal Parties

The new system bore marked similarities to the old. The franchise was extended: in the counties the forty shilling freeholders were joined by a number of new qualifications of which the most important were the £10 copyholders, £50 long leaseholders and £50 tenants-at-will. The more sweeping changes occurred in the boroughs where a uniform franchise, the £10 householder (occupant of a building worth £10 annual value) was introduced. Resident freemen retained the vote but those living more than seven miles from the constituency were disfranchised. This, along with the reduction of polling days to a maximum of two from the preceding fifteen and the creation of more polling stations to minimise the amount of travelling, was designed to cut the expense of elections, for voters had expected to travel and be fed and watered (or, more probably, 'beered') at the candidates' expense.[15] Another innovation was that electors had to be registered. But there were also significant continuities. Voting remained public for all to see and thus influence, both legitimate and illegitimate (i.e. deference to the opinions of one's betters or intimidation by them) continued to be exercised. Many freemen used to being indulged remained voters.

Within Kent changes were relatively modest. The county was divided into East and West, each returning two MPs. Queenborough and New Romney were disfranchised. Hythe, despite being extended to include Sandgate and Folkestone, lost one of its two seats. Sandwich was extended to include Deal and Walmer and, like Canterbury, Dover, Maidstone and Rochester, remained a double-member borough. Chatham was given one MP. Kent under the new system thus returned 16 MPs (the newly-created double-member constituency of Greenwich is best regarded as part of London) as against 18 before. In the

14 *Hansard's Parliamentary Debates*, 3rd ser., vol. 13, col. 349.
15 After 1835 borough elections were confined to one day.

boroughs freemen remained a significant proportion of the electorate, electorates which, unlike the county level, were little greater than before (See Table 2). The largest borough electorate in 1832, Dover, was smaller than Canterbury had been pre-1832; the loss of non-resident freemen was not matched by the new £10 householders.

Table 2a

Kent Electorates, 1832

East Kent	7,026	West Kent	6,678
Dover	1,651	Chatham	677 (single member)
Canterbury	1,511	Hythe	469 (single member)
Maidstone	1,108		
Rochester	973		
Sandwich	916		

a   The information in this table is derived from F.W.S. Craig, *British Parliamentary Election Results, 1832–1885*, Aldershot 1989.

Not surprisingly the Reformers did well at the first general election under the new system in December 1832, in Kent and nationally. All Kent seats were contested. In West Kent Hodges and Rider were re-elected; in East Kent Knatchbull reappeared under a new guise. In May 1832 he addressed a meeting of East Kent 'Conservatives' in Canterbury and in June he accepted a requisition to stand for election. He portrayed himself, in a premonition of Peel's terminology in his Tamworth Manifesto two years later, as 'an advocate for the removal of any existing abuse and a willing supporter of any improvement that may be suggested', adding:

> I desire the maintenance of the Constitution in its integrity and purity – I look to safety to persons and security to property; and I desire by every means in my power to promote the happiness of all classes of the people. Need I add the expression of my anxiety for the prosperity of the Agricultural interest? The welfare of the farmer I have long watched with anxious care – I will not desert him in his hour of difficulty.[16]

The Constitution – Crown, Lords, Commons, Protestant Church of England – and Land struck powerful Tory chords in Kent. But like Peel later, Knatchbull was seeking to appeal to a wider, *conservative* constituency. The *Gazette* had been using this word sparingly during 1831: on 29 April it referred to 'the friends of order and a conservative constitution' and on 3 January 1832, appearing with an enlarged format and in a new type, it avowed its principles in one word 'Conservative'. The 6 November edition enlarged upon the theme:

[16] *KG*, 5 June 1832.

'with the view of promoting the best interests of the country the propriety of abandoning the term *Tory* has been pressed upon our attention . . . let the broad standard of Conservatism be raised'. The point was hammered home on the hustings by Sir Edward Dering when he seconded Knatchbull's nomination, referring to him coming forward on 'Constitutional and Conservative principles'.[17]

Knatchbull was returned in second place behind J.P. Plumptre who the *Herald* chose to regard as a Liberal despite the vagueness of his address and his previous opposition to Catholic Emancipation. Plumptre had been careful to keep his distance from the defeated Reform candidate but in his speech of acceptance he claimed 'my principles are contained in two words – liberal but anti-revolutionary' (presumably his arithmetic had been undermined by the excitement of the moment). He also claimed that almost the whole of the gentry and clergy had been against him and that he had won because of the middling and poorer classes. He was thought to have had the support of the Dissenters. Knatchbull, clearly riled at coming second, spoke bitterly of Plumptre 'who by accident has been placed before me on the poll' calling him 'an enemy of mine'.[18] Plumptre responded in conciliatory vein and the healing passage of time and the fluidity of party politics were illustrated in 1835 when he was returned alongside Knatchbull as a Conservative.

To return to 1832, in the boroughs the Liberals swept the board save at Dover, where Thompson was successful (he in fact chose to sit for Manchester) but his Liberal partner was defeated by the Conservative who had stood down in 1831, and at Rochester where the Conservative captured the second seat. Kent thus returned 13 Liberals to three Conservatives.

Table 3 gives the Kent results in general elections before the Second Reform Act of 1867: the party designations are as given in Craig but should not be treated too rigidly, Liberal often meant Whig, Conservative Tory. It is striking that only twice, in 1841 and 1852, did Kent return a Conservative majority. There was a recovery to parity in 1835, perhaps responding to Peel's Tamworth Manifesto where he added to the traditional Tory defence of established institutions a commitment to 'the maintenance of order and good government' and a promise of 'a careful review of institutions, both civil and ecclesiastical . . . the correction of proved abuses and the redress of real grievances'.[19] Peel was portraying Conservatism as a middle way between Reaction and Radicalism in a bid to appeal to moderate Whigs and Liberals in much the same way as Knatchbull and the *Gazette* had done in 1832. He also wished to reintegrate the Ultra-Tories into the party and so included in his minority administration, formed after William IV dismissed the Whigs in 1834, Sir Edward Knatchbull, described by Gash as 'one of the most respected and respectable of the independent county members, high-minded, mediocre, diffident and dull . . .

17 *KG*, 21 December 1832.
18 *KG*, 25 December 1832.
19 N. Gash, *Sir Robert Peel*, London 1972, p. 96.

Table 3a

Kent General Election Results, 1835–65

	County		Borough		Total	
	Lib.	Con.	Lib.	Con.	Lib.	Con.
1835	1	3	7	5	8	8
1837	1	3	8	4	9	7
1841	0	4	4	8	4	12
1847	1	3	8	4	9	7
1852	1	3	3	9	4	12b
1857	3	1	8	4	11	5
1859	0	4	8	4	8	8
1865	1	3	8	4	9	7

a   The information in this table is derived from F.W.S. Craig, *British Parliamentary Election Results, 1832–1885*, Aldershot 1989.

b   Four of the 12 were unseated on petition.

eminently sensible and moderate'.[20] He became Paymaster-General. He did not hold office long. Despite gains in 1835 the Conservatives remained in a minority in the Commons and after an uneasy compromise between Whig, Liberal, Radical and Irish MPs Peel's government fell.

In 1837 the most interesting Kent result was at Maidstone where Wyndham Lewis who won a seat for the Conservatives in 1835 was joined at Westminster by a second Conservative, a rather raffish novelist of Jewish descent, one Benjamin Disraeli. Maidstone thus gave the future Conservative prime minister his parliamentary start in life. He also acquired his colleague's wealthy widow after Lewis's death in 1838, a marriage of convenience that turned into a love-match: 'a perfect wife' he called her in dedicating to her his novel *Sybil*.[21]

Maidstone had been highly politicised since the mid-eighteenth century, a feature intensified as the reform crisis encouraged the formation of party organisations, the Whig/Liberal Loyal True Blue Club and Maidstone Political Union competing with the Conservative Committee and the Constitution Club. Not that principle necessarily prevailed. John Phillips suggests that Conservative success in 1835 was attributable to the plentiful distribution of Lewis's sovereigns, the colour to which the voters responded being 'less Tory purple than Tory gold'.[22] In contrast two years later Disraeli pointed to the fact that the 'strength and property of the Boro' are on our side and opposition to the Poor

---

[20] *Ibid.*, p. 72.

[21] Quoted in R. Blake, *Disraeli*, London 1969, p. 161.

[22] John A. Phillips, *The Great Reform Bill in the Boroughs: English Electoral Behaviour 1818–1841*, Oxford 1992, p. 115.

Law makes us popular with the multitude'.[23] Even so, the Whigs (as in 1841) retained a loyal core of (unbribed) support, a third of the electorate plumping for their sole candidate.

In 1841, after years of increasingly ineffectual Whig government, the country returned a Conservative majority to the Commons. Kent experienced the full force of this tidal wave. Knatchbull and Plumptre were returned unopposed as were Sir E. Filmer, Bt, and Viscount Marsham in West Kent where Hodges did not even attempt to defend his seat. In the boroughs the Conservatives won both seats at Canterbury, Maidstone (though Disraeli migrated to Shrewsbury unable to afford the expense of satisfying what Blake calls 'the cupidity of the electors of Maidstone'[24]) and Rochester, and Dover and Sandwich returned one for each party. The Liberals retained Hythe (indeed Hythe returned a Liberal at every election from 1832 to 1880, on seven occasions unopposed) and Chatham where in a remarkably aristocratic contest the Hon. G.S. Byng (later Viscount Enfield) defeated Lord Dufferin and Claneboye (two lordships, only one candidate).

Peel's government took office at a time of much hardship and social discontent. Knatchbull resumed his old post but became increasingly disenchanted. He had never been really enthusiastic – when first appointed he told Peel not to expect too much of him because of inexperience and poor health: 'therefore I should go where I should have least labour and least work'.[25] He may have been upset at not getting promotion in 1841 but, while he accepted modification of the sliding scale of tariffs under which the Corn Laws operated, he was clearly disturbed that Peel's drift towards free trade would endanger the agricultural interest which he felt needed Protection. In July 1843 he lamented: 'Peel is not sufficiently bold for the times in which we live', a comment which would have seemed strange three years later, and the following month Knatchbull referred to his own exhaustion and desire to retire.[26]

Sir Edward was also uncomfortable with some of the official functions he was obliged to attend such as the christening of the Prince of Wales in January 1842. 'The banquet in St George's Hall was splendid – almost sinfully so – my heart misgave and sank within me when I drew the contrast between the guests present and the thousands absent who are starving. Why should such things be?'[27] In February 1845 he retired from both Cabinet and Commons (he was succeeded in the latter by William Deedes, unopposed). Earlier in the month his favourite child, Fanny, had died of consumption. It broke him. In his last diary entry, over 18 months later, he wrote: 'I feel as if my life was held by a thread.' As the family biographer touchingly put it: 'for three more years he lived on. It was not till 24 May 1849 that the thread broke.'[28]

23 Quoted *ibid.*, p. 118.
24 Blake, *op. cit.*, p. 163.
25 H. Knatchbull-Hugessen, *Kentish Family*, London 1960, p. 216.
26 *Ibid.*, esp. pp. 216, 251.
27 *Ibid.*, p. 239.
28 *Ibid.*, pp. 253–9.

By then the Conservative party was also broken. Stimulated by the Irish famine of 1845 Peel boldly resolved to repeal the Corn Laws. The landed interest within his own party was outraged, fearing the ruin of English agriculture. The atmosphere was embittered by venomous attacks on Peel by the erstwhile member for Maidstone, Disraeli. Repeal was carried since most of the opposition supported the government but in the vote on the third reading of the bill on 15 May 1846, of Kent's twelve Conservative MPs, eight, including all four Knights of the Shire and both MPs for the county town, voted against their government, the other four joining the four Liberals in the yes lobby. Clearly Peel was doomed and he resigned after losing a key vote on an Irish Coercion Bill. Though on that vote most Kent Conservatives supported the government, one, Bradshaw of Canterbury, voted against and Plumptre absented himself.

At the next election in 1847, of the eight Conservatives who had opposed Repeal, four, in Maidstone and East Kent were returned unopposed, clear recognition of the backing they enjoyed, but a seat was lost in West Kent to a returning T.L. Hodges whose son joined a returning R.Bernal in defeating the retiring members in Rochester (one pro-, one anti-Peel). Five of the Protectionist Conservatives were thus returned (the other, Bradshaw, died before the election), a much better result than that achieved by the Peelite four, only one of whom was successful. Two did not stand: Reid at Dover, MP since 1832, was certainly forced out, Lindsay at Sandwich probably so.[29]

The exception was at Canterbury where the Hon. George Smythe won a bitter contest. Smythe, 'our young and distinguished member', as the *Kentish Gazette* described him,[30] had joined the government in January 1846 as Under Secretary of State for Foreign Affairs. The situation in Canterbury was already heated before the general election. On Bradshaw's death the Liberals brought forward a former member for the city, Lord Alfred Conyngham, the Conservatives Henry Plumptre Gipps. Gipps, however, withdrew, alleging pressure exercised against his supporters by 'wealthy neighbouring residents' to which the *Gazette* added, surprisingly, the application of 'the screw' by the Archdeacon of Canterbury on behalf of the Dean and Chapter. The latter denied this and, in a revealing illustration of the customary link between the Church and Conservatism, issued a statement that they 'were fully prepared, with the exception of Archdeacon Croft, to have recorded their votes in favour of the Conservative candidate'.[31]

At the general election Smythe made a lengthy defence of his position arguing that true Toryism was based on a regard for progress and the interests of the people, both of these being represented by free trade. 'In the year 1846 he had the satisfaction of joining a government which was then in its dying moments. It lived but to complete its great measure of free trade.' He concluded by rejoicing that he had opposed Peel's administration 'when it was stagnating beneath the slime of aristocratic prohibition', rejoicing even more that he had

[29] See *KG*, 1 June and 20 July 1847.
[30] *KG*, 13 January 1846.
[31] *KG*, 16 and 23 March 1847.

joined it when it enabled 'the people of England to feel the invigorating influence of Liberal beneficence but not less ancient Tory policy'.[32]

Conyngham and Smythe were returned. The losing Conservatives hinted at dark reasons for their defeat: many who had promised their votes, failed to deliver 'and in numerous instances voted for our opponents – wherefore it is not for us to say'. The *Gazette* was typically gracious in defeat: 'False Conservative and hypocritical Whig alike came out in their true colours.'[33] The strength of party commitment was remarkable. Of the 1,456 who voted 759 polled for 'false Conservative and hypocritical Whig', 625 for the Conservatives. A mere fifteen split between Smythe and a Conservative, four fewer than split Conservative-Liberal.[34]

The political situation for the next twenty years was confused. With two Conservative parties, personality conflicts within the Whigs plus the presence in the Commons of Radical and Irish MPs, party labels did not count for much. The death of Peel in 1850 could have led to Conservative reunion but old bitterness prevailed. The situation was clarified in 1859 with the formation of the Liberal Party, the party of Peace, Retrenchment and Reform, though with Palmerston as prime minister Peace abroad was not always secure and political Reform at home was out of the question, though Gladstone at the Exchequer did useful work continuing the drive towards free trade. On Palmerston's death in 1865, however, parliamentary reform once more became an issue. In a confusing series of manoeuvres the Liberals failed to carry their Reform Bill because of internal divisions and Conservative opposition, only to see a minority Conservative government carry a reform measure of their own.

The Reform Act of 1867 extended the borough franchise to all householders who had been resident for a year, had paid their rates and were on the register, and the county franchise was extended to those occupying land worth £12 a year. Compared to the impact on some industrial towns in the Midlands and the North – the electorate in Leeds, for example, more than quintupled – that on Kentish boroughs was modest, as Table 4 shows. The greater effect was on the county as Kent was one of the ten shires to be given an additional two seats, Mid Kent being carved out of West. No Kent borough lost members and Gravesend was one of nine new constituencies created, returning one MP. Anomalies abounded: the 30,658 county electors in 1868 returned six MPs, the 23, 803 borough voters thirteen. The largest borough electorate, Chatham, returned one MP, Sandwich, with fewer than half Chatham's voters, two.

The emergence of Gladstone as leader of the Liberals and Disraeli as leader of the Conservatives clarified party divisions as did the need to appeal to a wider electorate, a function largely performed as it had been for generations by a highly partizan press. The 1868 election resulted in a Liberal victory as Gladstone reunited his party around a promise to disestablish the Anglican Church in

---

[32] *KG*, 13 July 1847.
[33] *KG*, 3 August 1847. The reference to corruption was justified, as will be seen below.
[34] *Pollbook*, 1847.

Table 4a

Impact of the 1867 Reform Act on Kent Electorates

Constituency	Size of Electorate	
	1865	1868
East Kent	8,250	13,107
Mid Kent		8,723
West Kent	9,811	8,828
Total county	**18,061**	**30,658**
Canterbury	1,603	3,001
Chatham	2,104	4,518
Dover	2,318	3,392
Gravesend		2,722
Hythe	1,291	2,275
Maidstone	1,817	3,420
Rochester	1,458	2,569
Sandwich	1,054	1,906
Total borough	**11,645**	**23,803**

a   Derived from Craig, *British Parliamentary Election Results*, Aldershot 1989.

Ireland which was popular with the Nonconformists, a vitally important element among the Liberal rank-and-file, who saw it as an attack on the privileged Established Church with which they were in competition and as an act of justice since the wealth of the Church of Ireland of the minority contrasted vividly with the poverty of the Roman Catholic Church of the vast majority. The Liberal ministry of 1868 to 1874 was a great reforming one. An Irish Land Act sought to improve the lot of the tenant farmers and important measures concerning the civil service, army, universities and elementary education attacked privilege in the interests of promoting efficiency and equality of opportunity. The Ballot Act introduced secret voting to free the elector from pressure from employer or land-lord. The Licensing Act sought to reduce drunkenness and poverty, which was held by many Nonconformist temperance reformers to result from drink, by modestly restricting public house opening hours. Abroad peace was promoted by using negotiation and arbitration to avoid conflict.

The problem with these reforms was that they alienated support. Whigs and moderate Liberals feared they would lead to more radical measures while Nonconformists felt that the 1870 Education Act was too conciliatory to the Anglican Church and the Licensing Act too timid. The drinking classes took a different view and the drink interest placed itself firmly in the Conservative camp. The comment attributed to Gladstone on his election defeat in 1874 is well known: 'we were swept away in a torrent of gin and beer'. Some may think there were worse ways to go.

Disraeli seized his opportunity. Conservative leader since 1868, he appointed John Gorst to improve party organisation and in 1872 made two keynote speeches at Manchester and the Crystal Palace, portraying the Conservatives as the party of the nation and empire. Essentially he was following Peel's strategy of forty years previously, waiting for his opponents to alienate support, presenting his party as moderate and safe. He did not, however, eschew reform. To quote from the Crystal Palace speech of 24 June 1872:

> I have referred to what I look upon as the first object of the Tory party – namely to maintain the institutions of the country . . . the second is . . . to uphold the Empire of England . . . Gentlemen, another great object of the Tory party, and one not inferior to the maintenance of the Empire, or the upholding of our institutions, is the elevation of the condition of the people.[35]

Thus was born 'one-nation Conservatism'. That it was a potent brew for Kentish electors is illustrated by Table 5. What is notable is not the Conservative gains in 1874 but the fact that these were not reversed in 1880 when the Liberals, on the back of Gladstone's Midlothian campaign, regained power nationally. Indeed, in Kent the Conservatives made further gains in 1880, long before Gladstone split his party over Irish Home Rule.

Table 5a

Kent General Election Results, 1868–80

	County		Borough		Total	
	Lib.	Con.	Lib.	Con.	Lib.	Con.
1868	0	6	11	2b	11	8
1874	0	6	7	6	7	12
1880	0	6	5	8	5	14

a   Derived from Craig, *British Parliamentary Election Results*, Aldershot 1989.
b   One of these was in fact Butler-Johnstone at Canterbury who had alienated Conservative support by voting to disestablish the Irish Church, stood as an Independent and was elected on Liberal votes: *Pollbook*, 1868.

Conservative domination was consolidated under a fundamentally changed political system. The 1880 election is reckoned to have been the most corrupt of the century as, fortified by the secrecy of the polling booth, those who were so inclined could receive favours not just from one side but from both. The remedy was the Corrupt Practices Act of 1883 which strictly limited the amount of money a candidate could spend and made him responsible for the actions of his agents. Even more important were the Reform and Redistribution of Seats Acts

---

[35]   Quoted in P. Adelman, *Gladstone, Disraeli and Later Victorian Politics*, London 1970, p. 89.

of 1884–5. The former, passed under pressure from the Radicals, extended the household franchise to the counties. The latter, passed under pressure from the Conservative leader, the Marquis of Salisbury, who was able to use Conservative dominance of the Lords as an important bargaining counter, largely replaced the old double-member constituencies with single-member seats. As Salisbury shrewdly calculated, this would enable Conservatives in the select, residential west ends of the cities to be represented instead of being swamped by the populous areas of the industrial east and also force the Liberals, who covered a broader ideological spectrum than their rivals, to choose either a moderate or a radical candidate instead of running both in double-harness, thus suffering loss of support from either left or right.

(3) Conservative Dominance

Gladstone's espousal of Home Rule for Ireland in 1885 divided his party, a significant minority placing preservation of the Union before Liberal unity. The following twenty years saw the Conservatives in government for all but a brief interlude in 1892–5 as the majority of Englishmen took the view that Irish Home Rule would lead to the break-up, not just of the Empire, but of the United Kingdom itself, to say nothing of handing over the Protestant minority in Ireland to the tender mercies of the Catholics: Home Rule means Rome Rule was a powerful slogan. However, in 1906, with Home Rule not an issue, a Conservative party divided over the reintroduction of protective tariffs suffered its worst electoral defeat since 1832, ushering in a period of productive Liberal government which lasted until the Great War. Driven largely by Lloyd George and Winston Churchill measures were passed such as old age pensions and national insurance, which laid the foundations of the future welfare state, and two years of ferocious political conflict from 1909 to 1911, the worst such crisis since 1831–2, eventually resulted in the passing of the People's Budget and the curbing of the powers of the House of Lords.

Conservatism in Kent sailed serenely through all of this, surviving even the hurricane of 1906 when it secured ten of the county's fifteen seats. Of the eight county constituencies which resulted from the redistribution of 1885, Ashford, Medway, St Augustine's, Sevenoaks and Thanet were solidly Conservative right up to 1914, as were Faversham and Tonbridge save for 1906. Of the seven boroughs (Woolwich, like Greenwich, is best regarded as a London borough), Canterbury, Dover and Gravesend had a similar unblemished Conservative record, as did Hythe after 1895, while the only blot on Chatham's escutcheon was 1906 when it returned a Labour member. Maidstone elected a Liberal in 1900 and again at a by-election the following year but was otherwise Conservative, even in 1906 when Viscount Castlereagh regained it against the national trend. Contests at Maidstone were close affairs, though: Castlereagh's majorities in 1906 and, January and December 1910 were 132, 247 and 70 in polls ranging from some 5,500 to 5,900. Only Rochester, Liberal in 1889, 1906 and December

1910 and the county seat of Dartford, Lib.-Lab. in 1906 and December 1910, deserted the Conservatives more than once in general election contests (see Table 6). Even the solitary Liberal from 1885 to 1892 was a dubious quantity, namely Sir Edward Watkin, Bt, on whom party affiliation sat extremely lightly compared with his obsession with the Channel Tunnel: he is probably better regarded as a Liberal Unionist.

Table 6a

Kent General Election Results, 1885–1910

| | County | | Borough | | Total | |
	Con.	Lib.	Con.	Lib.	Con.	Lib.
1885	8	0	6	1	14	1
1886	8	0	6	1	14	1
1892	8	0	6	1	14	1
1895	8	0	7	0	15	0
1900	8	0	6	1	14	1
1906	5	3	5	2b	10	5
1910(J)	8	0	7	0	15	0
1910(D)	7	1	6	1	13c	2

a   Derived from Craig, *British Parliamentary Election Results*, London 1974.
b   Includes one Labour.
c   Includes Sir Edward Sassoon, Bt, MP for Hythe from 1899, classified as Conservative by Craig, but as Liberal Unionist by M. Stenton and S. Lees, *Who's Who of British Members of Parliament, vol. II, 1886–1918*, Hassocks 1978.

Liberal weakness was further illustrated by the number of unopposed returns. In 1886 and 1895 six of the county seats were uncontested as were five in both 1900 and in December 1910. Five of Akers-Douglas's eight successes at St Augustine's were unopposed, including four in a row from 1886 to 1900; similarly Warde at Medway enjoyed untroubled returns in three of his six victories between 1892 and December 1910. Contests were more common in the boroughs: Heaton enjoyed unopposed returns four times in succession from 1886 to 1900 at Canterbury but this was an exception. The opposite extreme was Gravesend where the doggedness of the Liberals in always contesting a seat they never won can only be admired.

In such circumstances some Conservative MPs built up long periods of service. Sir William Hart Dyke, Bt, was first elected for West Kent in 1865, represented Mid Kent from 1868 to 1885, then Dartford until defeated in 1906 after over forty years in the House. Aretas Akers-Douglas, owner of 3,750 acres

Table 7a

Kent Borough Electorates, 1880, 1885 and 1910 (December)

Boroughs	1880	1885	1910(D)
Canterbury	3,671	3,107	3,836
Chatham	5,548	6,988*	15,799
Dover	4,239	4,885	6,247
Gravesend	3,286	4,200	6,733
Hythe	2,893	3,737*	6,541
Maidstone	3,878	4,273	6,260
Rochester	3,026	3,304	5,629

a   Derived from Craig, *British Parliamentary Election Results*, London 1974.
*   Double entries, i.e. voters qualified under more than one franchise, not eliminated, which inflates the size of the electorate.

in Kent plus a further 12,000 in Scotland[36] represented East Kent from 1880 to 1885 and St Augustine's from then until he was ennobled in 1911. Hardy was first elected for Ashford in 1892 and was still there in 1914 as were Warde at Medway and Forster at Sevenoaks over the same time span. In the boroughs Canterbury returned John Henniker Heaton from 1885 to January 1910, though having survived a challenge from an Independent Conservative, F. Bennett-Goldney, by only 21 votes on the last occasion he took it as his cue to retire. George, later the Rt Hon., George Wyndham sat for Dover from 1889 until his death in 1913.

With such power-bases several Kent MPs played prominent roles on the national stage. Wyndham was Chief Secretary for Ireland from 1900 to 1905 with a seat in the Cabinet from 1902. He was instrumental in passing the Land Purchase Act of 1903. He had been preceded in this position by Hart Dyke who held it from 1885 to 1886 having been a Conservative whip from 1868 to 1874 and chief whip from 1874 to 1880. Akers-Douglas also served as chief whip, from 1885 to 1895, then, after a spell as First Commissioner of Works, he became Home Secretary from 1902 to 1905. Finally, Sir John Gorst, MP for Chatham from 1875 to 1892 was Solicitor-General in 1885–6 and subsequently held a number of government posts.

In the main, Kent borough electorates (see Table 7) remained small and essentially manageable. Chatham stands out as the exception. The number of electors there increased markedly from 9,199 in 1895 to 13,432 in 1906. J.H. Jenkins, Kent's first Labour MP, thus had the honour of representing, if only for one Parliament, Kent's largest borough constituency.[37] The county electorates

[36] Viscount Chilston, *Chief Whip*, London 1961, p. 3 n.
[37] Jenkins was elected in the absence of a Liberal candidate, the two parties having done a deal; Labour did not contest Rochester.

were larger than the boroughs (see Table 8). Three of them were growing rapidly: Dartford, responding to industrial expansion; Sevenoaks, as London and its commuters spread into West Kent, the latter factor also affecting Tonbridge.

Table 8a

Kent County Electorates, 1885 and 1910 (December)

Constituency	1885	1910(D)
Ashford	13,389*	14,202
Dartford	11,173*	21,398
Faversham	11,370*	14,649
Isle of Thanet	7,941*	12,588
Medway	13,482*	15,181
St Augustine's	12,157*	16,614
Sevenoaks	11,098*	19,035
Tonbridge	10,703	17,116

a   Derived from Craig, *British Parliamentary Election Results*, London 1974.

*   Double entries, i.e. voters qualified under more than one franchise, not eliminated, which inflates the size of the electorate.

(4) Members, Party Organisation and Voters

(a) Members: (i) 1832–84[38]

Not surprisingly, Kent's MPs numbered many from the aristocracy and gentry. Of the ten sent by East Kent to Westminster, one was the eldest son of a peer, and four were baronets (including the sole Liberal), one of whom was ennobled as was one of the commoners. Kentish country seat and fashionable London address was the norm. A similar pattern applied in West Kent: of fifteen MPs, three were eldest sons of peers, five were baronets. The Liberals had greater strength here, at least until 1859, and none of their four MPs was titled but one (Hodges) married the only child of Sir Roger Twisden, Bt, and another the granddaughter of a marquess. Greater proximity to London was reflected in a slight intrusion of commerce: Hart Dyke, of Lullingstone Castle, Dartford, combined ownership of 9,000 acres with the deputy chairmanship of the London, Chatham and Dover Railway while Sir C.H. Mills, Bt, who married the eldest daughter of the Earl of Harewood, was a partner in the merchant bank

[38] The sections on Members are based upon M. Stenton and S. Lees, *Who's Who of British Members of Parliament*, vol. I *1832–1885*, vol. II *1886–1918*, vol. III *1919–1945*, Hassocks 1976–9.

Glyn Mills and Co. and made it to the peerage as Baron Hillingdon. Three West Kent MPs subsequently represented Mid Kent contributing to the social tone there: four MPs, three titled, one becoming so.

Equally unsurprisingly, the boroughs were not so socially well served, though even here Canterbury distinguished itself. Of its sixteen MPs ten (including four of the five Liberals) were either members of, or married into, the aristocracy, one (the remaining Liberal) was the youngest son of a knight, two were grandsons of peers and one's father was created an Earl. The most that can be said of the final two is that one married 'a celebrated actress',[39] the other was unseated for bribery.

Other boroughs were less exclusive, relatively. Chatham was dominated by people with service backgrounds (seven out of eight MPs) but as the services were frequently a refuge for younger sons of the upper class this did not preclude 'quality': the town was served by the eldest son of a peer and three baronets to accompany an Admiral, Major-General and Lieutenant-Colonel. Even the outsider, the political operator Gorst, was knighted. Neighbouring Rochester followed a different pattern: of its thirteen MPs only four were titled, and four were lawyers.

Sandwich, like Chatham, had service connections but to a lesser degree, numbering two Rear-Admirals and a Major-General among its thirteen MPs; four were descended from the aristocracy, a fifth married into it and a sixth was promoted into it (Lord Brabourne). Commerce was also notable: three of the early MPs had West or East India connections while of the later ones, one was a banker and chairman of the South Eastern Railway, another a merchant and shipowner, and Sandwich's last MP, H.A. Brassey, was the wealthy son of a well-known railway contractor. Sandwich was an expensive constituency. Dover had a similar mixture of the services, commerce and the titled: a viscount, three baronets, two knights. Of its first five MPs, two were London merchants, two Dover bankers. Among later ones, one was chairman of the Crystal Palace Company, another was the solicitor to the Bank of England and a third was Sir G. Jessel, son of a London merchant, Solicitor-General 1871–3, resigning to become Master of the Rolls, the first Jewish judge.

Hythe had but six MPs, all Liberal. The first married the widow of a lord, the second was the eldest son of an earl, the third was Recorder of Folkestone. Then Hythe became the refuge for the wealthy outsider: Sir J.W. Ramsden, Bt, who boasted five residences, including one in Huddersfield where the family had made its money, was followed by Baron M.A. de Rothschild of Jewish banking fame who in turn was succeeded by Watkin, the railway magnate.

As for the county town, the striking aspect is the paucity of the titled. Not until 1870 does Maidstone return one such, banker and author Sir John Lubbock, Bt, later Lord Avebury. He was joined by another Liberal baronet in

---

[39] Stenton and Lees, *op. cit.*, Bradshaw, J.

1874, Sir Sidney Waterlow, wealthy wholesale stationer and proponent of model lodging houses for urban workers. Admittedly earlier representatives had included A.J. Beresford-Hope, who married the eldest daughter of the Marquis of Salisbury, and C. Buxton, third son of a baronet and partner in Truman, Hanbury and Co., brewers. Maidstone typically returned London bankers and merchants. One final point: in contrast to the Knights of the Shire, few borough MPs resided in the county. Kent's function was to provide seats for the London-addressed landed elite, merchants, company directors, lawyers, those who had had careers in the armed services, even a Yorkshire industrialist. This was the advantage of its geographical location and facilitated some redistribution of wealth from economies more dynamic than its own.

(b) Members: (ii) 1885–1914

Again, not surprisingly, while aristocracy and gentry continue to make a contribution, increasingly Kent's MPs are drawn from the City, commerce and the professions. Leaving aside the survivors from before 1885, of the 21 county MPs only one was born into the aristocracy, though four others married into it, three were younger sons of baronets and one other, C.W. Mills, was a classic example of commerce ennobled, succeeding his father both as banker at Glyn Mills and Co. and as Baron Hillingdon. Of the rest, three were barristers, two company directors, one a banker, one a financier of dubious repute, one a Lieutenant-Colonel and one a working man. Only twelve had Kent addresses. Of the 25 borough MPs five were eldest sons of peers, one of whom doubled as a partner in Coutts Bank, three married into the aristocracy and one married the daughter of a baronet. Of the rest five were company directors and there was a banker, a contractor, a barrister, a Lieutenant-General and a former dockyard worker.

Of the individual constituencies, Maidstone stood out as being more aristocratic than before, boasting not only Castlereagh but also F.S.W. Cornwallis, who inherited the property of his great-grandfather, the last Earl Cornwallis, served Kent County Council as chairman for twenty years from 1910 and was created Lord Cornwallis in 1927. Maidstone was a difficult constituency: at six elections the majority was less than 200. By contrast Hythe was practically a pocket borough, being represented after Watkin by a knighted retired Lieutenant-General and two baronets, father and son, from the wealthy Jewish Sassoon family. As for once aristocratic Canterbury, its two MPs were Heaton, who had made his reputation in Australia and campaigned, with success in 1898, for the Imperial Penny Post, and Bennett-Goldney, six times mayor of the city, who won his seat initially as an Independent Conservative, defeating the official candidate.

(c) Party Organisation

There were two main links between members and voters. One was the press; the major towns had weekly papers, committed to each of the parties, which circulated in the neighbouring countryside and by the second half of the century the

London daily papers, which devoted much attention to politics, permeated Kent. The second was party organisation. Prior to 1832 this was tenuous. At elections committees were formed to organise the candidates' support and accompany them on their (very important) personal canvass of the electors, propose, second and back them at the hustings and bring up the voters if a contest resulted. The successful members were chaired around the principal thoroughfares, banquets were held to celebrate or commiserate and the committees then dissolved until the next vacancy. This continued after 1832 but the Reform Act introduced a new element, the electoral register. Voters had to be prepared to demonstrate that they had the necessary qualification to be registered, if challenged. It was obviously in the interests of each party to ensure that as many of its supporters as were qualified were placed on the register, as many of its opponents as possible challenged and struck off. Claims and objections were heard annually at a revision court conducted by a barrister. Solicitors dominated the proceedings and it was they who emerged as the first paid party agents. Their work was supplemented in places, as was noted above of Maidstone, by political clubs. It was not only Kent-based clubs that influenced Kent politics. The great London political clubs, the Carlton, the Reform, the National Liberal, could be contacted for advice and support. It was to the Carlton that Maidstone Conservatives turned when seeking a running-mate for Wyndham Lewis in 1837.

At election times, specific election agents might be appointed, again often solicitors, who in turn would appoint paid canvassers and messengers, a system which easily could and often did degenerate into outright bribery. It was also inefficient and thus fell victim to increasing professionalism, particularly among the Conservatives after their defeat in 1868. Even before then changes had been taking place for while the boroughs might be left to local agents the county constituencies with their numerous polling districts – thirteen in West Kent by 1860, including Blackheath and Lewisham, ten in East Kent – presented an organisational challenge. As early as 1836 proposals were afoot for a West Kent Conservative Association financed by annual subscriptions to work the revision courts, but this body seems to have lapsed and the task of watching the register left to local agents in the local polling districts. At least one, Blackheath, had a Conservative District Registration Committee and there was a West Kent Conservative Fund but the system was ineffective. The Liberals in West Kent took the initiative, appointing one agent to cover the whole constituency in the 1850s. Liberal successes in 1857 were attributed to his energy and the Conservatives immediately responded, setting up the West Kent Conservative Registration Society and appointing a London lawyer as constituency agent and secretary. There was some concern at the cost: he was paid £400 a year as against £340 paid to local agents the previous year, but the practice spread to East Kent in 1860 where the Registration Society had a large central committee with local committees in each polling district. Support was patchy: the 155 subscribers were located mainly in Ashford, Canterbury, Faversham and Sittingbourne and the Sheerness committee was unmanned. This society seems to have collapsed but it was replaced on similar lines three years later by the Central Conservative Registration Association for East Kent.[40]

Though Kent was only marginally affected, comparatively speaking, by the 1867 Reform Act, techniques developed in the North and Midlands to manage the mass electorates there were transplanted to the Garden of England. The process was aided by the fact that Hart Dyke and Akers-Douglas were prominent in the highest reaches of Conservative party management and the principal Tory agent, Gorst, appointed in 1870, became MP for Chatham five years later. Hart Dyke commented on the new spirit in 1873:

> I have a deal of trouble with our Kent boroughs: they have all been left for years in the hands of local attorneys, who have only cared for the filthy lucre, and have been content to lose any seat, so long as the victim they brought forward paid the bill. Now a spirit of energy has sprung up at Greenwich and Rochester and other places

By 1874 the solicitors had been driven out of Dover, Maidstone and Rochester.[41] In 1883 a full-time agent, Captain Middleton, was appointed for West Kent whose electorate was expanding rapidly: by 1880 it numbered 14,873. The close links between Kent and Conservative Central Office were further strengthened when Middleton became principal agent from 1885 to 1903. Operating from the county seat at Eridge, near Tunbridge Wells, of the former chief party manager, the Marquess of Abergavenny, Akers-Douglas, Hart Dyke and Middleton acquired the nickname, 'the Kent Gang'.[42]

After 1885 the basic pattern was established. Each constituency had its Conservative and Liberal Registration bodies and agents. These were supplemented by political clubs, especially among the Conservatives. By the early twentieth century such clubs were established in all the major towns and even in Hawkhurst and Malling. The Liberal presence was patchier but, as befitted tradition, Maidstone had a rich representation, the Maidstone and Mid-Kent Conservative Club (interestingly at Canterbury too the borough and neighbouring county constituencies combined in the East Kent and Canterbury Conservative Club, founded in 1884) confronting the similarly named Liberal Club. Rochester displayed a subtly interlocking Conservative structure, the Constitutional Association (president, Marquess of Abergavenny) secretary acting as registration agent from an office in the Rochester and Strood Conservative Club. A similar pattern prevailed at Dartford, the agent of the Division's Conservative Association trebling as secretary of the Conservative Hall and honorary secretary of the Constitutional Club. There was an interesting addition here, though, as befitted the industrial nature of the constituency, in the presence of two Dartford Working Men's Conservative Clubs. The only other similar

---

40 CKS, U1515, Romney of the Mote MSS.
41 H.J. Hanham, *Elections and Party Management*, Hassocks 1978, p. 243, from which the quotation is taken.
42 Chilston, *op. cit.*, p. 4.

body listed in *Kelly's Directory* was in the unlikely location of Tunbridge Wells with its Working Men's Conservative Association situated in uncomfortable proximity to the Liberal Association (Tonbridge Division) in Goods Station Road. No doubt in an emergency the Conservative working men could summon assistance from the Tunbridge Wells Conservative Association and the two local Constitutional Clubs.[43]

(d) Voters

Old customs died hard in the reformed Kent electoral system. As late as 1880 the election of Akers-Douglas for East Kent illustrated the semi-feudal nature of the county constituencies as the Tory gentry rallied to the cause and the tenant farmers did their duty. Borough electorates remained small and dominated by freemen voters long after 1832. In Canterbury, for example, in 1835 registered freemen outnumbered the £10 householders by 1,415 to 297. As late as 1854 there were 935 freemen to 717 householders but by 1865 the position had been reversed, 906 householders to 476 freemen. As at Maidstone party dominated Canterbury elections, those voting the ticket (i.e. supporting both candidates or where there was just one 'plumping' for that candidate) being the overwhelming majority (see Table 9).[44] 1847 is particularly impressive as it represented Liberal support for, and almost complete Conservative desertion of, the Peelite Smythe, a phenomenon demonstrated slightly less clearly in 1868 when the Liberals backed the maverick Butler-Johnstone. The comparatively low figures for 1854 and 1857 are explained by the Radical views of the second Liberal who thus alienated moderate support. The same party loyalty is discernible at Sand-wich,[45] especially after 1835 and seems to have continued at Maidstone: in 1865 'all but 60 out of 1,696 votes were straight party votes'.[46]

Table 9a

Percentage of Voters Supporting the Party Ticket in Canterbury Elections, 1835–68

Election	Percentage	Election	Percentage
1835	89	1854	73
1837	92	1857	78
1841	84	1865	96
1847	95	1868	76
1852	95		

a   Derived from the *Pollbooks*.

[43] *Kelly's Directory of Kent*, London 1903.
[44] *Pollbooks*, 1835, 1854, 1865.
[45] See F.W.G. Andrews, 'The Pollbooks of Sandwich, Kent, 1831–68', *Bulletin of the Institute of Historical Research*, lxxi (1998), pp. 75–107.
[46] J.R. Vincent, *Pollbooks: How Victorians Voted*, London 1967, p. 145.

Why did people vote the way they did? The clearest example of 'interest-group voting' was the clergy. In Kent pollbooks analysed by Vincent, every single dissenting minister's vote was Liberal, every Anglican clergyman, sexton, clerk, or organist voted Conservative save at Rochester and even here Conservative clergy predominated. Another determinant could be the employer-employee relationship: at Maidstone in 1870 the station master voted Liberal as did 40 of the 49 railwaymen, partly counterbalanced by the prison employees, all 22 of whom voted Conservative, as did the Deputy-Governor of the Gaol.[47] Whether such votes were freely given we cannot tell. At Canterbury in 1835 a prominent Liberal announced his conversion to the ballot after finding much intimidation in the canvass,[48] and it was well known that some tradesmen declined to vote rather than risk alienating customers. It was equally well known that many votes, far from being freely given, were expensively bought. Seven Kent borough elections were overturned on petition between 1832 and 1884 and this was only the tip of the iceberg: petitioning was expensive and often there were too many skeletons in the cupboards for close scrutiny to be welcome. Hanham, analysing the position in the period 1865 to 1884 placed Canterbury and Sandwich among the 21 'extensively corrupt' English boroughs and Gravesend, Maidstone and Rochester among the 43 with 'a corrupt element'.[49] The latter two were among the ten considered 'still more or less corrupt' after 1885.[50] The most recent historians of Maidstone believe the Liberals refrained from bribery until 1859 when they resumed the practice, their core support among nonconformist tradesmen and some of the skilled workers requiring augmenting if they were to succeed against the Conservative-inclined elite and Anglican Church.[51] A friend of Heaton's, hearing that he was standing for Canterbury in 1885, advised him: 'they are sure to ask you if you are in favour of payment of Members, but you must reply that you are in favour of the good old practice of payment for voters'.[52]

The most notorious example of the 'good old practice' was Sandwich where the Conservative elected at a by-election in 1880 was unseated for bribery. The subsequent Commission of Enquiry found 128 persons guilty of bribing, 1,005 guilty of being bribed, of whom 127 were bribed by both sides, and 48 guilty of treating though the latter practice was on a modest scale since the voters preferred hard cash, usually at £3 a head, to 'heavy wet'. The total electorate was about 2,000 when double entries were excluded. The Commission noted sadly: 'the actual distribution of money to individuals was effected without difficulty. We could find only one or two instances in which a bribe was refused.' The Conservatives spent £2,500 in direct bribery, the Liberals £1,500.

---

47 *Ibid.*, p. 146.
48 *Pollbook*, 1835.
49 Hanham, *op. cit.*, p. 263 n.
50 *Ibid.*, p. 281 n.
51 P. Clark and L. Murfin, *History of Maidstone*, Stroud 1995, pp. 178–81.
52 A. Porter, *The Life and Letters of Sir John Henniker Heaton, Bt*, London 1916, p. 13.

The Commission had no doubt 'that electoral corruption had long and extensively prevailed in the borough of Sandwich'. The consequences were severe: the constituency was disfranchised and ten of the bribers, including a Liberal agent and the clerk to the Conservative agent, were tried and sentenced to hard labour of between six and eighteen months.[53]

The experience of Sandwich demonstrates that corruption could be bubbling away merrily for many elections without petitions being pressed and also that, while it was usually the Conservatives who were caught, the Liberals were actively involved: Sandwich usually returned Liberal MPs.

Canterbury tells a similar tale. The two Conservatives elected in 1852 were unseated . The subsequent commission, to the consternation of the Liberals, insisted on going back beyond the uncontested by-election of 1850, which was relatively clean, to the contested election of 1847 which certainly was not. The commission thought the Liberals had been bribing since 1835. Both sides bribed in the 1841 by-election which cost Smythe £7,000, and his defeated opponent nearly £4,000, though not all on bribes. The verdict on 1847 was unequivocal: Conyngham and Smythe's return 'was obtained by direct money bribery' practised with the knowledge and consent of Smythe. Conservative success in 1852 was equally 'mainly due to bribery and corruption'. Smythe, who was in a good position to know, found no appreciable difference between the parties as regards electoral purity though he paid out more as a Tory in 1841 than he was called on to do as a Liberal in 1847.

Bribery was a well organised business. Groups of electors met to sell their votes in bulk to an intermediary who received payment from a party agent, charging commission, perhaps £20 to £30 for a dozen votes. Voters could get as much as £10 though £3 to £5 were more common. One family was said to have made £208 in the two elections of 1841. A less direct method of corruption was colour tickets, a practice going back way beyond 1832 and used by both sides until the Liberals gave it up in 1852, allegedly because they had discovered its illegality. An elector applied to a party for a colour ticket for two people, usually relatives (it was illegal if done directly), who would get ten shillings each for protecting the party colours. One grocer, owed money by two of his customers, sent them along for colour tickets as a way of recovering the debt. There were also refreshment tickets. For instance, a tailor's apprentice, aged fifteen, was sent by his master to get a shilling ticket which was exchanged at a Conservative public house for two bottles of ginger beer, some gin and a pot of beer. He also took home a shilling's worth of gin for the master's wife. Elections were a vital injection of money into the local economy, a form of wealth redistribution regarded as perfectly legitimate at a time when a labourer was lucky to get 2s 6d for a day's work.[54]

---

[53] *PP* 1881, xlv, *Reports from Commissions on Elections: Sandwich*, pp. 6ff. The quotations are on pp. 9, 15. W.B. Gwyn, *Democracy and the Cost of Politics in Britain*, London 1962, p. 91.

[54] *PP* 1852–3, ix, *Minutes of Evidence taken before the Select Committee on the Canterbury Election Petition, 1853*, pp. 98ff; xlvii, *Report of the Commissioners appointed to enquire into the Existence of Corrupt Practices in the City of Canterbury, 1853*, pp. 5ff, quotations on pp. 15, 22.

Canterbury also distinguished itself in 1880 when its two Conservative MPs were again unseated for bribery. Things were on a smaller scale, however, the colour men had gone and fewer people were involved. The tradition had been weakened. There was a suspicion of bribery in 1862 and 1865 but 1874 was thought to be clean and 1868 probably was. Bad habits returned at a by-election in 1879 when a Liberal outsider ran the Conservative, Laurie, exceedingly close, partly as a result of £140 spent by the Liberal agents on bribing and treating: 200 or 300 voters were involved, usually only a few shillings a vote; 'In many instances the same persons accepted bribes from the Conservative side in 1880.' Again it was small beer, 5 shillings to £1 a vote (deflation had taken its toll), perhaps £300 involved, paid by the Conservative agent via sub agents. Sixty-one people were deemed to have bribed, 180 to have been bribed. Laurie himself was among the 61, having continued to employ 'one Hart, a rat-catcher' to canvass for him even though aware that he was offering bribes. Treating was widely practised by both sides but the commission commented tartly that they did not want to prolong the inquiry 'by calling the whole of the constituency before us'. The commission was intrigued to uncover an attempted post-election deal whereby, in a bid to secure the petition's withdrawal, the Conservatives would yield one of the seats to the Liberals, pay the expenses of the defeated Independent Conservative, Butler-Johnstone, and £1,000 to cover the costs of the defeated Liberal: the deal collapsed when the latter held out for £2,500. They would no doubt have been even more intrigued had they learnt that the Liberal chief whip had contributed £500 to help Butler-Johnstone bring the petition.[55]

At Chatham influence rather than bribery was the issue. The Conservative elected in 1852 was unseated because he had obtained a position at the Post Office for the son of an elector but what really caused concern was the large number of voters employed at the dockyard and other public departments 'under the influence of the Government . . . it appears that there is no instance of a Candidate being elected for this Borough who has not had the support of the Government'.[56]

Bribery certainly occurred in constituencies where petitions were not sustained. For example, Gorst described Dover in 1873 as 'a place influenced much by private and corrupt motives, and little by public spirit'.[57] Nor did bribery cease after the 1883 Act. The Conservative elected for Rochester in 1892 was unseated, rather harshly, because of entertainments provided by the Constitutional Association of which his election agent was secretary, and the Liberal elected for Maidstone in 1900 was unseated for bribery by his agents: only 25 cases were proved and the sums expended were small, 7s 6d or 10 shil-

---

55 *PP* 1881, xxxix, *Report of the Commissioners appointed to inquire into the Existence of Corrupt Practices in the City of Canterbury*, pp. 5ff, quotations on pp. 6, 8; Hanham, *op. cit.*, p. 379.

56 *PP* 1852–3, ix, *op. cit.*, *Chatham 1853*, p. 216.

57 Quoted in Hanham, *op. cit.*, p. 348.

lings.[58] The electors do not seem to have been too concerned: the Liberals held Maidstone at the subsequent by-election with an increased majority, the Conservatives Rochester unopposed.

It seems reasonable to suppose that bribery and corruption were in decline even before 1883 and that the conclusion of the report into Canterbury in 1880 could be applied throughout Kent (except Sandwich); 'this constituency is not now as a whole corrupt. Out of about 3,000 voters perhaps 500 or 600 are at all times accessible to bribery, but there is no reason to suppose that the bulk of the voters is corrupt.'[59] When Heaton travelled to Canterbury in 1885 he did not need his friend's advice. Most voters cast their ballots actuated by the same indefinable mixture of principle, belief, self-interest and whimsy which their successors employ today.

(5) Conservative Kent

The reasons for Conservative dominance in Kent are clear. The landed interest, increasingly united as erstwhile Whigs deserted the Liberals, influenced not only the countryside but also the many market towns dependent upon it. It was buttressed by the Anglican Church and the drink interest, not only brewers and publicans but also hop farmers. The growth of what Lord Salisbury called Villa Toryism, the spread of suburban London into West Kent and the influx of commuters into such places as Sevenoaks and Bromley, was balanced in the East and South by expanding seaside resorts attracting the cautious retired. The development of industry along the Thames and Medway offered some hope to the Liberals but even here the presence of dockyards, especially at Chatham, favoured the Conservatives, as did military garrisons at Canterbury, Dover and Folkestone guarding a coastline so close to the Continent. But Conservative dominance was not total. The close nature of contests at Maidstone and the dogged persistence of the Gravesend Liberals have already been mentioned and even in January 1910, despite not winning a single seat, over one in three Kent voters was Liberal. In December 1910 the capture of Dartford and Rochester offered Liberals hope for the future. But that hope was illusory and the challenge to the Conservatives in the twentieth century would come not from them, but from Labour.[60]

---

[58] *PP* 1893–4, lxx, *Judgement on the Trial of the Election Petition for Rochester*, pp. 883ff; 1901, lix, *Judges' Report and Minutes of Evidence in the Maidstone Election Trial*, pp. 15ff.

[59] *PP* 1881, xxxix, *op. cit.*, p. 10.

[60] An example of defections to the Conservatives is provided by the first Lord Brabourne who, as Edward Knatchbull-Hugessen, third son of Sir Edward Knatchbull, Bt, had represented Sandwich as a Liberal from 1857 to his ennoblement in 1880, holding government office from 1859 to 1866 and again from 1868 to 1874. He left what he called 'Gladstone's Party' in 1880–1 over Irish policy which he feared would lead to separation and in 1886 he was referring to 'so many of my old Whig friends' confessing he was right. Chilston, *op. cit.*, pp. 68–9.

6

The Development of Independent Working Class Politics in the Medway Towns, 1859–1914

BRUCE AUBRY

The starting date for this study is the year 1859, which was an important date in the history of the labour movement within the City of Rochester and the towns of Chatham and Gillingham. It was in the summer of that year that the labouring classes, and their historians, benefited from the arrival of a regularly produced and truly 'local' weekly newspaper, made economically feasible by the repeal of the tax on newspaper advertisements, in 1853, and of the stamp duty, in 1855.[1] The first issue of the radical *Chatham News* appeared on 2 July, and with it a new era in the history of the labour movement had begun. Also, we should recall that 1859 was the year in which the new Medway Union Workhouse, at Luton opened; a physical manifestation of the first administrative step towards a unified 'Medway'.

(1) The Working Class Electorate and Reform

An anomaly in the parliamentary franchise dominated the political conscious-ness of an important section of the dockyard workforce, as Chatham was an unusual parliamentary constituency, in that it had a very high proportion of working class voters. Of the 2,104 voters, registered in 1866, 970 were workers, and of these 780 were government employees.[2] It was not surprising, in 1853, that proposals to disenfranchise these dockyardmen would lead to meetings and protests, more important than any demanding an extension of the parliamentary franchise to all male householders. Dockyard men, who possessed the vote, did not want to lose such a 'saleable' asset. In January 1859, a great reform meeting, in support of John Bright's unsuccessful Reform Bill, was held at Chatham, with

---

1   A.E. Musson, *The Typographical Association: Origins and History up to 1949*, London 1954, p. 77; E.L. Woodward, *The Age of Reform*, Oxford 1938, p. 179.
2   Mavis Waters, *Gleanings from the History of a Dockyard Town: Gillingham 1860–1910*, n.d., p. 5.

Ernest Jones, the celebrated Chartist, as the main speaker, and a Chatham and District Reform League was formed, encompassing a wide spectrum of Medway Towns social classes, including the former secretary of the local Chartist Association, George Pattison. When it was realised that the bill would disenfranchise the dockyard voter, this part of it was condemned at a later meeting.[3] Further 'Reform' agitation was unreported in the Medway Towns from 1859 until 1863, when a Chatham Reform Association was organised by working men to 'hold meetings, issue circulars, etc.', but very little was attempted, until the disenfranchisement issue reappeared in 1866, when Clause 16 of the new Reform Bill became known. W.E. Gladstone wished to eliminate the special and corrupting privilege possessed by workers at all the naval dockyards in elections before the Secret Ballot. Nevertheless, the local MP, Arthur Otway, and his fellow dockyard MPs, convinced the government to drop the clause.[4] In 1866, the National Reform League, which had been founded by the national trade union movement in 1865 to demand 'One Man, One Vote', reached Kent, and its first branch in the county was established at Strood, with thirty members.[5] Other branches were formed at Troy Town, at St Margaret's, Rochester, at New Brompton, at Chatham, at Luton, and at Ordnance Place, Chatham, with a Central Towns Committee co-ordinating these branches' activities.[6] When 'Reform' triumphed in 1867, doubling the electorate through the establishment of male household suffrage, the more radical campaigners began planning for the next instalments. The Strood branch resolved to maintain their organisation until manhood suffrage and the secret ballot had been won, whilst at Ordnance Place, the branch added local rate reform to these two electoral demands.[7]

(2) Republicanism

The first reaction of many of the Medway Towns' labour leaders, when they realised that the Reform Act of 1867 had failed to encourage 'social' reforms, and when they witnessed an actual worsening of the economic situation, due to lay-offs at the dockyard, was to turn to republicanism. All that Gladstone's first cabinet had suggested for the elimination of the poverty caused by unemployment was emigration, and this failure, on the part of a 'radical' government, led many working class reformers to doubt the feasibility of significant social amelioration under the existing constitution. By the end of 1871, a Chatham, Rochester and Strood Republican Club had sent a resolution of support to Sir

3   *SEG*, 17.5.53, 24.5.53, 7.6.53, 25.1.59, 1.3.59, 22.3.59.
4   *CN*, 31.3.66, 7.4.66.
5   *CN*, 1.9.66.
6   *CN*, 29.9.66, 13.10.66, 3.11.66, 10.11.66, 1.12.66, 22.12.66, 12.1.67, 2.2.67, 9.2.67, 23.2.67, 23.3.67, 27.4.67, 11.5.67, 8.6.67, 29.6.67, 27.7.67.
7   *CN*, 7.9.67, 19.10.67.

Charles Dilke, MP, in his opposition to the power of the monarchy. Republican meetings were held at Strood, near Thomas Aveling's factory, in which his Scots workshop manager, James Campbell, and many other old Reform Leaguers, took part. One may suppose that Campbell's radical employer sympathised with the republicanism of Sir Charles Dilke, of Joseph Chamberlain, MP, and of his own manager, for Thomas Aveling was an innovator, both industrially and socially.[8]

> He fitted up a part of the old works at Rochester as a lecture room for his men, and he and others read papers and delivered lectures there on educational, social and political subjects. Afterwards Mr. Aveling invited discussion, for he generally occupied the chair. At first the men delivered speeches of the most communistic type, but after a time they became capable of looking at questions from a different point of view . . . He used to say, 'There is nothing to fear from Radicalism, and I don't object to it; but there is a great deal to fear from uneducated Radicalism, and that I do object to.'[9]

George Odger, a ladies' shoemaker, who had been the secretary of the London Trades Council since 1867, five times an unsuccessful working man parliamentary candidate, and a member of the International Working Men's Association, spoke to the Republican Club at Rochester. Odger won top billing with the local republicans, though he did not speak solely on republicanism, but rather on general trade union themes. When he returned to lecture on 'Trades Unions v. Capital', the meeting was held at the Chatham Working Men's Hall, for the republicans had not been allowed the use of either the Lecture Hall or the New Corn Exchange, but, nevertheless, the local authorities did provide several policemen to stand at the entrance to the hall. George Odger's lectures were great successes, as he was booked for two more meetings, and one may wonder if he was considering Rochester for a sixth parliamentary campaign. However, as time passed, republicanism became part of the general radical-secularist underworld of Medway Towns' politics, and Queen Victoria and her large family were out of immediate danger.[10]

In the autumn of 1872, an early initiative was taken in the direction of independent working class politics, when the Rochester Working Men's Political Association was formed at a Borstal meeting. The Association's organisers wanted branches in all Rochester wards, open to Tory, Whig, radical or republican working men, though the chairman and vice chairman were themselves Reform Leaguers and republicans.[11] One of these branches met a month and a half later, at Strood, where John Campbell presided over fifty participants, who decided to endorse the Tory in the Strood Ward, though this was opposed by the

8   *CO*, 15.4.71, 22.4.71, 2.12.71, 9.12.71, 16.12.71, 23.12.71; *CN*, 6.1.73, 20.1.72, 9.3.72, 22.6.72.
9   *CO*, 15.7.82 (reprinted extract from obituary published in the *Journal of the Royal Agricultural Society*).
10 *CO*, 30.12.71, 6.1.72, 20.1.72, 27.1.72, 3.2.72, 10.2.72, 17.2.72, 9.3.72, 23.3.72, 30.3.72, 3.4.72, 11.5.72, 8.6.72, 15.6.72, 10.8.72; *CN*, 2.12.71, 9.12.71, 23.12.71.
11 *CN*, 14.9.72.

chairman. The Association next met at Rochester to discuss the endorsement of a candidate in the St Margaret's Ward, but the voting was tied 24–24, and neither Tory nor Liberal received their approval.[12]

A new working class 'Reform' organisation was born in May 1873 at a meeting in Aveling and Porter's Lecture Room, with Thomas Aveling, himself, in the chair. A placard had announced the meeting: 'all voters of Rochester are invited who wish to hear the exposition of an advanced political programme, and to form an Association for the purpose of securing Electoral Reform'. On that evening, the Rochester Working Men's Political Reform Association was established, and in October, a meeting was held in the Lecture Room with John Campbell presiding. A hundred members were claimed and James Claxton, an Aveling and Porter fitter-timekeeper, who later would succeed Campbell as the President of the Rochester and District Industrial Co-operative Society, moved a resolution favouring direct working class representation in the House of Commons, as well as on local bodies. The Association noted that the double-member Rochester constituency was two thirds working class and that it should have, at least, one working class MP. Both of the old political parties were criticised by speakers, and Thomas Aveling was in attendance to advise them, in detail, regarding strategy.[13]

At its next meeting, it was decided to nominate a 'Working Class' candidate for the newly-created Rochester School Board, and Joshua Black, a Cornish-born engine fitter, employed by Aveling, was selected.[14] Rochester's Liberal political establishment endorsed Joshua Black, who was elected at the top of the poll, with a claim to being the first working class member on any English school board.[15] The Political Reform Association met after their election victory to demand, unsuccessfully, a discretionary penny rate to establish a public library, but the Association continued its activities into 1875 with lectures on various radical topics.[16] At the next Rochester School Board elections in 1876, another working man was nominated to stand with Black. The new man, Thomas Carey of the Operative Bricklayers' Society, was selected by the recently-formed, but short-lived, Rochester, Strood and Chatham Trades Council, which had been formed, in April 1875, with the encouragement of its Maidstone counterpart. Black was re-elected, and Carey elected, to the School Board.[17]

In September 1879 a new political organisation, the Rochester and Chatham United Association for Ascertaining Public Opinion, also known as the Rochester and Chatham Radical Association, was founded by a meeting of working

12 *CO*, 26.10.72, 2.11.72.
13 *CO*, 4.10.73, 11.10.73; *CN*, 22.11.73.
14 *CO*, 22.11.73; *CN*, 22.11.73.
15 *CO*, 17.1.74; *CN*, 10.1.74.
16 *CO*, 28.3.74, 4.4.74, 3.4.75; *CN*, 28.3.74, 2.5.74.
17 *CO*, 16.12.76, 23.12.76, 6.1.77; *CN*, 16.12.76, 23.12.76, 30.12.76, 6.1.77; *Kent and Sussex Times and Herald*, henceforth *KSTH*, 26.3.75, 9.4.75, 16.4.75, 23.4.75.

men in Rochester.[18] Discussions were held on church disestablishment and on 'The Peoples' Representatives', and the Association organised the nomination and election of Mrs Katalena West to the Rochester School Board in 1879, the first woman elected to public office in the Medway Towns. The Association maintained some activity until 1882, and it took a great interest in the campaign of secularist-republican Charles Bradlaugh to occupy his Northampton seat in the House of Commons, after his refusal to take the religious oath.[19]

Thomas Aveling, the advanced radical and innovative capitalist, died in March 1882, as a result of a sailing accident. The workers of the Medway Towns had lost a true friend, as Aveling can justly be called 'the Foster Father of the Rochester and Strood labour movement'.[20] While the Aveling and Porter workmen were debating political and co-operative issues, a new Chatham, Brompton, and Rochester Radical Association was formed, during 1885, in preparation for the General Election of 1886. This organisation of working men radicals owed its success to the leadership of William Burnett Thompson, a New Brompton-based dockyard writer,[21] who was also a leading light in the very active Chatham Secular Society, a branch of Bradlaugh's national society.[22]

The General Election of July 1886 saw the last flowering of English radicalism, and at Chatham there was adopted an advanced radical, Major General Sir Andrew Clarke (Figure 5), who was the most distinguished and most experienced candidate ever to stand in the Medway Towns. Sir Andrew stood as a half-pay officer, for he could not conveniently retire from the Royal Engineers until a few weeks after polling day. Though voters in the constituency, as a whole, strongly opposed Irish Home Rule, Sir Andrew emphasised his loyal support for W.E. Gladstone's proposals, and this helped to defeat him, and to re-elect the sitting Tory Member, Sir John Gorst, by 3,187 to 2,422 votes.[23]

In 1888, the Chatham, Brompton and Rochester Radical Association voted to merge itself with the new Chatham Reform Club, though Thompson, warned fellow members of the Association that the new Reform Club was not solely 'a place of amusement'.[24] This warning regarding the temptations present in the Chatham Reform Club went unheeded, and within eighteen months, a New Brompton Radical Association had been organised with William Thompson's support, and it endorsed Sir Andrew Clarke, who continued as the prospective radical parliamentary candidate for Chatham. The New Brompton Radical Association discussed the new Legal Eight-Hours Campaign, and returned to the republican theme, when Thompson moved that no further grants be made to members of the Royal Family. During the exhilaration and euphoria which

[18] *CO*, 20.9.79; *CN*, 20.9.79.
[19] *CO*, 4.10.79, 18.10.79, 15.11.79, 13.12.79, 3.1.80, 7.5.81, 23.7.81, 27.8.81,11.2.82; *CN*,29.11.79, 20.12.79, 10.1.80.
[20] *CO*, 11.3.82, 15.7.82; *CN*, 11.3.82.
[21] *CN*, 19.9.85, 14.11.85, 21.11.85, 12.12.85, 3.10.85, 9.1.86, 23.1.86, 8.1.87, 21.1.88.
[22] *CO*, 9.5.85; 16.5.85; *CN*, 16.5.85.
[23] R.H. Vetch, *Life of Lieut.-General the Hon. Sir Andrew Clarke*, 1905, pp. 280–1; *CO*, 26.10.86.
[24] *CN*, 25.2.88.

THE LIBERAL CANDIDATE FOR CHATHAM.

Major-Genl. SIR ANDREW CLARKE, G.C.M.G., C.B., C.I.E., R.E.

Figure 5. Major General Sir Andrew Clarke, Liberal candidate for Chatham, 1886

followed the Great Dock Strike of 1889, the Radical Association scheduled a lecture, at the Reform Club, on 'The Future of Labour', but this subject attracted a crowd of unwelcome labourers, and the topic was quickly changed to 'Payment of Members of Parliament', so the 'ragged-trousered' aristocrats of labour could avoid unnecessary contact, outside of work, with the 'great unwashed'.[25]

(3) Trades Councils

In 1890, William J. Lewington, a dockyard labourer, took on the organisation of the first May Day demonstration in the Medway Towns, following the decision made at the 1889 International Socialist and Trade Union Congress in Paris, that May Day be designated as the Workers' Day, and that demonstrations be staged throughout the world in support of the eight-hour working day. A committee met to organise the local event, and although the Amalgamated Engineers branch had turned down their invitation to attend, there were promises from the Shipwrights and Bargebuilders' Union, the National Labour Electoral Association, and the Coal Porters' Union. Sir John Gorst, the Chatham Tory MP, decided not to speak at the demonstration, when he realised that the Legal Eight Hours would be the central demand on the day. The demonstration originally had been planned for the Chatham Lines, but as this was not allowed, the venue was changed to Mr Waters' Meadow, near Fort Clarence, where there were four platforms, from which four separate meetings were held, with resolutions favouring the Legal Eight Hours proposed and approved.[26]

During September 1890, following the Dockers' Union's strike victory on behalf of the cement labourers, another important event occurred. The Medway and District Trades Council was created by representatives of the Dockyard Labourers, the Bargebuilders, the Tailors, the Dockers' Union branches, the Dockyard Rivetters, the Kent and Sussex Agricultural Labourers' Union, and the Bricklayers, with an interest shown by the Bargemen's Society. The rules adopted were based upon those of the long-established London Trades Council, and in terms of numbers, the Trades Council must be seen as an initiative on the part of the labourers and the semi-skilled. However, by February 1891, trade unions of the skilled, as well as of the unskilled and semi-skilled, had affiliated, and a lasting voice of the Medway Towns working people had been established.[27]

The second great Medway Towns May Day demonstration was organised in 1891 by the new Medway and District Trades Council, and thirty four banners led the procession to the Recreation Ground, which they had been permitted to use. Four platforms were positioned for meetings addressed by both local and national labour leaders. In the following week the Trades Council affiliated to the National Labour Electoral Association, which had been created by the

25 *CO*, 15.6.89, 29.6.89, 27.7.89; *CN*, 28.9.89.
26 *CO*, 5.4.90, 10.5.90; *CN*, 5.4.90, 26.4.90, 3.5.90, 10.5.90.
27 *CO*, 13.9.90, 4.10.90, 21.2.91; *CN*, 4.10.90, 27.12.90, 21.2.91.

Trades Union Congress in order to help elect working men as Liberal MPs, but the Association was opposed to independent labour candidates.[28]

In June 1891, a new type of trades council was proposed, at a protest meeting called by the Ship Constructive Association, when Sir Andrew Clarke presided, and the dockyard's unpopular classification scheme was condemned. A fitter took the floor to praise the 'New Trades Unionism', and a dockyard labourer moved that a 'Dockyard Trade and Labour Council' be formed, seconded by a dockyard shipwright.[29] However, within a few weeks another district trades council had been established, but not the all-encompassing dockyard trades council, which had been proposed. A meeting had created a new Chatham, Rochester and Strood Trades' Council for 'mechanics', as the Medway and District Trades Council was considered to be an organisation for 'labourers'.[30] Thus a reaction against the recent domination of the Medway Towns labour movement by the labourers had occurred, and the Medway and District Trades Council lost many of its affiliates, at a moment when the new unions were beginning their own decline. Nothing more was heard of the new 'skilled' Trades Council until December 1891.[31]

The first political success of the immediate period following the Great Dock Strike was the election of Robert Powell, as a 'Liberal', to the Rochester City Council, for in November 1890, nominated by the Dockers' Union,[32] and endorsed by the local Liberals, he had won Strood Ward with a large majority. Although he was the manager of the Bridge Cement Works, the victorious cement labourers appreciated his brave efforts in bringing their recent strike to a successful conclusion, and Powell was well-known as the President of the Rochester Co-operative Society. After the success of Powell's by-election campaign, the Medway and District Trades Council made preparations for the forthcoming municipal elections, and, in March 1891, decided to endorse candidates for all three Town Councils. In July, four test questions were sent by the Trades Council to all candidates, with endorsements decided according to their replies.

1.   In the event of your being elected to the Corporation, will you use your vote and influence to obtain for all workmen employed by the Corporation trades union rates of pay?
2.   And vote in favour of the hours of labour for all municipal employees being limited to 48 hours per week on six days?
3.   Are you willing to assist in the return of working men to fill all the vacancies that may arise in the future, until a fair proportion of working men are members of the Corporation?
4.   Are you in favour of evening meetings?[33]

28   *CO*, 9.5.91, 16.5.91; *CN*, 7.3.91, 9.5.91, 16.5.91.
29   *CN*, 20.6.91.
30   *CN*, 18.7.91.
31   *CO*, 5.12.91.
32   *CO*, 8.11.90; *CN*, 8.11.90.
33   *CO*, 7.11.91; *CN*, 17.10.91, 31.10.91.

These four test questions were distilled from the Medway Towns' first modern Labour programme, which the Trades Council had divided into two sections.

> LOCAL: 1. the trade union rate of pay for all municipal employees; 2. the 48 hour week for all municipal employees; 3. a trade union clause in all municipal contracts; 4. municipal workshops to give jobs to the unemployed; 5. the enforcement of sanitary regulations regarding workshops and dwellings; 6. the granting of allotments to workingmen; 7. free libraries, baths and wash-houses.
>
> IMPERIAL: 1. payment for MPs; 2. election expenses to be borne by the local rates; 3. a triennial Parliament and a Second Ballot; 4. the 48 hour week in all Government Establishments; 5. Adult Suffrage; 6. free democrati-cally-controlled education and technical training; 7. a Department of Labour with a Minister of Industry, incorporating a National Arbitration Council; 8. District and Parish Councils with real powers; 9. nationalisation of the land, railways and canals; 10. popular control of the Liquor Trade.[34]

Lewington was criticised for the support given by his Trades Council to a Tory municipal candidate, but he answered that they had not been ready to run their own candidates, and they had supported all who agreed formally with the 'Labour Programme'. The Tory, a local barber, became an unsuccessful 'Inde-pendent Labour' candidate, and Lewington's action was defended by William Packer of the Bargebuilders', and by James Burke of the Dockers' Union.[35] In the previous year, Lewington, whilst moving a vote of thanks to Sir John Gorst, MP, had called himself a 'non-party man', and as he progressed towards the idea of an independent labour party, he may have been tempted to back a 'good Tory', rather than automatically supporting all Liberals, good or bad.[36] When interviewed in May 1891, Lewington was asked which party he supported: '[p]ut me down blue or black, pink or primrose . . . I'm an out-and-out prohibi-tionist, or was until I got mixed up in labour questions; now I have to consider that as well before I can support any candidate'.[37] However, by the end of October 1891, Lewington was speaking at Gillingham, alongside the socialist pioneers, Henry H. Champion of London, and Arthur Field of Maidstone, when a resolution was passed favouring the formation of a Gillingham Labour Party, and such was founded, with Lewington as one of its joint secretaries.[38]

At the beginning of 1892, the Trades Council began interviewing possible 'labour' parliamentary candidates, and William C. Steadman of the Barge-builders' Union, and Fred Maddison, a printer, who was the editor of the Amal-gamated Society of Railway Servants' journal, were questioned regarding the 'Labour Programme'. Steadman was endorsed for the Medway Division, and at the next Trades Council meeting, Maddison won the 'ticket' for Rochester,

34 *CN*, 18.7.91.
35 *CO*, 24.10.91, 7.11.91; *CN*, 17.10.91, 31.10.91.
36 *CO*, 27.9.90; *CN*, 27.9.90.
37 *CO*, 23.5.91.
38 *CO*, 31.10.91; *CN*, 7.11.91.

though the Tory candidate also was interviewed. The May meeting questioned and endorsed Sir Andrew Clarke for his second attempt at Chatham.[39] The 'Irish Question' no longer dominated Sir Andrew's election campaign, as he expressed a carefully considered advanced radicalism, and, at one meeting, spoke of his belief in the government's duty to be a 'Model Employer', for which '(h)e was held up as an agitator, as interfering with the capitalists of this country, and as a propagator of socialist doctrines. At this next election, the workmen must prove that it was a democratic doctrine.' At a Liberal Association meeting, the 'Agitator-General' spoke to the workingmen in the audience: 'I would advise even government workmen to join trades unions. I feel that little by little you have thrown off your past apathy in the matter, and are beginning to recognise that you must unite to protect your own individual interests.'[40]

In 1892, the Trades Council's third annual May Day demonstration had smaller support than the two previous ones, with an estimated 3,000 participants, but these did include Steadman, Maddison, and Clarke.[41] In the General Election campaign of summer 1892, a Labour Cycle Corps, formed by Lewington and Trades Council colleagues from the Dockers' Union, organised meetings for Steadman in the riverside villages, where a good result was obtained. In Gillingham, a 'Great Labour Meeting' was held to support Sir Andrew's candidature, but all three endorsed candidates were defeated though three Labour MPs had been elected elsewhere in England.[42]

After these disappointing results, a controversy developed, when Lewington, in an interview for a local paper, claimed with some reason, that there had been only one 'labour' candidate: Steadman, and that the other two were 'Liberals', of the 'liberal–labour' ilk. 'We did not look upon Mr. Steadman as an Independent Labour candidate. [The three] were called Liberal and Labour candidates until the election was over, but now the defeat has come they are simply Labour candidates – no doubt they would have been Liberal candidates had they been victorious.' Lewington explained that the Trades Council, having endorsed the three candidates, was unable to deliver the votes of unaffilated trade unions. He claimed that the coal porters' votes had gone solidly to the Tory in Rochester, as well as had a large part of the bargemen. At the time of the campaign, the local Dockers' Union had been involved in a leadership crisis, after the arrest of the Strood secretary, who was charged with embezzlement. The branch was in a 'rather weak and disorganised condition', and without the active participation of the Dockers' Union, the Trades Council was seriously weakened. Nevertheless, Lewington announced,

> In the future we intend to form an independent labour party, working irrespective of either political party, for an independent Labour candidate . . . Our

39 *CO*, 19.3.92, 21.5.92; *CN*, 12.3.92.
40 *CN*, 2.4.92, 25.6.92; Vetch, *op. cit.*, pp. 281–2.
41 *CO*, 7.5.92; *CN*, 7.5.92.
42 *CO*, 2.7.92; *CN*, 18.6.92, 25.6.92, 9.7.92.

tactics here in the future will be similar to those pursued at Battersea, West Ham, and Middlesboro', where an independent labour candidate has stood distinct from the two political parties. In adopting Liberal and Conservative candidates we cannot work with the assurance of success, for Liberal working men won't vote for a Conservative-Labour candidate, and vice versa. In the event of a pure-Labour candidate putting up, working men of both shades of political opinion would vote for him.

Lewington went on to blame the Liberals in the boroughs for failing to campaign and vote for the liberal–labour candidates. Steadman had been opposed by the Liberal establishment because he was a 'labour' trade unionist, and Lewington criticised the dockyardmen who had rejected their 'best friend', when they failed to vote for Sir Andrew: 'Chatham has pronounced against him, and thus made itself conspicuous amongst the other dockyard towns by its verdict, which says in effect "the Tories are not a bad lot of fellows, so we will stick with them". What short memories, or forgiving spirits, the men of Chatham must have to be sure – perhaps both. We have indeed lost our best friend. I had been building my hopes on great things for Sir Andrew Clarke.'[43] The Rochester result provoked a petition alleging serious corruption on the part of Rochester's Tories.[44]

The dockyard plumber and Rochester radical, Michael Sankey, who had resigned from Lewington's trade union, replied to his former comrade, dismissing all hope of independent labour success, outside of its traditional loyal service to the Liberal Party. Sankey called the Trades Council 'a donkey masquerading in the lion's skin', which could not be the basis of local labour politics, and Lewington countered with the examples of John Burns, MP, Keir Hardie, MP, and Havelock Wilson, MP, and ended with the fable of the fox who 'abused the grapes for being sour, and not worthy of his notice'.[45] The correspondence continued for some weeks, but at the end of the exchange Arthur Field of the Dockers' Union National Executive intervened, criticising Lewington for siding with the rebels in the local Dockers' Union, but he did not blame him for causing that crisis. Field agreed that the Dockers' Union was in decline, awaiting a second wave of industrial militancy, as had occurred in 1889. Returning to the Lewington-Sankey controversy, he dismissed Sankey as 'a political blackleg to the Labour party'. The real cause of the 'Labour' defeats, according to Field, was the Trades Council's 'Labour Programme', which may have won a few Tory working men's votes, but frightened off the money and votes of the 'shopkeepers and master tallowchandlers'. At the next General Election, he predicted the Liberal Party would lose more working class votes by courting middle class voters, than it had lost middle class ones by adopting the 'Labour Programme' in 1892.[46]

---

43 *CN*, 23.7.92.
44 Rochester Election Petition Enquiry, 1892.
45 *CN*, 30.7.92.
46 *CN*, 6.8.92, 13.8.92, 20.8.92, 27.8.92, 3.9.92, 10.9.92.

(4) The Independent Labour Party

In July 1892, Lewington and Field were delegates to the annual conference of the Eight Hours' League of Kent, held at Sittingbourne, when the former represented the Chatham Eight Hours League, and the latter the Dockers' Union. The meeting approved unanimously the 'Abstention' advice given by the Maidstone Labour Party during the recent parliamentary election, and a resolution calling for 'a National Labour Convention to prepare an efficient political labour organisation and a practical labour programme' was seconded by Lewington, and passed without opposition.[47] In October 1892, the 'Kentish Labour Party', as the Eight Hours' League of Kent was renamed, met at Maidstone,[48] but the organisation again would be repackaged as the 'Kentish Independent Labour Party' by the time of its 1893 annual conference.[49] The result of this agitation was seen in January 1893, when Lewington was elected as the official delegate to the Bradford Conference, which founded the new national party, representing his Trades Council, the Gillingham Independent Labour Party, the Chatham Labour Party, which had been the Chatham Eight Hours League, and the Sheerness Dockyard Labourers' Union. He was instructed to move three resolutions regarding: 1. trade union rates for all government employees; 2. forty-eight-hour week in government establishments; 3. abolition of systematic overtime in government establishments. These were not 'socialist' resolutions, but they reflected the experience of permanent labourers employed in state-owned industry.[50]

Lewington and his small band of ILP enthusiasts, tried to exploit the 1892 General Election victory of James Keir Hardie, when they invited the charismatic leader of the new Party to speak at the Chatham Public Hall. This meeting was hopefully to serve as a launch for a large and active Medway Towns political movement. In February 1893, only weeks after the ILP's Bradford conference, Hardie spoke to the three resolutions which Lewington had moved at Bradford. But poor weather meant that the hall was half-empty when the new MP addressed Sir Andrew Clarke's old theme: 'The State as an Employer of Labour'.[51]

At the first county-wide conference in 1893 of the Kentish ILP held in Dover, the Medway Towns sent delegates from the Chatham Amalgamated Bakers, the Gillingham Dockers' Union and the New Brompton ILP, and Lewington was elected county president.[52] Renewed political impetus resulting from the Bradford Conference led to the formation of the New Brompton ILP, established at a meeting of six socialists in Lewington's front room on Copenhagen Road. The

[47] CO, 9.7.92.
[48] CN, 8.10.92.
[49] CN, 8.7.93.
[50] CO, 14.1.93; CN, 14.1.93; D. Howell, British Workers and the Independent Labour Party, 1888–1906, London 1983, pp. 283–300; H. Pelling, Origins of the Labour Party, 1880–1900, London 1965, pp. 112–24; ILP, Report of the First General Conference (1893) passim.
[51] CO, 25.2.93; CN, 11.2.93, 25.2.93.
[52] CN, 8.7.93.

branch had grown large enough to start its own club in the same house, but it came to very little. During the summer of 1893, a second branch of the ILP was formed in Gillingham, and for some years this would represent the extent of the new party within the Medway Towns.[53] The ILP had appeared in the district a few years after the Salvation Army, when these two organisations represented opposing approaches to the clearing up of the mess left behind by nineteenth century capitalism. They were out on the street offering rival routes to salvation, one worldly and the other spiritual, and both were harassed, at the beginning, by drunken hooligans and the forces of law and order. At this present moment in Medway Towns history, there remains a Salvation Army base in Chatham, but there is no longer more than a memory of the old ILP.

There were still two rival Trades Councils in the Medway Towns: the 'Medway and District', and the 'Rochester, Chatham and Strood', and unity would not come until 1894. By March 1893, the latter Trades Council had done very little to justify its existence,[54] but it was reported that a joint committee of the two Trades Councils would organise a united labour demonstration in May. Lewington's radical critic, Sankey, acted as chief marshall of the procession, which went to the Recreation Ground, where there were three platforms, at which the Devonport Liberal MP was the main speaker before a very small crowd.[55] There was some good news, as trades council unity came at long last, when negotiations, in January 1894, were successfully carried out between the 'Rochester, Chatham and Strood' and the 'Medway and District'. A joint delegate meeting unanimously decided on unification of the mechanics' and labourers' trades councils, and Lewington suggested the name of 'Chatham and District Trades Council', which was accepted. The new Trades Council would admit labourers' unions and would be empowered to collect strike levies, when required. Lewington was honoured by being chosen the first president of the unified Trades Council, with George Bates, a dockyard hammerman, as secretary.[56]

In the autumn of 1893, a new Rochester Radical Association was formed to support the old-style liberal–labourism, at a meeting of working men, when Sankey was the mover of the resolution. Some feared that the new Radical Association might split the Liberal vote, but nevertheless Sankey was elected its president, and in October he opposed any Tory–Liberal 'deal' over Rochester School Board elections. The Radical Association decided to run its own candidate, and when the Liberal stood down in St Margaret's Ward, Sankey, who had been nominated as the radical and Labour candidate, refused to leave the field open, as was usual, for the Tory, but the Tory still won.[57]

As the 1894 Gillingham District Council elections approached, independent

53   *CN*, 10.6.93, 22.7.93, 19.8.93, 26.8.93.
54   *CO*, 1.4.93.
55   *CO*, 13.5.93; *CN*, 29.4.93, 13.5.93.
56   *CO*, 27.1.94, 14.4.94; *CN*, 13.1.94, 27.1.94.
57   *CO*, 28.10.93; *CN*, 2.9.93, 14.10.93.

candidates were nominated. The New Brompton Co-operative Society and the Gillingham Ratepayers' Association endorsed a mixed political list, while the local ILP held a selection meeting, which chose Walter Cook, a dockyard ship-wright, and Lewington, who both failed to win their own Co-operative Society's endorsement. At that same moment, the Admiralty ordered their workers not to accept election to District Councils, for dockyardmen could not attend the daytime meetings. If this Order were allowed, five candidates would not have been able to take their Council seats, if elected, though they planned to amend the standing orders so as to allow evening meetings. The Trades Council met and endorsed the two Labour candidates at Gillingham, and their next meeting petitioned the Admiralty to rescind the proposed ban. This action was demanded also by the Ratepayers' Association, and by the local leader of the Liberal Party, George H. Leavey, who would become a significant influence in the growth of the Medway Towns labour movement, through his attempt, momentarily successful, at building an anti-Conservative progressive alliance of Liberals and Labour. In the December 1894 poll, all the Co-operative and Labour candidates were defeated, except for the Tory, Cllr Cock, who consistently opposed evening meetings.[58] In Rochester, Sankey again stood, unsuccessfully, as a 'progressive' candidate, in St Margaret's Ward.[59]

Though there was no electoral activity in 1895, Rochester, in January of that year, formed its first ILP branch, and Alfred Curling, who was employed in Aveling and Porter's fitting shop, was elected the branch chairman, with Arthur Ireland as secretary. In April 1895, the short-lived Rochester ILP branch took a census of the local unemployed, and in the following January a paper on 'Moses and the Social Problems' was read by Rabbi Bernard Salomons, who wished to be called comrade, and was 'promoted' out of Chatham in August 1897, after twelve years of service at the High Street synagogue.[60]

In April 1896, Lewington was a candidate in Gillingham Ward for Gillingham District Council, and was elected by 177 to 166. As soon as he had taken his seat, he demanded evening council meetings, but that battle would not be won for years. The new socialist Gillingham Town Councillor and the Trades Council demanded a 'Living Wage' for all municipal employees in the three Medway Towns.[61] At the 1896 Gillingham School Board Election, there were four 'socialist-progressive' candidates: the Royal Engineer, Major C.B. Mayne, who was an editorial board member of the Labour monthly, *Chatham Advance*, Cook, Chapman, and Lewington.

The 'socialist-progressive' educational programme was criticised by one of their opponents: 'the declared policy of Mr. Lewington, etc. is to give each classroom a certificated teacher . . . this outrageously extravagant increase

58 *CO*, 20.10.94, 27.10.94, 3.11.94, 19.11.94, 17.11.94, 24.11.94, 15.12.94, 22.12.94; *CN*, 10.11.94, 24.11.94, 15.12.94.
59 *CN*, 27.10.94.
60 *CO*, 21.8.97; *CN*, 12.1.95, 4.5.95, 1.2.96.
61 *CO*, 28.3.96, 4.4.96, 2.5.96, 16.5.96, 30.5.96; *CN*, 21.3.96, 4.4.96, 9.5.96.

would have the effect of raising the School Board rate to eight pence in the pound'. Thompson and Lewington both were re-elected, and Major Mayne joined them on the Gillingham School Board. At the end of that year, in a by-election for a Strood seat on the Rochester Council, Robert Powell, who had served on the City Council from November 1890 to November 1893, was returned unopposed.[62]

At Gillingham, in the 1897 municipal election, the Trades Council supported Chapman as Labour candidate in the Gillingham Ward, as well as Cook, its secretary, and Holmes, in the New Brompton Ward. Both Holmes and Cook were New Brompton Co-operative Society Committeemen. In addition to these three, the Trades Council endorsed the five progressive candidates for the Medway Board of Guardians. At the April 1897 poll, Holmes, described as 'burly, blunt, and unassuming', was a victor, but he was 'radical labour', not 'socialist', though he did possess excellent trade union credentials. Holmes' running mates lost, but three of the five 'progressives' were successful in the Board of Guardians poll.[63]

(5) Chatham and the ILP

Chatham came late to independent labour politics, as its first socialist organisa-tion was founded, after the new ILP had begun to fade, both locally and nation-ally. The Chatham, New Brompton and District Socialist Society was formed under the leadership of Egerton Percy Wake, in 1896, but it was short-lived.[64] Wake became a socialist candidate in the Luton Ward, in the November 1897 Council Election, and the Trades Council endorsed his candidature, but the erratic Irish Anglican priest, George Hitchcock, who had been supported by Lewington and Wake during the former's battle with the Board of Guardians over the treatment of pauper children, decided to support the incumbent Liberal councillors, and Hitchcock resigned from the 'Socialist Board' of the *Chatham Advance*. When the votes were counted, the Tories had won both of the Luton seats, with Wake in fifth place.[65]

In 1898, the New Brompton Co-operative Society voted to support once again direct representation on their Town Council, and to nominate candidates. William Barnett, the Co-operative's full-time secretary, and James Davis, a dockyard storehouse foreman and Liberal, were the Co-operative candidates for New Brompton Ward, with James Chapman, the Labour candidate, also

[62]   *CO*, 7.11.96, 14.11.96; *CN*, 24.10.96; Waters, *op. cit.*, p. 8.
[63]   *CO*, 13.3.97, 20.3.97, 10.4.97, 1.5.97; *CN*, 20.3.97, 10.4.97, 1.5.97.
[64]   *CN*, 14.8.97.
[65]   *CO*, 19.12.96, 25.9.97, 2.10.97, 23.10.97, 30.10.97, 6.11.97; *CN*, 19.12.96, 14. 8. 97.

endorsed by his Co-operative Society. Davis finished top of the poll, and Barnett won in second place, while Chapman came a close, but losing, third.[66]

The Chatham and District Trades Council, the voice of the Medway Towns labour movement, decided in 1898, to carry out its long-standing policy, demanding 'labour representation' on all elected bodies, and it organised a Gillingham electoral committee composed of local co-operative, temperance and other reform-minded societies. This was the Gillingham Civic Union, formed early in 1898, at a meeting chaired by Lewington.[67] Early in 1899, with William Wardle of the Amalgamated Society of Carpenters and Joiners as secretary, the Civic Union decided to endorse the 'progressive' ticket of William Herring, Lewington, Chapman and Cook. However, an electoral disaster occurred, when Lewington lost his Town Council seat, while Chapman and Cook failed to win additional seats. Herring, another dockyard writer, and a Tory, was elected in the New Brompton Ward as a Co-operative Councillor,[68] and the Rev. George Hitchcock was a winning candidate in the Medway Board of Guardians elections, and, with some justification, he labelled himself the only 'Labour' elected representative in Chatham.[69] At this very moment, the Chatham Co-operative Society considered it was time for them to select a candidate for their own Town Council, and William J. Brown, a dockyard smith, and a Liberal, was nominated for one of the Luton seats, with the blessing of Hitchcock. Brown lost, though with twice the number of votes that Wake had taken in the previous year.[70] Although Labour had lost its sole Gillingham Town Councillor in the April election, they had a chance to increase the 'progressive' representation on the Gillingham School Board, in November 1899, when they supported a five-man 'School Board Ticket', which was endorsed by the New Brompton ILP as well, and four of the five were elected.[71]

The 1900 Election at Gillingham occurred soon after the London Conference had established the National Labour Representation Committee, and there was a hint of the new approach, which that initiative represented, when yet another joint co-operative-trade union body was formed: the Gillingham Municipal Workers' Election Committee. This organisation nominated four candidates, but only Cllr Holmes was re-elected.[72] Commenting on the disappointing result, the Trades Council's secretary wrote in his 1899–1900 Report: 'we have shopkeepers and publicans on the Council who oppose evening meetings and other necessary reforms, and yet we vote them in, rather than men from our own ranks who we know would serve us better; let us amend this in the future by working in conjunction with the New Brompton Co-operative Society, which, in my

---

[66] *CO*, 5.2.98, 19.3.98, 26.3.98, 2.4.98, 9.4.98; *CN*, 26.3.98, 2.4.98, 9.4.98.

[67] *CO*, 5.2.98, 19.2.98; *CN*, 19.2.98.

[68] *CO*, 4.3.98, 11.3.99, 1.4.99; *CN*, 4.3.99, 11.3.99.

[69] *CO*, 25.3.99.

[70] *CO*, 25.3.99.

[71] *CO*, 14.10.99, 21.10.99, 28.10.99, 4.11.99, 11.11.99; *CN*, 14.10.99, 21.10.99, 28.10.99, 4.11.99, 11.11.99, 25.11.99.

[72] *CO*, 17.3.00, 7.4.00; *CN*, 31.3.00, 7.4.00.

opinion, is a wise plan, as it prevents the clashing of what is practically two working-class organisations'.[73]

The Trades Council was confident enough, even after these defeats, to fleetingly discuss the possibility of a Labour parliamentary candidate for Chatham, and George Barnes, the Amalgamated Society of Engineers' General Secretary, as well as an ILP member, was favoured by a meeting at the end of May 1900.[74] Working-class jingoism, which flared up during the Boer War, made Chatham an unattractive seat for any ambitious national politician, and any local Liberal would have put himself in jeopardy by opposing the Tory government during a popular, if bloody, colonial war. Nevertheless, the former mayor and wealthy merchant, George H. Leavey, who was retiring from the Chatham Town Council, suggested a liberal–labour candidate, when he himself was pressed to stand. Leavey brought Ben Jones, the manager of the London Co-operative Wholesale Society, down to his house, in December 1899. It was unlikely that the grocer, and new leader of Chatham's Liberals, Sydney Hart, who had acted as a scourge of the co-operatives, would have welcomed Jones as parliamentary candidate, even if he were recommended by the Liberal Federation Council, and had conducted an energetic campaign in Woolwich at the 1892 General Election. During his shopkeeping days in Woolwich, Leavey had learned through his work with the future Woolwich MP, Will Crooks, that the advance of labour representation could not be halted by old-fashioned Liberalism, even if well-seasoned with the piety of Sidney Hart and the Free Church Council. Leavey's first attempt had failed, but his second would be very successful.[75]

Powell was renominated for the Strood Ward by representatives of all three parties, as a 'compromise' candidate, with the task of 'securing increased representation for Strood'. Arthur Ireland of the Amalgamated Society of Carpenters and Joiners and the ILP was selected as the first 'real' Labour candidate for the Rochester City Council, in St Margaret's Ward. In 1900, Ireland stood for office, as the candidate of the Trades Council, and though an active member of the ILP, he may have thought of his party as a 'social movement' rather than a poltical party, for he explained his position in the following words: 'I contest this Election in the interests of no Political party, whatever, but in the interests of the welfare of the City of Rochester generally, and the workers of St. Margaret's Ward in particular. Seeing that all interests save those of labour have direct representation, and with that object in view I submit myself to your judgment.' He went on to demand that every worker should have adequate wages to ensure 'a healthy home, a complete meal, and a sufficiency of clothing, and with that end in view I should always support the insertion of a trade union clause in all municipal contracts, and current wages to all municipal employees'. He called for the municipalisation of gas and water supplies, as well as 'the Electric Light supply, the running of the Trams and supply of Telephonic Communications,

---

73 Chatham and District Trades Council Annual Report and Balance Sheet, July 1899/1900.
74 *CO*, 2.6.1900.
75 *CO*, 6.10.99, 2.12.99; see Leavey's obituary in *CN*, 20.1.05.

also the erection of Municipal Slaughter Houses, a Borough Market Place for the use of Butchers, Fish-mongers and Market-gardeners, etc.' Public health was a major issue, and Ireland demanded 'a thorough system of Main-drainage, a more careful and periodical inspection of the sanitary arrangements in the homes of the workers and the provision of thoroughly sanitary public conveniences, the demolition of slum property and the erection of suitable accommodation under and according to the Better Housing of the Working Classes Act . . . the erection of Public Baths, the providing of Music for the citizens on summer evenings, and with a view to cleansing and maintaining a good road in the High Street of Rochester and Strood I should support the idea of Paving with Wood throughout'. Ireland came bottom of the poll with 556 votes.[76]

After the cement workers' strike of 1901 had been broken,[77] Ireland was nominated for the Frindsbury by-election, in September 1901, but he lost on a small poll in a ward dominated by the cement trades. However, in November, Ireland reversed the result, achieving the first authentic Labour victory in the city's history.[78] At the same time, the Chatham Co-operative Society nominated its own candidate, Richard F. Palmer, an elderly iron and brass founder, for Luton Ward, which he won at the top of the poll.[79] During 1901, the first election activity in Gillingham was Lewington's candidature for the New Brompton Kent County Council seat, where he lost to the Tory, and at the Town Council election, when he and Chapman stood in Gillingham Ward, as New Brompton Co-operative Society's candidates. The two New Brompton Ward Co-operative Councillors, Barnett and Davis, were re-elected. Lewington and Chapman were defeated. The fact that the former, after his 1899 failure to be re-elected to the Town Council, was not an official 'Labour' candidate may be indicative of the ILP's weakest moment, both locally and nationally.[80] Lewington's own inventions, the Civic Union and the Municipal Workers Election Committee had both failed, and, significantly, at the end of 1901, after his electoral defeats, he was active within the National Democratic League, an upgraded vehicle for old-style 'liberal–labour' politics, organised, in 1900, by radicals and ex-members of the ILP. The new League's National Secretary was the ILP's former Secretary, Tom Mann, in a depressing period of British labour history.[81] Nevertheless, Lewington was very soon back in the wars on behalf of a resurgent Gillingham and New Brompton ILP, at a demonstration, where he moved a resolution favouring 'Direct Labour Representation'.[82] This commitment was carried further, when the Trades Council corresponded with Ramsay MacDonald, the

[76] *CO*, 20.10.00, 3.11.00; *CN*, 20.10.00, 27.10.00, 3.11.00; Election Handbill, Rochester City Council, 1900, St Margaret's Ward, Arthur W. Ireland.
[77] *CO*, 23.2.01, 16.3.01, 23.3.01, 6.4.01; *CN*, 16.2.01, 23.2.01, 2.3.01, 9.3.01, 16.3.01, 23.3.01, 30.3.01.
[78] *CO*, 24.8.01, 31.8.01, 7.9.01, 26.10.01, 2.11.01, 9.11.01; *CN*, 31.8.01, 7.9.01, 14.9.01, 26.10.01, 9.11.01.
[79] *CO*, 2.11.01, 9.11.01.
[80] *CO*, 16.3.01, 23.3.01, 30.3.01; *CN*, 16.3.01, 23.3.01, 30.3.01.
[81] *CO*, 18.1.02; *CN*, 18.1.02; Howell, *op. cit.*, p. 128.
[82] *CO*, 25.1.02; *CN*, 25.1.02.

National Secretary of the Labour Representation Committee, regarding affiliation to his organisation, which had been proposed by Lewington's Government Labourers' Union.

A Labour Representation conference, organised by the Trades Council, on 12 April 1902, included representatives from trade union, co-operative, and socialist organisations, with Ireland presiding over nearly a hundred delegates. Lewington moved another 'labour representation' resolution, a local Labour Representation Committee was unanimously established, and MacDonald, the future Labour Prime Minister, made his first speech in the Medway Towns. A new period of Labour politics had begun, and as a sign of the times, the Rochester Co-operative Society, in October, followed the advice of both Powell and Ireland, and affiliated their Society to the new Labour Representation Committee.[83]

(6) Labour and Local Government

In March 1902, the Chatham Co-operative Society, endorsed by the Trades Council, nominated an unsuccessful female candidate in Luton Ward for the Medway Board of Guardians. Lewington was the Labour candidate at Gillingham Ward, and he was elected at the top of the poll, while both the Co-operative Society's candidates lost. As the Chatham Town Council elections approached, the Trades Council nominated Wake as Labour candidate again in Luton Ward, with a shipwright, as his running-mate. Frederick Hills stood in the St John's Ward, where he was described as 'one of advanced socialistic views', and as he had stood unsuccessfully as an 'independent', his opinions may have been far too 'advanced' for the Medway Towns' labour leadership. At his second attempt in Luton Ward, Wake and his comrade both lost.[84]

In the years between the formation of the local Labour Representation Committee and the election of a Labour MP, the Medways Towns labour movement continued a generally unsuccessful attempt at establishing a beachhead within the three local councils. The 1903 municipal elections in the Medway Towns were the last before the 'maturity' of the local Labour Representation Committee, and these began in March, at Gillingham, when Holmes and William Collins, another dockyard fitter, won seats in New Brompton Ward at the last election for the old Gillingham District Council.[85] The New Brompton Co-operative Society decided to contest all the Wards, except Old Brompton Ward, in November 1903, which would be the first election of the new Chartered and Incorporated Town of Gillingham. There were fifteen prospective 'Labour' candidates listed, some of which were Labour Representation Committee men, who would stand even if not nominated by the Co-operative

83   *CO*, 22.3.02, 12.4.02, 19.4.02; *CN*, 22.3.02, 18.10.02.
84   *CO*, 15.3.02, 22.3.02, 29.3.02, 5.4.02; *CN*, 22.3.02, 29.3.02, 5.4.02, 12.4.02.
85   *CO*, 21.3.03, 11.4.03; *CN*, 21.3.03, 11.4.03.

Society: William Reynolds, a dockyard shipwright in North Ward, Lewington in East Ward, Chapman in West Ward, and Arthur Hill, a dockyard fitter in South Ward. The Co-operative Society selected Herring and William Reynolds in North Ward, Collins and Chapman in West Ward, Edmund Middleton and Robert Allison, a dockyard shipwright in South Ward, Holmes and Lewington in East Ward, and Cook and George Doughty, a dockyard shipwright in Medway Ward. The New Brompton Co-operative Society's influence within the community became the major issue in the local election campaign, as the old Town Council had become known as the 'Co-operative Council', even though their nominees held only six out of the fifteen seats. The 'Co-operative' Councillors' reputation as 'high raters' affected the result, and only three of their nominees were successful. Herring and Collins lost their seats, though Middleton won independently of the New Brompton Co-operative Society, and Holmes and Lewington were re-elected.[86]

At Rochester, in 1903, Powell had been expected to stand for Labour in the Strood Ward, after the public announcement of his resignation as a 'liberal–labour' Councillor, but he withdrew in favour of Alfred Curling. The Rochester Co-operative Society gave its own backing to Curling, but his subsequent defeat was more than a temporary setback, as the Co-operative Society decided neither to help with his election expenses, nor to renew their Labour Representation Committee affiliation.[87] At Chatham, Wake was at the top of the poll, winning one of the Luton Ward seats, and Labour had secured, at last, an official foothold on the Chatham Town Council.[88]

The autumn of 1904 saw the usual plans being made for the annual elections, at which the New Brompton Co-operative Society voted to support four municipal candidates in Gillingham, with Wake present at the meeting to deliver the Trades Council's endorsements. Chapman retired diplomatically from the election in favour of a Co-operative nominee, but nevertheless the Labour Representation Committee would be criticised for failing to organise the Labour vote. Collins lost his seat in West Ward, while George Crowe, a retired naval writer and a Tory, who was to play a very important part in J.H. Jenkins' first election campaign, won a seat.[89] At Chatham, Palmer had stood down in Luton Ward due to 'advanced age', and George Stroud, a dockyard smith, nominated by the Chatham Co-operative Society, failed to hold the seat.[90] In Rochester, Ireland was re-elected in Frindsbury Ward, opposed by neither Liberals nor Tories, who both sent in nomination papers for the ILP leader.[91]

[86] *CO*, 26.9.03, 3.10.03, 10.10.03, 24.10.03; *CN*, 26.9.03, 24.10.03, 31.10.03, 7.11.03.
[87] *CO*, 3.10.03, 10.10.03, 24.10.03, 31.10.03, 7.11.03; *CN*, 3.10.03, 24.10.03, 31.10.03, 7.11.03, 19.12.03.
[88] *CO*, 10.10.03, 24.10.03; *CN*, 26.9.03, 7.11.03.
[89] *CO*, 22.10.04, 29.10.04, 5.11.04; *CN*, 5.11.04.
[90] *CO*, 29.10.04, 5.11.04; *CN*, 29.10.04.
[91] *CO*, 29.10.04.

(7) The Rochester By-Election of 1903

During 1903 the local Labour Representation Committee had grown in strength. Its February meeting attracted delegates from the Boilermakers' Helpers' Society, the Shipwrights, the Carpenters and Joiners, the Gas Workers, the Government Labourers, the Engineers, the Chatham and District Trades Council, and the Rochester Labour Association. Powell accepted the presidency, and it was decided that local parliamentary seats should be contested, with rumours of the imminent announcement of a candidate. There had been no contest in either seat during the 1900 General Election, and the Liberals had not elected an MP in Chatham since Arthur Otway in 1868. The Rochester Labour Association became involved in the 1903 parliamentary by-election caused by the death of Lord Salisbury, whose son and heir, Lord Cranborne, had been Rochester's Tory MP since 1893. Ireland explained that Harry Johnston, the Liberal's parliamentary candidate, had met the committee of the Rochester Labour Association, and had agreed to 'nearly the whole of their programme'. The Labour Association decided that members could support Johnston as 'the Free Trade' candidate, but they would not become part of the Liberals' official election organisation. For this reason, Robert Powell and Arthur Ireland, though they had opposed any formal backing for the Liberal, had voted for the unsuccessful Liberal candidate, but they had not worked at 'getting out the Labour vote'. Both Powell and Ireland were accused by members of the Rochester Liberal Club of selling out the Liberal candidate, who had lost to Charles Tuff by only 521 votes.[92] The two Councillors, Powell and Ireland, who had been 'social members' of the Club, both resigned their memberships. Powell described the difficulties involved in Labour endorsing a Liberal parliamentary candidate. Unless a candidate to represent the constituency in Parliament declares himself in favour of the whole of the industrial programme, he would not have his support. But the candidate who did take that programme in its entirety, no matter what they chose to term themselves, would have his help, both by voice and vote . . . He intended henceforth to devote all his energies to Labour interests, and the improvement of its organisations, so as to put the industrial classes of this city and district in a position to dictate terms to candidates, instead of being dictated to by political parties as hitherto.

At a meeting of the Labour Representation Committee, in October 1903, Powell did the 'honourable thing'; he announced his retirement from the Rochester City Council, for 'I joined the Council . . . as a Liberal-Labour representative, and probably the cause of dissatisfaction has been that I have been misunderstood . . . Eight or nine years ago I left the Liberal Association.'[93] This dispute did not seem to auger well for future co-operation between the Rochester Labour Association and the more radical members of the Rochester Liberal Association. At the very same moment, the Chatham Liberal leadership

[92] *CO*, 31.1.03, 14.3.03, 4.4.03, 25.4.03, 20.6.03; *CN*, 14.3.03, 4.4.03, 18.4.03, 20.6.03; F.F. Smith, *Rochester in Parliament, 1295–1933*, Rochester 1933.
[93] *CO*, 3.10.03; *CN*, 3.10.03.

approached the Labour Representation Committee to see if a candidate could be adopted, who would be acceptable to both Liberal and Labour Parties, as it was believed that a Liberal-Labour man was 'the only candidate [with] the ghost of a chance in opposition to Sir Horatio Davies . . . A Labour candidate with official Liberalism holding aloof [as in 1900], or a Liberal . . . with the Trades and Labour Unions passive or hostile, would be nowhere.' However, the Labour Representation Committee, in the Medway Towns, preferred a 'bona fide worker, and a section at all events would fix its choice upon a past or present dockyard man'. Robert Powell presided at the Labour Repesentation Committee's April meeting, which appointed a sub-committee to interview possible parliamentary candidates, who would address a delegate conference as well.[94] The Rochester Co-operative Society's quarterly meeting, in June 1903, elected seven delegates to that committee, and the Chatham Co-operative Society was formally invited to affiliate. Two months later, the Labour Representative Committee decided to contest all but two local council seats, and electoral pacts with the co-operative societies were discussed.[95]

During the early part of September 1903, there was a joint meeting of Labour and Liberal activists, when George Leavey introduced a former Lancashire coal miner, Sam Woods, who was secretary of the Trades Union Congress' Parliamentary Committee. After he had been interviewed, Woods was unanimously accepted as a prospective candidate by this informal bi-partisan meeting. The other contestant, Alex Wilkie, the Associated Society of Shipwrights' General Secretary, had direct experience of Chatham's working environment, but he had made enemies in the local community, when he recommended that dockyardmen, because they could not strike, should not be accepted as ordinary members of his union. This 'slander' was based on the fact that dockyard shipwrights did not negotiate as did private shipwrights; they humbly petitioned the Admiralty. Alex Wilkie, who had been a Liberal candidate in the 1900 General Election, was interviewed and invited to speak to an Labour Representation Committee delegate meeting.[96]

In 1897, Wilkie, himself, had advised his Chatham branch to nominate a shipwright for election to the House of Commons, and he recommended a Southampton shipwright, named Wilson, who was not a dockyardman.[97] Wilkie made no commitment regarding the candidature, and in October 1903 he decided that he would not accept the nomination, and John Hogan Jenkins, his trade union colleague, was interviewed by the Medway Towns' Labour leaders. Within a week, the Medway Labour Representation Committee had met the Associated Society of Shipwright's National Executive's deputation, and Jenkins was unanimously adopted, with essential financial support promised by

94   *CO*, 11.4.03, 25.4.03; *CN*, 18.4.03.
95   *CO*, 20.6.03; *CN*, 20.6.03.
96   *CO*, 12.9.03; *CN*, 12.9.03.
97   Mavis Waters, 'Social History of the Chatham Dockyard Workforce 1860–1906', Essex Ph.D. 1979, p. 240.

his union.[98] Jenkins wrote to the local Labour Representation Committee, in February 1904, accepting their nomination, and came to the Medway Towns to make his first political speech to a local audience, at a meeting organised jointly by the Chatham and District Trades Council and the Committee, to protest against the use of Chinese labour in South Africa.[99] Jenkins' trade union, the Associated Society of Shipwrights, explained their reasons for sponsoring him, arguing that since their Chatham and Gillingham membership contained a large proportion of 'Orange' Belfast and Scots shipwrights a straight Tory v. Liberal contest, dominated by the issue of Home Rule for Ireland, would have split their branches.[100]

In July, the Labour Representation Committee held a conference where 200 delegates heard Jenkins speak, and in early August there were processions from Chatham Town Hall and from Gillingham Green to a meeting at the Hippodrome, where George Leavey spoke publicly in favour of the candidate. A few weeks later, at a Labour meeting in Gillingham's Vestry Hall, Lewington moved the resolution declaring John Hogan Jenkins to be 'a fit and proper person to be Labour candidate'. In seconding Lewington's resolution, George Leavey recalled an earlier election, when Sir Andrew Clarke had been 'ranked nominally as a Liberal, but who in the fullest sense of the word was in complete sympathy with the working man. It carried his mind back to the time when he said you need to have a working man in full and complete sympathy with the working men to contest this constituency, and if he had been there that night nobody, he was sure, would have been a heartier supporter of Alderman Jenkins than General Sir Andrew Clarke.' Leavey called for unity: '[t]here were a very large number of Liberals in Gillingham and Chatham who would cordially come and help them if they would only say "Come on". If they were to be successful at Chatham they must not begin to make enemies of those who would otherwise be their friends. Let them try to get rid of jealousies and work on one common platform, remembering this, that there were only two lobbies in the House of Commons, and if they got Alderman Jenkins in they knew which lobby he would be in.'[101]

As the campaign grew in momentum, the Medway Towns said goodbye to the first leader of their modern labour movement, and some may have felt that Lewington should have been the Labour candidate in the Chatham constituency, but a dockyard labourer could never have been selected or elected. His appointment in Hong Kong was, as an Established Storeman, both qualitatively and quantitatively, a promotion, and Lewington resigned, in September 1904, from both the Gillingham School Board and the Town Council.[102]

98 *CO*, 10.10.03; *CN*, 24.10.03.
99 *CO*, 30.1.04; Barbara Nield, 'John Jenkins Hogan (1852–1936)', *Dictionary of Labour Biography*, London 1977, vol. iv. pp. 109–10.
100 *CO*, 30.1.04, 20.2.04, 27.2.04, 12.3.04; *CN*, 12.3.04, 28.5.04.
101 *CO*, 30.7.04, 6.8.04; *CN*, 16.7.04, 30.7.04, 6.8.04.
102 *CO*, 17.9.04, 1.10.04, 15.10.04; *CN*, 17.9.04, 24.9.04, 15.10.04.

In the neighbouring Rochester constituency, there were no plans to field a Labour Representation Committee candidate, and the Rochester Labour Association, which was an affiliate, interviewed a very receptive and perceptive Ernest Henry Lamb, the prospective Liberal candidate. The bad feeling engendered by Arthur Ireland and Robert Powell's lukewarm support for the previous Liberal candidate seemed to have disappeared. A special membership meeting decided to give official support to Lamb, who joined the Labour Party in 1929, and ended his political life as Paymaster General in Ramsay MacDonald's National Government, in 1931, when Rochester's last Liberal MP became Lord Rochester, the first baron of the third creation.[103]

(8) The 1906 General Election

Unemployment became the prime issue in local politics during the months leading up to the 1906 General Election, in both constituencies, for the cement industry's structural decline, and the resultant reduction in its demand for unskilled and semi-skilled labour, was the cause of great social distress along the Medway. Moreover, Chatham dockyard had discharged workers, and in May 1905 a deputation of 'dischargees' approached the Chatham Town Council, through Cllr Wake, demanding public works to create jobs, as they had earlier requested of the Gillingham Town Council. A well supported May Day demonstration focused on the issue of unemployment, with processions from Chatham, Strood and Gillingham, and Jenkins supported the resolution on unemployment.[104]

The Tory, Cllr George Crowe, joined the speakers at the May Day demonstration on Rochester Recreation Grounds, and he moved a vote of no-confidence in the Conservative Party, at a Tory meeting in 1905, and it was carried overwhelmingly. He and Major R.L. Long were to lead the many Tories who broke tradition by supporting the 'Labour' candidate. Crowe moved the resolution thanking the Chairman, the Revd Tyssul Davis of the Chatham Unitarian Church.

> If all clergy and ministers of religion were of his stamp they would hear no more of Archbishops groaning of their poverty on £15,000 a year, while workmen from the Dockyard, in receipt of little more than fifteen "bob" a week were being deprived of that through their being discharged from their employment. He asked his hearers to think they need not take Mr. [Joseph] Chamberlain's advice and think Imperially – let them think locally, and resolve no longer to be represented in Parliament by men with grand titles who would grind them down and soar above them through the very power those whom they crushed had given them.[105]

103 *CO*, 5.3.04; *CN*, 27.2.04, 29.3.04.
104 *CO*, 10.12.04, 17.12.04, 6.5.05, 13.5.05, 20.5.05; *CN*, 17.12.04, 22.4.05, 13.5.05, 20.5.05.
105 *CO*, 6.8.04, 29.10.04, 5.11.04, 11.2.05, 6.5.05, 20.5.05, 14.10.05, 21.10.05, 28.10.05, 25.11.05,

During the following week, the Chatham and District Trades Council formed a relief committee, whose supporters came from a wide spectrum of political opinion within the constituency. When an unemployed workers' 'hunger march' to London was suggested, the relief committee insisted that its role was to relieve distress, not to protest. Throughout the summer distress increased, and Powell suggested that another committee be appointed to study the Unemployed Workmen's Act, which was the Tory government's last important piece of legislation, in response to the post-Boer-War depression of 1904.

Wake attempted to get the Chatham Town Council to implement the required public works, and the Admiralty Superintendent received unfavourable press coverage when he refused to allow a relief committee collection in the dockyard itself. However, Lewington remembered his friends in the dockyard, and organised a collection in Hong Kong, among the Medway Towns men working there, which raised £7 10s for the relief fund. By December, the unemployed had formed their own committee, but the unemployment issue would be ruthlessly utilised in the Jenkins election campaign.[106]

In October 1905, the Labour Representation Committee nominated Arthur Hill for South Ward, and James Chapman for East Ward, in the Gillingham Town Council election; Hill lost in second place, but Chapman was elected. Chatham had no Committee candidate, although Egerton Wake had endorsed Waldemar Jensen, the tramway company manager, as an unsuccessful independent candidate in Luton Ward.[107]

Hart credited the Tories with changing political attitudes: 'there was a time when by continuing a policy of concession and conciliation in local affairs, [the Tories] might have most effectually frustrated any sort of alliance and co-operation between the Liberal party and the Labour party, and they knew it. The Labour men distrusted the Liberals. The Liberals misunderstood the Labour men, and each was further from the other than the Liberals from the Tories.' But in the November 1905 municipal elections, the Conservative Party helped the Labour Party by driving 'the Liberals into an attitude of opposition and resentment'. Hart believed that the Tories had chosen the wrong candidate, Major John Eustace Jameson, after the sitting Conservative MP, Sir Horatio Davies, had withdrawn at the last moment. Jameson was 'a man whose Parliamentary record proves him to have never been in the least degree in sympathy with what the mass of Chatham men would require in a candidate'.[108]

At the end of 1905, the Labour Representation Committee appointed Arthur Ireland as organising secretary for the General Election, though Wake was the election agent.[109] Jenkins' campaign began early in December with large public

---

9.12.05, 16.12.05, 30.12.05, 6.1.06, 13.1.06, 20.1.06; *CN*, 6.8.04, 11.2.05, 20.5.05, 8.7.05, 21.10.05, 9.12.05, 13.1.06, 20.1.06.
106 *CO*, 20.5.05; *CN*, 20.5.05; Mavis Waters, *op. cit.*, pp. 242–3.
107 *CO*, 7.10.05, 14.10.05, 21.10.05, 28.10.05, 4.11.05; *CN*, 21.10.05, 28.10.05, 4.11.05.
108 *CO*, 20.1.06.
109 *CO*, 2.12.05.

meetings, and at the end of the year he was formally adopted as the Labour candidate. The Liberal Town Councillor, William Paine, gave the Committee the use of his house on Chatham High Street for use as election headquarters. During his campaign, Jenkins preached devolution for all of the nations of the United Kingdom, and free trade, which he believed would benefit the ship-building industry and his own shipwright trade. His enthusiasm for free trade helped to win many wavering Liberal voters.[110]

Free Church clergymen were frequently on Labour platforms, in support of the teetotal Methodist candidate and the founder of the Lord's Day Observance Society in Cardiff. The Labour candidate promised them his full support for their demands for the repeal of the Education Act of 1902, which forced local ratepayers to underpin the Church of England's and the Roman Catholics' schools, and the Licensing Act of 1904, which they denounced as the 'Brewers' Act', for it compensated the brewers whenever redundant public houses were de-licensed. On the other side, the working publicans, whose careers were threatened as their numbers were reduced by the 'Brewers' Act', lacked much enthusiasm for the Tory candidate, though previously the publicans had been loyal supporters of any Tory.[111]

The active Liberals of Chatham and Gillingham met at the Chatham Reform Club's Gladstone Hall to confirm their tactics at the poll. Hart was in the chair, and George Leavey, the worthiest of the worthy Liberals, moved the endorse-ment of Jenkins, who was described as a 'nominal member of the Labour Party'. The policy which Leavey had begun in 1899 was brought nearer to a successful conclusion, when his fellow Liberals, in the Gladstone Hall, agreed to support the Labour candidate, rather than run one of their own.[112]

At the poll, Jenkins had won the greatest majority in Chatham's history, with 6,692 to 4,020 for the Conservative, and a half-day dockyard holiday was granted. Nationally, the Labour Representation Committee, which would soon become the Labour Party, claimed thirty victories, including J.H. Jenkins'. Chatham may have sent a 'liberal–labour' man to the House of Commons, but Jenkins accepted the Labour Whip. Though the Liberals had planned to use him to undermine the Tory hold on the constituency, they killed off their own future chances, and would never again hold the Chatham or Gillingham seat.[113]

There was much to celebrate in the Medway Towns: the election of a Labour MP, with 'Dockyard connections', someone who could understand its problems and would propose solutions to a sympathetic Liberal government. In Rochester, the voters had rediscovered the City's radical tradition, and had elected a very Labour-friendly Liberal MP, Lamb, in harness with Jenkins, and the cause of

[110] *CO*, 9.12.05, 16.12.05, 30.12.05, 6.1.06; *CN*, 9.12.05, 6.1.06.

[111] *CO*, 6.1.06, 13.1.06; *CN*, 20.1.06.

[112] *CN*, 20.1.06.

[113] *CO*, 20.1.06; *CN*, 20.1.06, 27.1.06; Henry Pelling, *Social Geography of British Elections, 1885–1910*, London 1967, p. 77; Kenneth Lunn, *Labour Culture in Dockyard Towns: A Study of Portsmouth, Plymouth and Chatham, 1900–1950*, Amsterdam 1992, pp. 283–4.

Labour's political independence received significant encouragement.[114] At the next quarterly meeting of the Rochester Co-operative Society, when the enemies of the Labour Representation Committee moved that no politics be discussed at meetings, and that no funds be donated for elections, this motion was heavily defeated.[115] Gillingham Tories, realising their hold on the constituency was no longer unassailable, decided upon new tactics, including the emphasising of protectionist 'Fair Trade', by forming a branch of the Unionist Labour League, under the leadership of a former Gillingham 'Co-operative-Tory' Town Councillor.[116] The Chatham and District Trades Council commented on this development: 'we would urge the workers to recollect that the protection they require is protection against trusts and monopolies, the crushing of landlordism and the burden of heavy railway rates, mining rents and royalties, all of which would be perpetuated by the many "vested interests" which are striving to delude the workers into accepting a corrupt system of multiple taxes'.[117]

After a few years as a Labour Representation Committee, the Medway Towns movement was transformed into the Chatham, Gillingham and Rochester Labour Party, in May 1906, and affiliated to the National Labour Party. At that moment, its affiliates were the Chatham and District Trades Council, the Dockyard Hammermen, the Dockyard Engine Drivers and Stokers, the Government Labourers, the Chatham Shipwrights, the National Union of Smiths and Hammermen, the Plasterers, the Dockyard Iron Caulkers, the Bricklayers, the Carpenters and Joiners, the Iron Founders, the Engineers, the Steam Engine Makers, the Boilermakers, and the Independent Labour Party. Wake became its first president and Alfred William Tapp of the Amalgamated Engineers' Society its first secretary. As a step towards the individual membership of the post-war Labour Party, the new party made a constitutional dispensation allowing associate membership for those not belonging to an affiliated trade union or to the ILP, as had been done by the Woolwich and Barnard Castle constituency parties. 'In addition to affiliated members who belong to labour organisations, provision is made for associate members, who will be those in sympathy with labour needs, but who by virtue of their trade or profession are unable to belong to special labour organisations.' The new Labour Party was divided into the three historical sections of Rochester, Chatham and Gillingham, which were, in turn, divided into wards, and each ward would be organised with ward officers and committee.[118]

In August 1906, new affiliates were reported, including the Gillingham Amalgamated Union of Co-operative Employees, the Dockyard Rivetters, the Gillingham Shipwrights, and the Chatham Amalgamated Association of

---

[114] *CO*, 20.1.06; *CN*, 20.1.06.
[115] *CN*, 17.3.06.
[116] *CN*, 17.4.06.
[117] Chatham and District Trades Council Annual Report and Balance Sheet, July 1906.
[118] *CO*, 26.5.06; *CN*, 26.5.06.

Tramway and Vehicle Workers.[119] At the end of 1906, Jenkins clarified his position within the Labour Party, agreeing that he was part of the Labour Group in the House of Commons, but denying that he had ever belonged to the ILP. Moreover, he pointed out that he had seconded the trade unionist David Shackleton's nomination for Parliamentary Chairman, in opposition to the ILP's Keir Hardie, who had won.[120]

The new Labour Party faced the local elections of 1906 with great expectations, even though Wake announced his resignation as president, and refused his Co-operative Society's nomination in Luton Ward, as he was planning a career outside politics. In September, a hundred delegates attended a private conference of the party, and voted to contest all of the council wards in the three towns, but it was soon understood that this was not practical, and only seven candidates were chosen.[121] In addition, the unity of the local Labour movement was undermined when the railwaymen's leader, James Bunyard, decided to support the Liberal in Strood Ward, though the Amalgamated Society of Engineers did endorse the Labour Party's candidate. The results were not encouraging for the re-structured political organisation, as only Tapp won in Gillingham, while no seats were captured at Chatham or Rochester. There was some recovery when Hill won one of the three Gillingham by-elections, which followed.[122]

The Gillingham Labour Party, in 1907, sought to increase their representation on the Town Council, with five candidates, of whom three were members of the ILP: Henry Alexander, Walter Cook, and H.E. Davis. The other two were trade unionists: William Collins and George Gordon. All received the endorsement of the Chatham, Gillingham and Rochester Labour Party. The election handbill issued for all five illustrated the 'Labour' issues.

1. I pledge myself . . . to carefully watch all expenditure . . . to check all unnecessary increases of Officials and their salaries.
2. In educational matters, I would support equal opporunities for all children.
3. I would support municipal enterprise in any direction likely to benefit the community or to reduce the rates.
4. I would agitate in every possible way for a clean river.
5. I believe in the development of the town's resources either for pleasure, profit, or comfort.
6. I would support a living wage for all the Council's employees . . . [and] the fair wage clause in all contracts.
7. I would do all . . . to ensure healthy homes by a keener inspection of doubtful property, and . . . to prevent disease would strictly enforce all sanitary laws.

119 *CO*, 11.8.06.
120 *CO*, 3.11.06.
121 *CO*, 22.9.06; *CN*, 22.9.06.
122 *CO*, 3.11.06, 17.11.06, 1.12.06, 8.12.06; *CN*, 20.10.06, 3.11.06, 24.11.06, 8.12.06.

The result of the poll was a vote of 'no confidence' in the Labour Party. With the successful employment by the Tories of the 'bogey of socialism', all five were badly defeated.[123] In Chatham, the bad news continued, when a meeting of only 80 out of the 1,958 members of the Chatham Co-operative Society refused to endorse the Luton Ward candidature of the ILP activist, Robert Edwards.[124]

At the beginning of 1908, rumours began to circulate that J.H. Jenkins would not be standing for re-election. The tall, austere MP had been criticised for a lack of 'magnetism', and the local Liberals were not pleased, as they were never consulted on matters placed before the MP, who depended a great deal on the ex-Tories who had been crucial to his electoral success. Jenkins served the special interests of his dockyard constituency, when he used the House of Commons to press the Liberal Government to pay full trade union rates in the dockyards, and to adopt a fairer method for distributing Admiralty work, pressing for more dry and floating docks, large enough to service the new Dreadnoughts. Wake, who had returned to politics, denied at a Labour Church meeting, that Jenkins was to be replaced by a 'real' liberal–labour candidate, and the MP, interviewed by a Cardiff newspaper, refuted the rumour.[125] In May 1908, Wake announced that he was leaving the Medway Towns, to begin another career, as full-time secretary of the Barrow-in-Furness Labour Party.[126]

In October 1908, the Labour Party nominated R.P. Edwards and Alfred Dale, for wards in Chatham, but Dale's nomination papers were ruled invalid, though he did have another unsuccessful try during a by-election. The Gillingham candidates ended up as Cllr Chapman, Cllr Doughty, Cook and George Blackwell, all dockyardmen, while in Rochester, the only candidate was Edward Kite, a shipwright and ILP activist. The results of the November 1908 polls were depressing for Labour in Gillingham, where Chapman lost his seat, though Doughty hung on to his. Blackwell and Cook were also unsuccessful. Chapman's defeat was blamed on Free Churchmen who were offended by his support for the Sunday sale of refreshments at Gillingham Park. In Chatham, Edwards came in a losing third in Luton Ward, as did Kite in Rochester's St Peter's Ward.[127]

The Labour Party was financially strong enough, in November 1908, to hire a full-time organiser, Walter Speed of Canterbury, who was selected in preference to the local candidate, Arthur Ireland.[128] At a time when the 'Temple of Liberalism', which had been the Chatham Reform Club, was sold, and when there was no longer a Chatham Liberal Association, the Labour Party was itself busy occupying a permanent central headquarters. At the very moment when the Gillingham ILP was busy paying off debt caused by its purchase of the Secular

---

123 *CO*, 6.7.07, 28.9.07, 2.11.07, 9.11.07; *CN*, 28.9.07, 26.10.07, 9.11.07; Election Handbill, Borough of Gillingham,1907, East Ward, H. Alexander.
124 *CO*, 7.9.07, 5.10.07, 12.10.07, 26.10.07, 9.11.07; *CN*, 28.9.07, 26.10.07, 9.11.07.
125 *CO*, 4.1.08, 11.1.08; *CN*, 11.1.08.
126 *CN*, 16.5.08.
127 *CO*, 31.10.08, 7.11.08, 14.11.08; *CN*, 31.10.08, 7.11.08, 14.11.08, 28.11.08.
128 *CO*, 12.12.08, 19.12.08; *CN*, 5.12.08, 19.12.08.

Hall, in February 1909, a large Labour Party office and meeting space opened at 263 Chatham High Street, after much voluntary refurbishing work. A large meeting hall provided 'a convenient meeting place, and the Trades' Council, the Independent Order of Good Templars, the Women's Labour League, and the Progressive League regularly hire it for their meetings'. The Labour Party hired two members to be the resident caretakers.

However, such 'socialist' activity provoked a right-wing reaction when the Anti-Socialist Union's London leadership decided to target the Medway Towns, in September 1909. A campaign was started, at the very moment when the local Labour Party was holding their own much more ambitious, fortnight-long Labour Mission, with William Crawford Anderson, an up-and-coming ILP leader, as the main propagandist.[129] The first Anti-Socialist meeting was held in the Chatham Town Hall, on 16 September, with a Tory MP speaking on 'The Perils of Socialism'. However, the most publicity was gained by Gerald Hohler, who recited a nursery rhyme 'in alluding to the present Member for Chatham', J.H. Jenkins: 'Taffy was a Welshman, Taffy was a thief . . .' The Bible Christian Minister, the Revd Arundell Ralph, in the balcony, shouted out 'Withdraw!', but Hohler refused to do so. The Red Flag was then raised by a few members of the audience, but these were soon ejected. The final speaker said the socialists would reduce the English to the morality of the Hottentot. They would do away with all religion and dissolve marriage ties tomorrow, if they had the opportunity. At that moment, the remaining socialists in the hall began to sing the 'Red Flag'. A few days later, an outdoor meeting at Gillingham's Victoria Bridge was held by the Anti-Socialist Union with speakers from London. On 24 September, another meeting was held in Gillingham, at the Public Hall, at which Gerald Hohler insisted that the campaign was 'non-political', but it would set the tone for the forthcoming parliamentary election.[130]

A curious footnote to this labour history of Chatham was the visit of Sir John Gorst, the Chatham Tory MP from 1875 to 1892, to speak on 'The Social Problem' to an ILP meeting in late 1908, when J.H. Jenkins presided. Two years later, Gorst endorsed Jenkins at the time of his re-election campaign, and attacked his former party, which had 'adopted as the chief plank of its platform Tariff Reform. It has put social reform into the background, and opposed the social measures of the Government.'[131] Exactly a year after the first retirement rumour, it was again whispered, in the Medway Towns, that Jenkins would not be standing again, and that a local Labour leader would replace him as candidate. There was another rumour that Lamb, Rochester's Liberal MP, would leave his present seat to contest Chatham for the Labour Party, but this was immediately denied by Lamb.[132]

[129] *CO*, 11.9.09, 18.9.09, 25.9.09, 2.10.09; *CN*, 4.9.09, 11.9.09, 18.9.09, 25.9.09, 2.10.09.
[130] *CO*, 18.9.09, 25.9.09; *CN*, 4.9.09, 18.9.09, 25.9.09; *Essays in Anti-Labour History*, ed. K.D. Brown, London 1974, p. 242.
[131] *CO*, 5.12.08; *CN*, 5.12.08, 5.1.10.
[132] *CN*, 2.1.09.

In 1909, the only election campaign in Rochester was in St Peter's Ward, where Edward Kite (Figure 6) was the candidate. He pointed out that friendly Liberal national government was tending to 'legislate for the material welfare of the people. The measures passed are mostly permissive in character, and are generally adopted only by those Councils that have a fair proportion of Labour members.' Demands for municipal allotments in the Delce, and for the preservation of the Rochester Recreation Ground, which was threatened by residential developers, were strongly stated. The Fair Wage Clause for all Rochester Council contracts, and better street lighting, public lavatories and baths for St Peter's Ward were all listed among the Labour Party's proposals.[133] At the 1909 polls, Labour lost all of the Gillingham contests, except for Tapp's, but nevertheless the total Labour vote was 2,003 against 2,090 for all of the anti-Labour candidates. Edwards and Kite lost badly in their wards, but in the by-elections at Gillingham, Holmes stood in West Ward, and Hill in North Ward, and both won those seats with large majorities.[134]

(9) The January 1910 General Election

With the early symptoms of war-fever in the Medway Towns, the 1910 General Election approached. Before the previous General Election, and greatly to the benefit of Labour's campaign, the Chatham and Gillingham Liberals had been alienated by the Tories, through the latter's behaviour during the 1905 local elections. On the other hand, in the 1910 Chatham town elections, Labour Party relations with an important Liberal leader seemingly had been damaged during a 'robust' election campaign in Luton Ward. Sidney Hart believed he had been insulted by Labour's candidate, Edwards, who came within 48 votes of defeating him. In fact, Hart was looking for an excuse to break off the Liberals' cool, but still friendly, relations with Labour. Edwards tried to minimalise the 'insult', which had involved raising his hat whenever he mentioned Hart's name, and admitted that Hart had been the best of the non-Labour Town Councillors in Chatham.[135]

Jenkins was almost daily in Chatham, and while the Liberals and the Gillingham and Chatham Free Church Councils considered their own courses of action, the MP's first non-Labour endorsement arrived, in December 1909, from the Gillingham Temperance Council.[136] He was formally adopted as the Labour candidate, when the Chatham and District Trades and Labour Council, a fusion of the Trades Council and the Labour Party, nominated him, with Ireland as his election agent, at a meeting of forty delegates.[137] The heirs of the defunct

---

[133] *CO*, 6.11.09; *CN*, 23.10.09, 6.11.09.
[134] *CO*, 23.10.09, 30.10.09, 6.11.09, 27.11.09; *CN*, 23.10.09, 30.10.09, 6.11.09, 13.11.09.
[135] *CO*, 13.11.09; *CN*, 20.11.09.
[136] *CO*, 18.12.09; *CN*, 18.12.09.
[137] *CO*, 1.1.10; *CN*, 1.1.10.

Chatham, Gillingham and Rochester Labour Party

ROCHESTER DISTRICT COMMITTEE

ROCHESTER TOWN COUNCIL ELECTION
NOVEMBER 1ST, 1909

St. Peter's Ward

FELLOW CITIZENS AND BURGESSES,

I have been requested by a large number of Ratepayers in the Ward, as well as by the local Labour Party and the Chatham and District Trades and Labour Council, to offer my services as a Candidate to represent you on the local Council.

Since the advent of the Labour Party in Parliament, there has been an increasing tendency to legislate for the material welfare of the people. The measures passed are mostly permissive in character, and are generally adopted only by those Councils that have a fair proportion of Labour Members. Even where these measures are compulsory—such as Old Age Pensions—it is obvious that the needs of the workers are best appreciated and cared for by the direct representatives of their own class on the Committee.

Distress due to unemployment will be an urgent question during the coming winter; I appeal to the Burgesses to strengthen the hands of the Council by sending another Labour Councillor to the Guildhall, who is pledged to deal with the problem efficiently, and in the best interests of the community.

I am in favour of Municipal Allotments for Delce, and have actively supported the movement to secure the Rochester Recreation Ground as a playground for the children, and for the benefit of the health of the district.

I would support the insertion of the Fair Wage Clause in all Council contracts, and advocate that the work of the Council should be done by direct employment wherever possible. I would do my best to secure the extension and improvement of Municipal services, and in particular would work for the better lighting of the streets in the Ward and the establishment of public Lavatories and Baths.

On these grounds I appeal for your support at the Poll on November 1st, and if elected I will do my best by devoted service to merit your confidence.

Yours faithfully,

EDWARD KITE.

1 Holcombe Road,
Rochester.

Printed and Published by The Stanhope Press, Ltd., Strood, Rochester.

Figure 6. Election manifesto for Edward Kite, Labour candidate for St Peter's Ward in Rochester, 1909

Liberal Party of Gillingham and Chatham met in the Minor Hall at Chatham Town Hall, and decided to re-establish a Liberal Executive, but Jenkins was nevertheless formally endorsed by a unanimous vote of this resurrected Liberal Party. After this factional meeting was adjourned, leading Liberals went upstairs to the main auditorium and joined the platform at a Jenkins demonstration.[138] Though the Liberal government had failed to reform the education and licensing laws to the nonconformists' satisfaction, a mass meeting of Gillingham's Free Church Council was held and Jenkins was endorsed, with only three votes dissenting, while the Chatham Free Church Council's endorsement was unanimous. One might wonder if the domination of the local Labour Party by the 'godless' ILP, led by a heretical Unitarian minister, had frightened Free-churchmen, and forced them back, ultimately, to their former loyalties to Liberalism, even though the Labour candidate, in his Election Address, would state, 'My views with regard to the Education controversy, and in favour of real Temperance reform . . . remain the same.'[139]

Jenkins campaigned for re-election, with great confidence, on the issue which dominated the 1910 campaigns: Lloyd George's 'People's Budget' and its obstruction by the Tory-dominated House of Lords. Jenkins expressed his support for Liberal Free Trade: 'I am strongly opposed as ever to so-called Tariff "Reform", which would have a disastrous effect upon the prosperity of a constituency like Chatham. The taxation of raw materials for shipbuilding would . . . endanger our premier position in the shipbuilding and carrying trade . . . Tariff Reform can do nothing for the workers of Chatham, and the men of His Majesty's Army and Navy in active service or on pension, except increase the cost of living . . .' The time-served shipwright pledged to continue his work in the House of Commons for the re-vitalisation and expansion of construction work at Chatham. His enthusiasm for all things naval caused some embarrassment for the generally 'pacifist' Independent Labour Party MPs, and the Chatham Labour MP's nickname, 'Admiral Jenkins', would have made Keir Hardie cringe. Jenkins defended his record, between 1906 and the January 1910 election: 'there were on September 25th last 1848 more men employed in the Dockyard than when you returned me to the House of Commons, and I have been assured that there will be no discharges this winter . . . I was the first Member . . . to call the attention of the Government to the serious lack of dry dock accommodation for vessels of the Dreadnought type . . . I have also kept before the Admiralty the desirability of making the alterations considered necessary to adapt Chatham Dockyard for the building and repairing of Dreadnoughts and Super-Dreadnoughts.' However, the Mayor of Rochester pointed out that while the number of men employed in the dockyard had increased, none were 'established', and in addition to that, no ship had been built. Many others in the

---

[138] *CO*, 8.1.10; *CN*, 8.1.10.
[139] *CO*, 8.1.10, 15.1.10; *CN*, 15.1.10.

Medway Towns suspected that Jenkins' trade union loyalties were instinctively with the privately-employed shipwright, rather than with the dockyardman.[140]

Alderman De la Cour described the difficulties which had been faced by the local Tories in their search for a parliamentary candidate, to replace Major Jameson, in what had come to be considered to be a 'Labour' seat. Nine months passed before the Tories made a decision, but in the end, the Gillingham and Chatham Conservatives had the good fortune to nominate a much more effective candidate than the 'galloping Major from Clare'. Their new candidate, the barrister Gerald Fitzroy Hohler, had established good relations with the Gillingham elite, regardless of party, when he had supervised the complicated legal work involved in the incorporation of that town, a few years earlier.[141]

After four years of seemingly effective 'Fair Trade' propaganda, which offered the easy solution for unemployment through the abolition of the Liberals' (and many Tories') most 'sacred cow', Free Trade, a sufficient number of voters returned to their former Tory habits. In addition, Crowe was no longer available to organise the Tory supporters of 1906, as he had moved to Portsmouth in 1907, though the more reserved Major Long remained loyal to Jenkins.[142] The new Tory candidate's campaign emphasised the danger to the armed services and to the dockyard represented by both radicals and socialists, even though the two local MPs had fought successfully for these interests. Hohler countered Jenkins' assurances regarding the dockyard's future by asserting that the anti-patriotic 'Socialists would have England without a navy; and how could they understand people in a dockyard town being in favour of Socialistic principles. Socialists had a notion that they could make peace with the working men of other countries. That was absurd.' The Tories exploited the fears of the naval and dockyard communities, and their widespread anxieties regarding Free Trade, which was blamed for all social and economic evil. Hohler enthusiastically adopted the new Tariff Reform plank of twentieth-century Conservatism, and he proclaimed 'Vote for Hohler This Time and tax the Foreigner.'[143]

Nevertheless, the Labour Party, which had spent more than had Hohler's official election committee, remained confident until polling day, when Jenkins lost disastrously, with a local swing against Labour of 17.2%. This may seem very high, but the swing at Portsmouth had been 19.8%, and even Will Crooks had lost his Woolwich seat. The Labour Representation Committee's Secretary, Ramsay MacDonald, was surprised by the Chatham figures, believing that 'in some way or other the Conservatives have tapped a reserve of voters which had hitherto been untouched by both Parties'. Both the Liberals and Labour had been surpassed by Hohler's organisation, which was aided by 'non-political' allies from both the Anti-Socialist Union and the fair traders. Its superiority was

---

140   *CO*, 8.1.10, 15.1.10, 22.1.10; *CN*, 8.1.10, 15.1.10, 22.1.10.
141   *CN*, 30.7.10.
142   *CO*, 1.1.10, 8.1.10, 15.1.10, 22.1.10; *CN*, 1.1.10, 8.1.10, 15.1.10, 22.1.10; Lunn, *op. cit.*, pp. 285–7.
143   *CO*, 18.12.09, 3.1.10, 10.1.10, 17.1.10; *CN*, 3.1.10, 10.1.10, 17.1.10.

demonstrated by their effective registration of voters. The total Chatham and Gillingham votes cast had grown, between 1906 and 1910, from 10,712 to 13,541, but, in Rochester, it had declined by 123. A more efficient pre-election organisation on behalf of the Liberals and Labour would have been able to challenge 'dubious' registrations in St Mary's Ward, especially on the Brook, where widespread corruption was suspected. The Chatham Liberal, Cllr Paine, said 'the voting list for St. Mary's was a revelation to him ... Although no new house had been erected there were 200 more voters on the list. He believed two-thirds of Mr. Hohler's majority came from St. Mary's.' Hart agreed that there had been hundreds not on the voting lists 'who ought to be on, and there were hundreds on who had no sort of qualification to be on. The Labour party were largely to blame for this, for they believed in one man one vote, and so they did not object to anyone whose name was on the list. That was a great mistake.' Hart admitted his surprise when all the inmates of the Medway Union Workhouse, who were still on the electoral register, had voted Tory.[144] Regardless of the loss of Chatham, the Labour Party nationally could claim forty MPs after the January 1910 General Election, but no party had a majority in the 'balanced' House of Commons. The Liberal government would depend on the votes of Labour and Irish Nationalist MPs to win crucial votes in Parliament, and the Liberal Party would never again achieve a working majority in the House of Commons.

Immediately after Jenkins' and Lamb's joint-defeats, a local newspaper asserted that the local Labour Party had lost contact with their electorate. However, as had been the case in the 1892 defeat of Sir Andrew Clarke, the dockyardmen apparently had betrayed another of their 'best friends'. Lewington's reprimand of his fellow dockyardmen, when they failed to elect Sir Andrew Clarke, in 1892, could have been adapted for use in January 1910.

On the other hand, Sidney Hart gave three reasons for Hohler's triumph: 1. Liberal support was 'either lukewarm or non-existent'; 2. Tory organisation and effort had been very good, and that of Labour 'poor and inefficient'; 3. Labour contained 'certain men of extreme views, of loud speech, and of tactless action (who) do not possess the confidence of the majority'. He praised both Jenkins and Lamb for their great services on behalf of the two constituencies. These included 'large increases in the weekly wages in the dockyard and in the number of employees, coupled with conditions and scales of improvement'. The Tories' plans to remove the Royal Engineers from Brompton had been stopped by their joint efforts at Westminster, but nevertheless the dockyard and services' vote went back to the Tories.[145]

The Liberal leader recognised, at once, that there was a partisan advantage to be gained from both the Chatham defeat, as well as from the loss of Rochester by a Liberal MP who had allied himself closely to Labour. He announced that 'the old flag of Liberalism could be successfully hoisted', with, possibly, the

---

144   *CO*, 22.1.10; *CN*, 22.1.10; N. Blewett, *The Peers, the Parties and the People: The General Elections of 1910*, London 1972, pp. 298, 378–9; Lunn, *op. cit.*, pp. 285–7.
145   *CN*, 10.1.10, 22.1.10.

tory maverick, Sir John Gorst, or the defeated Lamb, as their candidate at the next Chatham Election.[146] On 24 February 1910, the resurrection of Chatham Liberalism occurred at a meeting in the Town Hall, as the Liberals had lost their Chatham Reform Club, with its Gladstone Hall. The meeting attracted a few hundred Liberals, and it was decided to form a political association. Frank Clements, a Chatham Methodist, moved the resolution, believing that 'if in the future they agreed upon one common candidate for the progressive forces, Chatham, which was a constituency of men who had to work for their bread and butter, instead of being represented by one of the rich class, would be represented by one more in sympathy with them. (A voice: Alderman Jenkins.) He voted for him and would do so again, but if they could find a stronger candidate to represent the constituency they should stand by him.'[147] A month later, the rules for the new 'Liberal and Radical Association for the Parliamentary Borough of Chatham, consisting of the Municipal Boroughs of Chatham and Gillingham' were adopted by another meeting of Liberals at Chatham Town Hall. The Association's Objects were

1. the spread of Liberal and Radical principles;
2. the reform of political abuses;
3. the maintenance of the purity of elections;
4. the superintendence and conduct of Parliamentary and Municipal registration;
5. and the consolidation of the Party in the Boroughs.

A proposition was made by the Chairman of February's meeting, Charles William Knight, the dockyard constructor, 'that the Parliamentary candidate be provisionally selected by the Executive in conjunction, if possible, with the representatives of the local trade and labour Association, the final adoption of the candidate being made at a full meeting of the Association'. Knight was loyal to Leavey's vision of Chatham's special anti-Tory politics, and 'did not think that it was likely that either the Liberal or the Labour parties would return a Member without the help of each other'. This clearly did not please Hart who wanted it understood that if the local Labour Party refused to meet their new Liberal and Radical Association, they should be free to act independently of Labour. W.B. Thompson opposed Knight, as he believed the Labour Party already had declared its political independence and would not work in conjunction with any other Party, and the proposal was defeated by a large majority. Hart was elected as Chairman of the Association's Executive Committee, with Cllr Doggett as the Organising Secretary.[148] In April 1910, Hohler took credit for this 'revival' of Liberalism, as his defeat of Jenkins had freed the local Liberals from their alliance with the Labour Party, which, by the way, would

[146] *CN*, 22.1.10.
[147] *CO*, 26.2.10.
[148] *CO*, 26.3.10.

split the anti-Tory vote in any future election.[149] The Medway Towns socialists 'despise all association with progressive Liberalism'. Out of the Labour Party's defeat, Hart hoped to build a new radical coalition, uniting 'the Liberal working man, the Liberal tradesman, professional man, public servant, and Service and State official'.[150] It was possible that those socialist 'extremists', represented by the ILP and the Herald League, might have found some satisfaction in the defeat of their 'liberal–labour' MP. They may have had plans for a new Labour candidate in the 'heroic' mould of Grayson, who had spoken to an ILP meeting in November 1909, and would return in October 1910, though he denied that he wanted to be their candidate.[151] A rumour circulated, after the January defeat, that Jenkins would remain the Labour candidate.[152] In the meantime, the Medway Towns' full-time Labour official, Speed, in July 1910, left for a post with the Yorkshire Division of the Independent Labour Party, and his local responsibilities were assumed, on a voluntary basis, by Edwards.[153] Another problem arose at the Gillingham Co-operative Society, which had published a pamphlet in support of Jenkins' candidature. Some members reacted to his defeat by electing an 'Anti-Politics' Tory Tariff Reformer at the top of the March 1910 ballot for members of its management committee, but the socialist, Chapman, did come second.[154]

After the disappointment of the General Election results in both Rochester and Chatham, the Labour Party prepared for the Kent County Council election in March 1910, when Tapp was nominated for Medway No. 4, and Chapman for Medway No. 5, divisions and, although only Tapp won, the Labour Party in the Medway Towns was represented, for the first time, on Kent Council.[155] The plans for the other local elections began, and Lewington, recently returned to Gillingham from Hong Kong, was expected to be once again a Town Councillor, and five other Labour candidates were nominated at Gillingham. There was some surprise when Lewington failed to be elected, though Chapman and Percy Davies, a dockyard fitter, were elected.[156] In Chatham, Edwards stood in Luton Ward again, while Robert W. Dale, a Quaker grocer and Adult School activist, nominated in Rochester's St Peter's Ward, was supported by Labour. Ireland was returned unopposed in Frindsbury Ward, and both Edwards and Dale were elected, and the Luton Ward victor was carried to the victory meeting at the Labour Party Rooms.[157]

---

[149] *CN*, 30.4.10.
[150] *CN*, 22.1.10.
[151] *CO*, 6.11.09, 13.11.09, 29.10.10; *CN*, 13.11.09, 29.10.10.
[152] *CO*, 29.1.10; *CN*, 2.4.10.
[153] *CO*, 16.7.10, 4.11.11.
[154] *CN*, 12.3.10, 19.3.10.
[155] *CO*, 5.3.10, 12.3.10.
[156] *CO*, 27.8.10, 1.10.10, 8.1.10, 22.10.10, 29.10.10, 5.11.10; *CN*, 17.9.10, 24.9.10, 8.10.10, 22.10.10, 29.10.10, 5.11.10.
[157] *CO*, 1.10.10, 29.10.10, 5.11.10; *CN*, 1.10.10, 29.10.10, 5.11.10.

(10) The December 1910 General Election

On 18 November 1910, Herbert Asquith, the Liberal Prime Minister, beset by conflicts over Irish Home Rule and Free Trade, announced the dissolution of the short-lived House of Commons, and a second General Election was called for December 1910.[158] At Chatham, Hart's re-established Liberal Party felt itself ready to take sole charge of anti-Tory politics once again, with a local candidate, George Leavey, who had agreed to stand only if there were no Labour nominee.[159] However, the Labour Party's National Agent, in April 1910, had recognised the Chatham constituency as one where it was 'advisable to keep the Liberals out, otherwise they may again assert themselves, the only result being to "spoil the pitch" for Labour altogether'.[160] Nevertheless, the Liberals expected to benefit from the divisions between the socialist ILP, and the traditionally liberal–labour or non-political trade unions. The *Chatham News* editor commented that

> [The local Liberals] hold that the strength of the Labour party, by itself, is comparatively small, and that the superior voting power of the Liberals entitles them to take the lead in introducing a candidate . . . [and] many Liberals . . . would rather risk the loss of the battle than allow themselves to be tied to the Socialist chariot. They consider that if the Labour wing will not join them, and will persist in running a candidate of their own, it will make for success in the long run to fight the matter out with them at the ensuing election . . . [L]arge numbers of trade unionists are strongly opposed to the Socialistic tendencies of the Independent Labour Party, and there must be a cleavage in the ranks of the two sections sooner or later . . . [the] I.L.P. wield an influence altogether out of proportion to their strength, owing to their wonderful zeal and energy and the aggressive spirit they display.[161]

The Chairman of the local Labour Party, the Revd John Morgan Whiteman of Chatham Unitarian Church, attempted the impossible task of defining the political position of his party. He pointed out that the Labour Party was not a 'socialist', a 'liberal', or a 'conservative' party. Its fundamental purpose was to represent the interest of the workers, especially 'organised' workers. Moreover, he was firm in his denial of the assertion that the Labour Party was an offspring of Liberalism, emphasising his party's essential independence. Whiteman admitted that he, personally, was a socialist member of the ILP, 'in spite of all my efforts to hide my shame, so I may as well brazen it out, and say Socialism is my religion – my life – a glad gospel which I hope to live and die proclaiming'.[162]

Hart's determination to end the local Liberal alliance with the Labour Party requires a careful examination, as it would influence the political development

[158] Roy Jenkins, *Asquith*, London 1964, pp. 222–3.
[159] *CN*, 3.12.10, 17.12.10.
[160] Labour Party Minutes, NEC, 13.4.10.
[161] *CN*, 19.11.10.
[162] *CO*, 17.12.10.

of the Medway Towns for decades. After Hart had found a Liberal candidate willing to stand at Chatham, Whiteman attempted an explanation of the events leading to the fracture in the informal alliance of the previous five years, through letters to the local press, in which he challenged Hart to refute seven statements.

(1) That he, Mr. Hart, approached our committee on Monday, November 21st, and submitted the name of Mr. George Leavey, as that of a gentleman who was willing to stand, failing the appearance of a Labour candidate, but not otherwise.

(2) That, being informed we were prepared to bring forward a candidate, he fell back upon Mr. Bernacchi – a stranger, who had no such scruples as those which restrained the local gentlemen, Mr. Lamb and Mr. Leavey, both of whom recognised Labour's prior claim to the seat.

(3) That, therefore, Mr. Bernacchi cannot up to that time have 'received' and accepted an official invitation to contest Chatham as the Liberal candidate.

(4) That Mr. Frank Smith's name was communicated to Mr. Hart on the following evening, Tuesday, 22nd.

(5) That the onus of producing the official communication referred to by Mr. Hart – from the National Labour Party and the National Liberal Party – rests with him and Mr. Bernacchi.

(6) That, if these are not forthcoming, Mr. MacDonald's expressed contradiction holds the field as far as the Labour Party is concerned; and [Alexander Murray, the Chief Liberal Whip] the Master of Elibank's belated telegram of November 29th speaks volumes as to the Liberal Party's official sanction, alleged to have been received ten days earlier.

(7) That Mr. Lamb, more than once during his campaign, has expressed his disapproval of the attempt of Chatham's Liberals to snatch a Labour seat, and publicly asserted that a candidate was unauthorised.[163]

Hart immediately replied to Whiteman.

It is untrue to say that 'Mr. Leavey said three months ago he would not stand', or that he knew even ten days ago that Mr. Smith would be the Labour candidate. I had it personally from a member of the Parliamentary Committee of the Labour Party at five p. m. on Monday, November 21st, that they had no candidate in view. We agreed to submit the names of Mr. Leavey and Mr. Bernacchi to the committee that night, and at 10.15 p. m. I went with Mr. Councillor Doggett to the Labour Party's office for some reply, and was told for the first time they 'would run their own candidate'. Mr. Alderman Jenkins . . . told me in Chatham ten or twelve days earlier there would be no Labour candidate. Mr. Bernacchi received the same assurance from Mr. Middleton, [assistant] secretary of the Labour Party, at the London office. My immediate answer to the committee on Monday night was this:– Your decision disposes of Mr. Leavey, but Mr. Bernacchi will be our candidate, and we adopted him next day. It was past eight o'clock on the Tuesday night before the name of the

163 *CO*, 3.12.10.

Labour candidate was sent by wire to Chatham by Mr. Whiteman and Mr. Ireland. It is wholly false to say the Liberal Party have broken any agreement of any kind in London or Chatham; on the contrary, the breach of faith is with the London Labour office.[164]

Later in the election campaign, Louis Bernacchi, a scientist and explorer, allowed his own version of the affair to be published.

My position with regard to Chatham is perfectly simple and straightforward. On Monday, November 21st, I was asked by the Secretary of the Home Counties' Liberal Federation to contest the borough, and on that day I met Mr. Hart, chairman of the Chatham Executive. Before accepting, I stipulated there should be no Labour candidate in the field. In order to make this quite clear I went down to the House of Commons on Monday afternoon, and saw both Mr. G.N. Barnes, MP, and Mr. Henderson, MP. Both expressed the opinion they did not think there was any intention of fighting Chatham. Both advised me to see Mr Middleton, under secretary of the Labour Party, for a definite Yes or No. Indeed, Mr. Henderson volunteered to telephone to Mr. Middleton to inform him of my proposed visit. On reaching the Labour Party's office in Victoria-street, 30 minutes later, I found Mr. Middleton expecting me, and he repeated exactly what Messrs. Barnes and Henderson had said. 'But', he added, 'We have a committee meeting this evening to submit the final list of candidates. I will, therefore, let you know definitely to-morrow.' On Tuesday, Mr. Middleton telephoned to me at the National Liberal Club, and said: 'The ground is clear for you at Chatham; we are not running a candidate.' On this statement I immediately accepted Chatham. With subsequent events, I am not concerned.[165]

Hart hinted at a law suit against the local Labour Party, and mentioned that £5,000 damages had been granted recently in a similar case of 'vilification'. Whiteman replied that it would be impossible to get '£5,000 damages out of the Chatham Labour Party!'[166]

Whiteman believed that there were 'terminological inexactitudes' within Hart's and Bernacchi's explanations, which the Labour Party chairman examined in detail.

Monday, November 21st – Mr. Bernacchi was asked by the Home Counties' Liberal Federation to contest Chatham, but, before accepting, stipulated there should be no Labour candidate in the field. In order to make this quite clear, he went to the House of Commons, and saw Mr. Barnes and Mr. Henderson, both of whom 'expressed the opinion they did not think [sic] there was any intention of fighting Chatham'. They, however, referred him to Mr. Middleton, who expressed the same opinion, but told him there was to be a committee meeting that evening, and he would let him know the result next day. Tuesday,

---

164 *Loc. cit.*
165 *CO*, 17.12.10.
166 *Loc. cit.*

November 22nd – Mr. Middleton (says Mr. Bernacchi) telephoned to him at the National Liberal Club: 'The ground is clear for you at Chatham; we are not running a candidate.'

Whitman pointed out the differences between Hart's and Bernacchi's version of events. Hart had written that Cllr Doggett and he had gone to the Labour Party's office on Monday evening (21st), when they were informed that there would be a Labour candidate. The Liberal deputation admitted that George Leavey must be ruled out, but that Bernacchi would agree to stand. Whiteman refuted Hart's claim that the Chatham Liberals, 'before and after' the January 1910 defeat, had told the local Labour Party that they were intending to run a candidate at the next General Election; he claimed that the first announcement was at the 21 November 'conference'. Whiteman felt that it was 'quite incredible' that Barnes and Henderson would have told Bernacchi, on Monday (21st) that they did not believe 'there was any intention of fighting Chatham'. Bernacchi disagreed with Hart's version when he wrote that he, like Leavey, would not stand, if there were a Labour candidate.

On Tuesday 22 November, Morgan Whiteman, who had lived in Chatham for two years, and Ireland, who never had lived in the constituency, went to London to find a Labour candidate for Chatham. They spoke with the Chairman and the Secretary of the National Labour Party Executive at their headquarters, as they wanted to learn if there were any truth in what Hart had told them. Ramsay MacDonald, the Party Secretary, 'ridiculed the idea that Messrs. Barnes and Henderson had wished Mr. Bernacchi success in his candidature, and assured us . . . that Mr. Bernacchi had had no such intimation as he claims to have had'. After speaking with MacDonald, Whiteman and Ireland were sent to speak with W.C. Anderson, the National Chairman of the Independent Labour Party, who saw the two men, later in the afternoon, after an ILP meeting which had endorsed Frank Smith's candidature. A telegram was sent to Hart, giving notice that there would be an official Labour candidature, so he could decide if he really wanted a three-cornered contest. Whiteman wrote that Hart's answer was 'All right! We fight, too, if you were standing down, we should run Mr. Leavey. As you are not doing so, Mr. Bernacchi is our man.' Whiteman had believed that the Liberals would not be standing, if Labour put forward a candidate, but Bernacchi had been adopted on the very day that the Liberals had been informed of Frank Smith's candidature. The local Labour Party assumed that Bernacchi was an 'unofficial' candidate, as he did not receive a telegram enabling him to call himself 'the authorised Liberal candidate' until the end of the campaign, on 29 November[167] Ramsay MacDonald immediately made a public statement, which was used in a newspaper advertisement before polling day, that if 'Mr. Bernacchi states that he received any communication from the Head Office that the coast was clear for him, he is not telling the truth'.[168] Both Whiteman and

---

167 *Loc. cit.*
168 *CN*, 3.12.10.

Lamb were probably correct in considering the Liberals' behaviour as a purely Chatham affair. Nevertheless, one may never know the whole truth regarding this pre-election fracas (or fiasco), which ended Leavey's 'progressive alliance'.

The new candidate offered to Whiteman and Ireland was a strange one for a dockyard town: the journalist Frank Smith, the spiritualist and Christian Socialist friend of Keir Hardie. Smith had already been nominated for the London seat of North Lambeth but, according to Keir Hardie, Smith had been withdrawn as the Liberals had nominated a working man for that constiuency, and the ILP wished to avoid splitting the vote.[169] Though the National Labour Party endorsed Smith for Chatham, little money was available for another campaign within a year, especially as the 'Osborne Judgement' questioned the legality of the trade unions' political levy.[170] The all-important Government Labourers' Union branch faced an injunction stopping them from using union funds to help Smith's campaign, and the branch could not afford the legal costs to fight its case in court.[171] More important was the fact that the Labour candidate would be an ILP member, unlike Jenkins, and local socialists could feel that the 'extremists' were, at long last, the 'masters' of the Medway Towns Labour movement.

Hardie came to speak for his friend, but the great socialist must have felt uncomfortable in the dockyard town,[172] after a summer spent campaigning at home and on the Continent against militarism and war. In September, Hardie had led the British Labour delegates to the Copenhagen Congress of the Socialist International, where he and the French socialist, Edouard Vaillant, proposed a resolution opposing all increases in armaments, as well as advocating a general strike on the outbreak of war, especially in industries which supply war materials. Though the resolution was shelved by the Congress, it provoked much discussion within the Socialist and Labour movements throughout the world.[173]

There was an obvious lack of local support and enthusiasm for the last minute candidature of Smith, an intellectual moderate, who neither appealed to the industrial constituency nor enthused the local 'left wing' ILP activists. Nevertheless, the father of the Medway Towns Labour Party, Lewington, came out loyally and solidly for him.

> Fellow Workers, for twenty-one years I have fought for you; I warned you against being led away by side issues, either by Liberals or Tories. I have cried out night and day, in season and out of season. How long halt ye between two opinions? If you honesty believe the Tory landlord or Liberal capitalistic employers can best serve you, then vote for them . . . Fellow Workers, it is being whispered in your ears not to vote for Labour, because there is a Liberal

[169] *CN*, 26.11.10; E.I. Champness, *Frank Smith, M.P., Pioneer and Mystic*, London 1944; F. Coutts, *Bread for my Neighbour: The Social Influence of William Booth*, London 1978, pp. 105–6.
[170] Blewett, *op. cit.*, p. 298.
[171] *CO*, 3.12.10; *CN*, 3.12.10.
[172] *CO*, 10.12.10; *KM*, 10.12.10.
[173] K. Morgan, *Keir Hardie, Radical and Socialist*, London 1975, pp. 260–2.

in the field; but to vote Tory as he is bound to win. Bunkum! Don't be misled this time, neither Tory nor Liberal has a ghost of a chance without your votes . . . FANCY A LAWYER AS A WORKING MAN'S FRIEND. Don't make me laugh.[174]

With Ireland acting as his Agent, Smith campaigned with a £5 cash grant in aid and £5 worth of posters from the National Labour Party, but without any Labour election literature provided by them.[175] Lamb, who was standing again at Rochester, maintained his good relations with the local Labour Party. He went to London to urge the Liberals' national leaders not to campaign in Chatham. With a Conservative majority of 132 in January 1910, Lamb needed every Labour vote available in Rochester, and he spoke with the leaders of the Rochester ILP, on 29 November. Lamb had earlier refused the Liberal nomination at Chatham, as he insisted, like Sir Andrew Clarke, that Chatham was a 'Labour' seat, and during the November–December campaign Lamb reiterated his opinion and he even suggested that Bernacchi was not an 'authorised' Liberal parliamentary candidate.[176]

Significantly, on polling day, Arthur Ireland had not a single vehicle available to ferry Labour supporters to voting stations. The result was an electoral disaster, with Labour holding on to only 1,103 votes, against Bernacchi's 4,302, and the triumphant Conservative's 6,989, representing a ten to one vote against the Labour Party, which had held on to only 8.9% of those voting. The public squabbling between Whiteman and Hart damaged both Smith's and Bernacchi's anti-Tory campaigns, but Lamb, who did not have to fight on 'two fronts', won back his Rochester seat, with a majority of 153, compared with his 593 vote lead in 1906.[177] Nationally, in the last pre-war general election, the Labour Party had gained two seats, which gave them a total of 42 MPs.

A local newspaper tried to explain the haemorrhage of votes from Labour: 'the Chairman of the local Labour Party [Morgan Whiteman] was altogether too advanced in his views to suit the tastes of the people of Gillingham; while many of the rank and file, by their Socialistic utterances and domineering and dictatorial attitude, had driven moderate men into the opposite camp'.[178] At the next meeting of the Chatham and District Trades and Labour Council, a Labour Party Report admitted that there had been a large number of defections during the second 1910 election.[179] The Chatham seat would not be regained by Labour until 1929.

The leader of the Chatham Liberals, Sidney J. Hart, died in January 1911, in the midst of his frantic efforts to rebuild local Liberalism. With him died the belief that a reborn, old-style Liberalism could become the dominant force in the Chatham constituency, for never again would his party have any chance of

174 *CN*, 3.12.10.
175 Blewett, *op. cit.*, p. 298.
176 *CO*, 3.12.10.
177 *CO*, 10.12.10.
178 *Loc. cit.*
179 *CO*, 24.12.10; *CN*, 24.12.10.

electing an MP. Hart's death caused a by-election in Luton Ward, where the Labour Party nominated William John Hedge, a master tailor, who was an active member of the ILP, and Hedge defeated the Conservative, with Liberal support.[180]

(11) Local Elections

The strategic planning for the municipal elections began in September 1911, when the Rochester ILP nominated Kite for St Peter's Ward and William Hurdman, a former iron founder turned insurance agent, was chosen for Troy Town Ward, but Kite decided to stand independently of the Labour Party.[181] The Chatham Labour Party nominated William Kirk, a dockyard engine fitter, for Luton Ward, and Alfred Dale, a dockyard shipwright, for St John's Ward, after the Co-operative Society had voted not to nominate their own candidate for the Town Council.[182] In Gillingham, Labour chose five candidates, and Blackwell decided to stand as an independent at Old Brompton. The results were mixed. In Rochester, Kite was third in St Peter's Ward, and Hurdman lost in Troy Town Ward. At Chatham, Kirk was top in Luton Ward, but Dale came fourth in St John's Ward. The Gillingham poll saw Blackwell elected by sixteen votes, Doughty re-elected in Medway Ward, and William Nelson won in South Ward. Hill lost his seat in North Ward, and Gordon lost in East Ward for the fourth time, while Holmes was re-elected unopposed.[183] After the elections, Gillingham chose its first working-class mayor, James Davis, a Liberal and a retired dockyard storehouse foreman.[184]

The 1912 local election campaign commenced in September, with the Liberal Party's endorsements for the pioneer secularist, William B. Thompson, who had retired from the dockyard, in Gillingham East Ward and for Allison in Brompton Ward.[185] Labour chose Tapp in South Ward; Joseph Banks, a dockyard fitter and future Communist, in West Ward; Hills, who had come into the 'official' fold, in Medway Ward; John Clitherow, a fitter, in East Ward; Thomas Pepin, a dockyard joiner and patternmaker, in Old Brompton; and Henry Lee, an insurance agent, in North Ward. Tapp was opposed by the Tory trade unionist, John Bate, and Pepin had Allison standing against him, though the latter withdrew before the election.[186] At Chatham, Hedge would be unopposed in Luton Ward, and Dale would stand at St John's Ward, but there was no Labour political activity in Rochester.[187] The results were not good for the Labour Party in

---

180 *CO*, 7.1.11, 14.1.11, 21.1.11, 4.2.11; *CN*, 7.1.11, 14.1.11, 4.2.11.
181 *CO*, 9.9.11, 16.9.11, 14.10.11, 28.10.11; *CN*, 9.9.11, 16.9.11, 28.10.11.
182 *CO*, 30.9.11, 28.10.11; *CN*, 9.9.11, 28.10.11.
183 *CO*, 4.11.11; *CN*, 4.11.11.
184 *CN*, 11.11.11.
185 *CO*, 17.8.12, 21.9.12, 26.10.12; *CN*, 25.5.12. 14.9.12, 28.9.12.
186 *CO*, 21.9.12, 12.10.12, 19.10.12, 26.10.12; *CN*, 21.9.12, 12.10.12, 19.10.12, 26.10.12.
187 *CO*, 28.9.12; *CN*, 19.10.12, 26.10.12.

Gillingham, as the Tories won every Ward. Tapp lost his South Ward seat to John Bate by 670 to 704, and it was thought Bate had taken more of the former Liberal vote than had Tapp. Pepin did badly in Old Brompton, though he had lived there all his life, and in Medway Ward, both Thompson and Hills lost, the former blaming his secularist views for his defeat. The remaining Labour councillors on the Gillingham Town Council were categorised by a local journalist into 'Labour' (Holmes, Doughty and Nelson) and 'Socialist' (Chapman, Davies and Blackwell). After the poll, Holmes was made an Alderman. In Chatham, Hedge held his Luton Ward unopposed, but Dale lost.[188] Lewington commented on Tapp's defeat, as it was indicative of the difficulties facing the Labour Party: 'Mr. Councillor Bate was honest, for he let out that the Tory and Liberal combination gave him the victory over Mr. Tapp, the representative of Labour, and the enemy of both orthodox political parties, and explained how Tories and Liberals must combine to keep out their common enemy, the Labour representative . . . Ninety percent of the Gillingham electors are workers, yet have only one-third direct representation.'[189] Tapp failed to be returned during the resultant by-elections.[190]

Tapp tried again in February 1913 as a candidate for the Kent County Council, in Medway No. 4, with Chapman standing for Medway No. 5, and in Chatham, Percy Terry, a dockyard shipwright, was selected for the No. 3 seat. The fear of war had created overtime at the dockyard, and this limited the Labour men's campaigns, but Tapp was re-elected, though both Chapman and Terry lost.[191] Percy Davies announced his retirement as a councillor representing Gillingham's South Ward, thus giving Tapp another chance of returning to the Town Council. Chapman was nominated for West Ward, and Blackwell for Old Brompton Ward. William James Brown, a retired dockyard master smith, would be the Liberal candidate in Medway Ward. Brown was the chairman of the Gillingham Liberal Association, but, unlike the late Sidney Hart, he believed in a new and better understanding with the Labour Party. Tapp was successful and was back on the Town Council, though Chapman and Brown lost.[192] In the Chatham election, where Edwards would be opposed by the Tories, there were no other Labour candidates, but he kept his council seat.[193] At Rochester, Ireland stood again in Frindsbury, amongst the cement labourers, which he had done so much to help, but he lost badly.[194]

In the autumn of 1914, the last pre-war local elections were being organised as the war began. At Gillingham, Nelson was not standing for re-election as he had moved from the town, and Doughty also decided not to stand for re-election, but Banks was the Labour candidate, replacing Nelson, in South Ward, and

188 *CO*, 9.11.12, 16.11.12; *CN*, 9.11.12, 16.11.12.
189 *CO*, 16.11.12.
190 *CO*, 23.11.12, 30.11.12; *CN*, 23.11.12, 30.11.12.
191 *CO*, 1.2.13, 15.2.13, 22.2.13, 1.3.13, 8.3.13; *CN*, 15.2.13, 22.2.13, 1.3.13, 8.3.13.
192 *CO*, 16.8.13, 18.10.13, 25.10.13, 8.11.13; *CN*, 26.7.13, 2.8.13, 11.10.13, 18.10.13, 1.11.13, 8.11.13.
193 *CO*, 25.10.13, 1.11.13, 8.11.13; *CN*, 26.7.13, 4.10.13, 25.10.13, 8.11.13.
194 *CO*, 25.10.13; *CN*, 18.10.13, 25.10.13, 8.11.13.

Blackwell stood for re-election in Old Brompton Ward. In Chatham, Kirk was unopposed in Luton Ward. At the polls, Blackwell lost his seat by a single vote, while Banks failed once again. There was no Labour electoral activity in Rochester.[195]

The four local elections in the Medway Towns, after the 1910 General Election defeats of Jenkins and Smith, could not have been encouraging to Labour Party activists. After the 1914 elections, in Chatham, there were only Cllrs Edwards, Hedge, and Kirk; in Rochester, no one; and at Gillingham, Alderman Holmes, with Cllr Tapp on both Town and County Councils. It must be noted that of these five representatives three were members of the ILP. Such were the fruits of a century of political struggle within the Medway Towns, and none of the three town councils would have a Labour majority until 1945.

---

[195] *CO*, 17.10.14, 24.10.14, 31.10.14, 7.11.14; *CN*, 24.10.14, 31.10.14, 7.11.14.

7

Crime and Public Order

PAUL HASTINGS

(1) Introduction

Prior to 1842 the dividing line between crimes tried at Quarter Sessions and Assizes varied according to custom and area. Parliament then specified by statute (5 & 6 Vic. c. 38) the jurisdiction of Quarter Sessions. While justice at Quarter Sessions was administered by justices of the peace, who were not required to have any legal knowledge before appointment, Assizes were conducted by judges who had been professional lawyers and were appointed officers of the crown. In Kent, county Quarter Sessions courts were held in the two divisions of East and West Kent. Individual boroughs within the county also had their own courts of Quarter Sessions, while from the nineteenth century less serious offences came increasingly to be tried summarily by justices of the peace either singly, or in small groups, at Petty Sessions, without a jury.

Theoretically justices of the peace could try felonies and trespass but not treason. Felonies, which were capital offences, tended to be reserved for the Assizes. In the first half of the seventeenth century, however, Kent justices of the peace held gaol delivery sessions, quite apart from their Quarter Sessions, at which felons were tried and executed.[1] For the remainder of the century felons, who could claim benefit of clergy and therefore avoid the death penalty, continued to be tried and sentenced at Quarter Sessions. Juries, too, could diminish a capital charge. By 1650–70 almost one third of juries' verdicts were partial and it was claimed that 'juries usurped the discretionary powers of judge and sovereign by this devise'.[2]

Throughout the eighteenth century and during the early decades of the nineteenth century the judicial work at Kent Quarter Sessions was concerned almost entirely with misdemeanors and petty larceny. But as the number of capital crimes was reduced and alternative punishments, such as transportation, were favoured, so the work of the justices again increased. After 1834, however, the

---

[1] E. Melling, *Crime and Punishment*, Maidstone 1969, pp. 2–3.
[2] *Twelve Good Men and True: The Criminal Trial Jury in England 1200–1800*, ed. J.S. Cockburn and T.A. Green, Princeton 1988, p. 172.

newly established Central Criminal Court dealt with much of the more serious crime committed in the parishes of Metropolitan Kent.[3]

Crimes in English law can be divided into indictable offences, which include felonies and indictable misdemeanors tried by jury, and non-indictable offences which may be tried summarily by the justices without a jury.[4] The surviving judicial records in Kent are the product of a variety of different courts and vary at different times in quality and quantity.[5] Their nature and complexity prevent any meaningful statistical analysis of crime before the nineteenth century.[6] After 1805 Parliamentary Papers and Chief Constables' Reports provide annual totals of committals for indictable crime up to 1900. These permit a study of trends and fluctuations in serious crime per 100,000 head of the population but little more.[7]

They need to be interpreted with caution. Nevertheless trends in Kent conform generally to the national pattern. A sharp rise in indictable committals in the years after the Napoleonic Wars was followed by a significant fall in the early 1820s. The steady upward movement then resumed, peaking in the Swing years, in 1838, and twice during the 'Hungry Forties', before dropping in the late 1850s. These peaks coincided with years of economic depression. Since theft constituted the bulk of serious nineteenth century offences the strong suggestion is that crime for survival increased with poverty and hunger and diminished when times improved. In the late 1850s a long term downward trend began characterised particularly by a decline in crimes of theft and violence in late Victorian and Edwardian England. This is attributed to a combination of more efficient policing after 1857 and an increase in prosperity which, although unevenly distributed, was sufficient to keep many out of the courts.[8]

Some corroboration of this quite spectacular decline is provided by written evidence. Baron Bramwell, the Lent Assize Judge and the Recorder of Canterbury both commented upon the unprecedented lightness of their respective criminal calendars as early as 1869. Similar plaudits followed. No case

---

3   Melling, *op. cit.*, pp. 3–4.
4   G. Cross and G.D.G. Hall, *Radcliffe and Cross: The English Legal System*, London 1964, p. 337. An indictment is a written accusation of a person of a crime, at the suit of the crown.
5   Quarter Sessions records are kept in county record offices, in Kent at the CKS; Assize records are kept in the PRO.
6   Melling, *op. cit.*, pp. 3–15.
7   *PP* 1819, viii, *Select Committee on Criminal Laws*, Appendix 1 (1805–1818); *PP* 1826–7, xix, to *PP* 1834, xlvii (1820–33); *PP* 1835, xlv, to *PP* 1856, xli (1834–55); CKS, Chief Constables' Annual Reports, uncatalogued 1857–70, C/POL/1/9/1 1870–98, C/POL/1/18/1 1899–1901. For the methodology and caveats see V.A.C. Gatrell and T.B. Hadden, 'Criminal Statistics and their Interpretation', in *Nineteenth Century Society*, ed. E.A.Wrigley, Cambridge 1972, pp. 339–42, 350–3, 361–2. For further comment and caveats see Clive Emsley, *Crime and Society in England 1750–1900*, London 1987, pp. 21–49.
8   See Figure 7. I am most grateful to Mike Chitty for gathering the early criminal statistics and to Gordon Morris and James K. Morton of New College, Durham, for producing the graph by computer. The computer was used to calculate the county population for inter-censal years and to calculate crime rates. See also Gatrell and Hadden, *op. cit.*, pp. 363–86 and V.A.C. Gatrell, 'The Decline of Theft and Violence in Victorian and Edwardian England', in *Crime and the Law*, ed. V.A.C. Gatrell, Bruce Lenman and Geoffrey Parker, London 1980, pp. 238–337, especially pp. 240, 278, 281–3.

warranted penal survitude at the 1905 Winter Assizes. In May 1908 the editor of the *Kent Express* wrote of the 'paucity of crime'. Three years later 'crime of any sort' was reported 'practically absent' from Maidstone 'proving the excellence of police supervision'. Justice Channell, reminiscing over his 49 years' experience in Kent at the Autumn Assizes in 1912, concluded that by that date crimes of violence had decreased.[9]

Certain crimes were commonplace. The Recorder of Folkestone condemned drunkenness as 'the cause of more than half the crimes of the country'.[10] Certainly it was a factor in most felonies, particularly crimes of violence. Seventeenth century authorities were well aware of the problems created by 'disorderly ale houses'. 'Poor men tipple and families suffer' read a Yalding petition for the restriction of unlicenced houses in 1653.[11] The 'monstrous evil of intemperance' grew throughout the eighteenth and nineteenth centuries. Water was unsafe: milk was dangerous. Alcohol made the life of the labourer bearable. It was believed to give extra energy and dulled the fatigue of hard toil and the pain of illness. It also heightened the enjoyment of dances and fairs, and acted as an aphrodisiac. The 1830 Beer Act created the beerhouse which was beyond the control of magistrates and drew its licence, if it had one, from the excisemen. Magistrates predicted that crime would increase as a result. Certainly some went straight from work to the beerhouse where they remained until the early hours or until wages ran out. Hard drinking, like obesity, was thought to be an indication of physical strength.[12]

'There is hardly a town or village where the number of public houses is not in excess of reasonable requirements', stated a group of West Kent clergy in 1870, in an abortive attempt to prevent further multiplication of drinking houses.[13] Arrests for drunkenness in Kent increased by 57% to an average of 1,888 per year in 1873–80, aided by the Intoxicating Liquors Act, which made public drunkenness a misdemeanour for the first time. Women were culprits as well as men. Catherine Cuthbert was so drunk that she lay incapable, cursing in a Faversham street. Maidstone and Canterbury police wheeled drunks to the lock-up in a wheelbarrow. They were wise. It took three persons and two officers in 1865 to drag the drunk and disorderly Elizabeth Skelton to Gravesend station house. Drink was pleaded as an excuse by Michael White, a hopper, who, in a drunken quarrel, treated his wife 'as he would a football'.[14] Wife beating often followed drinking. An Otford blacksmith knocked down his wife and blacked her eye when she refused to allow his adult nephew to sleep with them. Returning from

9 *KE*, 13.3.1869, 3.7.1869, 2.7.1870, 6.1.1906, 2.5.1908, 7.1.1911; *KM*, 30.11.1912.
10 *KE*, 12.10.1867.
11 CKS, Q/SB4/66.
12 Brian Harrison, *Drink and the Victorians*, London 1971, pp. 23, 37–9, 42, 45, 77, 308; *KE*, 23.7.1864.
13 *KE*, 5.2.1870.
14 Carolyn Conley, *The Unwritten Law: Criminal Justice in Victorian Kent*, New York 1991, pp. 170–1; *KE*, 1.7.1865, 7.10.1865, 18.6.1870, 25.9.1875.

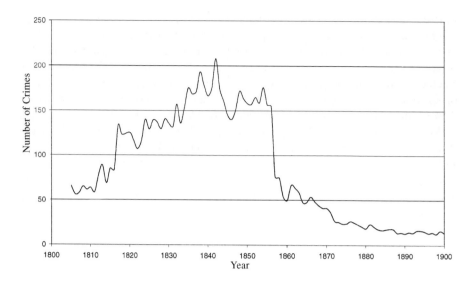

Figure 7. Kent criminal patterns, 1805–1900: indictable offences

the beerhouse he attempted to choke her. His defence was that he was drunk. Yet still the multiplication of licences continued.[15]

In the year ending 31 December 1908 Gravesend boasted 87 alehouses, 33 beerhouses, plus 4 beerhouses and 21 shops 'off', an average of 187 persons to each licence. This did not include inns and taverns which were classified as 'respectable'. An average of 342 persons per year between 1901 and 1908 were proceeded against for drunkenness. Maidstone with 73 alehouses, 49 beerhouses and 48 beerhouses 'off' had an average of 211 persons to every licence. In some of the smaller towns and large villages there was even more generous provision. West Malling had one licenced house to every 115 inhabitants and East Peckham one to 134.[16]

Theft was invariably the principal crime. Of the indictable offences tried in 1602 54.3% were for theft. Half these involved the stealing of livestock. The remainder were for theft of money, foodstuffs, linen cloth and clothing, agricultural, industrial, personal and household goods.[17] Sessions papers for 1639–77 again show that 67.8% of all offences involved theft of similar commodities. The seventeenth century thief stole anything that could be moved ranging from fuel, cattle, pigs, horses, sheep, silver plate, pewter and cash to a hive of bees (1669) and 200 eels (1670). Hop poles, scythes, saws, crops, firearms and household linen completed the range of articles.[18] In the eighteenth and early

[15] *KE*, 29.4.1865, 28.7.1866, 22.10.1870.
[16] *KE*, 6.2.1909, 3.3.1909.
[17] *Kent at Law 1602: The County Jurisdiction. Assizes and Sessions of the Peace*, ed. Louis A. Knafla, London 1994, p. xxi.
[18] CKS, Q/SB 1–12.

nineteenth centuries as the variety of household goods increased the thief was offered an even wider choice. Larceny still accounted for almost a third of all crime in March 1863 although by this time the figures had been distorted by large numbers of convictions for drunkenness (7.5%) and offences under the Vagrant, Army and Poor Law Acts.[19] By March 1886 larceny represented 13.8% of all indictable and summary offences. Drunkenness accounted for a massive 20% of all convictions, and offences under the Vagrant Act 9.7%.[20]

Most theft was petty. In March 1863 56% of larceny was dealt with summarily.[21] Agricultural produce was protected by the full weight of the law. William Morris, a Barham labourer, was sentenced to six months hard labour for stealing eight fowls. Another labourer got a month for theft of a faggot worth 3d. Young William Webb of Tenterden, imprisoned for six months for stealing six walnuts, had his sentence reduced to a month by the Home Secretary.[22] When a Lenham labourer stole three turnips in 1870 'because he was hungry' the farmer would not prosecute. This was unusual since 'farmers lost a great deal in this manner'.[23] The working classes were as much the victims as the perpetrators of theft. Frequently the pocket watch, often the working man's only possession of value, fell victim to the thief. Clothes and tools were the next most favourite targets. Theft of clothes was made easier by the practice of hanging them to dry on hedges. In 1651 three Ickham men confessed to stealing shirts from the hedgerow. David Richardson in 1750 even stole a wet shirt from a Dartford clothes line. A Nonington waggoner got three months hard labour for taking two eggs. Alfred Brown was prosecuted by a Charing farmer for taking food from the supper table to eat later.[24]

Heavier sentences were given for thefts implying greater professionalism such as burglary. Burglars themselves were sometimes at risk. Fred Solly, an unsuccessful burglar at Lee Priory, entered the dock 'bearing the marks of shot front and rear' sustained as he attempted escape through the shrubbery.[25] Disposal of stolen property was not always easy. Burglars at Barham Court, the residence of George Dering Esq., got away in 1870 with plate and wearing apparel, but all bore his crest and information was swiftly telegraphed to police stations throughout Kent. Pawnshops were the customary outlet for more ordinary items. As such they were immediately scrutinised by police. In 1867 a gang which had just robbed a house at Lower Hardres was arrested disposing of the stolen property in a Dover pawnshop.[26]

Assault was the second most common offence accounting for 18% of crime in 1602. In 1863 it represented 12% of all offences but with new legislation such

[19] CKS, Q/GP/b3.
[20] *Loc. cit.*
[21] *Loc. cit.*
[22] *KE*, 10.1.1857, 6.4.1861, 7.11.1863, 29.10.1864.
[23] *AA*, 13.9.1856; *KE*, 17.9.1857.
[24] *KE*, 10.11.1860, 23.4.1870; Melling, *op. cit.*, pp. 69–70, 104; CKS, Q/SB2/18–20, 3–4 October 1651.
[25] Conley, *op. cit.*, p. 140; *KE*, 30.7.1870.
[26] *KE*, 21.9.1867, 12.3.1870.

as the offences against the Elementary Education Acts it had dropped to 8.5% by 1886.[27] The authorities did little to curb such violence. It was regarded as a legitimate response to insult. Consequently it was often tolerated unless weapons were used or it was perpetrated against respectable citizens.[28] A typical Saturday night in Ashford commenced when two men emerged from the Fountain and began fighting. The contest was stopped by the police only to recommence in Castle Street before a large crowd. Robert Stubbs, a dockyard shipwright, and his adversary chose Chatham High Street on a Sunday when the congregations were leaving church for their confrontation before another massive audience.[29] Statistically women were convicted of only 6–10% of violent assaults. When they were involved they were no less violent than men. Elizabeth Thomas, when a brawl broke out in the Coach and Horses, Chatham, seized a poker 'with which she did such effective execution that three persons were hospitalised'. Superintendent Dewar, visiting the Rose and Crown, Ashford at 1.00a.m. on 30 November 1869, found it in uproar. Two shirtless men were fighting with seconds. Several women had bloody heads. The men were cleared by 1.15a.m. but ten drunken women were still fighting.[30] Yet in 91% of assault convictions arising from brawls between 1859 and 1880 sentences were under eighteen months. Even in the 63 cases in which people died 86% of those convicted still got less than a year and a half.[31]

John Boykett, husbandman of Westwell, accused of 'a violent rape' against Mary Boyce in 1666, was in grave difficulty since until 1841 the offence was punishable by death. Sentencing James Morgan to fifteen years penal servitude for the rape of Rose Uden in 1868 the judge stated that since its abolition as a capital crime the sentence for this offence was too light.[32] Yet rape or attempted rape constituted only 2.5% and 6.0% of indictable offences respectively. This was because the conviction rate was only 41% as opposed to 74% for felonies generally. Moreover only 21% of men charged with rape stood trial for that offence. The remaining cases were dismissed or heard as minor offences. Reduced charges were often introduced when 'respectable' men were accused. When fourteen-year-old Hannah Isaacs was appointed under-laundrymaid in the household of the Earl of Norbury, the Earl gave her £5 'for clothes' then went to her room and assaulted her. There would have been no prosecution had not the Society for the Protection of Women and Children undertaken it. As it was the charge was reduced to common assault and the Earl merely fined £5.[33]

Since consent was vital the verdict often hinged upon whether judge and jury believed the victim. Social status and respectability were crucial. Charges were often reduced if there were 'no . . . marks of violence to indicate the resistance

27 Knafla, *loc. cit.*; CKS, Q/GP/b3.
28 Conley, *op. cit.*, pp. 48–54.
29 *KE*, 5.11.1864, 28.12.1865.
30 Conley, *op. cit.*, pp. 70–1; *KE*, 11.12.1869.
31 Conley, *op. cit.*, pp. 50–1.
32 *Ibid.*, pp. 84–5; *KE*, 26.12.1868; CKS, Q/SB 10/10, 22 August 1666.
33 Conley, *op. cit.*, pp. 82–3; *KE*, 11.3.1865.

necessary to establish a charge'.[34] A young housemaid, attacked when walking home to Staplehurst, had a black eye and injuries to the chest and jaw. She admitted, under examination, familiarity with her sweetheart. Her attacker got only five years. In 1870, a groom was sentenced to eight years penal servitude for raping Mrs Mary Wood, 'a respectable married woman'. At the same Assizes four men who had gang-raped Mary Hockless at Whitstable were discharged since the prosecutrix was 'of dissolute character' and her evidence could not be relied on. Elizabeth Banks, an Irish hawker, was followed from the British Flag, Ashford and attacked by another gang. Her clothes were 'much torn', her face was gashed. Two policemen arrived as she 'lay struggling with her clothing round her waist and her face covered with blood'. Two men were kneeling beside her, one 'with his dress disarranged'. Despite police evidence they were discharged 'since the state she was found in might be the result of her drunken conduct alone'.[35]

Young domestic servants also got little protection from the law. Only one employer, a Tenterden tea dealer, was convicted between 1859 and 1880 of a violent outrage on a female servant. He committed the offence when his wife was away. Of employers accused of raping servants 65% were tried for indecent assault and half of those were acquitted.[36] When a retired army captain 'from a good county family' was given three months for indecently assaulting a domestic servant in a railway carriage it was hailed as a triumph for justice. The defendant was stunned since sexual assaults were usually regarded as 'drunken impulses' or 'regrettable lapses of self control'.[37]

If women, and working class women in particular, were disadvantaged, their female children were even more vulnerable. The age of consent was not raised from twelve to thirteen until 1875. Between 1859 and 1880 some 39 charges of sexual assault on girls under twelve were heard by magistrates who dismissed nine and heard the rest as aggravated assaults. In the same period 26 of 31 indictments for rape on girls between twelve and sixteen were dismissed, reduced or the defendant acquitted because the victims showed insufficient evidence of a violent struggle. When conviction was secured sentences were light. In 1870 a soldier got eighteen months hard labour for criminally assaulting a girl aged seven. There was no law against incest until 1908.[38]

In the first quarter of 1863 5.3% of summary offences concerned breaches of the Master and Servants' Statutes. These laws were used by employers to maintain deference and discipline. Masters accused of breach of contract were subject to civil action. Servants were liable to criminal prosecution. Kent magistrates, often landed gentry themselves, jailed absconding farm servants regularly. William Butt, in 1864, was given seven days hard labour for illegally

---

34 Conley, *op. cit.*, pp. 81–2, 84; *KE*, 23.12.1865.
35 *KE*, 24.11.1866, 1.12.1866, 7.8.1869, 9.10.1869, 12.3.1870.
36 Conley, *op. cit.*, p. 86; *KE*, 4.7.1868.
37 Conley, *op. cit.*, pp. 91–3; *KE*, 6.8.1870.
38 Conley, *op. cit.*, pp. 118, 120–1; *KE*, 30.7.1870.

leaving the service of a Milton farmer. Some farmers were relentless in the pursuit of offenders. William Rains absconded from a Marden farmer in November 1863 but was not taken until February 1866. Imprisonment did not end the labourer's contract. A servant who refused to complete it afterwards was liable to be gaoled again.[39] Magistrates were equally punctilious in imprisoning the disobedient. At Ashford a sixteen-year-old waggoner's mate was sent to the treadmill for three weeks. The bench 'wished it was in their power to have him flogged'. Two farm servants were presented who, after ploughing for four hours in torrential rain, refused to continue. Three labourers were charged with misconduct by James Tassell of Wye because they 'did not work . . . with the energy they might have done' and because they did not ask permission to go out after supper. 'Many farmers', wrote a contemporary 'esteem their labourers . . . below their cattle.'[40]

The Master and Servant Act 1867, intended to correct the worst inequities of this legislation, altered little. Servants could counterclaim but few were successful. A Northbourne farmer was accused of breach of contract by his farm servants for supplying them with bad food. Maggots crawled from the putrid meat. Their contracts were annulled but there was no other redress. Only after the foundation of the Kent and Sussex Agricultural Labourers' Union in 1872 did Kent magistrates slowly become more reluctant to accept the master's right to chastise. In 1863 a farmer was merely fined for assaulting a labourer. In 1875 an Eastchurch farmer received an £8 fine and fourteen days hard labour for a similar offence.[41]

(2) Factors Affecting Criminality in Kent

Thus far we have described patterns of criminal behaviour that were commonplace in any county. However, there were particular local conditions which shaped the pattern of crime in Kent.

(a) The Presence of the Military and Other Transients

The late seventeenth-century growth of royal naval dockyards at Chatham, Deptford, Woolwich and Sheerness had created a vast and tempting entrepot of naval supplies and enhanced Kent's position as England's 'frontline county' requiring a large, permanent military presence.[42] Barracks were built at Dover Castle in 1745. At Chatham accommodation was erected for five regiments between 1758 and 1806 to defend the dockyard. More barracks were

---

[39] See D.C. Woods, 'The Operation of the Master and Servant Act in the Black Country', *Midland History*, vii (1982), pp. 93–115; Conley, *op. cit.*, pp. 191–5; *KE*, 16.4.1864, 10.2.1866, 26.5.1866.

[40] Conley, *op. cit.*, pp. 191–2; *KE*, 24.3.1860, 7.4.1860, 23.3.1861, 31.1.1863, 11.4.1863, 17.4.1864.

[41] *KE*, 11.7.1863, 12.9.1868; *Kent and Sussex Times*, 18.6.1875, 20.8.1875.

[42] David Ormrod, 'Industry 1640–1800', in *The Economy of Kent 1640–1914*, ed. Alan Armstrong, Woodbridge 1995, p. 103.

constructed in the 1790s at Ashford, Canterbury, Dartford, Maidstone, Hythe, Deal and Walmer. The Napoleonic camp, established on Shorncliffe Heights in 1794, held almost 3,000 troops in 1901 when there were 18,000 soldiers and 9,500 sailors stationed throughout Kent.[43] A decade later 10% of adult males in Kent were members of the armed forces as opposed to 2% nationally.[44]

This situation had long influenced the county's criminal statistics. Dover was not only the port of entry and exit for troops serving overseas but after 1909 the base of the Atlantic Fleet. Chatham, 'a dirty, unpleasant town' was also 'devoted to the interests of soldiers and mariners'.[45] The Brook was notorious as its sink of iniquity. Three thousand books sent by the War Office in 1855 'for the benefit of soldiers in the winter evenings' had little appeal. Nor did a Citizens' League, formed to improve Chatham's morals, particularly after its objection to renewed licences for 45 beer houses.[46] Chatham remained a town where 'every third house is a beer house and every third man a soldier'.[47] Departing regiments were traditionally headed by prostitutes dancing to the music of the military bands. In 1906 a Brixton clergyman remarked that 'he had witnessed scenes of vice . . . which would not be tolerated in the worst quarters of London'.[48] Sheerness was similar. In 1865 a royal naval survey listed 53 brothels at Chatham, 39 at Dover and 33 at Sheerness. 8.3 per thousand of Dover's inhabitants were known prostitutes as opposed to 5.82 at Sheerness and 3.95 at Chatham.[49]

Sandgate's aspirations to become a watering place were frustrated by its proximity to Shorncliffe Camp. In the beerhouses lining the main street girls were kept nominally as servants but in reality for prostitution.[50] Visiting prostitutes slept in outhouses and in the fields in summer.[51] In 1867 Sandgate Local Board protested that the streets were unsafe after nightfall 'by reason of drunken soldiers inflamed by poisonous liquor'.[52]

Nor were brothels limited to the ports and garrison towns. Market towns, too, catered for the venal tastes of labourers and others on pay nights and at weekends. Gravel Walk, Ashford, was one such home of the 'unfortunates' and their 'bullies'. Beerhouses served their quarts at all hours and quarrels between and over 'the frail sisterhood' were frequent. 'There was a great disturbance . . .

43 *Ibid.*, pp. 222–3, 269; Jonathan Coad, *Hellfire Corner*, London 1993, pp. 3–5; Peter Bloomfield, *Kent and the Napoleonic Wars*, Gloucester 1957, pp. 23–30, 36–9; Michael Winstanley, *Life in Kent at the Turn of the Century*, Folkestone 1978, p. 166; George Bosworth, *Kent*, Cambridge 1909, p. 60.

44 Conley, *op. cit.*, p. 11.

45 *Loc. cit.*; G. Philips Bevan, *Handbook to the County of Kent 1876*, 1876, pp. 33–4.

46 *AA*, 29.12.1855; *KE*, 17.2.1906.

47 Winstanley, *op. cit.*, p. 164.

48 *CN*, 14.9.1901; *KE*, 10.2.1906; see also Brian Joyce, *The Chatham Scandal*, Rochester 1999.

49 *KE*, 8.4.1865.

50 *KE*, 22.10.1864.

51 *AA*, 4.9.1858.

52 *KE*, 19.10.1867.

which was often the case on Sunday evenings at Hadlow' stated Police Sergeant Mayne describing a brawl outside Bradley's beerhouse to the court.[53]

With three royal dockyards in Kent theft of naval stores was commonplace. The stealing of twenty pounds of sheet lead from *HMS Newark* at Chatham dockyard in 1741 is typical. Daniel Dunevan, a dockyard workman stopped by the watchman at the gate, was found to be carrying the lead in his basket. Mathew Wood, a marine store dealer, who sold seven cwt of new copper bolts stolen from Sheerness dockyard in 1866, was a much bigger 'fish'. A large, resident garrison also meant that traffic in military stores was frequent. Deserters often sold their uniforms. William Ferer, keeper of the Victoria beerhouse, Brompton, was found with the greatcoat, shell jacket and cap of Patrick Tawney of the 14th Regiment. Tawney had sold his kit twice before. For offering two pairs of military boots for sale, 'without the condemned mark which every Woolwich tradesman is expected to know', James Cable, shoemaker, was sentenced to a month's imprisonment.[54]

Despite the provosts, soldiers from the garrison towns were responsible for a vast amount of petty theft, violence and sexual offences against women and children from the early seventeenth century onwards. Commonwealth soldiers on a typical thieving spree in 1659 plundered poultry from Woodnesbrough farms. At East Kent Quarter Sessions in Summer 1858 nearly half the prisoners were from Shorncliffe Barracks. Most offenders at Dover Sessions in April 1860 were soldiers of Dover garrison. Twenty of 69 prisoners before the Lent Assizes in 1861 were also military men. Six were charged with rick burning. The principal objective of those offending was discharge from the army since the convict's condition 'was considered preferable to that of the soldier'. From 1859 to 1880 17% of all Kent arson cases involved soldiers.[55]

Bored and brutalised by army life, soldiers wrought havoc among Kent's civilians. In 1596 soldiers returning from France stole books, including a bible, from Charing Church. In Dover drinking bouts culminated in the plunder of shops. During the Crimean War the Swiss Legion, awaiting embarkation, nightly filled the streets brawling and chasing women 'as if they were wild animals'.[56] Between 1859 and 1880 soldiers were accused of 10% of indictable theft, 12% of indictable assaults and 10% of all sexual offences.[57] In the absence of opponents they fought each other. In a fight at Shorncliffe Camp between rival regiments in 1870 nine troopers were seriously injured. A sergeant who intervened almost lost his life and a private was later found dead.[58] Further depredations were committed by soldiers passing to and from the continent and by the

---

53 *KE*, 24.8.1861, 14.9.1861, 5.10.1861, 9.11.1861, 4.7.1863, 13.8.1864, 20.8.1864, 10.11.1866, 4.6.1870, 16.7.1870.
54 Melling, *op. cit.*, p. 68; *KE*, 10.11.1866, 26.6.1869.
55 *AA*, 3.7.1858; *KE*, 28.4.1860, 4.8.1860, 8.12.1860, 16.3.1861; Conley, *op. cit.*, p. 154; CKS, Q/SB 7/10 d–f, 26 January 1659–60.
56 Conley, *op. cit.*, pp. 154–5; *AA*, 19.1.1856; Melling, *op. cit.*, pp. 38–9.
57 Conley, *op. cit.*, p. 154.
58 *KE*, 1.1.1870.

constant flow of deserters. In 1874 Chatham deserters were being court-martialled at a rate of five a day. In the 1860s 11% of the inmates of Kent jails were soldiers, increasing to 14% by the 1870s.[59]

The military were not the only outsiders to swell Kent's criminal statistics. From the seventeenth century hordes of migrant hop pickers descended every autumn on the hop growing districts. This seasonal influx was sometimes estimated at 80,000.[60] The 'strangers' brought with them an annual outbreak of crime, violence and disease. Some came from the Medway towns. Many were London Irish. Before the railways most walked into Kent. Marshall complained in 1798 that they plundered 'the country of whatever they can'.[61] 'Since hop picking commenced', commented the *Maidstone Gazette* in 1831, 'many cottages owned by poor but industrious labourers have been broken open while they are at the plantations'[62] In 1870 the 'hoppers' arrived too soon. Consequently 'cases of brutality, drunkenness and robbery were "large beyond precedent" '.[63] Difficulties were worse, however, when the harvest was poor. In 1866 there were more violent clashes than usual between the 'home pickers' and the 'strangers' who were stranded jobless in Kent. In one such affray at Ide Hill a 'foreigner' died on his way to the union hospital. Two of his compatriots sustained fractured skulls. A 'home picker' was stabbed. Many others were 'more or less injured'. In the same year Irish hoppers, worsted in a Saturday night disturbance at Hadlow, returned armed with ripping hooks and attacked the three policemen on duty. Their womenfolk stood by their aprons filled with stones. A sergeant was severely wounded and two constables 'much hurt'.[64]

Arrests for drunkenness and riot soared every hopping. In 1855 drunken pickers tore out window frames and battered down the door of the Bull at East Farleigh to rescue the ringleader of a gang who had refused to pay the reckoning.[65] Irish pickers ejected from the Brickmakers Arms, Wrotham, in 1862 discharged pistols into the house. The inmates returned the fire seriously wounding two Irishmen. Two years later 300 'of the roughest class of hoppers' stripped a Mid-Kent fruit plantation in an orgy of wanton destruction.[66]

'The great work' was punctuated by strikes. An abundant crop led to wage demands. If concessions were made further demands followed. The usual response was to hire fresh pickers. If this occurred the original pickers tried to drive them off. In 1859 there were riots in the hop gardens at Leeds and Tudeley. In 1889, encouraged perhaps by the example of the London Dock Strike, labour disputes intensified. At Horsmonden a farm bailiff was stabbed by a striker. Two years later there were strikes at Newington and Upchurch. At the former,

---

[59] Conley, *op. cit.*, p. 155; *KE*, 5.12.1874.

[60] Winstanley, *op. cit.*, p. 79.

[61] J. Marshall, *Rural Economy of the Southern Counties*, London 1798, pp. 242–3.

[62] *MG*, 31.9.1831; see also Conley, *op. cit.*, p. 164.

[63] *KE*, 8.10.1870.

[64] *KE*, 6.10.1866, 13.10.1866, 27.10.1866.

[65] *MG*, 2.10.1855.

[66] *MG*, 14.9.1862; *SEG*, 15.9.1864.

strikers threatened to burn down the grower's house. The century ended with a strike of a thousand pickers at Offham and yet more at Farleigh.[67]

Even the hoppers' departure did not usually pass without incident. In 1862 two rival groups numbering almost a thousand, 'mostly inebriated', met near Maidstone West Station and decided to settle old scores. 'Showers of stones were hurled by the women . . . the men using their shillelaghs and bagging hooks in a most determined manner.' Twenty-four were injured including a baby in its mother's arms who later died. The police, though present, were powerless to intervene.[68]

Hoppers were not the only transient workers to bring violent crime. From the 1830s until the late 1880s navvy gangs were building Kent's railways. The majority followed the contractors who recruited them, living in damp and squalor alongside the tracks. Few survived beyond forty. Their only tools were picks, shovels and gunpowder. Accidents were frequent. Paid double the wage of the agricultural labourer they lived riotously while they could, bringing terror to rural communities.[69]

As the South Eastern Railway advanced across Mid Kent crime advanced with it.

> In Staplehurst and Marden scarcely a night passes without a robbery . . . by . . . excavators employed or seeking employment on the railroad.
> One night last week five farmers . . . lost their poultry and one two pigs . . . On Friday last a poor woman . . . returning from market . . . was robbed by five men of her week's provisions . . . Every woman who leaves her house unprotected is liable to be robbed or indecently assaulted.[70]

Builders of the Sevenoaks line gave the greatest trouble. Over one thousand labourers were expected and the town's anxieties heightened as the new beerhouses mushroomed. The contractor was more enlightened than most. He built an iron chapel and hired a full-time surgeon. When the navvies were granted a holiday, however, Superintendent Coleman of the county police confessed that 'he had never seen railwaymen so unruly'. A year later, when a sub-contractor decamped without paying them, an army of armed navvies entered the town to demand their money. The situation was only defused by the superintendent's timely intervention.[71]

Numerically the railway navvies never challenged the hop pickers. 760 men were employed between Folkestone and Dover and 580 in the Tonbridge district at the height of the SER's construction.[72] Many navvies, however, were also employed on public works, particularly sewers. These, too, made their presence

---

[67] *MG*, 11.10.1859; *SEG*, 3.2.1866; *KE*, 28.9.1889, 19.10.1889, 19.9.1891, 9.9.1899.

[68] *MG*, 30.9.1862.

[69] Armstrong, *op. cit.*, pp. 247, 255, 258; see also Terry Coleman, *The Railway Navvies*, Harmondsworth 1968.

[70] *MG*, 25.1.1842.

[71] *KE*, 31.10.1863; *SEG*, 2.6.1863, 12.1.1864, 7.2.1865, 11.7.1865.

[72] *MG*, 28.7.1840.

felt. Rioting occurred among a thousand navvies building the Sewerage Works at Erith Marshes in 1864. Strikers demanding the re-instatement of a colleague attacked men still working. Thirty 'fully armed' Woolwich police partly restored order but sporadic street fighting involving severe injuries continued for several days.[73] In 1869 a navvy gang working on the Tunbridge Wells sewerage works 'took over' the High Rocks beerhouse and threatened to kill the parish constable who hid until police arrived.[74]

(b) Geographical Location: The Proximity of London

London, the largest city in Western Europe and a centre of criminal activity, considerably influenced the incidence of crime in Kent. London criminals committed crimes in Kent escaping afterwards to the capital. In 1600 a woman from St Katherine's was taken for shoplifting in Gravesend, while in 1657 a thief from St Giles stole money and property from a house in Dover. As Metropolitan Kent became increasingly urbanised from the late seventeenth century crime here increased, providing the majority of serious offences at West Kent Sessions in the eighteenth and early nineteenth centuries.[75] Some 468 seats of the nobility and gentry were listed in the county in Bagshaw's *Directory* of 1847. These, plus the contents of the parsonage houses of some of Kent's 410 parishes, made attractive targets.[76] In 1656 an armed London gang raided the house of Bonham Faunce, a country gentleman at Cliffe, terrorised his household and stole plate and money. Four men were caught at Gravesend returning to London by waterway, the equivalent of the modern motorway. All were sentenced to death.[77]

In April 1870 Woodchurch rectory was burgled by another London gang who stole the silver. They also found the church keys but failed to find the communion plate.[78] Parish churches were soft options. In 1797 Boughton Monchelsea church was robbed of a surplice, two 'capital window curtains', some books 'and the strong chest attempted with Mr Marten's Coulter; as was two or three other churches with a like instrument stolen from the fields broken open'.[79]

When Queen Victoria embarked from Gravesend in 1858, London pickpockets took advantage of the crowds, as they did at Maidstone's Volunteer Review three years later. One of those arrested was described as 'a trainer of young thieves' and his London shop 'a den for the reception of stolen goods'.[80] When a professional pickpocket from Pentonville was sentenced in 1906 for stealing a watch at Kingsnorth Races he was stated to be one of twelve under the

[73] *KE*, 23.4.1864.
[74] *KE*, 24.7.1869.
[75] Clive Emsley, *Crime and Society in England 1750–1900*, Harlow 1996, p. 92; Melling, *op. cit.*, pp. 15, 32, 40–1; CKS, Q/SB 7/2, 7 December 1657.
[76] *Bagshaw's Directory of Kent*, vol. 2, Sheffield 1847, pp. 25–35.
[77] Melling, *op. cit.*, pp. 50–1, 63–6; CKS, Q/SB 6/42–49.
[78] *KE*, 4.4.1870.
[79] CKS, P39/1/2, Boughton Monchelsea Parish Registers.
[80] *AA*, 14.8.1858; *KE*, 21.9.1861.

training of a 'Father King'.[81] Another London pickpocket who preyed on steamer passengers at Ramsgate pier had ten previous convictions but, contrary to the popular belief that crime was the work of a professional criminal class of 'outsiders', most offences were committed by ordinary Kent citizens.[82]

(c) Geographical Location: The Kentish Coastline and the Continent
Kent's situation between London and the Continent and the length and variety of its coastline made it a major smuggling county. Smuggling in Kent was age-old and widely practiced. Supported openly or tacitly by entire communities, it was regarded as quite legitimate. Violence, intimidation and corruption were all part of the smuggling trade. From the outset smugglers were as likely to defeat excise officers by force as by stealth. Robert Jull, and two companions from Hythe custom house, who tried to seize wool from 'owlers' in 1657, were 'much disinabled'.[83] Between 1700 and 1840 smuggling was out of control as the gangs fought 'guerrilla' and often open warfare with the under-resourced authorities. In 1746 the notorious Hawkhurst Gang turned Wingham into a battlefield as they fought Wingham smugglers over a consignment of tea. Next year the gang attacked Goudhurst whose inhabitants, tired of intimidation, organised a militia and defeated the smugglers, three of whom were killed. Unabashed the gang regained credibility in a daring raid upon Poole Customs House.[84] In 1769 Joss Snelling and his Callis Court Gang fought the Battle of Botany Bay. A riding officer and ten smugglers were killed. Eight other smugglers were later hanged at Sandwich but similar bloody affrays continued throughout the century.[85]

The authorities enjoyed little success partly because they lacked effective manpower and partly because smuggling brought lower prices on illegally imported goods. A troop of dragoons quartered at Canterbury made little difference since 'setting soldiers to catch smugglers' was 'like setting elephants to catch eels'. In 1781 Deal was raided by a hundred cavalry and nine companies of infantry following the murder of a customs house officer. Three years later a troop of dragoons and the 38th foot, under orders from Pitt, burned the beached Deal luggers. The Deal smugglers remained undeterred. In 1801 the crew of a revenue cutter, which had intercepted a smuggling vessel near Deal beach, was forced to retreat by the townsfolk with an officer dead and several men wounded.[86]

Smugglers were not only regarded as public benefactors but were major

---

81 *KE*, 28.4.1906, 8.9.1906.
82 *KE*, 2.7.1870; see also Emsley, *op. cit.*, pp. 84–5, 168–75.
83 Melling, *op. cit.*, pp. 66–7; CKS, Q/SB 7/5–7, 7 October 1657.
84 Craig and Whyman, 'Kent and the Sea', in Armstrong, *op. cit.*, pp. 175–81; M. Waugh, *Smuggling in Kent and Sussex 1700–1840*, Newbury 1985.
85 W.H. Lapthorne, 'The Battle of Botany Bay, Kingsgate', *Bygone Kent*, vol. 3, no. 1 (January 1982), pp. 19–22.
86 William Honey, *Smuggling in Deal*, Deal n.d.; B. Collins, *Discovering Deal*, Deal 1969, p. 59; Stephen Pritchard, *History of Deal*, Deal 1864, pp. 249–50.

employers in an era of rural underemployment. Their 'runs' were highly organised. Sea smugglers brought the contraband close inshore. The landing party of several hundred men and horses remained concealed until the last moment. Most were local labourers hoping to earn more for a night's work than they could earn in a week. The 'tubsmen' who carried the cargo from the vessel to the horses were paid 10s 0d. They were protected by a line of 'batsmen' on either flank armed with bludgeons and often cutlasses and firearms. The going rate for a 'batsman' in 1800 was a guinea per night, money which was earned since smugglers were frequently attacked by revenue men. Large armed convoys, relying for protection on superior numbers, then headed for London. In 1744 the Canterbury customs officer reported that 'London smugglers almost daily stop in the city on their way to the coast'. In 1735 Kent coastal farmers were obliged to increase harvest wages to entice labourers back to the land owing to 'the great numbers who employ themselves in smuggling'. In August 1804 Birchington vestry denied 'gristing' that week to anyone neglecting 'a day's work on smuggling or wrecking without the leave of the master they work for'.[87]

In these circumstances there was complete disregard for the law. A decomposing and unidentified male corpse discovered in a pond at High Halden in May 1786 was generally 'supposed to be a smuggler . . . come for some contraband'. When the body of John Darby was found on the shore between Birchington and Reculver in 1818 it was simply thought 'he was engaged in his occupation of smuggling and . . . was brutally murdered by some Frenchmen for the sake of his watch'.[88] Magistrates would not convict either because they benefited from smugglers' activities or because they feared reprisals. Lord Holland of Kingsgate, who told the House of Lords it must compromise with smuggling, had a financial stake in a Kent smuggling gang.[89] Informers got short shrift. The remains of a man, who revealed the existence of a secret tunnel at Kingsgate, were uncovered 120 years later in a shallow grave.[90] Between 1834 and 1852 there were only ten local indictments and three convictions for smuggling. In 1823 a jury even discharged the survivors of *The Four Brothers*, a Folkestone lugger which had fought a running battle with a revenue cutter, losing four of its crew.[91]

Kent villagers were prepared to defend the county's 'chief industry'. When customs men descended on Wouldham they were driven out by the inhabitants. When they returned with troops they recovered 224 tubs of brandy, a greater

87 Sanca de Burca, 'Smuggler Gangs . . .', *KM*, 6.12.1985; J.P. Barrett, *History of the Ville of Birchington*, Margate 1893, p. 167; John Douch, *Smuggling: The Wicked Trade*, Dover 1980, pp. 53–5.

88 *Ibid.*, p. 114; *KG*, 28.4.1818.

89 William Webb, 'Kent Smugglers', *Bygone Kent*, vol. 1, no. 1 (January 1980), p. 21.

90 W.H. Lapthorne, 'A Ruse of the Most Ingenious', *Bygone Kent*, vol. 5, no. 10 (October 1984), pp. 601–4.

91 *Accounts and Papers* (1835) XLV–(1852–53) LXXXI, Criminal Statistics; John English, *The Cruise of the Four Brothers*, Folkestone 1875.

seizure than had been known for many years.[92] Excessive intimidation however, could be counter-productive. The brutal murder of Daniel Chater, who gave evidence against one of the Poole raiders, together with his escort, spelled the end for the Hawkhurst gang. In the wake of the public revulsion witnesses came forward. By 1749, with its leaders executed, the gang was broken.[93] Its successor, the Aldington Gang, which dominated the post-Napoleonic era, did not learn from its mistakes. The gang, led by George Ransley, had its own surgeon and lawyer. Its operations stretched from Walmer to Rye. Initially it 'forced the runs' despite heavy casualties. Eventually its excesses cost it public support. After the murder of Richard Morgan of the coastal blockade in 1826 a smuggler turned King's Evidence and the gang was transported.[94]

Smuggling continued for the next quarter of a century. As late as 1832 a company of the Rifle Brigade was stationed at Hythe 'to act against smugglers'. Increasingly contraband consisted of tobacco for which there was a ready market among Kent garrisons. Duty on tea was reduced by over three quarters in 1784 and the change to free trade after 1840 brought reduction or abolition of duties on wines, spirits and other much smuggled commodities. Eventually tobacco remained the only worthwhile proposition for smugglers.

Wrecking was not as prevalent as on the coast of South-West England. Nevertheless, the coast guard was regularly called out from Folkestone and Whitstable to prevent villagers pillaging wrecks. When the *Lord Sidmouth* was wrecked on the Goodwin Sands Deal coastguards fired over the heads of the crowd. The cargo of the *Francis*, which foundered off Dungeness Lighthouse in 1843, was carried away in cartloads for sale in Lydd and New Romney.[95]

(3) Responses to Economic Hardship

(a) Poaching

From the sixteenth century subsistence crises and escalating prices resulted in increasing misery for the urban and rural poor. Many inhabitants of early seventeeth-century Canterbury were reported to be 'starving through want of corn'.[96] In the nineteenth century an overpopulated county suffered acutely from unemployment, underemployment and poverty.[97] The seasonal and uncertain nature of their work and the gruelling aspects of their existence also drove many labourers to crime. If they were caught poverty was undoubtedly pleaded

[92] *MG*, 25.7.1843.
[93] A Gentleman of Chichester, *A Full and Genuine History of the inhuman . . . murders of William Galley . . . & Daniel Chater*, 1749.
[94] Douch, *op. cit.*, pp. 49–88; Webb, *op. cit.*, p. 22.
[95] *MG*, 13.3.1832; 18.4.1843; *KE*, 25.1.1873; *PP* 1839, *Report of the Constabulary Commissioners*, p. 61.
[96] CKS, Q/SB 1/30.
[97] See Paul Hastings, 'The Old Poor Law 1640–1834', N. Yates, R. Hume and P. Hastings, *Religion and Society in Kent 1640–1914*, Woodbridge 1994, pp. 112–53.

to enlist sympathy but many pleas were real. Robert Pryer, a Lynsted brick-maker, stole butter and cheese in 1657 because he was unable to feed his wife and four children. A Woodchurch labourer, who stole five turnips from a field in 1861, pleaded that he had no dinner for his family except 'a bit of bread'. Three men ferreting at Harrietsham in 1867 claimed they were unemployed 'and suffering very hard times'.[98] From the theft of crops, fuel and poultry it was a short step to sheep stealing, poaching and other major crimes of acquisition.

The relationship between crime and social protest has been much debated. Poaching was not widely perceived as criminal either by its perpetrators or by the public.[99] By the nineteenth century Kent poachers fell into two categories. Thomas Feakins, a labourer found at Charing using a terrier 'in search of conies', Henry Knott, another labourer, fined ten shillings for killing a pheasant at Lyminge, and the SER platelayer who set his traps beside the railway line at Ashford were all poachers feeding their families.[100] 'Every other man you met was a poacher', stated Joseph Arch.[101] One night's systematic poaching, however, earned more than several week's work. John Wyborn, a Canterbury labourer, caught at Godmersham with seven rabbits and 101 wires (snares) was a professional poacher supplying local tradesmen and innkeepers.[102] When professionals joined forces in organised gangs poaching became big business providing for poulterers and urban gentlemen. The more the Game Laws attempted to limit the right to hunt the more 'the Long Affray' between poachers and gamekeepers intensified.[103] Only eight poachers appeared before West Kent Sessions at Easter 1703. By the second half of the nineteenth century Kent magistrates heard summarily an average of 184 poaching cases a year.[104] This was only between 5 and 7% of all cases but the number was larger since the 'dark' figure for poaching offences is unknown.[105]

Gamekeepers were not popular. They earned three times the wage of an agri-cultural labourer. Moreover they often administered their own punishment. In 1860 a Rolvenden gamekeeper was fined for unlawfully beating a poacher.[106] Consequently gamekeepers and night poachers particularly fought it out in the woods with an assortment of weapons. William Clifford had a pistol in his pocket at full cock when arrested at Platts Heath. Two other 'old poachers' and a keeper were similarly armed.[107] The only poaching cases heard by juries involved violent confrontation. Even then conviction was not easy and sentences

[98]   CKS, Q SB7/3; *KE*, 21.12.1861, 7.12.1867.
[99]   John Rule, 'Social Crime in the Rural South in the Eighteenth and Early Nineteenth Centuries', *Southern History*, i (1979), pp. 135–53; see also Harry Hopkins, *The Long Affray: The Poaching Wars in Britain 1760–1914*, London 1986; Emsley, *op. cit.*, pp. 2–3, 39–40.
[100] *KE*, 14.1.1860, 8.8.1863; *SEG*, 6.1.1868.
[101] Hopkins, *op. cit.*, p. 24.
[102] *Ibid.*, pp. 25–6; *KE*, 31.10.1863.
[103] For legislation see Hopkins, *op. cit.*, pp. 305–7, and chapter 2 above.
[104] Melling, *op. cit.*, pp. 122–31; Conley, *op. cit.*, p. 200.
[105] CKS Q/GP/b 3.
[106] Hopkins, *op. cit.*, pp. 33–59; *KE*, 21.1.1860.
[107] *KE*, 7.11.1863, 23.12.1865, 26.10.1867.

were often light. Four members of a Cranbrook gang of twenty-two who fought
a pitched battle with six keepers were transported for fifteen years in 1838.[108]
Other sentences were less severe. Thomas Joslin who beat a gamekeeper in
Trinity Park Wood, fracturing his skull and breaking his arm, got six months
hard labour.[109] Three keepers were shot and killed between 1860 and 1880 but
there were no convictions for manslaughter. Alfred Burr, who murdered James
Gray, gamekeeper at Roydon Hall, Nettlestead, in 1862 was imprisoned for a
year. Members of his gang were poaching again within a few months.[110] Only
too often keepers encountered a 'wall of silence'. Chief Constable Ruxton noted
that poachers were 'looked upon as village heroes for their nocturnal expedi-
tions and assaults on keepers'. Henry Hart, accused with two others of poaching
at Great Chart, produced four witnesses who swore that he was working at that
time. He offered to produce twelve more.[111] At times the poaching wars, as
bitter in Kent as elsewhere, spilled over into village life. The head keeper at
Surrenden Park and William Terry, whom he had charged with poaching, fought
in a tavern while Charles Oliver of Boughton Monchelsea threatened to 'wring
the nose from the face' of Thomas Rider's keeper, who had successfully prosecuted his sons.[112]

(b) Sheep Stealing

Sheep stealing, which was endemic, was partly a protest crime but there were
other motives too.[113] Hunger was the motivating factor for Robert Bishop of
Capel-le-Ferne in whose house joints of a 'fat sheep' stolen from Folkestone
were discovered in 1650. Similarly in 1865 William Seager and Robert Jell,
labourers, were convicted of stealing a lamb from John Day, a previous
employer. In both cases the number of sheep stolen was small. In the last case
the carcass was reconstructed by a butcher acting for the prosecution and the
meat pronounced to be cut in an 'unbutcherlike' fashion. There were also more
professional motives. Organised gangs and large numbers of sheep stolen meant
rustling for re-sale, an arrangement with a local butcher or the stocking of farms
with stolen livestock. Richard Holland, who stole 30 sheep 'to the north of
Canterbury' in 1601 was a professional rustler. Twenty-five wethers stolen by
two Lenham labourers in 1602 were obviously not for personal consumption.
Five butchers, accused of theft in various parts of Kent in 1601–2, were
engaging in professional theft which was still common in the nineteenth
century. A Paddock Wood butcher and his assistant were convicted of sheep
stealing as late as 1911. Professional motivation, too, brought about the down-

108 MG, 27.3.1838.
109 KE, 4.12.1869.
110 Conley, op. cit., p. 201; SEG, 28.1.1862, 12.8.1862; KE, 10.1.1863, 12.3.1864.
111 CKS, Chief Constable's Annual and Quarterly Reports 1857–70, uncatalogued, Report dated
     7.1.1862; KE, 9.12.1865.
112 KE, 5.10.1861, 8.1.1870, 22.1.1870.
113 J.G. Rule, 'The Manifold Causes of Rural Crime: Sheep Stealing in England c.1740–1840', in
     Outside the Law, ed. J.G. Rule, Exeter 1983, pp. 102–29.

fall of William Steer, a butcher and meat contractor for Dover garrison, who in 1865 was given seven years' penal servitude for receiving stolen sheep.[114]

Sheep stealing reached its height during the years of harvest failure in the eighteenth century and the prolonged hardship among Kent labourers in the first half of the nineteenth century. It was widespread in 1817 and 1827 and prior to the onset of the Swing Riots. Another peak followed in 1837–8. Farmers suffered nightly losses in districts as widely separated as Gravesend, Sevenoaks, Malling, Maidstone and Tunbridge Wells. Over a hundred graziers were robbed in January 1837 alone. Twelve months later it was still so rife that a night watch was established around Sittingbourne. Like arson, extensive sheep rustling recommenced in 1842, continuing throughout the 'hungry forties'. Brenchley was a notable victim in 1843–4 as was Faversham in 1849. At the latter scarcely a night passed without reports of some fresh case but generally this category of theft was county-wide. Sometimes the number taken was large. In 1841 152 sheep and lambs were stolen from Court Lodge, Hunton. In 1845 49 sheep disappeared from Bradbourne Farm, Sevenoaks, but most thefts involved single animals which were slaughtered on the spot and the head, entrails and fleece abandoned nearby.[115]

> Potatoes are scarce and turnips are thin
> We take the carcass and leave you the skin

Thus read a message from Brasted sheep stealers in 1847. It was easy thieving. Discovery of concealed skins was the most frequent cause of detection. After 1850 sheep stealing declined but it was still common enough for Chief Constable Ruxton to order his constables in 1866 to take full particulars of all droves of sheep encountered on the highway and, if suspicious, to follow them to their journey's end.[116]

Sheep stealing remained a capital offence until 1832. Most rustlers were reprieved and transported but some were hanged. Convictions, although greater than for arson, were few in relation to the offence. 'For every man convicted there are . . . 50 sheep stolen in Kent which has no rural police', complained the *Maidstone Gazette* (see Table 10).[117]

---

114 CKS, Q/SB1/6, 25 March 1650; *KE*, 3.12.1864, 7.1.1865, 11.3.1865, 15.4.1865, 8.7.1869, 10.9.1869, 6.5.1911, 15.7.1911; Knafla, *op. cit.*, pp. 9, 18, 28, 131, 171, 175.
115 Rule, *op. cit.*, p. 108; Shirley Burgoyne Black, 'Swing: The Years 1827–30 as Reflected in a West Kent Newspaper', *Archaeologia Cantiana*, cvii (1989), p. 92; *MG*, 12.1.1830, 23.2.1830, 16.3.1830, 23.3.1830, 24.1.1837, 21.2.1837, 28.2.1837, 1.4.1837, 16.1.1838, 17.8.1841, 1.2.1842, 22.2.1842, 11.4.1843, 18.4.1843, 12.12.1843, 9.1.1844, 4.3.1845, 17.4.1849, 9.6.1849.
116 *MG*, 26.1.1847; Rule, *op. cit.*, p. 120; CKS, Kent County Constabulary General Order Book 1861–75, General Order dated 14.9.1866.
117 Rule, *op. cit.*, pp. 107–8; *MG*, 9.1.1849.

Table 10

Committals and Convictions for Sheep Stealing in Kent, 1834–55

	Committals	Convictions		Committals	Convictions
1834	12	7	1845	8	6
1835	1	0	1846	3	3
1836	14	12	1847	9	9
1837	9	6	1848	10	8
1838	17	13	1849	11	10
1839	25	17	1850	14	12
1840	27	22	1851	10	8
1841	10	10	1852	9	5
1842	13	9	1853	7	6
1843	20	16	1854	10	8
1844	15	9	1855	14	12

Source: *PP, Criminal Statistics* 1835 XLV p. 38 to 1856 XLIX p. 18.

(c) Incendiarism and Machine Breaking

Incendiarism had a variety of motives. Susan Colgate, who in 1602 threw 'coles of fyer' into William Baker's barn at Fawkham, was probably motivated by personal vengeance. So, too, were James Barber who fired Christopher Hamon's malt house in 1651 and William Ward 'committed of fireing a barne' in 1704.[118] By December 1800, when John Boghurst's rick was burned at Delce, arson had become a 'prime weapon of rural war'. One Victorian commentator described 1816 as the first year of incendiarism . In Kent the Swing Riots produced some 141 fires between 1 January 1830 and 3 September 1832. After the defeat of Swing arson became the characteristic mode of protest in a bitter guerrilla war against unemployment, underemployment, low wages and the New Poor Law which lasted until the second half of the century.[119]

Aided by the 'lucifer' match, incendiarism was a quick and effective weapon of terrorism against which farmers and the authorities were powerless. Horse-drawn fire engines were slow to arrive. When Parish Farm, Benenden, was fired in 1864 the Kent Fire Engine was stationed four miles away. Operations began half an hour after its arrival. Meanwhile 200 men and women formed a bucket chain. With no leader to direct them much water was wasted

---

[118] Knafla, *op. cit.*, p. 28; Melling, *op. cit.*, p. 102; CKS, Q/SB2/2, 22 July 1651.

[119] Richard Grover, 'Social Discontent during the Napoleonic Wars', *Cantium*, Winter 1974, p. 72; John E. Archer, *By a Flash and a Scare: Arson, Animal Maiming and Poaching in East Anglia 1815–1870*, Oxford 1990, pp. 69, 72; John E. Archer, 'Under Cover of Night: Arson and Animal Maiming', in *The Unquiet Countryside*, ed. G.E. Mingay, London 1989, pp. 65–6, 69; David Jones, 'Thomas Campbell Foster and the Rural Labourer: Incendiarism in East Anglia in the 1840s', *Social History*, i (1976), pp. 5–43; see also pp. 103–25 above.

and the farm and its produce were lost.[120] Ponds or wells were the usual source of water supply. These were frequently pumped dry. Chalk Pit Farm, Bekesbourne lost an entire range of buildings because the only water was a quarter of a mile away. Given sufficient warning a farm fire could be curtailed by cutting away the burning outer stack with hay cutters while the surrounding stacks were covered with saturated blankets. If the middle of the stack was free from fire a considerable portion could be saved. It was also proof that the fire was the work of an incendiary and not caused by spontaneous combustion which began in the centre.[121] Farmers were fortunate to obtain the help of their labourers in fire fighting during the Swing Riots. The same tradition of non-cooperation continued afterwards. 'Labourers looked on with indifference' at two fires at Chalk in 1837. An appeal for help to a crowd of labourers at Crowhurst Farm, East Peckham, in 1876 met with 'dogged refusal'. At an incendiary fire at Great Chart in 1869 waggon shafts were placed across Great Chart street with the intention of overturning the fire engine.[122] A farm fire was

> a hell above ground . . . Half scorched pigs in the agonies of death; dead ducks and fowls mingled with the smoking ruins of their roosting house . . . four fine young horses burnt to death . . . their bowels protruding as if the carcasses had burst with the excessive heat . . .[123]

The scale and cost of the destruction could be immense. A fire at Bickley Farm, Bromley, in 1835 cost John Wells, the former Maidstone MP, £10,000. He was only insured for £5,000. Two years later another fire at the same farm cost him £3,000 more. Damage to the value of £5,000 was sustained in 1884 at a farm near Ramsgate in which over a hundred animals were destroyed.[124]

While open protest often meant imprisonment or transportation, rural terrorism frequently brought a favourable result. Tonbridge farmers agreed in 1835 to pay wages on a scale regulated by wheat prices. Chislet farmers increased labourers' wages 'in consequence of the high price of provisions' the following year.[125]

All arson was a capital offence until 1837. Thereafter only firing a dwelling house remained punishable by death. Other incendiarism was punishable by transportation and from the mid-1850s by penal servitude. There were few convictions. Between 1834 and 1859 there were at least 439 recorded fires in Kent. There were 74 persons committed but only 27 were convicted. Thus about 6% of all incendiaries were punished. Of those arrested 42% were employees, former employees or received poor relief from their victims. Farm workers or members of their families were 73%. Almost 60% fell into the 17–30 age group

---

120 *KE*, 27.8.1864, 22.9.1866.
121 *KE*, 22.8.1863, 21.9.1867, 2.5.1868; *SEG*, 26.8.1862.
122 *MG*, 10.10.1837, *KE*, 11.12.1869, 27.5.1876.
123 Archer, 'Under Cover . . .', p. 65; *SEG*, 6.5.1862; *KE*, 21.5.1865.
124 *MG*, 18.8.1835, 12.9.1837; *SEG*, 18.2.1884.
125 *MG*, 16.6.1835, 22.11.1836.

who, if single, found work difficult to obtain from rates-conscious farmers.[126] Cries for the return of mantraps and spring guns, only made illegal in 1827, were rejected. The authorities, however, met the same wall of silence as over poaching and smuggling.[127] Incendiarism was often a crime of protest committed by an individual but expressing a collective grievance. The applause which greeted James Gardner's acquittal of firing a Marden wheat stack in 1849 was not an uncommon reaction.[128]

Before the mid-nineteenth century fires were largely the result of arson, accident or overheating. After 1850 an increasing number were caused by children, by vagrants seeking the security of imprisonment or by soldiers wishing to escape from the army. In 1861 two seven-year-olds fired a lodge at Cooling Castle Farm 'for the purpose of seeing a blaze'. 'The mischief caused by children . . . with lucifer matches is quite alarming', stated the *South Eastern Gazette*. A fifth of children under twelve who appeared before grand juries between 1859 and 1880 were charged with arson. In 1875 a fire at Egerton, started by children, destroyed a thousand trusses of straw.[129] Many vagrants also awaited arrest alongside burning stacks. For them 'penal servitude represented the only hope'. Others started fires accidentally but still paid the price. 'Nine tenths of fires at this season . . . are caused by men of your class lying about in . . . outbuildings', stated an Ashford magistrate sentencing a vagrant in 1861.[130]

The ranks of incendiaries were also swollen by hoppers. Oasts had always been susceptible to accidental fire during drying. After 1850 disgruntled hoppers and harvesters consciously used arson in their dealings with employers. A fire which destroyed a waggon load of corn in 1859 was started by lucifers secreted by harvesters. The same trick accounted for many oasts burnt down without apparent explanation. In 1875 several fires were caused by matches placed among the hops. The heat of the oast then ignited them. Such fires could be highly costly. When an eight-kiln oast was destroyed by incendiarism at East Peckham in 1876 over 200 pockets of hops were lost.[131]

The peaks in Kent's post-Swing incendiarism coincided generally with national peaks. An initial peak marked the anti-Poor Law riots of 1835, followed by a fall in the late 1830s, created partly by repression and partly by attempts to improve the labourers' lot through Labourers' Friend Societies and allotment schemes.[132] The 1840s marked the re-appearance of threshing machines. A farm at Charing was burned to the ground in 1844 and 1846. 'Much prejudice existed against a threshing machine which the farmer lately had at work.' In 1847 a

---

[126] *PP* 1835 xlv – *PP* 1852–3 lxxxi, Criminal Statistics.

[127] *MG*, 20.9.1831.

[128] *MG*, 31.7.1849.

[129] Conley, *op. cit.*, p. 128; *KE*, 30.3.1861, 5.6.1875; *SEG*, 15.9.1863.

[130] *KE*, 17.8.1861.

[131] *SEG*, 16.8.1859; *KE*, 25.9.1875, 22.5.1876.

[132] By 1839 there were branches of the Labourers' Friend Society in 40 West Kent parishes alone. Many had allotment schemes, *MG*, 17.9.1839. At Bearsted an allotment scheme had existed since 1834, *MG*, 15.10.1844.

threshing machine manufactured by Garratt of Maidstone, threshed 22 quarters of corn in three hours. Henceforth the long, bitter rearguard action against farm mechanisation was an important element in Kent incendiarism. Two Sheppey farmers, who lost their straw to incendiaries in 1849, 'had been using threshing machines'. Mechanisation was not the only cause of the incendiary peaks of 1844 and 1849–50. Wage reductions and high unemployment also played their part although these in turn were linked to mechanisation. In May 1849 wage reductions and growing distress were reported among agricultural labourers. Class bitterness was emphasised when shots were fired into the bedchambers of a Lamberhurst farmer and a Linton overseer.[133]

With the onset of steam, fires continued peaking again in 1863, 1865 and 1868. Sometimes it was sparks from the machine which caused the fire.[134] More frequently the barn in which the offending engine stood was the target. A steam threshing machine, hired by a Denton farmer, had its gauge broken and was then discovered on fire together with a large stack two nights later. Another machine hired to a Faversham farmer was fired and destroyed on the same night. It was not only threshing machines which suffered. 'Owing to the great prejudice against reaping machines . . . on the part of labourers', stated Thomas Aveling, the Kent manufacturer of farm machinery, 'farmers have . . . found difficulty in selecting men to walk behind'. At the lawless village of Great Chart incendiaries first destroyed 14 cwt of wheat followed by 1,200 bales of straw belonging to Henry Andrews of Chart Court Lodge. A few months later labourers smashed his mowing machine. In April 1879 the destruction of his new farm buildings was again attributed to his introduction of steam driven machinery for ploughing and other agricultural work.[135]

A final peak in incendiarism occurred in 1876. Despite a labourers' strike in the parishes of Romney Marsh, this had more to do with the retrenchment of farmers facing agricultural depression than the growth of the Kent and Sussex Labourers' Union. As late as 1909 three cases of arson arose from disputes between employers and their workers, while during the wage cuts of 1921 Edward Croft, chairman of the local branch of the Agricultural Workers' Union, received three years penal servitude for firing the stack of the farmer who had dismissed him.[136]

While Kent between 1834 and 1890 averaged just over seventeen reported cases of arson per year, which was approximately the same as Norfolk and Suffolk between 1815 and 1870, other reported 'crimes of protest' were fewer. The only recorded cases of poisoning involved cattle at Upper Hardres Court in 1852 and poultry at Chilham in 1874. Animal maiming was much less common

[133] *MG*, 16.3.1841, 24.8.1841, 17.2.1846, 16.2.1847, 27.11.1847, 4.1.1848, 22.5.1849, 29.5.1849, 11.9.1849, 2.10.1849, 4.12.1849.
[134] *MG*, 6.8.1850; *SEG*, 6.2.1855, 17.3.1857, 27.8.1861, 27.8.1868, 22.10.1877.
[135] *MG*, 1.1.1850, 21.10.1851; *SEG*, 28.9.1856, 10.3.1857, 27.4.1858, 11.5.1858, 23.9.1862, 28.2.1871; *KE*, 6.11.1869, 11.12.1869, 9.7.1870, 5.5.1877, 26.4.1879; *SEG*, 13.9.1859, 11.9.1860.
[136] *KE*, 15.4.1876, 1.5.1909, 31.7.1909, 23.10.1909; *KM*, 3.12.1921.

in Kent than in East Anglia. In 1835 twelve sheep were found in their fold with their throats cut in the disturbed parish of Ash but committals for this 'fiendish outrage' numbered only seventeen between 1834 and 1855. Far more common was the slashing of hop bines, still punishable by transportation in 1863. In 1834 the bines of a hundred hills of hops were slashed at Petham. Bines of 116 hills were cut at Goudhurst in 1843. The cutting of hop bines tended to peak in the incendiary years when class tensions were at their highest.[137]

Not only hop bines were destroyed. In 1835 five thousand furze faggots were burnt near Tonbridge. Lord Stanhope, Viscount Falmouth and Lord Cornwallis lost large acreages of underwood to incendiaries in the 1850s. At West Malling 15,000 hop poles surrounding a tar tank created an inferno when the tank was ignited, one of several costly fires of its kind.[138]

Thus incendiarism, often arising from the bitterness created by the labourers' diminished economic standing, became the most malign form of rural unrest in nineteenth century Kent. Usually, however, a distinction was made between the torching of ricks and barns and burning a farm house, between destroying property and endangering life. 'The labourers' scale of values was thus the diametrical opposite of their betters', for whom property was more precious to the law than life.[139]

(4) Law Enforcement to 1857

Law enforcement rested in the parishes in the hands of unpaid borsholders or petty constables. In large parishes or groups of parishes a high constable was sometimes appointed whose duties were wider and to whom the borsholders were deputies. The borsholder had the duty of raising the hue and cry and enforcing the laws against vagrancy and Sabbath defamation. He served warrants, brought offenders before the magistrates, dealt with affrays, guarded suspects and was required to administer punishment. Farningham's borsholder patrolled the village on Saturday nights and with three deputies supervised the annual fair. In 1828 he was called out three times in a month to deal with 'riot' in the streets and inns. At Whitstable and Seasalter the borsholders attended the streets, pubs and shops on Sundays. The borsholder had to exercise care in executing his office. Richard Bastocke, Kennington's borsholder, was assaulted when serving a warrant in 1605. George Burton, borsholder of St Mary Cray, found himself accused of manslaughter after ejecting a drunk from an alehouse in 1653. Since the office changed hands annually someone he arrested one year might be borsholder the next. Many refused to undertake such a thankless and unpaid task. Sometimes the responsibility was passed to those least able to

137 Archer, 'By a Flash', pp. 70–1, 202–3, 208–9; *PP* 1835 xlv – *PP* 1856 xvix, Criminal Statistics; *MG*, 22.7.1834, 14.7.1835, 29.5.1843, 27.1.1852; *KE*, 3.1.1874.
138 *MG*, 28.7.1835, 31.5.1853; *SEG*, 3.7.1855, 29.4.1856; *KE*, 28.11.1863.
139 E.J. Hobsbawn and G. Rudé, *Captain Swing*, Harmondsworth 1973, pp. 244–7.

resist. In the Upper Hundred of Boughton in 1652 the constable was reported to Quarter Sessions as being 'sick and nearly eighty'. The situation was little changed in 1834.[140]

> The . . . constables are usually village artisans totally unacquainted with the business of police . . . They are changed every year and seldom willing to serve a second time. The state of the rural police is altogether inefficient . particularly in those districts where the intimidation caused by the . . . riots of 1830 still remains.[141]

In the boroughs and some small towns law and order was often vested in watchmen after dark. Canterbury from 1679 employed sixteen watchmen between 10.00p.m. and 4.00a.m. The Canterbury Improvement Act of 1787 enabled a rate to be levied for this watch but the quality of the watchmen was indifferent and there was a high turnover. Dismissal for intoxication was common. A riding officer, attacked by smugglers near the West Gate, reported that 'the watchman, instead of giving assistance, put his candle out'. By 1829 three watchmen were so senile that they were incapable of discharging their duties. While the magistrates controlled the borsholders of the city's six wards the Pavement Commissioners controlled the watchmen. A similar situation prevailed at Dover.[142] Folkestone, like Gravesend and Milton, had only two Town Watchmen. Dartford employed four in 1812 and Ashford three under a local Act in 1824. Rochester had only two constables, elected by the resident freemen, who acted in conjunction with the borsholders. Deal, throughout the eighteenth century, preserved order with a Town Sergeant, twelve constables and a varying number of watchmen. At Sandwich twelve 'fit and able bodied' volunteer constables and their deputies, sworn in annually on a part-time basis, were considered adequate. Two West Malling watchmen made their nightly patrol arresting vagrants, quieting drunks and reporting suspicious characters. They were given lanthorns on dark nights and paid extra by subscribers during bad weather. In summer they were reduced to one.[143] It is indicative of the lack

---

[140] Bryan Keith-Lucas, *Parish Affairs*, Maidstone 1986, pp. 153–4; Frank Gallagher, *The Foundations of our Police Force*, typescript, 1983, p. 3; Shirley Burgoyne Black, *Local Government, Law and Order in a Pre-Reform Kentish Parish: Farningham 1790–1834*, Kent Ph.D. 1991, pp. 148–9; F.D. Johns, 'A Petty Constable's Account Book', *Archaeologia Cantiana*, civ (1987), pp. 9–24; CKS, Q/GPa, Returns of Peace Officers 1832; Melling, *op. cit.*, pp. 43, 58–9; CKS, Q/SB 3/15,16,19, 1652.

[141] *Select Committee on the Poor Laws (1834)*, XXVIII, Evidence of Ashurst Majendie, Commissioner for Kent, pp. 175, 211.

[142] L. Poole, 'The Canterbury City Police 1835–1888', Kent Extended Essay 092 (1974), pp. 5–6; Paul Muskett, 'Policing Dover 1800–1860', *Cantium*, vol. 2 (October 1970), pp. 82–4.

[143] W.H. Bishop, 'Folkestone Borough Police from 1836 to 1943', *Bygone Kent*, vol. 17, no. 8 (1996), p. 443; Cruden, *op. cit.*, p. 445; Peter Boreham, *Dartford through Time*, Dartford n.d., p. 49; A. Ruderman, *A History of Ashford*, Ashford 1994, p. 58; F.F. Smith, *A History of Rochester*, London 1928, pp. 171–2; W.H. Gillespie, 'An Old Force', *Police Journal*, October 1954, p. 307; Sandwich Local History Society, *Sandwich Charters and Local Government*, Occasional Paper no. 3, Sandwich 1976, p. 28; CKS, P243/10/1 West Malling Night Watchman's Report Book 1822–23.

of zeal of underpaid watchmen that 60 (31%) of the cases before West Kent Sessions at Easter 1703 were concerned with their neglect of duty.[144]

Discontent with the existing system caused some to adopt other means of law enforcement. A mid-seventeenth-century Sutton Valence 'private investigator' used a book of 'mug shots' (painted portraits) of horse thieves to successfully recover stolen animals. More common, however, by the late eighteenth century was the creation of voluntary associations funded by subscription. Confronted with the difficulty and expense of detection and arrest, and the ensuing cost of prosecution, local property owners formed Associations for the Prosecution of Felons and raised funds to arrest and prosecute offenders themselves.[145] Some established their own police forces or patrols. Most worked with the parish constables and later the new police. They were normally conducted by elected committees. Membership consisted largely of 'Gentlemen, Farmers, and Tradesmen' although the Goudhurst Prosecuting Society could extend its benefits to any labourer or poor person resident in the township. Handbills were printed and newspaper advertisements placed offering rewards for information leading to conviction for a particular offence. Each association had a graduated table of rewards for the most common offences ranging from petty theft to murder and arson.[146] There were at least twenty known associations in Kent (see Table 11) and probably more.

Many were formed during or immediately after Swing and others during the incendiarism of the 1840s. The majority covered a small area. Members of the Charing Society had to reside in Charing, Little Chart, Pluckley, Stalisfield or Westwell. Most were energetic in their pursuit of criminals. The Cranbrook Association captured two members of the Hawkhurst Gang in 1747. The Goudhurst Society between 1816 and 1855 prosecuted in 70% of offences. The Charing and Tenterden Societies each secured a formal death sentence commuted to life transportation. When the authorities refused to charge James Joy for arson the East Kent Association initiated the prosecution and Joy was hanged. Normal business was less dramatic but the Associations formed a supplement to the existing law enforcement system.[147] No Kent Association

---

[144] Melling, *op. cit.*, pp. 122–31.

[145] David Philips, 'Good Men to Associate and Bad Men to Conspire: Associations for the Prosecution of Felons in England 1760–1860', in *Policing and Prosecution in Britain 1750–1850*, ed. Douglas Hay and Francis Snyder, Oxford 1989, pp. 115, 118; R.P. Hastings, 'Private Law-Enforcement Associations', *The Local Historian*, vol. 14. no. 4 (1980), pp. 226–32; Melling, *op. cit.*, pp. 57–8; CKS, Q/SB4/12, 19 March 1652/3.

[146] CKS, U442 066 and U129 307 Charing Society for the Prosecution of Thieves, Minutes; U769 L6, Goudhurst Prosecuting Society, Articles and Minutes 1815–63; Te/24 Articles of Tenterden Prosecuting Society 1802, Journal of Tenterden Association for Preventing Depredations; F. Giraud and Charles Donne, *Visitors' Guide to Faversham*, Faversham 1876, p. 41; *AA*, 20.9.1856; CKS P390/31/1 Minutes of Westwell Association for Prosecuting Felons.

[147] Waugh, *op. cit.*, p. 160; CKS, U442/066 Minutes of Charing Prosecuting Society 1799; TE/24 Journal of Tenterden Association . . . 1824; U 769/L6 Goudhurst Prosecuting Society, Articles and Minutes; P400/25/1 Articles of Woodchurch Society for Prosecuting Felons 18 June 1800; P222B Rules of Leeds Prosecuting Society 11 December 1840; *MG*, 15.9.1835, 22.9.1835, 22.3.1836, 5.4.1836; Philips, *op. cit.*, pp. 144, 169.

Table 11

Kent Associations for the Prosecution of Felons
in the Eighteenth and Nineteenth Centuries

Name of association	Known date of operation
Association for Protection of Property in NE Division of Aylesford	1827–35
Benenden Prosecuting Society	1819
Charing Society for Prosecuting Thieves	1799
Cranbrook Society for Prosecuting Thieves	1747–1800
East Kent Association for Protection of Property	1834–5
Farningham Prosecuting Society	1842
Faversham Association for Protection of Property against Incendiarism	1831–45
Goudhurst Prosecuting Society	1815–63
Higham Association for Protection against Incendiarism	1834
High Halden Prosecution Society	1866
Hythe Mutual Protection Society	1842
Leeds Prosecuting Society	1840–90
Leigh Prosecuting Society	1837–44
Pembury Society for Prosecution of Felons	1836–66
Sevenoaks Association for Detecting Incendiaries and Protecting Property	1830–39
Smeeth Prosecuting Association	1856
Tenterden Association for Preventing Depredations	1824–62
Tonbridge Association for Prosecution of Felons	1845
Westwell Association for the Prosecution of Felons	1844
Woodchurch Society for Prosecuting Felons	1800–44

established a full subscription police force. Few night patrols, such as the Brenchley patrols of 1840 and 1848, outlasted the crises that had brought about their foundation. Tenterden, however, in 1824 established a group of hired men and householders which nightly patrolled the town's three divisions. From this emerged the Tenterden borough police force.[148]

The establishment of the Metropolitan Police in 1829 increasingly drove London criminals into Kent. By the late 1830s thirteen Kent boroughs had created their own police forces ranging in size from 25 officers at Rochester to a single constable at Hythe. The principal catalyst was the Municipal Corporations Act 1835 which empowered them to establish watch committees and appoint police. Many borough forces like Dover, Ramsgate, Tenterden and Faversham developed from a body of night constables. Ashford replaced its three watchmen with a force established under the Lighting and Watching Act in 1841. Tonbridge also considered its adoption but did not proceed. In 1840 Rochester Watch Committee, alarmed by theft on the Medway, established a Water

---

[148] *MG*, 18.2.1840, 19.12.1848; Philips, *op. cit.*, p. 147.

Guard. Three constables, transferred from the borough force, henceforth nightly patrolled the river in an open boat.[149]

Other specialist policing emerged in Kent's dockyards where theft had always been rife. At Chatham dockyard the ineffectual 'Porters, rounders, warders and watchmen' credited to Samuel Pepys in the 1680s, were replaced in 1834 by the Admiralty's Dockyard Police Force. These had full police powers in the dockyard and later within a five mile radius outside. They were replaced in 1860 by the Dockyard Division of the Metropolitan Police whose superintendents exercised summary jurisdiction within the yard and also policed Sheerness dockyard. Policing of Deptford and Woolwich dockyards was handed to Greenwich Division of the 'New Police' in 1841 when the parishes became part of the Metropolitan Police District.[150]

Dockyard policing was much superior to maintenance of order in Chatham where before 1857 there were neither resident magistrates nor a police force apart from a patrol of local parishioners. Crime was rife. Since the nearest magistrates sat at Rochester or Gadshill even those criminals who were taken frequently escaped.[151] Chatham's problems arose from the parsimony of its ratepayers but, even where they existed, borough forces met with no great enthusiasm. At Canterbury, substitution of a 24-hour coverage by paid policemen for the system of watchmen provoked a hostile reaction. Policing costs rose from £343 in 1834 to over £1,000 in 1837. In 1842 the force was reduced. Recruitment was largely local, drawing upon former labourers, soldiers and police from other areas. Long hours of shift work without leave or meal breaks produced a high turnover. Six of the eighteen officers who inaugurated the force were dismissed within three and a half years. 127 officers were appointed between 1836 and 1888. Constables often had 25 public houses on a beat which they could walk in fifteen minutes. Consequently over half the disciplinary cases resulted from drink. In 1888 police drunkenness and corruption were so common that the Watch Committee considered amalgamation with the county force. Running fights between police and soldiers were frequent.[152] Other borough forces had similar problems. In July 1837 three of Tunbridge Wells' five constables were suspended for drunkenness. The tiny borough force at Hythe was plagued by intemperance until 1878. While the larger boroughs were considered to be satisfactorily policed the forces of Deal, Faversham, Hythe,

---

149 Muskett, *op. cit.*; *Kent Police Centenary 1857–1957*, ed. R.L. Thomas, Maidstone 1957, p. 120; Ruderman, *op. cit.*, p. 58; Hugh Roberts, *Tenterden – The First Thousand Years*, Tugby, pp. 217–18; *MG*, 7.10.1834; Frank Gallagher, 'Policing the Medway', *Bygone Kent*, vol. 2, no. 10 (October 1981), pp. 615–20; Frank Gallagher, *The Foundations of our Police Force*, p. 15. I am indebted to Inspector Frank Gallagher and to John Endicott, Curator of the Kent Police Museum, for the assistance which they have given me with the history of the Kent County Constabulary.

150 Tom Pearse, 'Policing Chatham Naval Base', *Bygone Kent*, vol. 5, no. 3 (March 1984), pp. 174–80; Bernard Brown, 'The Maritime Duties of London's Bobbies', *Bygone Kent*, vol. 13, no. 4 (April 1992), pp. 211–16; A.R. Salter, *The Protection of Chatham Dockyard throughout the Ages*, Gillingham 1983.

151 *Wright's Topography*, 1838, pp. 63–4.

152 Poole, *op. cit.*, pp. 10, 16, 25, 55, 57, 59, 63–5, 95; *KG*, 28.1.1836, 8.3.1836.

Sandwich and Tenterden were criticised as 'insufficient in number and inefficient in organisation', until absorbed into the county police in 1888. At Tenterden the superintendent was a tradesman who undertook no active police duties. At Sandwich in 1857 duties for the only constable were undefined and he 'occasionally followed his trade as a hairdresser'. Yet in 1839 Maidstone reported 'the peace and good order of the town greatly improved' while the clear-up rate for reported indictable crime in Canterbury never fell below 66%.[153]

In rural Kent half the magisterial divisions reporting in 1836 had local police of some kind. The Lewisham, Lee, Kidbrooke and Charlton United District Watch, formed under the 1833 Act, functioned on the edge of the Metropolitan Police District. It operated a well-defined beat system 'to check . . . evil doers'. Alderman Wilson, Lord Mayor of London, spoke eloquently of the benefits derived in his seat at Beckenham from a small force paid by subscription and recruited from the Metropolitan Police. Agricultural theft and vagrancy had been suppressed and neighbouring parishes such as Bromley and Hayes had been forced to follow Beckenham's example. Kent witnesses were almost unanimous in their condemnation of parish constables who they found 'disinclined to an active discharge . . . of their duty' and 'quite inadequate to the protection of inhabitants and . . . their property'. 'The parish constable likes to be at home with his family: he does not think it his duty to go and look after crime, to repress or prevent it. If any party . . . brings him an offender he will take him, but not otherwise: he asks who is to pay him.' More perceptive contributors emphasised that the cost of an 'efficient constabulary' was less than the cost of damage resulting from the Swing Riots and could have prevented the Bosenden Wood Massacre in 1838.[154]

These feelings were evident when the Kent magistrates met to debate adoption of the Rural Police Act 1839. Protagonists of 'a good, active force of thief takers' stressed the notorious inadequacy of the existing constables and the need for a young and effective preventative police. Their opponents, led by Sir E. Knatchbull, chairman of the county magistrates, emphasised the cost of such a body and, whilst maintaining that parish constables were not as ineffectual as represented, were also conscious that behind the Act lay the centralising ambitions of Edwin Chadwick, secretary of the Poor Law Commissioners, for a full-time, uniformed force which would dilute magisterial power locally. A Return of Peace Officers made in 1832 certainly shows that Kent's 550 parish constables were not a geriatric force. Only 5% were over sixty. The average age of the 108 high constables was 48.3 years as opposed to 41.3 years for the 442 borsholders giving a combined average age of 42.7 years. Constables, however,

153 Gallagher, *op. cit.*, p. 10; W.H. Bishop, 'Under the Influence . . .', *Bygone Kent*, vol. 13, no. 11 (November 1992), pp. 683–8; Helen Bentwich, *History of Sandwich in Kent*, Sandwich 1991, p. 94; Gillespie, *op. cit.*, pp. 311–12; Poole, *op. cit.*, p. 103; *Report of the Constabulary Commissioners* (1839) XIX, p. 139.

154 Robert D. Storch, 'Policing Rural Southern England before the Police', in Hay and Snyder, *op. cit.*, pp. 233, 252; *Report of the Constabulary Commissioners* (1839) XIX, 46, 102, 133–5, 162; Poole, *op. cit.*, p. 131.

were usually ordinary householders hindered by local connections. They were paid on a fee-for-service basis. The borsholder of Loose was 'paid what he can get'. At Petham he was 'paid sometimes'. Most would have echoed Cranbrook's high constable whose amateur officers 'were not sufficiently paid to cause a man to exert himself'. They could rarely be persuaded to pursue suspects beyond their parish boundaries and would never become a preventative police force. Twelve parishes had no peace officer at all.[155]

Kent declined to adopt the Rural Police Act by three votes in 1840. Thereafter magisterial opposition grew. It was rejected by thirty votes in 1849. Meanwhile Kent justices, not averse to police reform provided their own position was safeguarded, sought an alternative. A Poor Law police force, mooted in 1847 by Sir John Tylden in the parishes of Milton Union, came to naught but the Superintending Constable Act 1850 was adopted since magisterial control over parish constables was increased by the appointment of paid superintendents. By October 1850 a Superintendent of Constables had been appointed in each of Kent's twelve petty sessional divisions.[156] The system was condemned as 'inefficient' and 'impossible to ever become effective' by John Dunne, former superintending constable of Bearsted division who subsequently became Chief Constable of Norwich. While parish constables refused to co-operate, the divisions were too large for the superintendents to exercise effective supervision. Wingham, Kent's largest division, consisted of 56 parishes. Watchmen, appointed by vestries, were entirely independent of the superintending constables and suppression of vagrancy was impossible.[157] When Ashford division refused aid to Tonbridge in a local riot and Tonbridge magistrates called on the Metropolitan Police, the weakness of the system was completely exposed. As a result of the County and Borough Police Act 1856 Kent was forced to accept compulsory policing, as were the remaining counties that had refused to adopt rural police at an earlier date.[158]

(5) The Kent County Constabulary, 1857–1914

Kent's first chief constable, Captain John Henry Ruxton of Broad Oak, Brenchley, was selected by his fellow Kent magistrates in January 1857. His local magisterial connection and his scheme to drill the county police as a defensive volunteer force aided his candidature in a maritime county fearful of invasion. Ultimately his attempt to transform Kent's rural police into an armed rifle corps was squashed by the Home Office. By this time Ruxton, who had served

---

[155] *MG*, 3.12.1839; CKS, Q/GPa Return of Peace Officers 1832; Storch, *op. cit.*, pp. 221–5; Carolyn Steedman, *Policing the Victorian Community*, London 1984, p. 18.

[156] *Ibid.*, p. 19; Storch, *op. cit.*, pp. 216, 253; Gallagher, *op. cit.*, Appendix 1, Appointment of Superintending Constables 14 October 1850; *MG*, 23.3.1847.

[157] *First Report of Select Committee on the Police* (1852–53) XXXVI, pp. 115–23, Evidence of John Dunne.

[158] Steedman, *op. cit.*, pp. 20–1.

in India and controlled convicts in Australia, had begun laying the foundation of his police force.[159]

While the Kent borough forces, which remained independent, recruited considerably from ex-soldiers, Ruxton considered the best recruits to be married agricultural labourers aged 25–45 years. Former soldiers saw drinking as part of institutional life. In Kent their criminal record was deplorable. Agricultural labourers could walk twelve miles a night. They understood rural life and accepted its social relationships. Francis Mallalieu, Superintendent of R Division Metropolitan Police, who at one time had employed large numbers of ex-soldiers, similarly admitted 'that the intelligent part of the agricultural labouring community, after training, make the best policemen'.[160] Ruxton's preferences are reflected in the previous occupations of his early recruits (see Table 12).

Table 12

Previous Experience of early Kent Police Recruits,
as a percentage of the total police force

	Super/Insp.	Sergeant	Constable
Police	43.7	11.3	4.3
Military	0	3.7	0.7
Labourers	12.5	20.7	51.0
Craftsmen/Tradesmen/ Professional	25.1	36	30.7
Others	18.7	28.3	13.3
	100	100	100

Source: CKS, C/POL/20/01, Record of Service, Kent County Constabulary, 1857–70.

While in the East Riding Constabulary almost half the initial recruits had either police or military experience,[161] Ruxton selected only part of his senior officers from the former and largely avoided the latter, with former labourers constituting the backbone of his force. Most constables were recruited locally but senior officers were recruited further afield with a strong emphasis on married status. The average age of the force was well below that of constables in the unreformed parochial system (see Table 13).

---

159 Steedman, *op. cit.*, pp. 19–20, 29; Gallagher, *op. cit.*, pp. 17–19; Thomas, *op. cit.*, pp. 21, 34–5; *KE*, 14.1.1860, 21.1.1860.
160 Steedman, *op. cit.*, pp. 70–1, 89–90; *Second Report of Select Committee on the Police* (1852–53), pp. 16–21, evidence of Mr M. Mallalieu.
161 D. Foster, 'The East Riding Constabulary in the Nineteenth Century', *Northern History*, xxi (1985), pp. 202–3.

Table 13

*Age, Marital Status and Birthplace of early Recruits
to Kent County Constabulary*

	Super/Insp.	Sergeant	Constable
Average age (yrs)	29	29.8	26.7
Married (%)	90.6	90.5	41.3
Born in Kent (%)	31.2	54.7	69.2

Source: CKS, C/POL/20/01, Record of Service, Kent County Constabulary, 1857–70.

In the early years it was difficult to find men with suitable experience. The village policeman was a lonely man occupying a difficult position between his neighbours and the authorities. In the formative years discipline was harsh. A constable was on duty 24 hours a day. Rest days and meal breaks were unknown. Sandwiches were eaten in some public convenience. Policemen not in their lodgings during official sleeping time were in serious breach of regulations. Church attendance on Sundays was compulsory. Pay was a constant source of irritation, although the Kent Constabulary was not attracted by trade unionism as was the Rochester Borough Force in the 1890s. The sergeant commanding 23s 4d a week was comfortable but the constable earning 18s 0d a week was little better off than a labourer in the 1860s. Nonetheless agricultural labourers seem to have been attracted by the security of work, provision of clothing and accommodation and, after 1861, a superannuation fund. The disadvantages during the early years, however, produced a high turnover and numbers surviving to enjoy their superannuation were not large (see Table 14).[162]

Table 14

Fate of early Recruits to Kent County Constabulary

	Super/Insp.	Sergeant	Constable
Resigned (%)	10.3	20	41.4
Dismissed (%)	3.4	12	28.7
Promoted (%)	17.2	28	13.2
Discharged (ill health) (%)	10.3	10	5.9
Deceased (%)	10.3	4	1.1
Superannuated (%)	48.5	26	9.7
	100	100	100

Source: CKS, C/POL/20/01, Record of Service, Kent County Constabulary, 1857–70.

---

[162] Foster, *op. cit.*, p. 203; Thomas, *op. cit.*, p. 34; Gallagher, *op. cit.*, p. 20; *KE*, 6.4.1861; *Maidstone and Kent Journal*, 15.7.1890; *CO*, 27.6.1891.

Table 15

Punishment of Disciplinary Breaches in the Kent County Constabulary,
April–December 1857

Dismissed	31	Severe reprimand	5
Fined	24	Suspended with loss of pay	2
Demoted	7	Not guilty: re-instated	2
		Total	71

Source: CKS, Kent County Constabulary Discipline Book, 1857–80.

Of the total force 31% resigned or were dismissed between April and December 1857 as Ruxton attempted to impose the discipline and high standards of conduct which would command public respect. Table 15 shows how the 71 disciplinary breaches were punished. Offences ranged from neglect of duty, disobeying orders, and lying, to failing to keep a journal, missing conference points and warning beerhouse keepers of the approach of their superiors. John Kennedy of Wingham Division was found in bed during duty. Another constable was discovered playing a drum in a public house band. Two others were dismissed for patronising brothels. Despite Ruxton's exclusion of soldiery some 40% of offences arose from drink-related problems. George Hamilton was even dismissed for creating a disturbance in the yard of the Bell at Maidstone while on duty. Before the county police were deployed in their thirteen divisions Ruxton secured the use of Maidstone Barracks where he drilled his men to accustom them to discipline. He also issued a simple manual on the proper and legal manner of performing their duties. Initially literacy was only demanded of senior officers. Later schoolmasters were employed to teach penmanship to new recruits. Drilling continued on the parade ground at Police Headquarters, Wrens Cross, Maidstone. Gradually discipline became less harsh and offences fewer. Nonetheless 32 offences produced 19 dismissals in 1879 (see Table 16). They included 14 cases of drunkenness and 4 of sexual assault. In 1880 there was still a 10% turnover of the total force.[163]

Mid-Victorian police forces were small. Ruxton's original force consisted of 222 men policing some 915,500 acres. Each constable was responsible for an average area of 4,124 acres. In 1860 the Force absorbed Romney Marsh adding a sergeant and three constables. By 1866 it had increased to 262 with each constable responsible for an average of 1,384 people. Two years later the relentless increase in population had swollen their number to 300 with one constable to an average of 3,039 acres and 1,272 persons. In 1894 the Force increased to 412 but the volume of work was still great. In 1867 Ruxton had indicated that

163 Steedman, *op. cit.*, pp. 93, 103; Thomas, *op. cit.*, pp. 21, 26–7; CKS, Kent County Constabulary Record of Service Book 1857–70, Discipline Book 1857–80, Chief Constable's Reports 1857–70; *KE*, 13.6.1868.

Table 16

Kent County Constabulary: Total Number of Disciplinary Offences, 1857–79

1857	71
1864	54
1874	33
1879	32

Source: CKS, Kent County Constabulary Discipline Book, 1857–80.

Chatham, Strood and Gillingham were seriously underpoliced but the necessary rate increase prevented any expansion. Similar constraints frustrated attempts by Hythe to amalgamate with the county force before small borough forces were compelled to merge with county forces in 1889.[164]

Ruxton, at the outset, warned the public that the size of the county and the severity of night duties would limit police activities in daylight. He also emphasised the prompt completion of police returns to keep him abreast of every occurrence. Parish constables were still appointed to cover for county police. Many parishes considered parish constables an unnecessary expense and often constables had neither staves nor handbolts until the county constabulary supplied them.[165] Ratepayers, well-aware of the cost of the new police, were quick to complain of the 'insufficiency of policing'. In Ashford, attacks on women and the behaviour of hooligans who took over the streets in the evenings, led to demands for a return to a local force by 'respectable citizens'. When Ruxton drafted extra constables into Ashford at weekends there were immediate protests from rural parishes. Appledore claimed that public order was better kept by two parish constables costing 48s 0d than under the county police costing £85 0s 0d per year. 'Where are the police?' demanded the 'respectable' inhabitants of Challock and Molash, who had no policeman within five miles, after an outbreak of housebreaking and petty theft. Ruxton responded that his system enabled a large body of police to be concentrated anywhere 'in times of excitement'. Separate local police establishments could not offer the same service. Ratepayers, concerned with their own lesser but immediate problems, took a long time to convince.[166]

'Respectable' members of the community required their 'persons, property and sensibilities' to be protected from the 'lawless and immoral'. This involved suppression of the drunkenness, vice and riotous behaviour created by an under-

---

[164] Thomas, *op. cit.*, pp. 156–7; *CO*, 17.4.1880; *KE*, 10.3.1860, 6.4.1861, 23.2.1867, 2.3.1867, 11.5.1867, 25.5.1867, 22.6.1867, 16.11.1867, 7.12.1867, 11.1.1868, 4.7.1868.

[165] Kent Police Museum, Kent County Constabulary General Order Book 16.4.1864; *AA*, 30.5.1856; *KE*, 13.4.1861, 11.4.1863, 8.4.1865, 22.4.1865.

[166] *KE*, 24.8.1861, 14.9.1861, 14.12.1861, 17.1.1863, 11.4.1863, 17.9.1864, 3.4.1869, 9.10.1869, 16.10.1869, 4.12.1869, 19.3.1870; *AA*, 10.1.1857, 2.3.1867, 26.7.1870.

employed and disaffected generation of young men which Victorian morality would not tolerate. Consequently the basic aim of the Kent Constabulary was prevention of crime and the maintenance of good order. There was little time for detective work. Some borough forces used policemen in plain clothes in the 1860s. In 1878 county police superintendents were empowered to borrow constables from other divisions to work in plain clothes on licensing matters where their own policemen were too well-known. There was no official detective branch until 1896.[167]

The first step was to establish some control over the taverns and beerhouses which frequently served as brothels. Physical strength was an important pre-requisite in recruiting. Its value quickly became evident in the countless confrontations of the 1860s and 1870s as Ruxton's policemen battled for superiority in scenes reminiscent of the American frontier. When Sergeant Bates and PC Oliver attempted the arrest of a party of seamen in the Bricklayers Arms, Whitstable, 'a . . . fight ensued in which chairs, pewter pots, glasses . . . were freely used. Both policemen were severely handled as was evidenced by their heads and faces. The knuckles on two of Bates' fingers were displaced . . . One man held him while others struck him with a chair . . .'. Despite magisterial promises to protect the police the offenders got only the statutory month's hard labour.[168]

Simultaneously the police were called upon to crush the riotous fall-out from popular festivity, which had been treated more tolerantly a century earlier, and to suppress prize fights and youthful hooliganism which incensed the respectable. The traditional celebrations of 5 November had long degenerated into an orgy of drunkenness and disorder. Possession of the streets passed to the mob; fireballs were thrown; tar barrels lit; and attacks launched on the borough police in most Kent towns. When it was rumoured in 1865 that the Folkestone mob intended to fire the new ritualist church of St Michael and All Angels on 5 November dragoons were placed on standby and the local police re-inforced with twenty county constabulary. The troops were not needed. When the county police were showered with stones they dispersed the crowd with a baton charge. The following day there were insufficient magistrates to hear the overwhelming number of resulting cases.[169]

Prize fights, organised in London, had come with the railways. Trains carrying hundreds of passengers travelled into Kent stopping at an unguarded spot to erect the ring. If the spectators were disturbed they re-boarded their train and the fight continued elsewhere. Police usually arrived to stop the contest before it was over but patrolling the railway lines was irksome and created much hostility. An undermanned police force was also often diverted from other

---

[167] Conley, *op. cit.*, pp. 202–4; B.J. Davey, *Lawless and Immoral: Policing a Country Town 1838–1857*, Leicester 1983, pp. 6, 27, 30–1, 36, 42, 60–1, 182; Thomas, *op. cit.*, pp. 33, 63, 119; *KE*, 15.9.1866, 17.11.1866, 16.7.1867.

[168] *KE*, 6.2.1864, 2.12.1865.

[169] *KE*, 14.11.1863, 21.11.1863, 5.12.1863, 11.11.1865.

duties in order to curb youthful delinquents. Pluckley hooligans stoned a respectable resident who complained when they 'abominably molested' his wife and daughter. At Ashford, Brabourne and Folkestone youths obstructed thoroughfares and insulted churchgoers. At Seasalter the new policeman was obliged to attend Sunday services to keep order among 200 teenagers who threw peas, nutshells and tobacco 'as if in a theatre'.[170]

A serious riot at Cowden among 'navvies' on the Sussex and Surrey Junction Railway in 1866 tested the ability of the county constabulary to maintain public order. The contractors unwisely imported 500 French navvies on lower pay. Sacked Englishmen drove them to Edenbridge railway station having demolished their huts. When the French retaliated the army stood by. Ruxton and county police re-inforcements arrived and protected the French until the situation was defused.[171] Preservation of order at general elections was another thankless police responsibility. Election riots were nothing new to Kent. A polling booth was demolished and a thousand panes of glass broken in Gravesend when Liberal supporters went on the rampage in 1868. At the 1880 election, as 500 roughs began smashing up Tonbridge after the Liberal defeat, Ruxton arrived by train with 94 police. Twelve policemen, including the Chief Constable, were injured in an all-day struggle but the mob was contained.[172]

The new police were unpopular for other reasons besides their attack on boisterous working class pleasures. Ruxton believed the police should not be employed in the preservation of game. After the Night Poaching Prevention Act 1862 gave wide powers to policemen to stop and search, the constabulary became involved in poaching matters and became even more unpopular. This was increased by rumours that policemen brought trivial cases before the magistrates to boost their pensions, since fines for drunkenness and assaults on the police could be paid by the justices into the Police Superannuation Fund, and divisional registers of offences and detections helped to determine pension levels. The high level of dismissals brought the force into further disrepute whether it was Superintendent English, brought back from Australia charged with embezzlement and desertion, or PC Valentine Betts found seated in the road at Sutton-at-Hone, drunk on duty with an unknown 'lady' and singing that music hall favourite 'Slap, Bang, Here we are Again'.[173]

Gradually the virtues of less colourful constables began to make a favourable public impression. PC Antonio in 1861 was presented with a silver watch by the residents of Bearsted division for 'his zeal, courage and integrity'. PC Dobson received a similar gift in 1867 for 'the energetic manner in which he performed

---

[170] Gallagher, op. cit., p. 20; Thomas, op. cit., pp. 37–40; KE, 6.1.1864, 5.11.1864, 31.12.1864, 13.5.1865, 20.11.1869.
[171] Conley, op. cit., pp. 27–8; SEG, 14.8.1866.
[172] KE, 31.7.1869; Thomas, op. cit., p. 156; Frank Chapman, The Book of Tonbridge, Tonbridge 1976, p. 43.
[173] Chief Constable's Report, 7.1.1862; Steedman, op. cit., pp. 63, 150; Conley, op. cit., p. 32; KE, 3.7.1858, 6.4.1861, 9.12.1865, 2.7.1867, 4.1.1868, 11.1.1868, 17.9.1870; Dartford Reference Library, Memorandum from Chief Constable to Dartford Division Constabulary, 4.11.1875.

his duties' at St Lawrence, Ramsgate. Sgt Coppinger, transferred from Sutton Valence to Great Chart in 1870, received a framed address stating that 'for the whole ten years we have found you eminently fitted for your post'. Many policemen impressed, too, by their bravery. 'The pluck of the rural policeman is not appreciated . . .', commented the *Kentish Express*. 'Alone and practically defenceless . . . he does his duty by day and night . . . often . . . being attacked by half a dozen men.' PC Barker received the Chief Constable's Merit Award for single-handedly stopping the prize fight Sullivan v. Tyler in 1860. PC John Kennedy, attempting to end a dance at Barham Fair, was almost drowned in a cess pool before striking down his assailants with his staff. Police could appeal to the public for help but it was often not forthcoming. PC Crittenden took two and a half hours to conduct a man he had arrested in the Woolpack, Smeeth, the six miles to Ashford lock-up . He was followed in the darkness by the man's friends hurling abuse. 'They were going to assault me,' he told magistrates, 'but their hearts failed them. I kept them off with my staff.'[174]

Serious injuries were common. The navvies' riot at Cowden produced two merit awards but PC Willian Solley resigned 'partly paralysed and most severely ruptured' by the beating he took. PC John Regis was stabbed in the slums of Sheerness. Between 1859 and 1880 170 persons were indicted by Kentish grand juries for assaulting the police but the number of attacks was much higher. In 1878 67 persons were convicted and 71 in 1879. Only one officer was killed on duty, PC Israel May, murdered by a drunken Kingsdown labourer in 1873.[175] One of the most tragic cases was that of PC Waller. Ruxton stationed married men with families in the rural districts in the hope that they would integrate into their local communities. Waller was a single man stationed alone in the notorious village of Great Chart. He testified against the local gang. The following night he was beaten senseless outside his cottage by three men with heavy stones and pieces of iron. Villagers watched unmoved. Paralysed and scarcely able to speak he was granted a pension of £20 per year from the Superannuation Fund. His attackers received the statutory month's hard labour.[176]

The policeman's staff was a formidable weapon and there is no doubt that the Kent constabulary on occasions meted out rough justice themselves. PC William Barnes, when threatened in Chatham by a soldier with his belt, struck first with his staff. Pte Dogherty, a thrice court-martialled prize fighter, was hospitalized for a fortnight. On this occasion Barnes was supported by the bench. There was perhaps less justification for the treatment of a habitual drunk ejected from the George at Ashford: 'they threw me on the causeway . . . and dragged me through the mud . . . They as nigh killed me as could be.' PC Couchman was dismissed in 1879 'for throwing . . . a labourer on the ground

---

[174] Chief Constable's Report, 7.1.1861; *KE*, 17.7.1858, 13.4.1861, 6.8.1864, 20.8.1864, 6.4.1867, 11.1.1868, 29.1.1870, 9.4.1870, 9.5.1908.

[175] Chief Constable's Report, 27.10.1868; *KE*, 30.3.1867, 8.10.1870; Conley, *op. cit.*, p. 33; *CO*, 17.4.1880; Thomas, *op. cit.*, pp. 59–60.

[176] *KE*, 28.12.1867, 4.1.1868, 11.1.1868, 4.7.1868.

several times at Cliffe' but disciplinary action for excessive violence was rare. The Metropolitan Police at Chatham dockyard were temporarily issued with cutlasses in 1867 but they were never given to the county police.[177]

In 1857 many divisions were without adequate police stations or lock-ups. Tonbridge lock-up was 'hardly fit to put a dog into'. Ashford and Sevenoaks were equally defective. Where there was no lock-up keeper's accommodation prisoners were left alone all night. At Sheerness, without a station house, constables were 'hard put to find lodgings of the most . . . undesirable description'. By 1914 all divisions had station houses with accommodation for single men. When Ruxton retired in 1894 the county constabulary stood at 412. By 1921 it had grown to 621. There were no female officers until some were acquired when the remaining boroughs amalgamated with the county in 1943. Until then female searchers were employed or the duty was performed by policemen's wives. Working conditions very slowly improved. In 1912 one rest day was granted in fourteen. There were still assaults on policemen but Kent had become a more 'policed' society. The need for a professional police force was generally accepted. Co-operation between county and borough forces improved and in the last decades of the nineteenth century serious crime began to fall (see Figure 7).[178]

[177] For a general introduction to this subject see Clive Emsley, 'The Thump of Wood on a Swede Turnip: Police Violence in Nineteenth Century England', *Criminal Justice History*, vi (1985), pp. 125–49; *KE*, 13.4.1867, 26.10.1867, 16.11.1867, 23.11.1867; Chief Constable's Report, 13.6.1879.

[178] Thomas, *op. cit.*, pp. 32, 44, 86, 156–7; Chief Constable's Report, 13.1.1863; *KE*, 6.7.1861, 22.2.1867, 25.5.1909, 7.8.1909, 4.3.1911, 13.5.1911.

I am particularly grateful to the following for help during the difficult circumstances of my illness. Without the aid of Bruce Aubry, Mike Chitty, Ian Coulson, Christine Dunn, Inspector Frank Gallagher, Dr Fred Lansberry, and Gordon Morris this contribution could not have been written. I am also indebted for assistance to Janet Cousins, K. Irving, C. Pobgee, L. Pratt, Sue Samson, P.M. Stevens and Hilary Streeter of the Kent Library Service and to Michael Carter at the Centre for Kentish Studies, John Endicott, Curator of the Kent Police Museum, and Eva Newman of the Templeman Library, University of Kent.

8

County Administration in Kent, 1814–1914

ELIZABETH MELLING

(1) General Sessions Administration

Comparatively little has been written about county administration in England in the nineteenth century prior to the creation of county councils in 1889. Historians have preferred to study the new authorities set up to administer such services as poor law and public health or the reformed municipal boroughs. The administration of local government by the unelected justices of the peace at county level, which remained unreformed, has attracted less attention.[1] Yet the administrative work of the justices grew during the mid-nineteenth century, most notably when they became responsible for county police forces, which greatly increased their expenditure and the manpower they employed. Increased responsibilities brought changes to the way the administrative work was organised and how it was financed. Government grants brought more central government control over local government.

Kent before 1889 was a larger county than later and included the expanding urban area of south-east London. Geographically Kent reached from London to the English Channel and the North Sea, was well populated and contained a number of towns which were chartered boroughs. Four of the five Cinque Ports and their 'limbs' were geographically in Kent but were outside the county administration, and the city of Canterbury formed a separate county, which became a county borough in 1889.

For justice and administration by the county justices, the county was divided into two divisions, East and West Kent, with quarter sessions held at both Canterbury and Maidstone. There was only one commission of the peace for the whole county but in practice justices usually acted only for their own division. In addition there were petty sessional divisions where local justices met regularly to deal with minor administrative and judicial matters for their localities. Meetings of petty sessions had developed in Kent as early as the seventeenth century and were well established before nineteenth century legislation made alterations to these courts.

---

[1] A notable exception are the chapters on county government in *Victoria County History of Wiltshire*, vol. 5, Oxford 1957.

East Kent and West Kent each had a treasurer, kept their own accounts and raised separate rates. In the late eighteenth century rising costs, particularly in connection with the county gaol at Maidstone, led to the West Kent justices asking those of East Kent to pay a proportion of their gaoler's salary. This request was refused leading to years of dispute, a law suit won by West Kent and several local Acts of Parliament which attempted to make a more equitable financial arrangement between East and West Kent.[2] The culmination was an Act of 1814 which established a court of 'Annual General Session' to be held at Maidstone for the whole county to deal with financial matters.

The wording of the Act implied a meeting once a year on a specified day, the Thursday before Midsummer quarter sessions, with provision for adjournment from time to time 'as occasion shall require'. Provision was also made for the calling of emergency meetings at the request of three or more justices to the clerk of the peace. In practice the court met frequently, usually monthly, in the early years. Later quarterly meetings gradually became the established practice with some smaller meetings for specific purposes in between. Numbers attending rose as transport improved, a committee structure evolved, additional clerical help was employed and the court came to function much as a county council except that the people attending were not elected.

Kent was not the only county with the problem of two judicial divisions. Sussex had one commission of the peace but also separate quarter sessions courts for East and West Sussex. The Sussex justices by resolutions in 1818 and 1819 decided to hold an annual meeting of justices acting for both divisions to consider matters relating to the whole county, in an attempt to obtain more uniformity of practice. This, however, did not lead to the significant developments found in Kent and the holding of general sessions in Sussex lapsed after about twenty years.[3]

Another county, Lancashire, which though not divided formally for quarter sessions purposes like Kent and Sussex, also set up an annual general sessions for dealing with business relating to the county as a whole in 1787. This was due to Lancashire being geographically a large county leading to quarter sessions being held in a number of places, which resulted in lack of uniformity. As in Kent disputes followed but in Lancashire's case they were over whether the meeting place for general sessions should be at Preston or Lancaster. This was resolved by obtaining a local Act of Parliament in 1798.[4] The general sessions, unlike that of Sussex, survived until 1889 but did not have the range of duties which general sessions had in Kent.[5]

In Kent, as in Lancashire but unlike Sussex, general sessions was established by legislation. The long years of dispute with the expense of a law suit and four

2   *Guide to Kent County Archives Office*, ed. F. Hull, Maidstone 1958, pp. 2–3, 17.
3   *A Descriptive Report on . . . the Official and Ecclesiastical Records in the West and East Sussex Record Offices*, Chichester and Lewes 1954, pp. 2, 38.
4   S. and B. Webb, *The Parish and the County*, London 1963, pp. 432–3.
5   *Guide to the Lancashire Record Office*, ed. R. Sharpe France, Preston 1985, p. 21.

Acts of Parliament had, no doubt, disposed the justices to make the new arrangement work. The justices of East Kent, having established a right theoretically to participation in the control of the finances of the whole county, were less ready to attend general sessions than those of West Kent. The first meeting on 5 July 1814 was attended by twenty justices from West Kent but only six from East Kent. Charles, second Earl of Romney, of Mote House, Maidstone, chairman of West Kent quarter sessions, was elected chairman of the new court but a resolution was passed that the next chairman should come from East Kent. Joint county treasurers were appointed including the existing East Kent treasurer. It would appear that efforts were being made to reassure the justices from East Kent.

In the three years between the initial meeting in July 1814 and the annual meeting in July 1817, 43 meetings were held at 23 of which no East Kent justices attended. At the rest there were between one and three East Kent justices except for two meetings when four or five people came from the east out of a total attendance of 23 on both days. The reason for the larger than usual attendance was that consideration was being given as to what was to happen to the money raised by the sale of the old county gaol in Canterbury.

There are several probable reasons for the new court being dominated by people from the western division. The meetings were held in Maidstone in West Kent, which was the larger division containing more magistrates living within it than in the eastern division. There were quite a number of West Kent justices living within comparatively easy reach of Maidstone. This was not so for those from the eastern part of the county, who probably felt that it was not worth the journey to attend meetings dealing with routine uncontroversial matters, a larger proportion of which affected West Kent rather than East Kent. In addition the court must have been dominated by the chairman, Lord Romney, who during the nineteen years he was chairman attended almost every meeting presiding over numbers which were usually small.

As time went on the number attending general sessions rose. Fewer meetings of the court, better transport and more non-routine business, some of it of a controversial nature, contributed to this factor. Meetings on 17 February and 15 March 1824 which considered the question of whether female prisoners should work on treadmills drew attendances of 61 and 62 justices. There were 63 justices at the meeting on 28 May 1824 to discuss whether gaol alterations should be financed by a separate gaol rate or paid for out of the county rate. For the appointment of a new county treasurer in October 1832 57 attended. A series of meetings in 1839 and 1840 on whether to have a county constabulary were attended by between 36 and 59 justices. One of the largest attendances during these years was of 81 justices on 14 December 1843, again to appoint a new county treasurer. The largest attendance of the whole period was in November 1862 when 102 justices attended to discuss a motion by an East Kent justice that the 1814 Act should be amended so that general sessions could meet in towns other than Maidstone. The motion was lost.

Editorial comment in the local press deprecated decisions which affected ratepayers being taken by a handfull of justices while there were big attendances when the justices were bestowing their patronage. The editor of the *Maidstone Gazette* in the edition of 25 March 1845 questioned why ten or twelve unelected people should have power to place a big charge on ratepayers. A recent proposal for a new county prison in the metropolitan area of Kent had been considered by only 21 out of 200 magistrates but at a meeting to appoint a county treasurer, where patronage was exercised, there were about 100 present. Reference was made by the editor to, 'no taxation without representation'. The figures given in the newspaper were somewhat exaggerated but do not affect the general principle being stated.

By the mid-century quarterly meetings of the court in January, March or April, July and October or November, together with the Midsummer annual meeting, had become more important and better attended than the smaller meetings in between for specific limited business such as receiving tenders and signing contracts. At the quarterly meetings rates were set and committees appointed. The attendance at these meetings was between 35 and 45 justices many of whom attended regularly.

The figures mentioned, however, were still small compared with the number of justices named in the commissions of the peace for Kent or of the smaller number listed as 'acting justices'. The Kent commissions for the county dating from the early to mid-nineteenth century contained over 600 names.[6] Some of these were figures of national importance such as members of the royal family, officers of state, judges and privy councillors named in most county commissions. These people did not take part in the affairs of counties other than their own. Others named did not go through the process of qualifying themselves to act. Of those who qualified many still took no active part at county level. The Kent commissions of the nineteenth century also contained the names of stipendiary magistrates sitting in police courts in the metropolitan area of Kent and in Sheerness and Chatham, who were involved with judicial rather than administrative work. The mid-nineteenth century lists of 'acting justices' among the general sessions records or printed in county directories show that there were between approximately 200 and 260 acting justices for the administrative county. In Wiltshire in 1854 there were 185 acting justices out of a total commission of 509 justices.[7]

(2) People Attending General Sessions

Who then were the justices who took an active part in county administration? As might be expected there were land owning peers and country gentry, some of whom were also qualified lawyers, but there were also people engaged in busi-

---

6   S.B. Black, *The Kentish Justices 1791–1834*, Otford 1987.
7   *VCH Wiltshire*, vol. 5, pp. 177, 232.

ness and commerce particularly from the part of Kent near London. Clerical justices were active in county administration throughout the whole period under consideration, though in diminishing numbers. Some were very regular attenders, chaired committees and sat on the important finance committee. Some were related to the main county families.

The most influential people in the period up to 1873 were the second and third Earls of Romney, members of the Marsham family. Charles, the second Earl, was, as has been mentioned, the first chairman of general sessions. He had been chairman of West Kent quarter sessions since 1809 and continued in that office until 1820 as well as being chairman of general sessions. He retired from the latter in 1833 dying in 1845.

The new chairman was from East Kent, in accordance with the resolution made at the first meeting in 1814. He was Sir Edward Knatchbull (ninth Baronet) of Mersham Le Hatch near Ashford, who was chairman of East Kent quarter sessions from 1819 to 1835. Living further from the meeting place and also having a London residence as he was an MP and held government office, he did not attend as regularly as his predecessor, while Lord Marsham, Lord Romney's eldest son, though also an MP from 1841 to 1845, seldom missed a meeting.

Press comment indicates that Lord Marsham was an influential justice at general sessions. The editorial in the *Maidstone Gazette* on 25 March 1845, already quoted in part, mentions Lord Marsham as one of the few on whom the bulk of county business rested and though 'obliged to him for the close attention he pays to the more irksome part of the duties of a magistrate' the editor considered that the public was not on that account bound to follow him on expending money unnecessarily.

When Sir Edward retired as chairman in 1848, a year before his death, the former Lord Marsham, from 1845 the third Earl of Romney, did not succeed him as chairman. The office went to another justice from East Kent, William Deedes, thus breaking the original agreement that the chairmanship should alternate between the two divisions of the county. Lord Romney continued as a regular attender and influential member finally becoming chairman from 1863 to 1873, a year before his death. He was also chairman of West Kent quarter sessions from 1847 for over twenty years. His son, Charles, fourth Earl of Romney, took little part in county affairs in Kent, though a magistrate and a deputy lieutenant. He attended general sessions only in the early 1860s. After that he lived mainly in London and ultimately on the family's estates in Norfolk having sold part of the estate in Kent to settle debts.

Other members of the Marsham family were also active at general sessions including Jacob Joseph Marsham, a grandson of the second Baron Romney (1712–93), Vicar of Shorne from 1837 to 1889, who attended regularly in the 1850s and 1860s. Also there was Henry Shovell Marsham of Loose, who attended during the 1840s and 1850s while Admiral (Shovell) Jones Marsham, also of Loose, was active during the 1860s. He was also vice-chairman of West Kent quarter sessions to Lord Romney during his later years as quarter sessions chairman. George Marsham of Loose was a great-grandson of the second Baron Romney and son of George Frederick John Marsham, rector of Allington. He was influential during the 1870s and 1880s and became an important member of the county council.

Sir Edward Knatchbull, the second chairman of general sessions from 1833 to 1848, came from a family which had been prominent in Kent from late medieval times both in local affairs and as members of parliament for the county. Sir Edward succeeded his father, another Sir Edward, in 1819 and was also elected to his parliamentary seat for the county of Kent. He continued as an MP until 1845 sitting after the Reform Act of 1832 for East Kent. He was a member of the government as Paymaster of the Forces in Peel's two adminis-trations. In 1820 he married, as his second wife, Fanny Knight, Jane Austen's niece and sons from both his marriages took part in general sessions adminis-tration.

As mentioned before, Sir Edward was succeeded as chairman in 1848 by another justice from East Kent, William Deedes of Sandling Park, Saltwood. The family had been involved in county affairs for some time, William Deedes' grandfather, another William Deedes, having been chairman of East Kent quarter sessions from 1776 to 1792. William Deedes, like Sir Edward, was an MP and his main residence during the 1850s was in London. He managed, however, to attend general sessions with some regularity. William Deedes' brother, Julius Deedes, rector of Wittersham and then of Marden, also went to general sessions with some frequency during the 1840s and 1850s. William's son, also William Deedes, started attending in 1862, overlapping with his father for one meeting before the latter's death.

The last chairman of general sessions from 1873 to 1889, who was to become the first chairman of the county council, was not initially a country gentleman but a professional army officer. Colonel John Farnaby Lennard (a baronet from 1880) had been born John Farnaby Cator, son of General John Cator of Beck-enham. His mother was heiress of the Farnaby Lennard estate in West Wickham and John Farnaby Cator succeeded to the estates in 1861 assuming the Lennard name. He had retired from the army in 1852, became a magistrate in 1854 and attended general sessions from that date. He soon established himself as one of the important participants at general sessions. He became a member and then chairman of the finance committee. When Lord Romney resigned as chairman in 1873 Colonel Lennard had had almost twenty years experience in county ad-ministration.

The chairmen of East and West Kent quarter sessions often played a part at general sessions and when a committee structure evolved were placed on some committees by right of their offices, no doubt to improve liaison between the three courts. They included for West Kent Thomas Law Hodges of Hempstead in Benenden, a lawyer who became MP for Kent and then West Kent, and Joseph Berens of Chislehurst. Later there was Gathorne Gathorne-Hardy (1878 Viscount Cranbrook, 1892 Earl of Cranbrook) a barrister and politician, at one time President of the Poor Law Board. He was an immigrant to Kent and lived at

Hempstead, Thomas Law Hodges' former seat. John Gilbert Talbot of Falconhurst near Edenbridge was also a lawyer and an MP.

For East Kent quarter sessions the chairmen included James Beckford Wildman of Chilham Castle in the 1850s and Sir Brook William Bridges (1868 Lord Fitzwalter) of Goodnestone in the 1860s. Then a member of the Knatchbull family took over again. This was Edward Hugessen Knatchbull-Hugessen (1880 first Lord Brabourne) a son of Sir Edward Knatchbull (ninth Baronet) by his second wife. He was an MP from 1857 to 1880 and several times held minor government offices.

The Lord Lieutenant of Kent and *custos rotulorum* when general sessions began was the first Marquess Camden. He attended the first meeting and occasionally thereafter when business he considered important was being discussed. He also offered advice by letter and on one occasion in October 1832 was asked to meet a committee of justices for a discussion. A later Lord Lieutenant was a very regular attender over a long period. This was Viscount Sydney (1874 Earl Sydney) of Frognal near Footscray, who was Lord Lieutenant from 1856 to 1890. He was related to the second Earl of Romney through the marriage of his sister to Lord Romney as his second wife. This personal link may have encouraged him to attend regularly. Viscount Sydney had been involved in the court's business before becoming Lord Lieutenant and attended for over fifty years.

The justices who came to general sessions included some people who had business experience such as members of the Best family, originally Chatham brewers, and the Whatman family of Boxley, papermakers, though by the mid-nineteenth century these families had acquired land and become country gentry as well. Even though living at a distance from Maidstone justices from the part of Kent near London, some with London banking and business connections, came to general sessions.

A regular attender during the first decade of the court was Benjamin Harenc (*sic*) of Footscray Place, who had become a justice of the peace in 1806. The same name appears as High Sheriff of Kent in 1777, so the family had been established in Kent for some years. David Salomons (a baronet from 1869) of Broomhill near Tunbridge Wells, a London financier, first attended general sessions during 1839 when he was High Sheriff. He continued attending from time to time during the 1840s and in 1849 suggested that a proper agenda for each meeting should be prepared in advance. He was Lord Mayor of London in 1855 and became an MP in 1859.

The varied members of the commission of the peace who attended general sessions also included clergymen. At one time there had been no clergy on the commission in Kent.[8] By the late eighteenth century this had changed and there were an increasing number of clerical justices in Kent. The chairman of West Kent quarter sessions between 1778 and 1795 was the Revd Pierrepoint Cromp of Frinsted. He probably held the office more as a landed gentleman than as a

8   Webb, *op. cit.*, p. 384.

clergyman. He had come to Kent from Gloucestershire after marrying a Kentish heiress and lived on her estate. He was not an incumbent of a living in Kent. The early nineteenth century commissions for Kent named about seventy clergy, over 10% of the total number of justices.[9] This percentage was small compared with some counties where over half the justices were clergymen.[10] The Webbs calculated that in 1832 a quarter of the justices in England and Wales were clergymen.[11]

At the first meeting of general sessions in 1814 seven clergymen attended out of a total attendance of 26 justices. During the first five years there were only two meetings without any clergy present and between one and five clergymen attended meetings which had a total number of less than ten people present. The pattern was the same in the 1820s except that the overall numbers of justices attending rose. In the 1830s and 1840s there were more meetings with no clergy present and at the other meetings one to three clergy attended except when there were big meetings such as in November 1839 when there were eleven clergymen out of 59 justices and in December 1848 when there were fourteen out of 81 present. In the 1850s four to six clergymen came to general sessions out of normally twenty to thirty people present and there were ten in April 1857 out of 116 attending. Lists of acting justices of 1855 and 1859 both name eighteen clergymen out of 239 and 241 magistrates respectively. In the 1860s usually only one clergyman attended regularly but right up to 1889 there were often one or two clergy present.

In the early years of general sessions the parish clergy had relatively light pastoral duties, were not responsible for running sizeable estates like the country gentry and could not be MPs, so they had leisure to attend and inclination to do so through family links with the secular justices attending. A few country gentlemen were themselves in holy orders though not incumbents. The continuing clerical presence in the later years of general sessions was probably due to the personality of the individual clergymen involved. The involvement of the clergy at general sessions was on at least one occasion subject to criticism. A letter to the editor, dated 10 November 1832, appeared in the *Maidstone Gazette* of 13 November 1832, signed 'A Constant Reader and Friends' complaining that at the recent appointment of a new county treasurer the successful candidate, who did not live in Maidstone, had been chosen over two applicants who lived in the town. This was attributed to clerical influence

> We regret to say, that through the influence of one or more Reverend Divines, who have sacrificed private worth to party motives, this important office has been diverted from its legitimate source and unfairly smuggled from us; and while we deeply lament this disgrace to our County Town, and abuse of clerical influence, we trust the time is not far distant, when members of our

9   Black, *op. cit.*, p. 6.
10 E. Moir, *The Justices of the Peace*, London 1969, pp. 106–7.
11 Webb, *op. cit.*, p. 383 n. 1, p. 384 n. 2.

Church will be restored to their proper sphere, by having their care and attention to their religious duties.

There had been eleven clerical justices attending out of 57 justices on 23 October 1822 when the appointment was made. In a close contest, however, a group of some of them acting together may have swayed the balance. Voting figures were not given either in the court minutes or the newspaper.

Among the clerical justices who attended general sessions there were some who were there regularly over a long period of time. These included Edward Hasted, son of the county historian, and rector of Hollingbourne until his death aged 94 in 1855. He attended the first meeting in 1814 and often went to meetings until 1845. Another clergyman who attended the first meeting was George Moore, rector of Wrotham from 1805 to his death in 1846. He was the eldest son of John Moore, Dean of Canterbury, then Bishop of Bangor, who became Archbishop of Canterbury in 1783. George, the son, was made a prebendary of Canterbury in 1795. His wife was a daughter of the Earl of Errol. Socially he must have been very acceptable to the gentry among the justices. He attended regularly from 1819 to 1831, on one occasion in 1826 taking the chair. John Poore DD, rector of Murston, became a magistrate in 1818 and attended general sessions from 1819 to 1850. He was an active member of the finance committee from its formation in 1836 and was also in 1841 put on the county rates committee. Another member of the Moore family, George Bridges Moore or George Moore, junior, as he was described in the press, rector of Tunstall from 1837 to 1885, began attending general sessions in 1840 making his last appearance in 1881. He was chairman of the asylum committee for many years. Then when a second county asylum was built in 1874 he switched to be chairman of the committee for that institution. He was also a member of the finance committee. In October 1878 another clergyman, who was to become a regular attender during the final decade of general sessions, first came to the court. This was Robert Whiston, who was a retired schoolmaster. He had been headmaster of Rochester Cathedral Grammar School, later Kings School, from 1844 to 1877. A colourful character, he engaged in a bitter legal battle with the Dean and Chapter of Rochester between 1848 and 1853 over the terms of the trust under which the school was run. He became known nationally through this and Trollope based the plot of his novel *The Warden* on what became known as the 'Whiston Matter'. Robert Whiston became a county councillor and was active in public affairs until his death aged 87 in 1895.[12]

12 R. Arnold, *The Whiston Matter*, London 1961.

(3) Functions of General Sessions

The duties which these varied justices performed were much concerned with erecting and maintaining buildings and bridges and with running the institutions which occupied some of the buildings. During the years 1814 to 1889 the county justices were responsible for the building of a large prison, two lunatic asylums of some size, an industrial school, a courthouse and numerous lock-up houses and police stations. They were also responsible for the maintenance of an increasing number of the more important bridges, known as county bridges.

General sessions had been set up mainly due to a dispute over the finances of the West Kent county gaol in Maidstone. In 1814 when general sessions began to operate the West Kent justices were in the process of having a new county gaol built in Maidstone. This work was taken over by general sessions. In the late eighteenth and early nineteenth centuries the spread of the prison reform movement led to most county gaols being rebuilt or radically altered to adhere to the principles of John Howard. In 1806 both the East Kent and the West Kent justices considered building new county gaols and courthouses at Canterbury and Maidstone in their respective divisions. The building of the new gaol and courthouse at Canterbury was implemented quite quickly but the work at Maidstone was postponed due to the inability of the West Kent justices to obtain financial help from East Kent for the projects which would benefit the whole county, assizes being held in Maidstone.

In 1810 the West Kent justices decided to buy a site for a new gaol and in 1811 purchased fourteen acres of land from a number of different owners at a total cost of £10,442. Daniel Alexander had been appointed as the architect. He had rebuilt Mote House, Maidstone, for Lord Romney's father and already acted as a consultant in connection with repairs to the county bridges. The new gaol was to bring together on one site the gaol, the house of correction and the debtor's prison, providing for 452 prisoners in 27 classes. The numbers were 167 higher than the greatest number held in the old prison. The estimated cost was £163,467 but the estimate was much exceeded. The money was raised by rates. The justices did not borrow money for the project because of the difficulty of borrowing money in wartime. This led to very strong protests from ratepayers against the proposed expenditure.[13]

Building work, however, started in 1811 and lasted until 1819. The justices wished to stagger the building work so as to spread the cost over a number of years. The prisoners were transferred to the new gaol at the end of 1818 and beginning of 1819. By July 1819 when the prison was fully operational, £194,159 had been spent. Fraud, however, had been discovered which led to Alexander's dismissal and the prosecution of his clerk of works, who was found guilty and imprisoned. One of Alexander's pupils, John Whichcord, who had drawn up the detailed plans for the gaol, took over responsibility for the building, later being appointed county surveyor. In a sense the prison was never

---

[13] *New Maidstone Gaol Order Book 1805–23*, ed. C.W. Chalklin, Maidstone 1984, pp. 19–22, Appendix II.

finished; alterations both minor and major were almost continuous from 1819 to 1878 when the government took over all county gaols. The alterations were partly due to the increased supervision by the Home Office of local prisons following continuing legislation on the regulation of prisons and prisoners.

Running the county prisons at Maidstone and Canterbury involved both administration and money. The justices at general sessions took over from the two courts of quarter sessions the appointment of the visiting justices to each prison and received their reports. The visiting justices, about half a dozen for each prison, often included some clergymen. They acted in each location as a committee which supervised the day to day running of the prisons. The staff were few when the new prisons opened. The ratio of staff to prisoners was assisted by the use of trusted prisoners or warders who helped to keep order in the wards into which the prisons were divided. Each unit at Maidstone, for example, had a day room, a workroom, sleeping cells and an arcaded exercise yard which could be used in fine or wet weather. The justices at general sessions, being primarily concerned with finance, dealt with tenders for food, fuel and equipment and the payment of the contractors who supplied these. They appointed and dismissed staff and paid the pensions of those who served until they retired. They also entered into contracts with many of the boroughs in Kent who wished to pay the county to look after their prisoners rather than up-grade their own prisons.

By 1824 the justices were ready to go ahead with building a new court or sessions house in Maidstone, first considered in 1806. The courts including general sessions were being held in Maidstone town hall, which had been built at the cost of both the borough and the county in the 1760s for joint use. The new courts for the use of the county for sessions and assizes were built in front of the prison and designed by Sir Robert Smirke, the architect of, among other buildings, the original part of the British Museum. Sir Robert had already been advising on the completion of the gaol following Alexander's dismissal. The court house was a relatively small project compared with the prison and was again financed from the rates. The main rooms were two courts and a large room called the Grand Jury room which could be used for other meetings and was where general sessions and later the county council met. The building was ready for use in 1827.

In July 1825 the justices decided to build a county lunatic asylum but no plans were to be drawn up before the court house was finished. In 1829 John Whichcord, now county surveyor, produced plans for a building to contain 174 inmates and land was purchased at Barming Heath near Maidstone. The estimated cost of the land and buildings was approximately £13,000 to be paid from the rates. The asylum opened in January 1833. A permanent asylum committee of justices supervised the building and then the running of the institution. The number of inmates grew steadily so that extra wings to take a further 250 people were added in 1842. In 1850 an additional separate building accommodated another 200 inmates. In 1867 another new building to take 400 people was built. By 1874 there were 1,236 patients.

In 1872, however, the justices had decided to build another asylum in East Kent. A site was acquired in Chartham near Canterbury in that year and the asylum opened in 1875. Some patients were transferred from the asylum at Barming. A separate committee of justices was formed to supervise the new asylum. Loans of £125,000 had been taken to cover the cost of the land and buildings.

General sessions had taken over from quarter sessions the appointment of visiting justices to inspect private asylums, of which there were only a few small ones in Kent, the best known one being at West Malling, founded in the mid-eighteenth century by Dr William Perfect who became well known for caring for and curing the insane.[14] The fact that there was a shortage of private asylum accommodation in Kent had meant that the justices had had to build county asylums rather than place pauper lunatics in private asylums as had been done in Wiltshire.[15]

The last institution which the justices built was an Industrial School for boys at Kingsnorth near Ashford as a result of the Industrial Schools Act 1872, which enabled prison authorities to erect and manage these schools. A committee was set up in 1872, land was acquired in 1874 and the school opened in 1875. The boys received education and also worked on the school farm. The justices also bought musical instruments in 1877 and appointed a music master to teach some of the boys to play them. For the girls a house was leased in Greenwich as a girls school in 1873 but few cases were sent for admission so the school was on a very small scale. It was closed in 1884 and the girls were transferred to a school in Essex. Under reformatory schools legislation the justices also became financially responsible for children who were to be sent to reformatories. No reformatory was built in Kent but use was made of existing institutions in a number of other counties some at a distance from Kent.

Compared with the expenditure on the building work just described, the maintenance of the county bridges was on a small scale but was an ongoing responsibility which the county justices had undertaken for several centuries. There were over twenty of these bridges in Kent, many more than in the adjoining counties of Sussex and Surrey. This was due to the number of rivers in Kent. Most of these larger bridges, for which the county was responsible, were over the River Medway and its tributaries, excluding Rochester and Maidstone bridges looked after by a bridge trust and a borough respectively. There were several bridges on the Darent, three on the Stour and the important Deptford bridge on the Ravensbourne. The cost, which came from the county rates, fluctuated according to the work which needed doing and was highest when the rebuilding of a major bridge was required. From 1815 to 1839 for example, between around £200 and £1600 a year was spent.[16] Increasing traffic of a heavy

---

[14] S.B. Black, *An 18th Century Mad-Doctor: William Perfect of West Malling*, Otford 1995.

[15] *VCH Wiltshire*, vol. 5, pp. 246–8.

[16] C.W. Chalklin, 'Bridge Building in Kent 1700–1830: The Work of the Justices of the Peace', in *Studies in Modern Kentish History*, ed. A. Detsicas and N. Yates, Maidstone 1983, pp. 49–63.

nature led to more repairs and by the mid-nineteenth century there were few quarterly meetings when orders about bridges were not made. Under the Turnpike Continuance Act 1875, responsibility for the less important Hundred bridges, hitherto financed on a more local basis, was transferred to the county, greatly increasing the number of county bridges.

The county was not responsible for road repairs except for short lengths at either end of the county bridges. As, however, turnpike roads came to an end, from 1879 the county had to contribute towards the cost of maintaining main roads undertaken by the Highway Boards established in 1862 and a separate county rate called the Main Road rate was levied. County justices had been responsible for dividing the county into Highway Districts, a committee for this purpose having been appointed by General Sessions in October 1862.

The establishment of a county police force in 1857 was a major new departure in the administrative work of the county justices. The number of people employed and the amount of money spent greatly increased. The existing ways of keeping law and order, particularly in rural areas, were generally felt to be unsatisfactory as the nineteenth century progressed. The parts of Kent nearest to London fell within the Metropolitan Police District set up in 1829 and later extended. The Municipal Corporations Act 1835 stated that borough councils should have a Watch Committee and appoint a paid police force. Some urban areas which were not incorporated obtained Improvement Commissioners who could introduce better lighting and watching in the areas concerned. There was a perception that while urban crime was falling it was increasing in rural areas as criminals began to operate there instead of in the more efficiently policed towns.

The unpaid local constables had in the past been appointed at manorial courts but with decreasing manorial court activity these officers, who were usually small traders or craftsmen, were chosen by the solicitor who was steward of the manor. The job was unpopular. If the local constable was too assiduous in his duties he risked retaliation by criminals. If he was too lax those who had been the victims of crime complained. These constables, unpaid and unpopular, disinclined towards holding the post in the first place, were for the most part unsatisfactory. 'The present state of our county's police is a disgrace to the name of Kent' wrote the editor of the *Maidstone Gazette* in an editorial of 13 October 1840, while individual justices in the debates in 1839 and 1840 on whether a county police force should be established told of personal experiences of unsatisfactory constables.

Two police Acts of Parliament were passed in 1839 and 1840, the latter amending the former, which was found to be unsatisfactory in some respects. These Acts, which were adoptive not prescriptive, allowed county justices to establish county police forces paid for by county rates. As many as 31 counties took advantage of the Acts to have police forces. In Kent the Acts led to bitter and lively debates at general sessions. Surrey, bordering on Kent, was considering having a police force and this alarmed the justices of Sevenoaks petty sessional division, one of the most westerly divisions in Kent. They feared that criminals would be driven from a well policed Surrey into a badly policed Kent.

A special meeting of general sessions was requisitioned by five justices, three from Sevenoaks division supported by one from Malling division and by Lord Marsham.

The meeting took place on 29 November 1839 and was attended by 59 justices, a much larger number than usual, indicating the interest which the proposal aroused. The debate was reported at some length in the *Maidstone Gazette* of 3 December 1839, showing well the strong views held for and against the proposal. After the motion had been proposed and seconded, Joseph Berens, chairman of West Kent quarter sessions, moved an amendment that a police for the whole county, not just for one petty sessional division, should be established. The chairman of general sessions, Sir Edward Knatchbull, said that the subject was the most important to come before the court since he had been connected with the magistracy but he was against the proposal which would be expensive and lead to the end of the magistracy in its present form. The decision should be postponed for enquiries to be made. He also thought the Act needed amending. The speakers divided sharply between the views of the main protagonists. Thomas Law Hodges said the police force would be too expensive and consideration should be postponed in view of an expected revised assessment for the county rate. Joseph Berens stated that duty should be put before money and it was important to protect the property and persons of their poorer fellow subjects. William Deedes, chairman of East Kent quarter sessions, was for deferring a decision while more enquiries were made. When Berens' amendment was put to the vote it was carried. This led to Sir Edward's son, Norton Knatchbull, moving that the meeting be adjourned *sine die* but some present were indignant at this, pointing out that some of the justices, who had travelled from 30 or 40 miles away, had left to return home. Even William Deedes, who had opposed the resolution, did not want to vote to negate the resolution passed. T.L. Hodges then moved a motion that a committee should be appointed to enquire into the state of policing in the county and report back to the court. After further discussion this motion was put resulting in a tie, followed by the chairman giving his casting vote for the motion. There was a protest at the overthrowing of the previous resolution but a committee of 22 justices was appointed including five justices who were members of parliament. The whole meeting had lasted five hours. The editor of the *Maidstone Gazette*, writing in the edition of 10 December 1839, was indignant at the outcome of the meeting and took up the point that it was the poor who needed police protection. The rich could look after themselves. They had servants to protect their property and themselves when travelling.

On 9 March 1840 the committee appointed reported to the general sessions that they were of an unanimous view that 'an entire and complete change was absolutely necessary in the constabulary force of the county and should be carried out in the course of the present year.'[17] Yet at general sessions on 20

---

[17] CKS, General Sessions Minutes, Q/GO4.

August 1840 the committee reported further that, having looked more closely at the returns from the localities and found them unsatisfactory, they did not feel there were sufficient reasons for establishing a paid constabulary. At the same meeting, however, a requisition for a special meeting had been received from the justices of Wingham petty sessional division wishing to have paid police within their own division. In an editorial of 25 August 1840 in the *Maidstone Gazette*, the editor, in commenting on the meeting of 20 August, stated that the opposition 'in our county parliament' primarily related to the unconstitutional character of a paid police, the imminent danger of centralisation and the horror of a paid magistracy. The general session meeting requisitioned by the Wingham petty sessional division justices was held on 27 October 1840, attended by 45 justices. It resulted in a debate which closely followed that of November 1839 with additional complaints that there were no particular circumstances in Wingham division which showed a need for a paid police. The result of the debate was a resolution not to adopt the Constabulary Acts of 1839 and 1840.

No further consideration was given to having a county constabulary until 1856, following further legislation. In the meantime some attempt was made to improve the old system of policing. On 28 September 1842 a specially requisitioned meeting was held to consider building lock-up houses. This resulted in a committee being appointed to communicate with the justices in each petty sessional division to find out their views. The committee reported on 13 March 1843 that several divisions would like lock-up houses and it was agreed that the county should organise and finance the building of these. The building of lock-up houses was to continue. Then in 1850 the county justices decided to employ a paid superintendent constable in each petty sessional division to oversee the work of the existing constables. A constabulary committee of general sessions was also appointed.

The Police Act 1856 made it obligatory for counties to have police forces. Government grants were made available to pay for a quarter (from 1874 a half) of the cost of the pay and clothing of the police subject to certification by Home Office inspectors that the force was efficient. A committee was appointed at general sessions on 21 October 1856 to enquire into establishing a police force. It consisted of the Lord Lieutenant, the chairmen of general sessions and West Kent and East Kent quarter sessions together with one justice from each petty sessional division chosen by their own divisions. The committee was also to enquire if any municipal boroughs would like to join with the county for police purposes. The committee reported on 3 December 1856 recommending a force of 222 men and that the chief constable should be paid £400 a year with £200 for expenses. A committee was set up to deal with the preliminary work for appointing a chief constable. The committee reported to the court on 13 January 1857 that there had been 66 applications for the post. A short list of 22 had been made and the suggested voting procedure to be used at general sessions was explained. A police rate of a half penny in the pound was also made by the court. This rate had to be separate from the county rate as a different area was involved since the part of Kent in the metropolitan police area was not subject to the county's police rate. Soon four small boroughs – Fordwich, Lydd, New Romney and Queenborough – came under the county police force paying police rates but not county rates. The Hythe police force amalgamated with the county in 1874 and further boroughs joined after the Municipal Corporations Act 1883.

On 14 January 1857 the court met again to appoint the chief constable in a special session for business under the Police Acts. Captain John Henry Hay Ruxton of Brenchley was appointed as chief constable and a police committee of justices appointed. Captain Ruxton remained Chief Constable until 1893 retiring when 77 years of age. He had joined the army in 1834 and seen service in Australia.[18] Buildings at Wrens Cross in Maidstone were leased as a county police headquarters, being purchased by the county in 1860. The one acre site included a house for officers and room for a barracks to be built to house unmarried constables and for a parade ground, stables and a horse paddock. The members of the force were appointed during February and March. The annual cost for the first year was estimated as £16,641. A superannuation fund was also established to which the police employed contributed 2½% of their pay. After years of indecision, when the time came the police force was established very quickly.

A new function brought new building work. In April 1862 the Inspector of Constabulary for the southern district criticised poor police stations in Kent. This was referred to the police committee and in June 1862 the police and finance committees appointed a joint committee to consider the matter. Money for the building work was obtained by borrowing partly from the police superannuation fund and partly from an insurance company. When the new police stations had been built the old lock-up houses were sold.

The county justices meeting at general sessions also had more minor functions some of which they had inherited from quarter sessions and others which were new duties. Some related to consumer protection including appointing and supervising inspectors of weights and measures and, from 1873, appointing a county analyst. During the eighteenth century the justices of the peace had been involved with outbreaks of cattle plague, paying compensation for the slaughter of diseased animals. This work continued in the nineteenth century under new legislation. Stores for the equipment of the militia had been provided by the county during the Napoleonic wars and responsibility for them continued. Coroners responsible for holding inquests were paid by general sessions.

(4) Organisation of General Sessions

As has been shown, one of the ways the justices dealt with all their tasks was to appoint permanent standing committees of general sessions. This was something which other counties also did by appointing committees of quarter

---

[18] *Kent Police Centenary*, ed. R.L. Thomas, Maidstone 1957, pp. 21, 34–5.

sessions. In Kent when general sessions began in 1814, there were only the committees formed by the visiting justices of the county gaols. In 1828 the asylums committee was established to supervise the building of the county asylum and then the running of the institution and to act as visitors of it.

In the early years of general sessions a number of *ad hoc* short lived committees were appointed to consider specific matters and report back. This practice was less used once a permanent finance committee was appointed in March 1836, to which many matters were referred so that the committee became in fact, and in the 1860s in name, a finance and general purposes committee. The committee grew in size from six or seven to eighteen or nineteen members.In January 1841 the county rates committee was appointed in connection with re-valuing the rate basis of the administrative county. The committee was re-appointed each time this needed doing, the name being changed to the basis of rates committee.

In October 1850 the constabulary committee was set up as a regular committee to deal with matters concerning the superintending constables in the petty sessional divisions. This was followed by the police committee appointed in January 1857 on the founding of the county constabulary. It was abolished and its work taken over by the finance committee at the end of 1862. In 1859 the county works committee was formed but was short lived, also becoming absorbed by the finance committee.

Committees for the new institutions opened in the 1870s, Chartham asylum and the industrial schools, were established. The cattle plague committee of the 1860s became the diseases of animals committee in 1878. A parliamentary committee to study the effect of proposed legislation on Kent started in 1874. A number of these committees were continued by the county council, the same minute books being used.

Business at general sessions in its early years was slow and some time was taken to reach more important decisions. A proposal at one meeting would be postponed until the next meeting. This was probably to give justices, who were not at the original meeting, a chance to come to a subsequent meeting if they wished to join in the debate. Justices were notified of meetings by advertisements placed in about half a dozen county newspapers. There is also some evidence that the clerks of the petty sessional divisions were notified to inform justices attending petty sessions. On 13 March 1848 general sessions decided that acting justices should be informed in advance of non-routine business to be considered at general sessions. It was not until the middle of the century that there was a formal agenda paper for meetings. The form this should take was re-considered from time to time. In April 1860 it was resolved at general sessions that in future routine business should be taken first followed by business on which discussion was likely.

There was no fixed day for holding general sessions meetings apart from the Midsummer annual meeting which always took place on a Thursday in accordance with the wording of the 1814 Act. The only day on which meetings did not take place was Sunday. It was usual to hold the quarterly meetings in the same week that quarter sessions was held at Maidstone.

General sessions meetings by the 1860s were becoming more streamlined. At the quarterly meetings reports were received from committees starting with the finance committee. This committee's report was from April 1867 divided into sections for finance, police and works, which reflected the work of the committee. Reports were also made by some of the chief officers such as the county surveyor and the chief constable. Rates were also set.

(5) Employees of General Sessions

The justices had only a limited number of people to execute and administer the decisions which they took at general sessions. The oldest post was that of clerk of the peace. Technically the appointment was made by the *custos rotulorum*, that is the lord lieutenant, but the entries in the general sessions minutes concerning appointments of clerks of the peace do not reflect this fact. Usually in Kent the clerk of the peace was a local lawyer from law firms operating in various towns in Kent. During the late eighteenth and early nineteenth centuries three clerks of the peace in succession came from the same firm in Sevenoaks. When general sessions started the last of these, John Fellows Claridge, was in the post, dying in 1822.[19] At this stage payment was made by means of the county being charged legal fees for the work done. The clerk also took fees for judicial work at quarter sessions from individuals and the justices. It was not until the middle of the century that consideration was given to paying the clerk a salary in place of some or all of the fees but no firm conclusion was reached.

The appointment of the clerk of the peace was made for life but clerks sometimes resigned when elderly and on one occasion in the mid-nineteenth century the Kent justices dismissed the clerk of the peace. The occupant of the office, H.A. Wildes from a partnership in Maidstone, was appointed in 1855. He was also clerk to the lieutenancy. It was not until May 1863 that there is a hint of trouble appearing in the general sessions minutes, when it was recorded that the Examiners of the Criminal Law Accounts disallowed certain fees which had been wrongly charged by the clerk in connection with the transportation of prisoners. In September 1863 it was found that the clerk was using two rooms in the Sessions House for his private work and he was said to be in financial difficulties. A committee of justices was appointed to investigate and in the meantime the clerk was not to be employed as a solicitor on any county business. The court arranged for Frederick Scudamore of Maidstone, attorney, to do legal business and he became designated county solicitor.[20]

In January 1864 an order was made at general sessions for the solicitor to

[19] B. Keith-Lucas, 'Francis and Francis Motley Austen, Clerks of the Peace for Kent', in *Studies in Modern Kentish History*, ed. A. Detsicas and N. Yates, Maidstone 1983, pp. 87–102.
[20] CKS, Q/GO 10.

attend all general sessions meetings and papers were to be handed over to him. Correspondence was also taking place with the Home Secretary about the clerk of the peace's disputed fees. In June 1864 the Home Secretary wrote suggesting that the clerk's salary should be £600 a year in lieu of fees. The finance committee recommended in July a salary of £450, with the rider that the money in dispute over the fees for prisoners should be deducted from the salary. Court proceedings taken by the clerk of the peace against the county followed, together with non-cooperation by him in certain matters, such as refusing to authorise the county treasurer to pay the county solicitor's bill. In 1865 the clerk of the peace was finally dismissed and a new one appointed, against whom the former clerk also took legal action, but none of these law suits succeeded. The new clerk of the peace was Francis Russell of Maidstone who was also to become, in addition, clerk of the county council in 1889.

County treasurers were local bankers or lawyers. At the first meeting of general sessions on 5 July 1814 joint treasurers were appointed, William Scudamore of Maidstone and Mawer (*sic*) Cowtan of Canterbury, the latter being the existing treasurer for East Kent. As was customary they entered into a bond with the county justices in the large sums of £10,000 each and provided two sureties of £2,500 each. They were paid a small honorarium for their trouble and expenses and were to be resident and have an office in both Maidstone and Canterbury.[21]

In 1821 Cowtan was dismissed and in 1822 William Scudamore became sole treasurer until his death in 1832. Then there was a hard fought election by three candidates who had applied for the post. Each advertised in the local press prior to the meeting of general sessions on 23 October 1832, at which the appointment was to be made, canvassing support and also after the meeting thanking their supporters through advertisements. It was evidently considered well worthwhile to obtain the county's financial business.

In 1845 there began the county's association with a local bank and the families linked to it, which lasted into the time of the county council. John Mercer of Maidstone, banker, was appointed county treasurer, the first of three Mercers, fathers and sons, to hold the office. The firm became Randall, Mercer, Wigan and Company and continued to provide county treasurers.

The first county surveyor had been appointed in 1796 primarily to supervise work on county bridges, being paid by the day plus travelling expenses. The next surveyor appointed in 1810 received an annual salary and travelling expenses and was the first county surveyor to general sessions. The building of the county gaol at Maidstone brought John Whichcord to Kent. In 1819 he became surveyor of that gaol and in 1821 surveyor of Canterbury gaol as well. The county surveyor was dismissed in 1825 and Whichcord became 'surveyor of the county for all purposes'.[22] He was both a salaried official for routine county

---

21 CKS, Q/GO 1.
22 CKS, Q/GO 3, 22 Aug. 1825.

work and also had a private architectural practice. When working for the county as an architect he was paid fees. He died in 1860 to be succeeded by Martin Bulmer. Then from 1878 two members of the firm of Ruck, Son and Smith of Maidstone, George Ruck and F.W. Ruck, succeeded each other. The latter was also to work for the county council.

The keepers or governors of the county prisons were technically appointed by the High Sheriff but in practice by the justices who controlled them and in due course paid them. Gaolers originally ran prisons as commercial enterprises charging the prisoners for food and drink and collecting various fees from them. The West Kent justices began to pay their gaoler a salary in 1785. When general sessions started in 1814 the West Kent gaoler's salary was £400 a year. As has already been mentioned the staff numbers at the prisons were small, but rose at Maidstone from fifteen in 1820 to thirty in the 1840s and more in the next decade.[23]

Increasing legislation concerning prisons and Home Office oversight brought a change in the type of persons appointed as governors. From 1824 onwards the governor of Maidstone gaol either had army experience or previous experience of running a prison or both. The government took over county prisons on 1 April 1878 and the county no longer had responsibility for the staff apart from paying the pensions of former employees who had been in the prison superannuation scheme when they retired.

The county justices appointed the medical superintendents of the county lunatic asylums and the masters and mistresses of the industrial schools. Again these institutions had a small but increasing total staff.

The appointment of a salaried chief constable in 1857 in charge of a police force of several hundred men increased the number of staff the county justices employed considerably. Police numbers were to rise as population in Kent increased and as more borough police forces were amalgamated with the county police.

In 1873, under recent legislation, a county analyst was appointed on an annual contract to be paid by fees. Initially, the arrangement did not work well as the analyst's laboratory was in London and the justices felt that he, and the colleague whom he had asked to be appointed joint analyst with him, could not give enough time to this work for the county. In 1874, another analyst operating in Maidstone was appointed and re-appointed each year for many years. He was paid a fee for each sample examined on a sliding scale.

The justices of the peace had appointed and supervised inspectors of weights and measures from before general sessions began. They had been paid by taking half the fines imposed on those found with false weights but they became salaried. Coroners expenses for holding inquests had long been paid but they too came to be paid a fixed salary instead of charging fees, which had led on occasion to disputes over coroners' bills. Fees were replaced by salaries for the

23 E. Melling, *Kentish Sources VI: Crime and Punishment*, Maidstone 1969, pp. 225, 227, 250.

justices' clerks in the petty sessional divisions in 1863. So the wages bill of the justices steadily rose, though they had more control over paying fixed salaries than fluctuating fees.

As committees of general sessions grew in number some of them needed clerical help, particularly the finance committee. In January 1848 a clerk was appointed for this committee, being paid 10s for summoning and attending each meeting. In 1886 John Henry Turner, who had been clerk to the finance committee and some other committees for many years, was appointed assistant treasurer with a salary which was to include his providing clerks and also covering postage. In addition he was to be paid a salary as secretary of the finance committee and the vagrancy and rate basis committees instead of submitting a quarterly bill of charges.

The county solicitor was clerk of the parliamentary committee being paid according to the work done. The lunatic asylum committee for the first asylum at Barming used a Maidstone firm of solicitors as their clerk. So varied means were used to provide committee clerks as suited individual committees.

(6) General Sessions Finance

The administrative duties of the county justices had to be financed and this finance in itself needed organising. The basic means of raising money was by levying rates on property, to which was added from the mid-nineteenth century government grants, while the cost of expenditure on capital projects led to sums of money being borrowed on the security of the county rates.

The expenditure financed from the county rate in the first full year of general sessions administration between Easter 1815 and Easter 1816 was £12,350. The headings in the accounts, under which the payments were grouped, consisted of conveying vagrants and prisoners, the current costs of running the county gaols and houses of correction and also the court houses, payments in connection with the maintenance of county bridges, the inspection of weights and measures, the holding of coroners' inquests and the salaries of county officers. There were also payments for the expenses of prosecutors at quarter sessions and assizes which had begun under legislation of 1752. The legacy of the recent war was reflected in payments headed militia and military baggage.

In addition to the county rate expenditure there was expenditure financed by a gaol rate for building the new county gaol at Maidstone. For the years 1816–17 expenditure from the gaol rate was £23,785 and from the county rate £13,462, making a total expenditure of £37,247. Expenditure on the county rates between 1816 and 1839 varied between £12,350 and £23,653 but was usually between £15,000 and £18,000. The rates set varied between ½d and 2d in the pound levied three or four times a year. The product of a 1d rate in 1827 was £4,403.

The gaol rate was as much as 3d in the pound in October 1817 and November 1819. As has been mentioned, building work continued at Maidstone gaol after it opened and what was now called a special county rate was levied during the

1820s and early 1830s to pay for this. The same rate was also used for the building of the Sessions House at Maidstone and then for building the county lunatic asylum. The rates varied between ¼d and 2d but were usually 1d raised from one to four times a year.

After a lull in capital expenditure between 1836 and 1840 there was again a special county rate from 1840 to 1845 of between ¼d and 1d, levied infrequently in connection with erecting an additional building at the county lunatic asylum. In 1848 when further buildings were needed at the asylum the justices in Kent at last decided to borrow the finance required, something which other counties, such as Wiltshire, had done since the late eighteenth century.[24] The money was borrowed from the Public Works Loan Commissioners at 5% interest. During the next thirty years the justices usually borrowed from insurance companies, either local or London-based, paying between 4 and 5% interest. In June 1875 the justices were arranging to pay a financial agent £200 to negotiate loans.

The reluctance of the justices to finance capital expenditure from loans instead of rates, resulted, in part, from the difficulties of borrowing money at reasonable rates in wartime when work started on the county gaol at Maidstone. A matter of principle was also involved. In a speech at general sessions on 29 November 1839, reported in the *Maidstone Gazette* of 3 December 1839, Thomas Law Hodges MP referred to the 'enormous sums' which had been raised in the county for a county gaol and lunatic asylum and is reported as saying that 'it has been always the practice in this county to pay for such things within the year in preference to burdening those who come after them with a debt'. Between 1846 and 1857 there was only the county rate being levied. The rate levels were between ½d and 1½d. The product of 1d rate in 1852 was £7,950. Expenditure was between £21,247 and £37,271. The ending of the financial year was changed from Easter to September in 1852.

Several improvements to the county's finances occurred during the 1840s. There was a revaluation of the basis of the county rate in 1841 and the collection of the rates passed in 1845 from the High Constables to the staff of the Boards of Guardians, leading to fewer arrears in rate payment. Government grants had already begun, when from 1835 the government paid half the expenses of prosecutions at quarter sessions and assizes. There was also a grant for the conveyance of transports. From 1846 the government grant covered the full cost of prosecutions. There was also a grant towards the keep of prisoners from 1846.

The budgeting for receipts and payments and the level and frequency of levying rates was done on a quarterly basis. The reports of the finance committee from 1836 show, particularly in its early years, a small group of justices taking into account the balance in hand, estimating how much would be needed for expenditure in the next quarter and recommending to general sessions the level of rates to be raised. If a good balance had been built up and

24 *VCH Wiltshire*, vol. 5, pp. 193–4.

no extraordinary payments were expected, no rates were levied in some quarters.[25]

The auditing of the accounts were done by the justices themselves, at first at the Midsummer annual general sessions meeting, then at a preliminary meeting on the preceeding day. When the county's financial year was changed to end in September the audit was approved at the quarterly meeting held the following January. The spending of government grants was checked by the civil service.

In January 1857 when a county police force was established a separate police rate was levied as the area in which the police operated was different from the area of the administrative county. The produce of 1d police rate in 1859 was £6,053. In the first fifteen years the police rate was usually levied at ¾d in the pound but could vary between ¼d and 1½d. Expenditure rose from £17,856 in 1858 to almost £30,000 in 1869 and then dropped back a little. County rate expenditure for the same period was between £31,770 and £51,665. Overall the expenditure of the justices increased considerably. There was a government grant of one quarter of the cost of the pay and clothing of the police which increased to half the cost in 1874. Growing numbers of men in the force and rises in pay caused the cost of running the county constabulary to rise steadily. Loans were also raised to build police stations.

Other rates besides the county rate and the police rate were levied during the last 25 years of the administration of general sessions. An outbreak of cattle disease in the late 1860s led to having a modest and occasional cattle disease rate of ¼d to compensate owners of the diseased cattle which had been slaughtered. In 1870 a lunatic asylum rate, usually of ¼d, began to be levied, partly to pay towards the interest and repayment of loans raised to build the second county asylum at Chartham. In 1874 the government began to make a grant towards the keep of the lunatics in the asylums. Another new rate was the main road rate which began in 1878. The turnpike roads were coming to an end and in that year disturnpiked roads were declared main roads. Counties were to pay half the cost of repairs to the highway boards responsible for these roads.

Running the county prisons was the largest expenditure on the county rate but on 1 April 1878 the government took over the administration and financing of these local prisons causing a drop of over £20,000 in the county's expenditure in 1879. Despite this total annual expenditure on the rates continued to rise. In 1886–7 it was £94,924 including £24,522 for main road repairs. Receipts from rates, government grants and other miscellaneous sources were £111,024. The loan debt was still high at £351,994 in 1885–6 resulting from building work at the lunatic asylum and Kingsnorth industrial school.[26]

---

[25] CKS Q/GCz 1.
[26] CKS, Q/GFa 30.

(7) The End of General Sessions

The increasing cost of county government was one of the reasons why it was felt that an elected authority was needed in the counties. There were elected boards administering other aspects of local government. Two reform Acts in 1867 and 1884 had enlarged the parliamentary suffrage thereby increasing democracy. Both the main political parties were in favour of local government reform and in 1888 an Act to establish elected county councils was passed. There was also a County Electors Act in 1888 to deal with the mechanics of the election process. The Kent justices were in favour of the proposals for reform and on 10 April 1888 passed a resolution that the Home Secretary be informed that they expressed general support for the local government Bill before parliament. At the same meeting a small committee of justices was appointed to monitor the Bill. The committee was re-appointed in June 1888 to consider the establish-ment of the electoral divisions for electing a county council, reporting on this matter on 18 September and 2 October 1888.

The last meeting of general sessions before the county council elections was held on 8 January 1889. There were 44 justices present to pass a vote of thanks to the chairman, Sir John Farnaby-Lennard, for his care of the county finances and for presiding over 'an economical and efficient administration'.[27] Certainly the county administration had developed considerably since 1814. A pattern had been set which the county council was to follow, holding quarterly meetings and having a number of permanent committees for specific purposes which met regularly and reported to general sesssions. The justices had also lost some of their independence, being required to send statistics and reports on many of their functions to civil servants and also to ask ministerial approval for their building work. Government grants were dependent on meeting standards set by central government. Legislation had also increased their duties. Seven further meetings were held between March and November 1889 attended by a few justices dealing with financial matters as they prepared to hand over to the county council already in being. A balance of £10,756 went to the council but also a £5,723 debt to the highway boards, as well as £6,592 principle and interest on outstanding loans. The minutes of the final meeting end with the adjournment of general sessions to 2 January 1890 but no further meeting took place. The administration of the county of Kent by the justices of the peace meeting at general sessions had come to an end.

(8) County Council Administration

Though there was continuity between general sessions and the county council in a core of membership belonging to both organisations and a similar committee structure for continuing functions, there were differences, apart from the

27 CKS, Q/GO 18.

obvious one of an elected body replacing an unelected one. These differences included the area of the administrative county, the larger numbers attending meetings and the bringing of people from urban areas into county administration.

Kent lost 35% of the rateable value of the county through the area of Greenwich, Woolwich, Deptford and Lewisham becoming part of the newly formed London County Council area. Kent also had to compensate the LCC for one third of the value of the county buildings and cash balances for which the rate payers of the metropolitan part of Kent had paid. After prolonged negotiations, a sum of £164,729 was agreed in 1892 and Kent County Council borrowed £140,000 towards making the payment.

On the other hand, however, apart from Canterbury, which became a county borough, all the other boroughs in Kent, including the Cinque Ports, became part of the administrative county. This brought a better balance between East and West Kent. The rivalry between the two parts of the county, which had resulted in general sessions coming into being in 1814, still existed. Prior to the first meeting of the provisional county council on 31 January 1889, the members from each division held preliminary meetings to discuss whom to nominate as aldermen from their part of the county.

There were 72 elected county councillors, who then elected 24 aldermen to make a council of 96 members. One more member was added in 1901 after Penge was transferred from Surrey to Kent. Of the 72 elected councillors, 33 represented rural areas and 39 urban ones, including eighteen from nine corporate boroughs. Thirteen of the councillors were elected as aldermen, others being chosen from notable people in the county. In the original elections there had been only 30 contests in the 72 electoral divisions and then five contests for the vacancies created by the election of some county councillors as aldermen. Kent was not unusual in this. There were only a small number of contests in other counties. In the county council elections of 1889 nationally 44% of the seats were uncontested.[28] The contests in Kent were even fewer in the succeeding triennial elections up to 1914. In 1892 there were only eight, in 1895 nine, in 1898 four, 1901 seven, 1904 eleven, 1907 seven, 1910 eleven, and 1913 fifteen.[29]

About a quarter of the council members in 1889 had been county justices who had attended general sessions. They were initially to dominate the workings of the council through their presence on committees and by being chairmen of all the committees. The eighteen borough members were precluded from voting on, or initially from sitting on committees dealing with matters involving expenditure for purposes for which the boroughs they represented did not contribute to the county rates.

The chairman and vice-chairman of the county council selected the members

[28] *New Directions for County Government*, ed. K. Young, London 1989, p. 31.
[29] P.A. Moylan, *The Form and Reform of County Government: Kent 1889–1914*, Leicester 1978, p. 25.

of the original committees after asking members to state their preferences. Despite this 23 members were not placed on a committee and 45 were on only one, while several with general sessions experience were on three or four. Protests followed which led to a more even distribution of committee member-ship after the next elections in 1892. A selection committee was formed in 1898 consisting of the chairman and vice-chairman of the council and the existing committee chairmen.[30]

In 1889 there was part of one more committee to which appointments had to be made. This was the Standing Joint Committee of county council members and county justices which was to be responsible for the county constabulary, though the county council financed the police force. Eight members were chosen from each organisation. There was some discussion on who to choose and the county council's eight members were deliberately selected from those who were not county magistrates.

(9) Members of the County Council
The first chairman of the Kent County Council was Sir John Farnaby-Lennard, who had been chairman of general sessions. Twenty six other counties elected the chairman of their quarter sessions as chairman of the county council.[31] Sir John presided over the first meeting of the permanent county council on 1 April 1889 and remained chairman until 1899. It must have needed some adjustment on Sir John's part to chair meetings considerably bigger than the 30 or 40 justices who had attended general sessions, most of whom he had known socially. Some of the new councillors, particularly from the urban areas, were very vocal and argumentative. At the last meeting of the first county council in February 1892, prior to the first triennial elections, Sir John said in a speech that people with whom he had worked at general sessions were brother justices and all personal friends who had known each other for many years and it was like a family gathering, but he felt that the new system of bringing together more people from all over the county was working well.[32]

Another veteran of general sessions administration who joined the county council was George Marsham of Loose, who had been chairman of the finance committee of general sessions. He became chairman of the county council's first finance committee, then from 1890 to 1900 was vice-chairman of the county council, succeeding Sir John as chairman from 1900 to 1910. He remained a county alderman until 1925 so continuing the links between the Marsham family and the administration of Kent, which had begun in the early nineteenth century, well into the twentieth century.

The first vice-chairman of the county council in 1889 was another regular

---

[30] *Ibid.*, pp. 45–7.
[31] Young, *op. cit.*, p. 34.
[32] E. Melling, *The History of Kent County Council 1889–1974*, Maidstone 1975, p. 5.

attender at general sessions, the fourth Baron Harris of Belmont near Faversham. His tenure was short as he was appointed Governor of Bombay in 1890. After his return from India he became an alderman in 1895 and took an active part in county affairs. He was noted for his interest in cricket in Kent. Another cricketing member was the eighth Earl of Darnley, county alderman from 1906 to 1925. He had played for England against Australia in the team which brought the original 'ashes' back to England. His father, the sixth Earl of Darnley, was a county alderman from 1889 to 1896, while the Honourable and Reverend Edward Vesey Bligh, his uncle, was an alderman from 1897 to 1908. The latter took an active part in the reform of the system of road maintenance in the county. He had been a frequent attender at general sessions. Another alderman with general sessions service was the sixth Lord Stanhope. His great interest was the industrial school at Kingsnorth, later named after him.

Two further people who had personal and family links with general sessions were the Honourable John Stewart Gathorne-Hardy (1892 Viscount Medway, 1906 second Earl of Cranbrook), who was elected a county alderman in 1889 and took an active part in debates until 1911. The other was Sir David Salomons, the nephew and heir of Sir David Salomons, first baronet. The second Sir David was an elected member of the county council from 1889 to 1904. He was a pioneer motorist and also carried out experiments into the use of electricity, thus having technical knowledge that was on occasion useful to the council.

Charles Whitehead of Barming (knighted 1907) was another talented member with specialist knowledge. He was an authority on agriculture, was on the Council of the Royal Agricultural Society, also agricultural adviser to the Privy Council and a writer on agriculture. He was elected as a county councillor in 1889 and immediately chosen as an alderman. He became chairman of two of the four committees on which he sat, having had experience at general sessions.

One of the most influential people on the county council was George Arnold, a Gravesend solicitor who was several times mayor of Gravesend. He was one of the original aldermen in 1889 remaining one until 1908. He was chairman of the Kent Technical Education Committee from its formation in 1891 until 1903 when he became first chairman of the Kent Education Committee from 1903 to 1904. His vice-chairman on both these committees was Frederick Wingent of Rochester, who had been mayor of the city and was a flour miller.

Among other councillors, who had not been county justices but who made a mark at county council meetings through being vocal and putting forward opposing views to the ruling elite, were Charles Smith of Chatham, a councillor from 1889 to 1910 who was a draper. There was also Adam Stigant, councillor from 1889 to 1907, another draper. He was critical among other matters of aldermen but became one himself in 1907. Two members of the Labour Party were elected to the council before 1914. William Ling, a carpenter and trade unionist, who was on Erith Urban District Council, had only one term from 1907 to 1910 but Alfred Tapp, a shipwright, was elected for Gillingham in 1910 and remained on the council until 1938 apart from a few years in the 1920s.

Both men were strong advocates of minimum wages and better conditions for county council staff.[33] The county council was not organised on party political lines until after 1945 and in the early years members were more likely to split into rural members against urban members or East Kent against West Kent.

The early members of the county council were thus a very varied group of people including some talented aristocracy and gentry, also professional men, farmers, manufacturers, tradesmen and craftsmen, many of whom had experience on other local authorities such as borough councils, boards of guardians, highway boards and the rural and urban district councils formed in 1894. For the most part the traditional rulers of the county continued to rule through dominating the main offices but a wide variety of views were expressed in debate.

(10) Functions of the County Council

The county council continued the routine administrative work which general sessions had done but acquired new functions in connection with education, road maintenance and public health. In 1891 the county council established a Technical Education Committee of 21 members, the government having made finance available for this purpose from the customs and excise revenues, to be administered by county councils. George Arnold wrote a report on how the money could be used and was appointed chairman of the committee. When the committee first met over sixty requests for assistance had already been received from local authorities and private organisations. In urban areas the local authorities did the organising while the county gave grants of money but in the rural areas the county council arranged lectures and demonstrations on a wide range of practical subjects. One of the lasting legacies of the committee's work was the foundation with Surrey County Council of the South Eastern Agricultural College at Wye, better known as Wye College, which became affiliated to London University. Because the committee had its own source of money, it had a high degree of autonomy. This did not prevent the council twice trying to divert some of the money to aid the rates but without success. George Arnold on one occasion made an eloquent speech containing classical allusions and appealing to the parliament of Kent not to take such a retrograde step.[34]

In 1903, as a result of the Education Act 1902, the county council became responsible for the education of school children. For Kent County Council this was a milestone comparable to that of having a county police force in 1857 had been for the justices of the peace at general sessions. The county's expenditure and the number of people employed increased greatly. The county council, through the Kent Education Committee, took over the employment of 2,600

---

[33] See Moylan, *op. cit.*, pp. 31–43, and Melling, *History of Kent County Cpuncil*, pp. 4–6, for further information on early members of Kent County Council.

[34] *Kent County Council Record 1889–97*, Maidstone c.1898, p. 154.

teachers and the education of 80,000 children. There were 432 elementary schools, of which 90 were board schools transferred from 68 school boards, the rest being church or charity schools. Secondary schools were far fewer. The provision of evening classes continued and more was done to train teachers. In 1903 the county rate was 9d, in 1904 1s 3¾d. Expenditure rose from £329,373 in 1903 to £497,126 in 1904. The county council was not responsible for elementary education in sixteen boroughs and urban districts which under the Act had independent powers in this respect, otherwise the increase in expenditure would have been even higher.

The county council delegated to the education committee all its powers under the Education Acts, 1870 to 1902, except the powers of raising rates or borrowing money. Annual and quarterly accounts, estimates and reports were to be submitted to the county council by the education committee. This wide delegation of powers was to lead to future trouble. The committee was a large and powerful one consisting of 26 county councillors and twelve co-opted members representing various educational interests. Among the co-opted members were two women. The committee had seven sub-committees. The secretary of the technical education committee became secretary of the education committee and George Arnold became chairman. There were 31 school attendance districts under the supervision of local committees and also 21 local sub-committees for higher education in the larger boroughs and urban districts, under the education committee. Thus a large bureaucratic structure was set up. The education committee met in London and established its headquarters office for administrative staff there. This was another matter which was to concern the county council later.

Being responsible for education also involved capital expenditure. The provision of secondary education in the county was uneven geographically and there was little for girls. By 1905 the education committee had built seven secondary schools for girls to add to the three existing ones. By 1913 there were sixteen maintained secondary schools for boys and girls and the county aided seventeen old endowed grammar schools which took pupils on Kent Education Committee scholarships. The increased building activity led to a works department, under the education committee's own architect, being set up. There was also established a stores department for supplies to the schools. The education committee also had its own finance department.

It was not long before there were criticisms at county council meetings of the size of the committee's staff, the location of the head office, whether the stores, works and finance departments were needed and also the committee's own structure, concentrated on whether more work could not be delegated to local committees and questioning the wide powers delegated to the main committee. From the beginning of 1905 a prolonged attack began on these points. The education committee was asked to enquire into decentralising the system and moving the head office from London to Maidstone. The resulting report defended the existing system and this was accepted by the county council. In 1906 a resolution from 16 district and 25 parish councils, complaining of the rising cost of education to ratepayers, was received by the county council and referred to the education committee.

In 1907 a resolution calling for a new education office in Maidstone was passed by the county council and a committee was appointed to consider this as well as the reduction of the staff. An accountant was brought in to make a report. He had some criticisms but the special committee did not feel radical alterations were required. The report was debated at length at a meeting of the county council in February 1909 and finally accepted after several amendments had been defeated, but some staff cuts were made as a result.

Another resolution from 42 district and parish councils was received in 1909 criticising what was described as the education committee's continued exorbitant expenditure. This led to another motion being passed that the offices should move to Maidstone. In May 1910 the county offices committee was formed, ironically holding its first meeting in the education committee's office in London. This was to lead, ultimately, to a new office being built in front of the Sessions House at Maidstone in 1913.

The other controversial subject, which led to lengthy debates at county council meetings, was how best to organise the maintenance of the rural main roads. The cost of this service was the county's largest expenditure before becoming responsible for education in 1903. After 1890 the roads expenditure was over £100,000 a year rising to £155,000 in 1899. Kent had over 600 miles of rural main roads, more than most counties.

In the first year, 1889–90, arrangements were made with local highway authorities to continue to repair these roads as they had prior to 1889 with the county council paying the whole instead of half the cost. After further consideration of the matter, in the next year the county was divided into five divisions and in three divisions the work was to be contracted out to private firms. In 1892 it was decided that both firms and local authorities should be allowed to tender for contracts but the local authorities found it difficult to compete with the firms. Few counties other than Kent operated a contract system but used either a direct labour force or made arrangements with district authorities. All three methods had their advocates on the county council. By 1893, however, the bridges and roads committee had a new chairman who was an enthusiastic supporter of the contract system. He was Thomas Powell, a substantial farmer who became chairman of Hollingbourne Rural District Council. He was the first chairman of a mainstream county council committee who had not been a county justice with general sessions experience. He was evidently trusted and liked and was elected an alderman in 1894.

In February 1893, after a debate on rising costs and methods of organisation of road maintenance, it was resolved to try direct management in the most easterly of the five divisions, which was the least easy to contract out, and to use contractors for the rest of the divisions. This system lasted until 1899.

In 1898 the Honourable and Reverend Edward Vesey Bligh became a county alderman and from then until 1903 he was a persistent critic of the contract system and one of the leaders of the opposition to it on the county council. For several years Bligh and his supporters made little headway despite obtaining the appointment of a special committee to report on the matter in 1898. In February 1902 the bridges and roads committee's proposal to let the road maintenance contracts on a three yearly not an annual basis was accepted by the county council. In April 1902, however, there was a special county council meeting, which had been requisitioned by a group of members, to discuss a mistake which had been discovered in the documentation connected with the specifications for tenders drawn up by the county surveyor. During the debate, Lord Harris moved a resolution that an outside expert should be brought in to report on the management of the roads and this was passed. Another resolution moved by Lord Medway (formerly J.S. Gathorne-Hardy) that a new full time surveyor should be appointed was not passed. In November 1902 Douglas Joscelyne, formerly chief engineer and secretary to the Public Works Department of the Government of Bengal, was selected to make a report. A year later this was presented and accepted. It was in many respects a critical report giving detailed descriptions of how the existing long-used ways of maintaining roads were no longer suitable for roads used by increasingly heavy and motorised traffic.

In March 1904 the bridges and roads committee was re-constituted, eight changes were made in the membership of the committee and Thomas Powell ceased to be chairman. In April 1904 a new full-time county surveyor was appointed. He was Henry Maybury, surveyor to Malvern Urban District Council in Worcestershire since 1895 and with previous experience with other local authorities and private firms. His salary on appointment was £700 a year but was £1,500 by the time he left in 1913. A motor car was bought for him. Sir David Salomons advised on the purchase as an expert on cars and the county surveyor was given an allowance of £60 a year to cover 'housing the county's motor car' and the wages of a driver.

Henry Maybury was one of the most effective and distinguished officials the county council ever employed. In 1913 he became chief engineer to the government Road Board established in 1909. During the First World War he supervised road building in France for the allied armies, becoming a Brigadier General. He was knighted in 1919 and became Director General of the Road Department of the Ministry of Transport after the war. The policies he introduced revolutionised the roads of Kent. Tar was sprayed on to the surface of roads to give a better surface and settle dust. Then tarmacadam was used to provide a better foundation for the roads. Kent came to have more macadamised roads than any other county during Maybury's time as county surveyor. The work was done by a direct labour force.

The other new service for which the county council became responsible between 1889 and 1914 was public health. This was a much less controversial service than education or road maintenance, partly because it was on a small scale up to 1914 and so less expensive. The Local Government Act 1888 had given county councils permissive powers to appoint medical officers of health but only about a quarter of the county councils had done so by 1898. The councils' role in public health matters was largely confined to supervising the district authorities by receiving reports from district medical officers of health and taking action if necessary. Under the Midwives Act 1902, county councils were made the supervising authorities for the inspection of midwifery. Initially, in Kent, the county council delegated this function to the districts, paying them an agreed amount for the costs and receiving annual reports on the service from them.

In 1907 a new situation arose. Under an Education Act of that year, medical inspection of school children was introduced and a Board of Education circular urged the appointment of county medical officers of health. This led to the county council in Kent making such an appointment. In 1908 the delegation to district councils under the Midwives Act was ended and two women inspectors were appointed on the county medical officer's staff and the work of the health department began to expand. The National Insurance Act 1911 led to schemes for the prevention and treatment of tuberculosis, culminating in the building of Lenham Sanatorium, used during the war as a military hospital but opened for its intended purpose in 1919.

(11) Employees of the County Council

One of the most important aspects of county council administration between 1903 and 1914 was the establishment of departments for specific services headed by a professional full-time salaried chief officer supported by staff with local government experience, in some cases from outside Kent. In 1903 the education department, as mentioned, was established with an increasing staff numbering 93 by 1906. Then in 1904 came the county surveyor's department already described. In 1907 a county accountant was appointed, though bankers remained as county treasurers. Starting with five staff there were 21 by 1910. The health department grew from three staff in 1908 to ten in 1910.

Prior to 1900 most county councillors had been unwilling to employ many staff directly. Any suggestion for employing full-time professional officers was met with similar arguments to those used in 1839 and 1840 against establishing a county police force. The argument was that the officers would become the masters not the servants of the members of the county council. Some county councils smaller than Kent continued to use local firms rather than their own employees for many more years.

The departments, apart from the education department in London, were housed in scattered offices in various parts of Maidstone. In 1911 the county surveyor's department was moved to purpose built accommodation near the River Medway with a wharf and yard for the delivery and storage of road building stone. The decision to build new offices near the Sessions House, primarily in order to move the education department from London, made it possible to transfer the staff of other departments, apart from that of the county surveyor, on to one central site. The building designed by the county architect and former county surveyor, F.W. Ruck, was opened in 1913. It cost £68,000 paid for out of revenue with the help of £10,000 adjustment money paid by London County Council when Penge moved into Kent. The building included, in addition to offices, a new council chamber.

(12) County Council Finance

The basis of the county council's revenue, like that of the justices, remained the money received by levying a variety of rates. The need for several rates was still that some parts of the county were exempt from paying for certain services, despite the change in the area of the administrative county. In 1889–90, the first year, the product of a 1d rate from the four rates concerned was: general county rate £17,578, special county rate about £14,000, the lunatic asylums rate about £14,000 and the police rate £10,878.

The other main source of money came from the government. A provision had been made under the 1888 Act that government grants for specific purposes should cease, being replaced by what was known as the 'assigned revenues'. These came from a percentage of the proceeds of local taxation licences, with a smaller amount from probate duty, which was set aside by the Exchequer to be distributed to county councils. Much of this money had to be handed over by county councils to boards of guardians and other lesser local authorities to help pay for the cost of such items, among others, as their medical officers of health, vaccination programmes, the registration of births, marriages and deaths and a proportion of the costs of the police at borough and county level.

The amount received by Kent County Council in 1889–90 from this source was £121,556. This was less than the £162,000 anticipated. In spite of that, when the payments had been made there was a surplus of £39,881 available for transfer to the general rate account. The rates had brought in £110,046 during this first year which was £33,000 more than expected. Estimating the money to be received from a new system even though it had similarities to the old one had not been easy.

Expenditure by the county council of £103,392 for 1889–90 rose to £300,695 in 1893 and varied between £220,000 and £270,000 during the rest of the decade 1890–1900. Spending on the old services remained, in some cases, fairly constant, £3,000 to £4,000 a year being spent on the industrial school and £15,000 for the administration of justice. Expenditure on the asylums was between £14,000 and £58,000 and on the police force £47,000 to £57,000. The largest expenditure was on main roads, £100,000 to £172,000. Technical education had its own separate source of income. For the first three years from 1891 the technical education committee spent £12,000 to £17,000 a year. Reserves built up which could be carried forward. Spending after that was between £22,000 and £25,000 as the service developed, rising to £32,000 in 1896 and was £31,000 in the two years to 1901. After 1903 the county council had to provide for another high-spending service, general education. Expenditure on elementary education which was £171,000 in 1903–4 had risen to £300,000 a year from 1907 to 1914. The secondary education costs were £52,000 in 1904, £75,000 in 1905 and over £100,000 between 1909 and 1914. The assigned revenues in lieu of government grants provided since 1889 were not flexible enough to support the rising costs of expensive services, so the assigned revenues had again to be supplemented by government grants for specific purposes. Grants were given for education and from 1912 for road maintenance, the two highest spending services. Overall expenditure by the county council rose from £103,392 in 1890 to £852,110 in 1914, the highest expenditure being £897,117 in 1912. In 1890 the general county rate was 7½d and in 1914 2s 0½d.

(13) Conclusion

In surveying the administration of Kent during the century under consideration it has to be said that the justices acting through general sessions were somewhat lacking in initiative. They were later than most counties in providing the new gaols resulting from the prison reform movement, though this was partly due to the financial dispute between East and West Kent. They did not establish a police force until mandatory legislation was enacted though 31 other counties had done so under permissive legislation, including the neighbouring counties of Surrey and East Sussex. They did not appoint a finance committee until pressured to do so by the government. In financing big capital projects they were reluctant to use loans until the mid-nineteenth century though some counties had done so from the late eighteenth century.

Once a function was taken over, however, it was conscientiously undertaken but always with an eye to the cost to the ratepayers. Many of the justices themselves were big ratepayers. The development of general sessions into, in effect, a miniature unelected county council, with the administrative work of the justices separated from the judicial work, was an achievement. The quarter sessions of other counties also developed a committee structure to deal with administrative matters but the divorce between administrative and judicial work was not so clear cut as in Kent. The early development of general sessions with its many small meetings and *ad hoc* committees in the first two decades, must have been largely due to the determination of the first chairman, Lord Romney, to make general sessions a success after the long dispute between East and West Kent over finance.

The middle years of the century were more turbulent with disputes among the justices over whether to have a police force and a long quarrel with the clerk of the peace leading to legal action. A more efficient and streamlined administration under the chairmanship of Sir John Farnaby-Lennard, and with Francis Russell as clerk of the peace, was evident in the last two decades of general sessions.

The replacement of general sessions by an elected county council as Kent's administrative body at county level was a time of continuity and change. Some of the justices became members of the county council but new voices were heard. A larger body formed the county's parliament, as both general sessions and the county council were called by the justices, council members and the press. The old functions were taken over by the county council and some new ones added. These grew in importance. There was a relatively quiet first decade and then a big expansion with main road repairs and education being costly services which led to dispute over their management. A very important feature was the employment of full-time salaried professional and clerical staff and an abandonment of the contracting out of services, so bringing most work 'in house'. This was a significant development which gave the county council the ability to develop new services quickly and efficiently.

What were the motives of the justices and then the elected councillors in giving their time and energy free? The county gentry who were justices no doubt enjoyed meeting their fellow justices, known to them socially, at the meetings of general sessions and its committees, particularly those who were comparatively new county justices and had not lived in the county for long. It gave them an entry into county society. The people who were county justices also lived in an age when public service was taken for granted and sons followed fathers in helping to administer the county. The service involved travelling to a central meeting point at a time when travel was slow until a railway network was developed in Kent. It also involved attending meetings which must often have been routine and lacking in interest. There were no material rewards and little patronage to bestow. It can only be concluded that there was no other motive but custom and duty.

The membership of the county council embraced a wider cross-section of society, even in its earlier days, than general sessions had. Those inside the circle of the old style administration carried on doing what they had been doing for years. Those from outside wanted to have county-wide power and influence instead of just in their own localities on smaller local councils. The detailed press reports of meetings published at the time show that there were quite a number of county council members who evidently enjoyed joining in debates, had views on the topics discussed and wished to express them. They had not yet become lobby fodder. The speeches embraced the elegant orations of the gentry and professional people, who had had a classical education, through the more robust speeches of those used to the less gentlemanly debates of some borough councils, to the speeches of the few Labour members demanding social justice. In one way the county council in its early days was not a particularly democratic institution, in that there were so few contests at elections but the mechanism was in place for more democracy when the time was ripe. By the end of the period under consideration many of those who had known the administration of general sessions had died or left the council and new people with new ideas were taking over from them.

Further Reading

(1) Kent and the Civil Wars

A succinct overview of the events from 1640 to 1660 can be found in I. Roots, *The Great Rebellion, 1642–1660*, London 1966, and G. Aylmer, *Rebellion or Revolution? England 1640–1660*, Oxford 1986. M. Bennett, *The Civil Wars in Britain and Ireland, 1638–1651*, Oxford 1997, integrates the findings of more recent studies on the relationship between the English Civil Wars and the rebellions in the other Stuart kingdoms of Scotland and Ireland. The most recent military account of the civil wars in all three kingdoms is contained in J. Kenyon and J. Ohlmeyer (eds), *The Civil Wars: A Military History of England, Scotland and Ireland, 1638–1660*, Oxford 1998. Information about individual royalist officers can be found in P.R. Newman, *Royalist Officers in England and Wales, 1642–60: A Biographical Dictionary*, New York 1981. The progress of the Civil Wars in the English counties is the subject of J. Morrill, *The Revolt of the Provinces: Conservatives and Radicals in the English Civil War, 1630–1650*, London 1976 (2nd edn 1998).

The background to the civil wars in Kent is explored in depth in P. Clark, *English Provincial Society from the Reformation to the Revolution: Religion, Politics and Society in Kent, 1500–1640*, Hassocks 1977. The history of Kent during the years 1640–60 has been dealt with at greatest length in print in H.F. Abell, *Kent and the Great Civil War*, Ashford 1901; A. Everitt, *The Community of Kent and the Great Rebellion, 1640–60*, Leicester 1966; and T.P.S. Woods, *Prelude to Civil War, 1642: Mr Justice Malet and the Kentish Petitions*, Salisbury 1980. For an interpretation of the intellectual activities of the gentry which is at odds with that of Everitt see P. Laslett, 'The Gentry of Kent in 1640', *Cambridge Historical Journal*, ix (1948), pp. 148–64. Political issues in Kent are dealt with in F. Jessup, 'The Kentish Election of March 1640', *Archaeologia Cantiana*, lxxxvi (1971), pp. 1–10, and M.V. Jones, 'Election Issues and the Borough Electorates in mid-Seventeenth Century Kent', *Archaeologia Cantiana*, lxxxv (1970), pp. 19–27. For biographies of individual members of parliament see M.F. Keeler, *The Long Parliament, 1640–1641: A Biographical Study of its Members*, Philadelphia 1954, and B.D. Henning (ed.), *The History of Parliament: The House of Commons, 1660–1690*, 3 vols, London 1983. The political stance of the constitutional royalists, including Sir John Culpeper, the Earl of Dorset and the Duke of Richmond and Lennox, are discussed in D.L. Smith, *Constitutional Royalism and the Search for Settlement, c.1640–1649*, Cambridge 1994. The political affiliations of influential individuals are considered in F.W. Jessup, *Sir Roger Twysden, 1597–1672*, London 1965; D. Hirst, 'The Defection of Sir Edward Dering, 1640–1641', *Historical Journal*, xv (1972), pp. 193–208; and S.P. Salt, 'The Origins of Sir Edward Dering's Attack on the Ecclesiastical Hierarchy c.1625–1640', *Historical Journal*, xxx (1987), pp. 21–52. Church affairs and religious dissent in civil war Kent are discussed in P. Collinson, 'The Protestant Cathedral, 1541–1660', in *A History of Canterbury Cathedral*, ed. P. Collinson, N. Ramsay and M. Sparks, Oxford 1995; and G.F. Nuttall, 'Dissenting Churches in Kent before 1700', *Journal of Ecclesiastical History*, xiv (1963), pp. 175–89. For information about individual ejected ministers see *Calamy Revised*, ed. A.G. Matthews, Oxford 1988, for dissenters and *Walker Revised*, ed. A.G. Matthews, Oxford 1988, for Anglican conformists.

(2) The Government of the County

The History of Parliament Trust is publishing the most detailed account of the constituencies and members represented in parliament for the period 1640–1832. So far it has published *The House of Commons 1660–1690*, ed. B.D. Henning, London 1983; *The House of Commons 1715–1754*, ed. Romney Sedgwick, London 1970; *The House of Commons 1754–1790*, ed. Sir Lewis Naimier and John Brooke, London 1964; and *The House of Commons 1790–1820*, ed. R.G. Thorne, London 1986. These volumes contain an analysis of the constituencies, the parties, and biographies of every county and borough member of parliament.

Kent's gentry as magistrates are described in Norma Landau, *The Justices of the Peace 1679–1760*, California 1984. The seats of the gentry are described architecturally in John Newman, *The Buildings of England: North and East Kent* and *West Kent and the Weald*, Harmondsworth 1969. Some of them are depicted and their artists described in John Harris, *The Artist and the Country House*, London 1979.

For national politics there is Tim Harris, *Politics under the Later Stuarts: Party Conflict in a Divided Society 1660–1715*, London 1993, and in the constituencies, W.A. Speck, *Tory and Whig: The Struggle in the Constituencies, 1701–1715*, London 1970. Attention should also be drawn to R.L. Greaves, *Deliver us from Evil: The Radical Underground in Britain 1660–1663*, Oxford 1986. *The Diaries and Papers of Sir Edward Dering Second Baronet, 1644 to 1684*, ed. M.F. Bond, London 1976, indicate the scope of material that older gentry families accumulated.

(3) Government in the Boroughs

The most readily available printed account of all the corporations is the *Report of the Royal Commissioners to Inquire into Municipal Corporations* (1835). For a concise commentary upon the report see G.B.A.M. Finlayson, 'The Municipal Corporation Commission and Report, 1833–35', *Bulletin of the Institute of Historical Research*, xxxvi (1963), pp. 36–52. S. and B. Webb, *English Local Government from the Revolution to the Municipal Corporations Act: The Manor and the Borough*, London 1908; F.H. Spencer, *Municipal Origins 1740–1835*, London 1911; and Bryan Keith-Lucas, *The Unreformed Local Government System*, London 1980, set out the origins and main principles of borough government before 1835.

(4) Radical Movements and Workers' Protests

A national overview is provided by E.H. Hunt, *British Labour History 1815–1914*. E.P. Thompson, *The Making of the English Working Class*, Harmondsworth 1968, furnishes a stimulating and often controversial account of working class society in its formative years 1780–1832. C. Gill, *The Naval Mutinies of 1797*, Manchester 1913, still provides an objective account of these events, while E.J. Hobsbawm and George Rudé, *Captain Swing*, Harmondsworth 1973, is a masterly analysis of the Swing Riots. A shorter and more recent account of the latter is given by G.E. Mingay, ' "Rural War": The Life and Times of Captain Swing', in *The Unquiet Countryside*, ed. G.E. Mingay, London 1989, pp. 36–51. Barry Reay, *The Last Rising of the Agricultural Labourers*, Oxford 1990, is the definitive study of the Courtenay Rising of 1838, while J.T. Ward *Chartism*, London 1973; David Jones, *Chartism and the Chartists*, London 1975; and Edward Royle, *Chartism*, Harlow 1980, between them capture the appeal, assorted policies and general complexity of the Chartist Movement.

(5) National Politics in Kent

Developments at the national level can be approached through R. Blake, *The Conservative Party from Peel to Major*, London 1997, and B.I. Coleman, *Conservatism and the Conservative Party in Nineteenth-Century Britain*, London 1988. For the Liberals see J. Vincent, *The Formation of the British Liberal Party 1857–1868*, Hassocks 1976, and M. Bentley, *The Climax of Liberal Politics: British Liberalism in Theory and Practice 1868–1918*, London 1987. H. Pelling, *Social Geography of British Elections 1885–1910*, London 1967, discusses the characteristics and political complexion of the various Kent constituencies, enabling them to be placed in the national context, while H.J. Hanham, *Elections and Party Management*, Hassocks 1978, permits a similar contextualisation of Kent political practice, including the corrupt and seamy side.

Turning specifically to Kent, there is a biography of Sir Edward Knatchbull, Bt, in H. Knatchbull-Hugesson, *Kentish Family*, London 1960, and of A. Aretas-Douglas in Viscount Chilston, *Chief Whip*, London 1961. At constituency level, there is useful material on Maidstone in P. Clark and L. Murfin, *The History of Maidstone*, Stroud 1995, and on Sandwich in F.W.G. Andrews, 'The Pollbooks of Sandwich, Kent, 1831–68', *Bulletin of the Institute of Historical Research*, lxxi (1998), pp. 75–107.

(6) Working Class Politics in the Medway Towns

Nationally, the formulation and organisation of working class movements and the origins of the Labour Party may be followed in D. Howell, *British Workers and the Independent Labour Party 1888–1906*, Manchester 1983; H. Pelling, *Origins of the Labour Party, 1880–1900*, Oxford 1965; E. Royle, *Radicals, Secularists and Republicans: Popular Freethought in Britain, 1866–1915*, Manchester 1980; and C. Waters, *British Socialists and the Politics of Popular Culture, 1884–1914*, Manchester 1990.

For some of the personalities connected with the rise of the labour movement see: T. Mann, *Tom Mann's Memoirs*, London 1967; D. Marquand, *Ramsay Macdonald*, London 1977; K. Morgan, *Keir Hardie: Radical Socialist*, London 1975; L. Thompson, *The Enthusiasts: A Biography of John and Katharine Glazier*, London 1971; and *Dictionary of Labour Biography*, ed. J.M. Bellamy and J. Saville, London 1977.

(7) Crime and Public Order

Clive Emsley, *Crime and Society in England 1750–1900*, London 1996, provides an excellent introduction to the subject. Carolyn A. Conley, *The Unwritten Law*, New York 1991, is a fascinating study of criminal justice in Victorian Kent. M. Waugh, *Smuggling in Kent and Sussex 1700–1840*, Newbury 1985, and J.G. Rule, 'The Manifold Causes of Rural Crime: Sheep Stealing in England 1740–1840', in *Outside the Law*, ed. J.G. Rule, Exeter 1983, deal with the specific offences, as does John E. Archer, *By a Flash and a Scare: Arson, Animal Maiming and Poaching in East Anglia 1815–1870*, Oxford 1990. The latter also considers the same offences in essays entitled, 'Poachers Abroad' and 'Under cover of Night: arson and animal maiming' published in *The Unquiet Countryside*, ed. G.E. Mingay, London 1989, pp. 52–79. Associations for the Protection of Property are described by David Philips, 'Good Men to Associate and Bad Men to Conspire: Associations for the Prosecution of Felons in England 1760–1860', in *Policing and Prosecution in Britain 1750–1850*, ed. D. Hay and F. Snyder, Oxford 1989, pp. 113–51. The development of mid-nineteenth-century police forces and the men who became the earliest provincial policemen are analysed by Carolyn Steedman, *Policing the Victorian Community*, London 1984.

(8) County Administration, 1814–1914

Little has been written about county government in the nineteenth century. The best overview for a single county is to be found in the *Victoria County History of Wiltshire*, vol. 5, Oxford 1957. The writings of Sidney and Beatrice Webb on English local government remain useful and local details can be found in the voluminous footnotes. The volume *The Parish and the County* only covers the early nineteenth century but *The Story of the King's Highway* and *English Prisons under Local Government* cover the whole century. The complete series of volumes was republished in 1963.

Information about the early years of Kent County Council can be found in E. Melling, *The History of Kent County Council 1889–1974*, Maidstone 1975, concentrating mainly on administrative developments, and in P.A. Moylan, *The Form and Reform of County Government: Kent 1889–1914*, Leicester 1978, dealing mainly with the political background.

Index

Personal names are indexed selectively.